Superheroes, Strip Artists, & Talking Animals

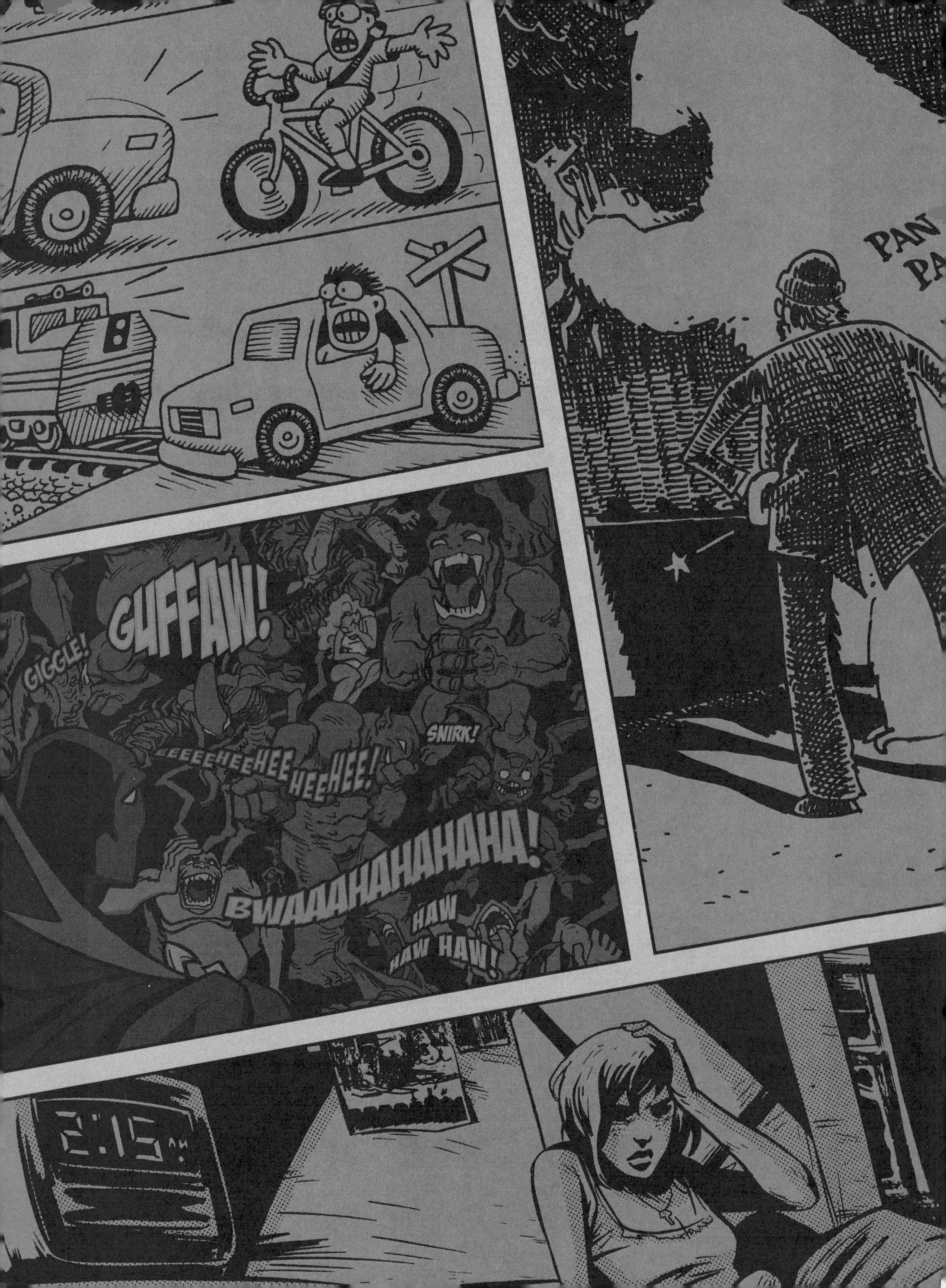
PAN
GIGGLE!
GUFFAW!
SNIRK!
EEEEEHEEHEEHEEHEE!
BWAAAHAHAHAHA!
HAW HAW HAW!
2:15 AM

SUPERHEROES, STRIP ARTISTS, & TALKING ANIMALS

MINNESOTA'S CONTEMPORARY CARTOONISTS

Britt Aamodt

Minnesota Historical
Society Press

THIS BOOK IS DEDICATED TO CARTOONISTS PAST AND PRESENT, WHO BUILD DREAMS ON A DIME, WORK TOO MUCH, SLEEP TOO LITTLE, AND HAVE ALWAYS APPRECIATED LIFE FOR WHAT IT REALLY IS— THE BEST SOURCE MATERIAL FOR ART EVER CONCEIVED BY HUMANKIND.

THIS BOOK IS MOST ESPECIALLY DEDICATED TO MOM, DAD, AND GRANDMA JUNE, BECAUSE THEY'RE THE TOPS.

For information, write to Minnesota Historical Society Press, 345 Kellogg Blvd. W., St. Paul, MN 55102–1906.

The Minnesota Historical Society Press is a member of the Association of American University Presses.

Manufactured in the United States of America

10 9 8 7 6 5 4 3 2 1

♾ The paper used in this publication meets the minimum requirements of the American National Standard for Information Sciences—Permanence for Printed Library Materials, ANSI Z39.48–1984.

International Standard Book Number
ISBN 13: 978-0-87351-777-5

Library of Congress Cataloging-in-Publication Data

Aamodt, Britt.
Superheroes, strip artists, & talking animals : Minnesota's contemporary cartoonists / Britt Aamodt.
p. cm.
Includes index.
ISBN 978-0-87351-777-5 (pbk. : alk. paper)
1. Comic books, strips, etc.—Minnesota—History—21st century. 2. Cartoonists—Minnesota—Biography. I. Title. II. Title: Superheroes, strip artists, and talking animals. III. Title: Minnesota's contemporary cartoonists.
NC1305.A22 2011
741.5'9776—dc22
2010030563

CONTENTS

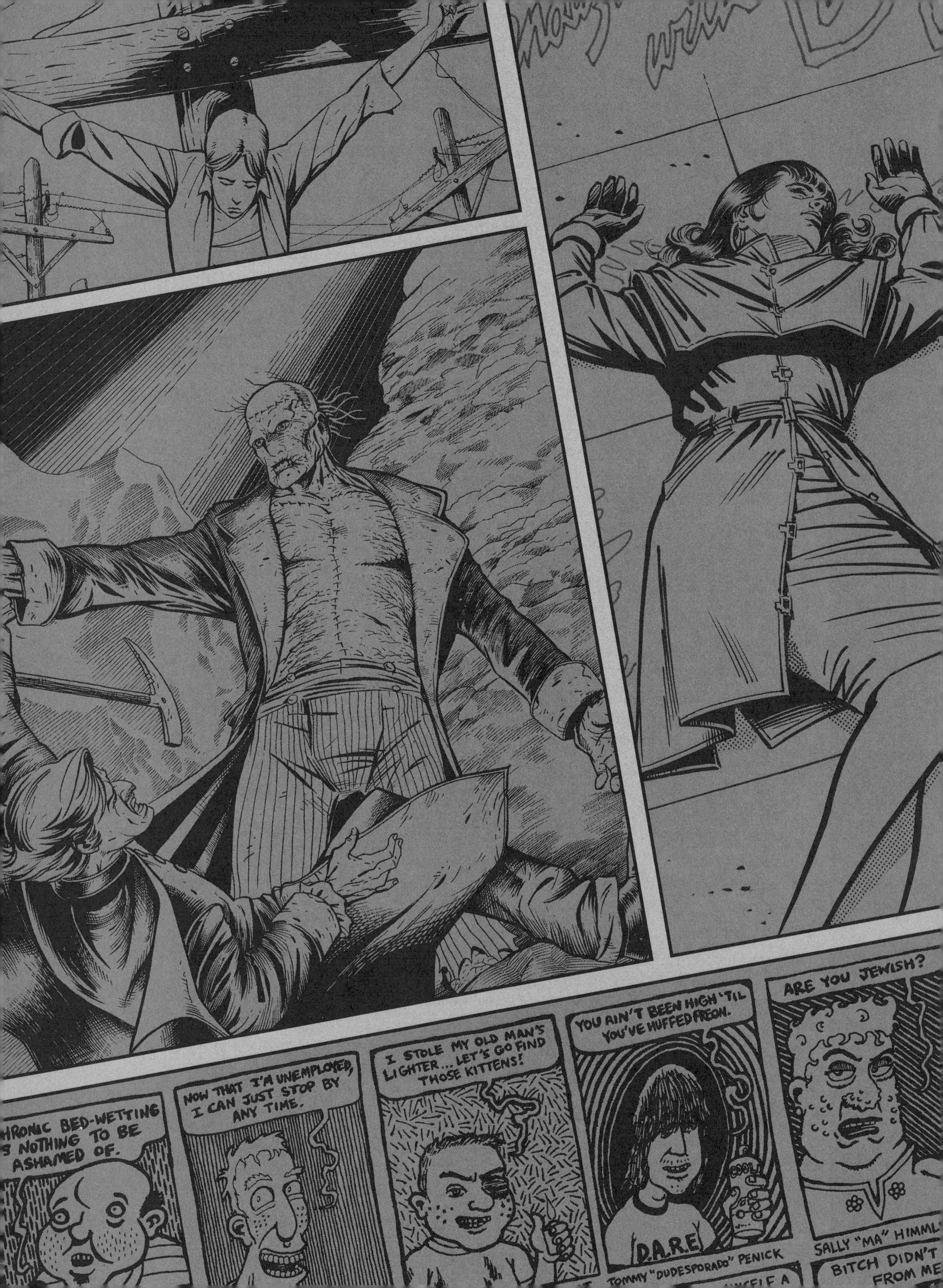

HRONIC BED-WETTING
S NOTHING TO BE
ASHAMED OF.
NOW THAT I'M UNEMPLOYED, I CAN JUST STOP BY ANY TIME.
I STOLE MY OLD MAN'S LIGHTER... LET'S GO FIND THOSE KITTENS!
YOU AIN'T BEEN HIGH 'TIL YOU'VE HUFFED FREON.
D.A.R.E.
TOMMY "DUDESPORADO" PENICK
ARE YOU JEWISH?
SALLY "MA" HIMML
BITCH DIDN'T
FROM ME

INTRODUCTION

Where do you begin a book about cartoonists? Well, first, you can pare down the numbers a bit. After all, the world is lousy with cartoonists. Just lousy. You open the alternative weekly, and there they are. You find them on editorial pages, in Hollywood movies, on television, on library shelving carts, in between sofa cushions, in comic book stores, and, for crying out loud, on the Internet. Next thing you know, they'll be turning up on the doorstep with copies of *The Watchtower*.

But wait a second. That's their art turning up in all those places. Their comic strips, political cartoons, graphic novels, 'zines, comic books, minicomics, webcomics, comical comics. What about the cartoonists themselves? Probably back at home, hard at work on the next great American whatchamacallit.

Cartoonists spend a lot of time at the drawing board. Sure, they get out and move among you, but like the awesomely disguised Clark Kent (That guy? Superman? Get outta here!), you wouldn't know it to look at them. Quite unlike the stereotypes of scruffy dudes with drooping pants and hanging shirttails, cartoonists look like everyone else. They might even resemble the person you just cut off with your grocery cart, making him wait in line while you pay your bill in nickels and dimes. Only difference is, this offended grocer goes home and mercilessly parodies you in art, posting the result online so everybody in the universe knows you have nostrils the size of wind tunnels and a forehead that blinks "Passive-Aggressive."

The world is just lousy with cartoonists, but you would never know it. So, it comes down to a book like this to pull them out of their comfy obscurity for a spell and stand them front and center. Alongside their work, of course. Because you can't talk cartoonists without showing the cartoonists' art. And really, the art is the point of this book. It's great art. It's Minnesota art.

Oh, that's right. Did anyone mention this book singles out Minnesota cartoonists? Specifically *contemporary* Minnesota cartoonists? Had to draw the line somewhere. Because, as mentioned elsewhere, cartoonists abound. Not so numerous as Twins baseball fans or Ponzi-scheming, white-collar crooks, but then art is long and arduous. You don't get to be a cartoonist overnight. You don't arrive at a promised land of effortless creation—ever. Because for cartoonists, the art is earned every day, through a multitude of failed pages and a self-discipline that sputters fiercely and always refuses to quit. Many are called; few are chosen.

The cartoonists featured in this book were selected with a few basic criteria in mind. First, their art needed to stand on its own, to draw the reader in with a certain spark, whether that spark was technical mastery, individual style, storytelling, or humor. Too, the cartoonists were chosen to represent categories within the larger scope of comic art.

Dan Jurgens works in mainstream superhero comic books. He's the guy who killed Superman in the early 1990s. Likewise, Christopher Jones draws superheroes for the mainstreams (*Batman*, for one. Could the guy be any cooler?), but he has also gravitated to indies, penciling the far-out *Dr. Blink: Superhero Shrink* about—what else?—a psychiatrist to superpowered beings. Kirk Anderson kicks off the section on Minnesota comic strip artists. He applied his keen-eyed talent to "Banana Republic," a strip about a misguided and wholly immoral Third World government that, quite coincidentally, mirrored policies instituted by the contemporary Bush administration.

> YOU DON'T GET TO BE A CARTOONIST OVERNIGHT. YOU DON'T ARRIVE AT A PROMISED LAND OF EFFORTLESS CREATION—EVER.

Selected cartoonists were also singled out to illustrate trends in comics and roles in the creative process. Peter Gross jumped into comics at the height of the self-published, black-and-white boom, exemplified by the *Teenage Mutant Ninja Turtles,* in the 1980s. He did it all. He scripted, penciled, inked, lettered, printed, and distributed his monthly comic *Empire Lanes* nationwide. This all-in-one approach departed from the assembly-line process, which continues to dictate mainstream comic book publishing. One person writes a script, which others pencil, ink, letter, and color in sequence. Apart from penciling work produced with writer-collaborator Max Allan Collins (*Ms. Tree, Return to Perdition),* Terry Beatty has devoted eleven years to inking a number of *Batman* titles. Melissa Kaercher letters and colors scanned pencil-and-inks with her computer. In true do-it-yourself fashion, Danno Klonowski photocopies his self-produced minicomic series *Manly Tales of Cowardice,* which he sells at regional conventions.

Spring and fall, the Midwest Comic Book Association hosts conventions at the Minnesota State Fairgrounds. But cartoonists get around. They make appearances at conventions and small press expos throughout the United States, in particular Comic-Con, the large national convention held every summer in San Diego. The conventions, along with comic book stores (The Source, Big Brain Comics, Comic Book College, DreamHaven, etc.) and the Minneapolis College of Art and Design's comic art program, supply the infrastructure for Minnesota's comics scene. Cartoonist Steven Stwalley further developed the scene in 2002 with the Cartoonist Conspiracy, an organization he founded to provide a common meeting ground for Minnesota-based cartoonists.

Lastly, these cartoonists were chosen because they live in Minnesota. This leads to another question: Where did all these Minnesota cartoonists come from? Some moved here for school. Some married into the state. Some sailed in on job offers or on recommendations of friends already ensconced in the Cities. Some woke up one day and said, "What the #$@?! Where am I?" Many cartoonists arrived the old-fashioned way: They were born here.

If you're talking Minnesota cartoonists, "Peanuts" creator Charles Schulz tops the list. Though this book isn't about Schulz or the generations that preceded him, in small ways it trades on that legacy in the section chapters and artist profiles. The sections are divided into strip artists, comic book artists, and independent cartoonists, who work with non-mainstream publishers and self-publish books, webcomics, and minicomics.

By the way, this isn't *just* an art book. You will encounter blocks of text as you leaf through the pages. But admit it: You're only thumbing through to scope the art. That's the nature of comics. They steal the show. Providing text for a shapely body of art is like reciting poetry after a sexy topless act exits stage left.

For the same reason, cartoonists tend to recede behind their work. It's hard for a cartooning Joe or Jane to compete against Superman, the Green Lantern, hot-tempered Arctic pirates, and dead chickens. So, the biographical profiles attempt to yank them from the shadow of their creations to talk about themselves—as a child, Doug Mahnke fought crime in the guise of his super-sudsy alter ego Soap Man—and their careers—Christopher Jones published his first comic strip at age ten.

These contemporary cartoonists share only a state of residence and a dedication to a singular art form that has been variously praised, put down, demonized, popularized, ghettoized, refined, revamped, and adored for over a century now. They do not constitute the be-all and end-all of Minnesota contemporary cartooning, but a sly incitement to search beyond the pages of this book for work by Duane Barnhart, Sam Hiti, Peter Krause, Chris Monroe, Daniel J. Olson, Tom Richmond, Steve Sack, Mike Sgier, David Steinlicht, and Jerry Van Amerongen, among many, many more.

Don't know who these folks are? You're in luck. Luck, incidentally, is spelled "web search." Cartoonists have blogs, websites, and social networking personas; and you can find a list of sites at the end of the book. Again, not a comprehensive list, but who wants to snore through a ten-page inventory? (Certainly not the publisher of this book.)

So sit back, relax, enjoy the art. Bone up on the histories of these Minnesota cartoonists. And oh yeah, if some day you bump into your friendly neighborhood cartoonist at the store, remember to observe proper grocery cart etiquette. These cartoonists, they have sharp pencils and sharper wits. ∎

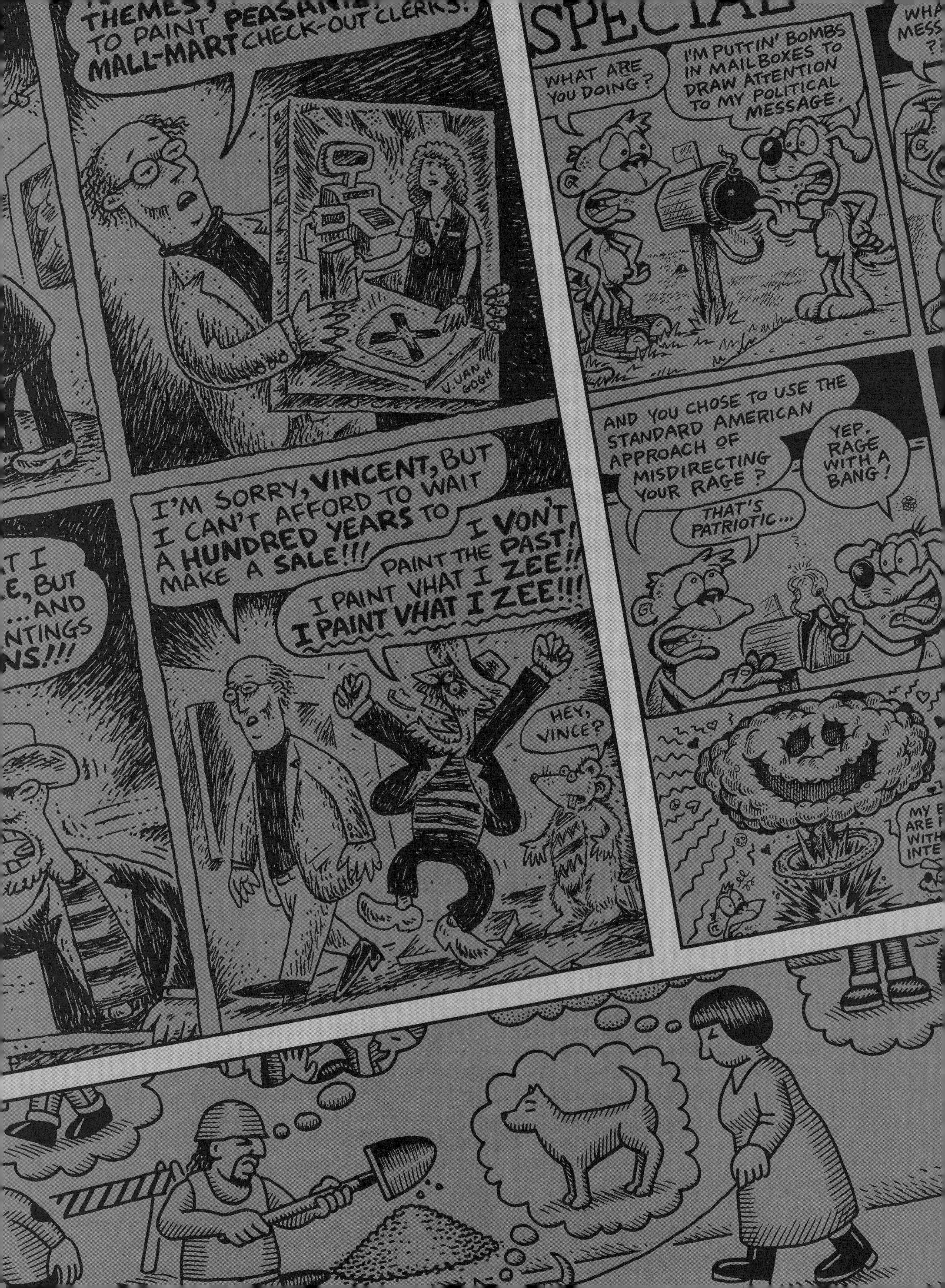
TO PAINT PEASANTS, TO PAINT MALL-MART CHECK-OUT CLERKS!
V. VAN GOGH
I'M SORRY, VINCENT, BUT I CAN'T AFFORD TO WAIT A HUNDRED YEARS TO MAKE A SALE!!!
I VON'T PAINT THE PAST! I PAINT VHAT I ZEE!! I PAINT VHAT I ZEE!!!
HEY, VINCE?
SPECIAL
WHAT ARE YOU DOING?
I'M PUTTIN' BOMBS IN MAILBOXES TO DRAW ATTENTION TO MY POLITICAL MESSAGE.
AND YOU CHOSE TO USE THE STANDARD AMERICAN APPROACH OF MISDIRECTING YOUR RAGE?
YEP. RAGE WITH A BANG!
THAT'S PATRIOTIC...

STRIP ARTISTS

The House That Charlie Built

Comic strips exist in a realm of romance and nostalgia few pursuits can claim to inhabit. Maybe baseball comes close, but then only baseball prior to the era of bizarrely named corporate stadiums and gazillion-dollar salaries, when Babe Ruth was the Bam and Ty Cobb filed his spikes to side-sticking, uniform-slashing weapons of intimidation.

Comic strips are as American as hot dogs, rock and roll, and mom's apple pie. They induce a glow of affection in admirers born out of shared experience, of kids chattering at recess about "Garfield" and "Calvin and Hobbes," of cubicle-mates sharing a laugh over "Dilbert," of mom and dad exchanging newspaper sections over coffee cups and breakfast dishes.

In a lakeside artist studio, Duane Barnhart holds up a reproduction of a 1930s Sunday Funnies insert. "Krazy Kat," a strip created by George Herriman in 1913 and considered one of the best ever made, spreads across the page.

"Look at the size of that comic," says Barnhart, an editorial cartoonist for his paper in Aitkin, Minnesota, and the author of the how-to book *Cartooning Basics*. "What a beautiful piece of art. What a wonderful thing. And full of those bright primary colors they used back then. What a joy to wake up on a Sunday morning and run out and grab that. I still get a joy doing that. It brings me back to my childhood."

American kids and adults have been enjoying comic strips since the late nineteenth century, when Hearst and Pulitzer were the undisputed newspaper barons and Richard Outcault's "Hogan's Alley," a.k.a. "The Yellow Kid," ran in the *New York Journal*. And as American as they feel, strips had their antecedents in Europe. The British "Alley Sloper's Half Holiday" (1884) is generally considered the first comic.

Ever since Gutenberg mechanized the printing press, artists have been drawing comics for a mass medium, either as entertainment or commentary. Benjamin Franklin, a printer long before he devoted himself to revolution, is credited with drawing an early political cartoon, showing a snake segmented into the American colonies.

COMIC STRIPS ARE AS AMERICAN AS HOT DOGS, ROCK AND ROLL, AND MOM'S APPLE PIE.

For comics historian David Mruz, the story of Minnesota comic strips begins with a little-known figure who cast a large shadow in his day: Charles Lewis Bartholomew, or Bart. Born in 1869 in Charlton, Iowa, Bart made a name with strips like "George and His Conscience" (1907), "Cousin Bill" (1909), and "Bud Smith, the Boy Who Does Stunts" (1908–12) and editorial cartoons printed in the *Minneapolis Journal*.

Bart was significant for three things, says Mruz: his art, his mentorship of young cartoonists, and the years he spent as dean at the Federal School of Illustration and Cartooning in Minneapolis. One of the cartoonists Bart mentored was Frank King, a Wisconsin boy born in 1883.

"A traveling salesman saw some of the work King had done and told King that if he wanted a job, he should go to Minneapolis. So he went there, and Bart took him under his wing," says Mruz.

From 1901 to 1905, King sharpened his skills working in the art department at the *Minneapolis Times*. King would later move to Chicago, where in 1918 he debuted the strip for which he will always be remembered, "Gasoline Alley." Significantly, it was one of the first strips to acknowledge the passage of time in characters' lives.

Barnhart teaches cartooning in schools. He gets a ground-zero report on the new generation's favorite doodlers. "Kids tell me their favorite cartoonist is Bill Watterson. Well, that's great. Bill Watterson is a genius with 'Calvin and Hobbes.' But Bill Watterson was influenced by Cliff Sterrett."

Born in Fergus Falls, Minnesota, Cliff Sterrett (1883–1964) possessed a fire to pursue his own comic strip. Instead, he languished for eight long years in the bullpen at the *New York Herald,* designing photo borders, pasting pages, and sketching news illustrations. At last, in 1911, the *New York Telegram* hired him to draw strips.

A year later, Sterrett came up with "Positive Polly," later renamed "Polly and Her Pals." The strip featured Polly, a flirtatious college girl; her parents, Maw and Paw Perkins; and a wacky supporting cast that included the butler Neewah, Cousin Carrie, Angel, Kitty the cat, and Paw's infuriating nephew Asher. "Polly and Her Pals" is considered one of the better strips to come out of that era, though it is little remembered today.

The name Charles Schulz has attained legendary status in comics circles. His strip "Peanuts" ran for over fifty years, earned millions, and saw a run of TV adaptations. But the story always came first, for Schulz and for his fans. The story was simple, too, just the doings of a group of kids and a few self-realized animals.

Schulz (1922–2000) was born in Minneapolis, grew up in St. Paul, and attended St. Paul's Central High School. After serving in World War II, he returned to Minnesota as a teacher at Art Instruction Schools. There he worked alongside a number of talented cartoonists, including Frank Wing (1873–1956), who had created the single-panel comic "Yesterdays" for the *Minneapolis Journal.*

Wing encouraged Schulz to submit his strip, "Li'l Folks," to the *St. Paul Pioneer Press,* where it ran from 1947 to 1950. In 1950, Schulz pitched his strip to the United Features Syndicate, which renamed it "Peanuts" and syndicated it around the country.

Schulz was a Minnesota cartoonist who, like many of his contemporaries, eventually moved to the coast in search of bigger markets. But his time in Minnesota, his contacts and his experiences, forged the artist who would create "Peanuts." Many of the characters in "Peanuts" are based on people Schulz knew in Minnesota, according to Mruz, who was interviewed by David Michealis for his book, *Schulz and Peanuts: A Biography.*

WHERE THERE'S A WILL TO DRAW, THERE'S AN ARTIST LOOKING FOR A MEANS TO MAKE A LIVING AT IT.

Quite a few characters originated from Schulz's teaching stint at the art school. Charlie Brown was the name of a staffer. Another colleague, Linus Maurer, became the strip's Linus Van Pelt. Donna Johnson, an accountant, became the model for the Little Red-Haired Girl. Apparently, Johnson rebuffed Schulz's marriage proposal, which may explain Charlie Brown's unrequited love for the Little Red-Haired Girl.

In 1999, Schulz was diagnosed with colon cancer. He tended to work three months ahead of publication, so the last "Peanuts" daily strip didn't appear in print until January 2000 and the last Sunday page until February 13, the day after his death. Schulz always pledged that no one else would draw his strip. A tall order when you consider that his contract gave the syndicate rights to hire a replacement. Though "Peanuts" remains in syndication, no one but Schulz has ever drawn it.

Yet, for all his success, how would Schulz fare if he were starting in comics today? Minnesota's contemporary cartoonists are speculating on the end of the newspaper comic strip artist and editorial cartoonist. The Internet and craigslist have nearly replaced the classified ad sections of newspapers, drying up an important source of revenue. Papers are trimming down, cutting corners, and laying off staff cartoonists. The *Minneapolis Star Tribune,* which ran Kirk Anderson's "Banana Republic" strip from 2005 to 2007, survived a bankruptcy in 2009.

Still, where there's a will to draw, there's an artist looking for a means to make a living at it. Newspaper cartoonists remain, despite the downsizing. Steve Sack draws editorials for the *Star Tribune.* David Steinlicht's "In This Corner" and Chris Monroe's "Violet Days" appear weekly in the *Pioneer Press,* and the *Star Tribune* and the *Duluth News Tribune* respectively. Jerry

Van Amerongen's "Ballard Street" strips are now collected in paperback. Andy Singer has discovered a niche in the reprint market, where comics turn up in everything from economics textbooks to corporate PowerPoint presentations. Other cartoonists like Roger Lootine and Ken Avidor are uncovering new audiences in specialty markets—bike enthusiasts, political causes, environmental campaigns.

And today's cartoonists self-publish. Digital printing technology has brought down production costs, while specialty bookstores, comic book conventions, and the web provide distribution outlets. Cartoonists are also posting comics online. For the first time in history, strip artists can reach a worldwide audience without the intermediary of a publisher or syndicate. Better yet, people are still reading, still collecting, and still running out to buy their favorite strips. ∎

KIRK ANDERSON

The land of Amnesia lies south of the United States border. Amnesia is a country of dichotomies where the palaces of the wealthy bask in a landscape richly populated by hovels and shantytowns; where the benevolent dictator, Generalissimo Wally, roughhouses the populace with gentle swats of his velvet fist; where surveillance, corruption, massive foreign debt, and mindless war are the order of the day—every day.

No one knows Amnesia better than St. Paul political cartoonist Kirk Anderson. From 2005 to 2007, Anderson documented the policies of Generalissimo Wally and the travails of Amnesia's state-sponsored opposition party (Los Cause) in "Banana Republic," a weekly comic strip for the *Minneapolis Star Tribune*. Amnesia, "the small backward Third World nation with hearts of silver and mines of gold," promised a pinch of habanero and a dash of jalapeno with the morning breakfast routine.

For two years, the strip's sharp political satire piqued the curious and jolted the complacent—this at a time when America had gone to war in the Middle East and national media were reporting on prisoner abuses at Abu Ghraib and suspected terrorist detainees at Guantanamo. Not surprisingly, secret prisons, prisoner abuse, indefinite detention, and domestic spying would play out in the panels of "Banana Republic," though Anderson, with tongue firmly planted in cheek, swears, "Amnesian politics have nothing in common with American politics. Nothing whatsoever."

HE KNEW NEXT TO NOTHING ABOUT POLITICS, BUT HE COULD PRETEND HE DID IF THE POSITION LED SOMEWHERE.

Born outside Madison, Wisconsin, Anderson cut his cartooning teeth at the University of Wisconsin–Eau Claire's student paper. After graduation, with the optimism of inexperience, he blanketed editorial offices with his strips. And he got a break, too, sort of. "As luck would have it, the first place I tried, an alt weekly in Milwaukee, called me back. I thought, *This is easy. I'm going to freelance strips full-time.* Of course, that was the last break I had for a couple months."

To supplement his income, the college grad rented his body to science. "There was a place in Madison where you could test drugs for money. Most of the drugs were benign, like aspirin or whatever. Ours was an anti-psychotic, which meant you couldn't be psychotic in order to test it."

Anderson floated through the week on a mild buzz and then cannibalized his experience for a comic strip in the *Daily Cardinal,* one of Madison's student papers. He laid it all out for *Cardinal* readers—the free high, the institutional housing, the $1,000 payday, and the fellow guinea pig who had all the behavioral traits of the anti-psychotic's target market.

Political cartooning came into Anderson's life accidentally. The *Daily Cardinal's* political cartoonist departed, and Anderson slid into the job.

He knew next to nothing about politics, but he could pretend he did if the position led somewhere.

In 1995, Anderson moved to Minnesota, eventually putting in eight years as staff cartoonist for the *St. Paul Pioneer Press* before returning to life as a freelancer. His editorial cartoons appeared in the *New York Times,* the *Washington Post,* and the *Onion.* All told, Anderson spent nearly fifteen years refining his political satire to a single-panel format. So, in 2005 when the *Star Tribune* asked him to create a quarter-page weekly strip, Anderson had to push himself to "think outside the box, literally."

The result was "Banana Republic." Anderson's Amnesia boasts a colorful cast of characters (an epaulette-wearing generalissimo, a long-suffering activist, terror suspects, gutless opposition leaders, and a war vet whose amputated arms are fitted with prosthetic bazookas) and a reporter's field day of political blunders, social turmoil, and bureaucratic wrongheadedness. For inspiration, Anderson only had to turn on the TV. In 2008, he collected the strips in a trade paperback, *Banana Republic: Adventures in Amnesia.*

"I took whatever was going on in the world and shoved it into the paradigm of 'Banana Republic,'" says Anderson. He took pokes at the Bush administration and the wars in Iraq and Afghanistan. He riffed on social stratification. Yet he never once presumed his cartoons, with all their messaging, would change a reader's mind, much less change the world. "The way I see it, an editorial cartoon is like a grain of sand. It's a grain of sand along with other grains of sand—from editorial columns, news stories, talking to friends and family—that can eventually form a rock that clocks you in the head." ■

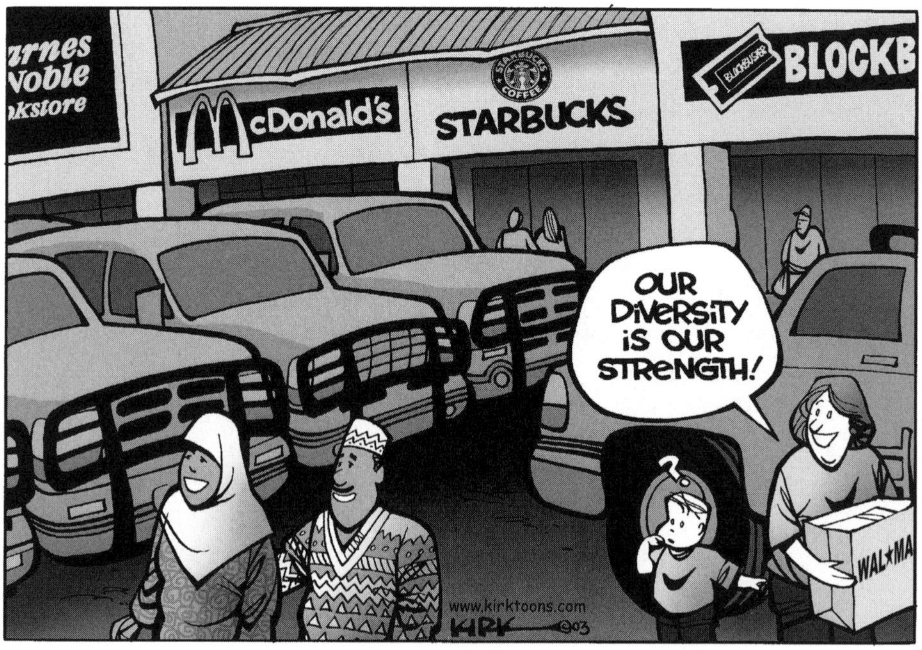
arnes
Noble
okstore
McDonald's
STARBUCKS
BLOCKB
OUR DIVERSITY IS OUR STRENGTH!
WAL★MA
www.kirktoons.com
KIRK ©03

Editorial cartoon by Kirk Anderson. © Kirk Anderson

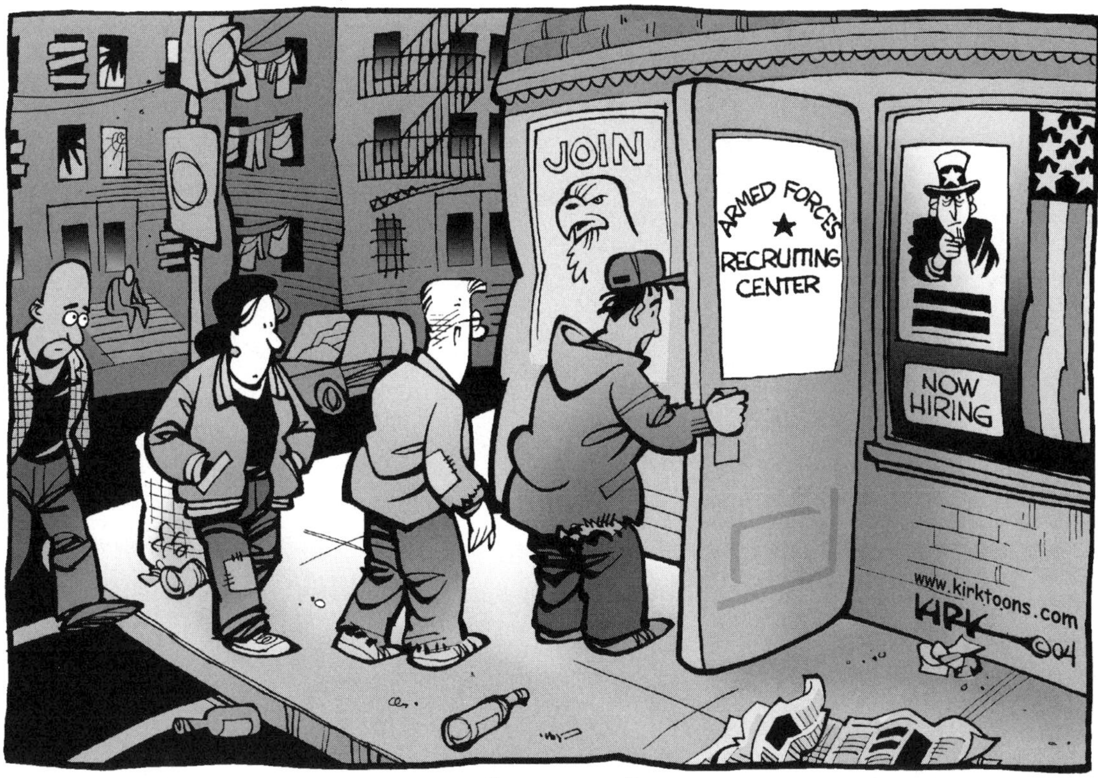
JOIN
ARMED FORCES ★ RECRUITING CENTER
NOW HIRING
www.kirktoons.com
KIRK ©04

CLASS WAR

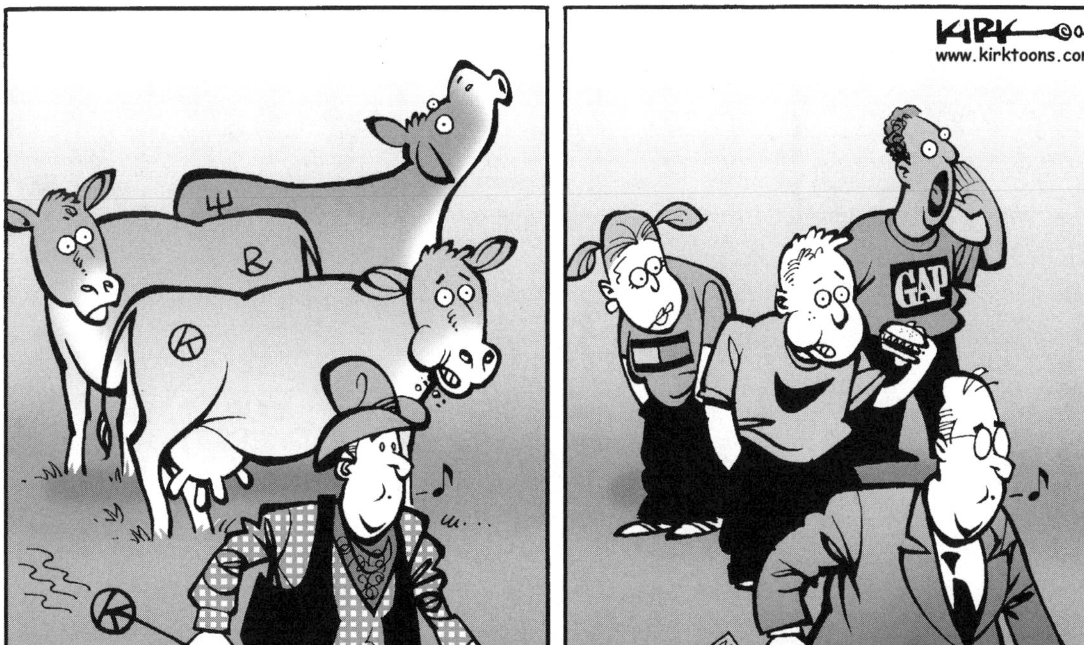
KIRK ©04
www.kirktoons.com
GAP

BRANDING

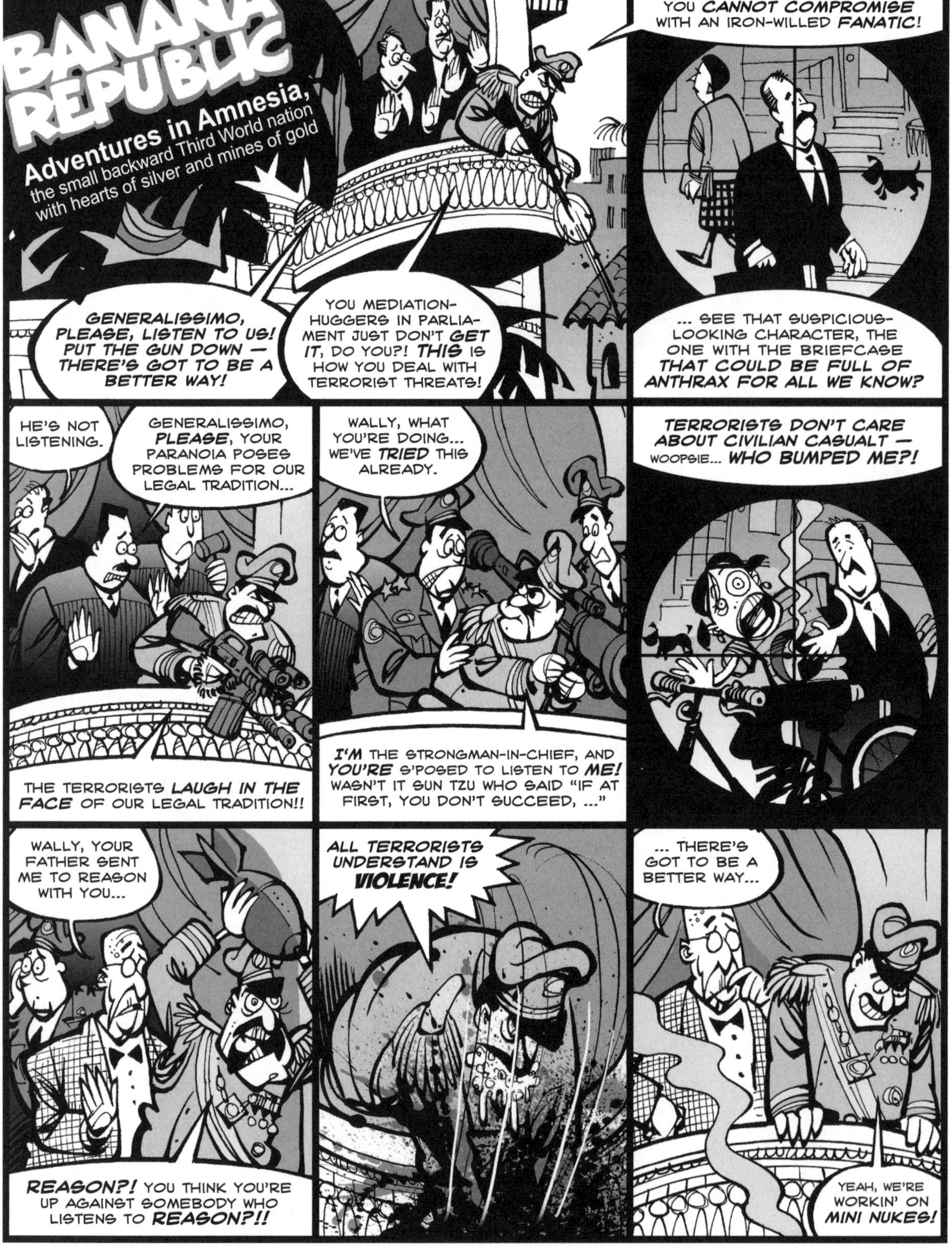
BANANA REPUBLIC
Adventures in Amnesia,
the small backward Third World nation with hearts of silver and mines of gold
GENERALISSIMO, PLEASE, LISTEN TO US! PUT THE GUN DOWN — THERE'S GOT TO BE A BETTER WAY!
YOU MEDIATION-HUGGERS IN PARLIAMENT JUST DON'T GET IT, DO YOU?! THIS IS HOW YOU DEAL WITH TERRORIST THREATS!
YOU CANNOT COMPROMISE WITH AN IRON-WILLED FANATIC!
... SEE THAT SUSPICIOUS-LOOKING CHARACTER, THE ONE WITH THE BRIEFCASE THAT COULD BE FULL OF ANTHRAX FOR ALL WE KNOW?
HE'S NOT LISTENING.
GENERALISSIMO, PLEASE, YOUR PARANOIA POSES PROBLEMS FOR OUR LEGAL TRADITION...
THE TERRORISTS LAUGH IN THE FACE OF OUR LEGAL TRADITION!!
WALLY, WHAT YOU'RE DOING... WE'VE TRIED THIS ALREADY.
I'M THE STRONGMAN-IN-CHIEF, AND YOU'RE S'POSED TO LISTEN TO ME! WASN'T IT SUN TZU WHO SAID "IF AT FIRST, YOU DON'T SUCCEED, ..."
TERRORISTS DON'T CARE ABOUT CIVILIAN CASUALT — WOOPSIE... WHO BUMPED ME?!
WALLY, YOUR FATHER SENT ME TO REASON WITH YOU...
REASON?! YOU THINK YOU'RE UP AGAINST SOMEBODY WHO LISTENS TO REASON?!!
ALL TERRORISTS UNDERSTAND IS VIOLENCE!
... THERE'S GOT TO BE A BETTER WAY...
YEAH, WE'RE WORKIN' ON MINI NUKES!

"Banana Republic," Kirk Anderson. © Kirk Anderson

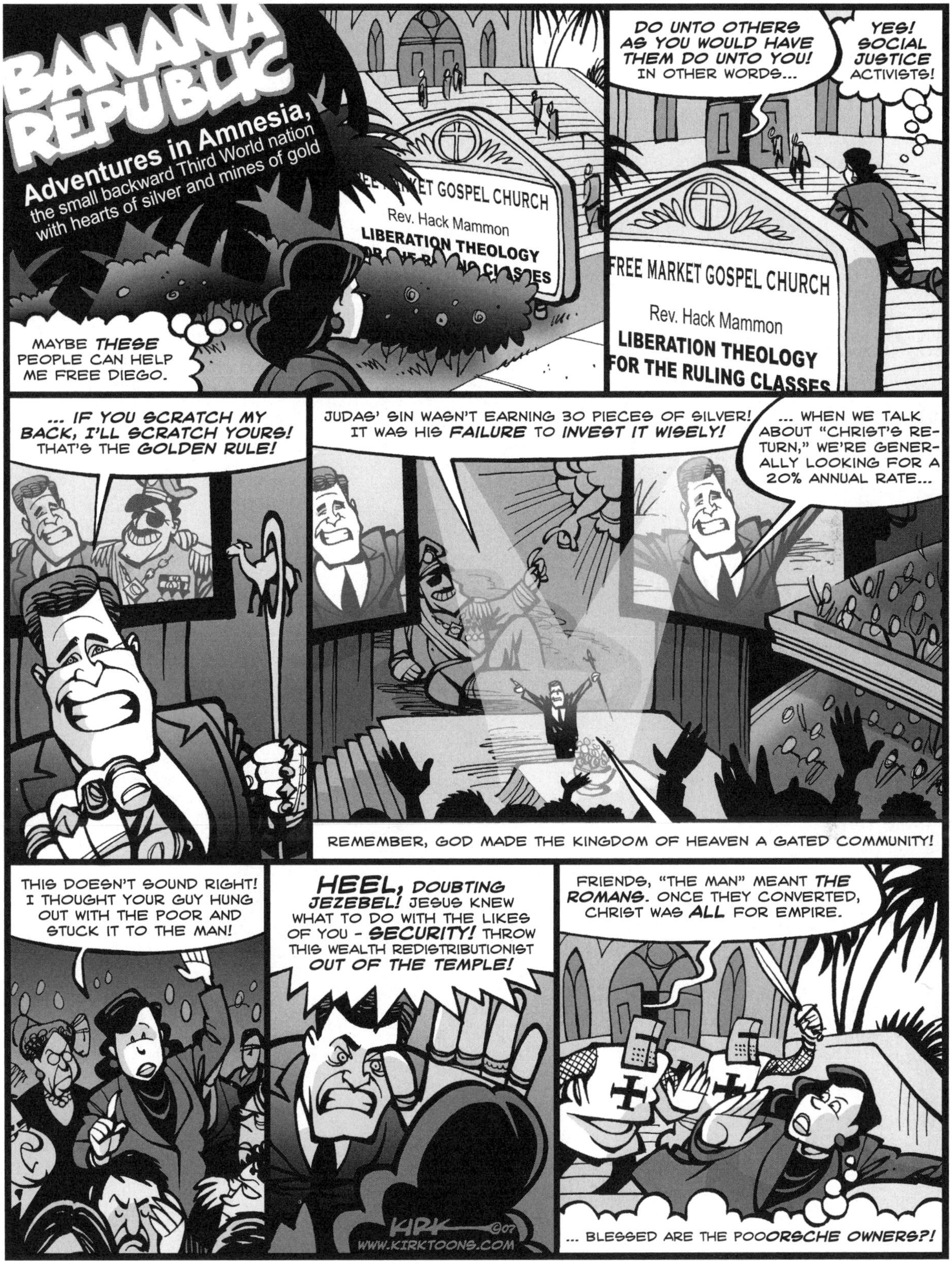
BANANA REPUBLIC
Adventures in Amnesia,
the small backward Third World nation with hearts of silver and mines of gold
Rev. Hack Mammon
LIBERATION THEOLOGY
MAYBE THESE PEOPLE CAN HELP ME FREE DIEGO.
DO UNTO OTHERS AS YOU WOULD HAVE THEM DO UNTO YOU! IN OTHER WORDS...
YES! SOCIAL JUSTICE ACTIVISTS!
FREE MARKET GOSPEL CHURCH
Rev. Hack Mammon
LIBERATION THEOLOGY FOR THE RULING CLASSES
... IF YOU SCRATCH MY BACK, I'LL SCRATCH YOURS! THAT'S THE GOLDEN RULE!
JUDAS' SIN WASN'T EARNING 30 PIECES OF SILVER! IT WAS HIS FAILURE TO INVEST IT WISELY!
... WHEN WE TALK ABOUT "CHRIST'S RETURN," WE'RE GENERALLY LOOKING FOR A 20% ANNUAL RATE...
REMEMBER, GOD MADE THE KINGDOM OF HEAVEN A GATED COMMUNITY!
THIS DOESN'T SOUND RIGHT! I THOUGHT YOUR GUY HUNG OUT WITH THE POOR AND STUCK IT TO THE MAN!
HEEL, DOUBTING JEZEBEL! JESUS KNEW WHAT TO DO WITH THE LIKES OF YOU - SECURITY! THROW THIS WEALTH REDISTRIBUTIONIST OUT OF THE TEMPLE!
KIRK ©07
WWW.KIRKTOONS.COM
FRIENDS, "THE MAN" MEANT THE ROMANS. ONCE THEY CONVERTED, CHRIST WAS ALL FOR EMPIRE.
... BLESSED ARE THE POOORSCHE OWNERS?!

"Banana Republic," Kirk Anderson. © Kirk Anderson

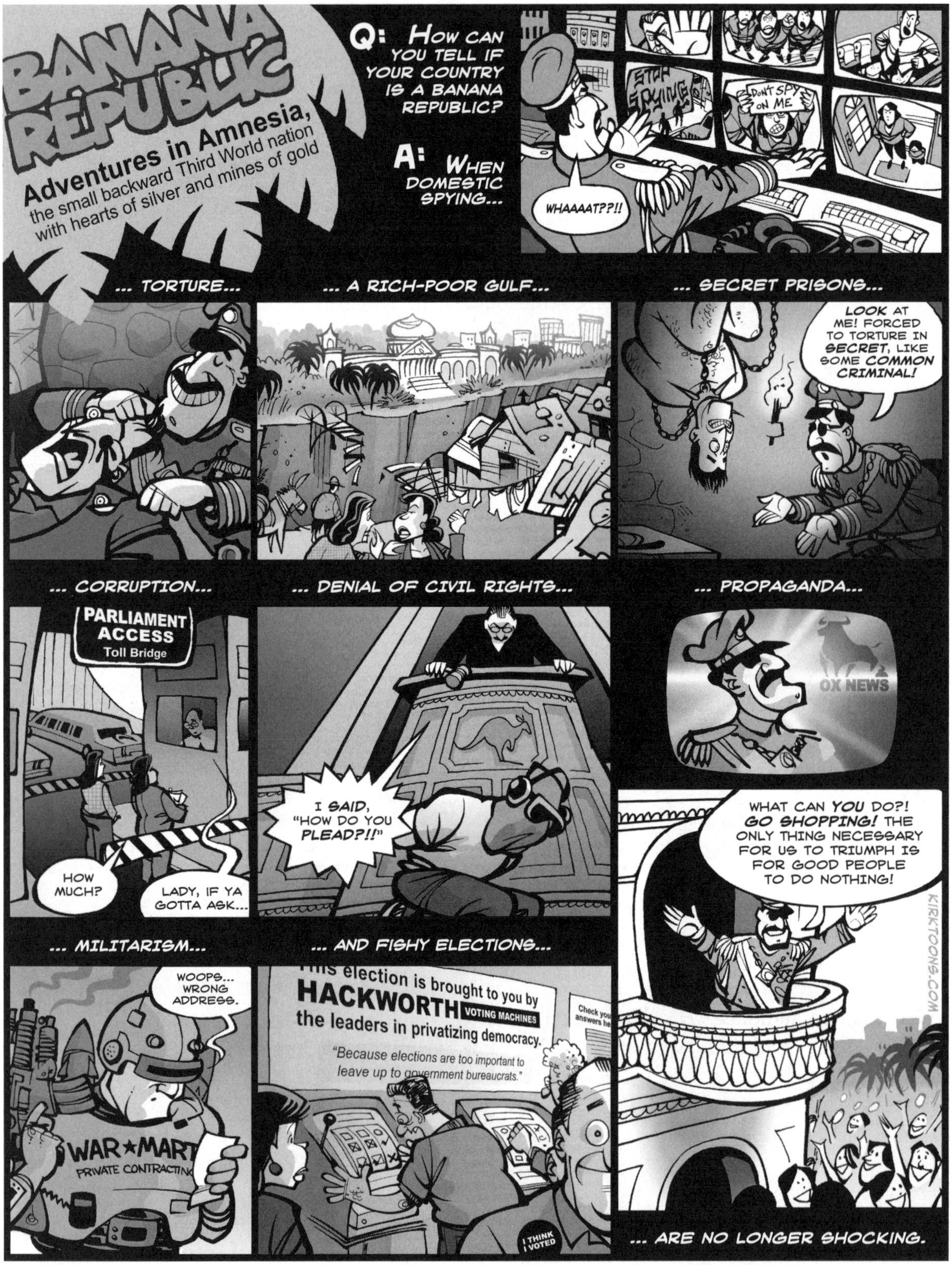
BANANA REPUBLIC
Adventures in Amnesia,
the small backward Third World nation with hearts of silver and mines of gold
Q: How can you tell if your country is a banana republic?
A: When domestic spying...
STOP SPYING
DON'T SPY ON ME
WHAAAAT??!!
... TORTURE...
... A RICH-POOR GULF...
... SECRET PRISONS...
LOOK AT ME! FORCED TO TORTURE IN SECRET, LIKE SOME COMMON CRIMINAL!
... CORRUPTION...
PARLIAMENT ACCESS
Toll Bridge
HOW MUCH?
LADY, IF YA GOTTA ASK...
... DENIAL OF CIVIL RIGHTS...
I SAID, "HOW DO YOU PLEAD?!!"
... PROPAGANDA...
OX NEWS
WHAT CAN YOU DO?! GO SHOPPING! THE ONLY THING NECESSARY FOR US TO TRIUMPH IS FOR GOOD PEOPLE TO DO NOTHING!
KIRKTOONS.COM
... MILITARISM...
WOOPS... WRONG ADDRESS.
WAR★MART
PRIVATE CONTRACTING
... AND FISHY ELECTIONS...
This election is brought to you by
HACKWORTH VOTING MACHINES
the leaders in privatizing democracy.
"Because elections are too important to leave up to government bureaucrats."
I THINK I VOTED
... ARE NO LONGER SHOCKING.

"Banana Republic," Kirk Anderson. © Kirk Anderson

KEN AVIDOR

The creator of the "Roadkill Bill" weekly strip, which ran for nearly four years in the alternative newspaper *Pulse of the Twin Cities,* goes by Ken Avidor these days. But when he was born in 1950s Brooklyn, Ken Avidor was Ken Weiner. The name change took place three decades later when Weiner and his wife Roberta, also an artist, moved to South Minneapolis.

Researching Avidor online, you find two identities—at least. There's Ken Weiner, the New York artist working in 1970s alternative publications like *Punk* and *Screw*. There's Ken Avidor, Minneapolis artist and creator of the "Roadkill Bill" strip. There's also Ken Avidor, the bike enthusiast, the concerned public citizen, the anti–Public Rapid Transit blogger, the lightning rod for conservative political bloggers, and the artist behind the ongoing graphic novel *Bicyclopolis.*

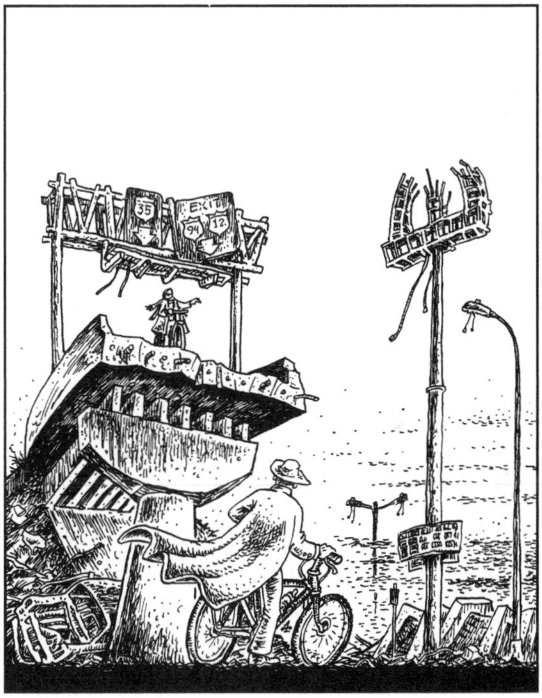
35
EXIT
94
12
Bicyclopolis by Ken Avidor. © Ken Avidor

Weiner/Avidor gets around, on- and offline. He's a talented cartoonist and a sometimes controversial figure, which to him is all in a day's work. His cartooning, even from the very early days, tended to land him in a fix.

"Probably the first time I got into trouble with my artwork was in third grade," recalls Avidor, as he settles into the upstairs room that serves as his studio. It's neat, as far as artist studios go. Traces of his artistic history paper the walls and are crammed into stacked boxes. An Apple computer occupies a desk with only a modicum of clutter. "I had two friends. We always did stuff together," he recalls. "One day, one of my friends said, 'I have a friend who has a brother who has a cousin who actually saw a copy of *Playboy.*' We didn't know what *Playboy* meant, but we knew it was something forbidden."

Avidor's friend described the notorious magazine to his rapt audience. "His description was so bizarre: *Playboy* had nude women in it. That blew our minds. We knew we couldn't get a copy. So we decided to create one ourselves."

The boys set to work. Some kids caricature their teachers in classroom doodles. Others scrawl graffiti on trains. Avidor and his friends, at the tender ages of eight and nine, composed a skin rag. They divided the labor of producing a magazine, with Avidor taking on the roles of art director and artist. The art included his version of a *Playboy* Playmate.

"But I really didn't know what a nude woman looked like," says the artist. "We put our heads together. We'd been to the beach, and we'd seen topless

guys with hair on their chests. So I drew a woman with hair between her breasts. It was freaky, but that's what we thought they looked like. We were trying to figure something out. It was a wonderful experiment."

Enthusiastically, the boys premiered their masterpiece in the school cafeteria. Small fingers flew over the pages. "Kids were raving. 'This is great.' 'This is wonderful.' My friends and I were already planning issue number two," says Avidor. He and his pals had produced a great first issue, all in all, save for one oversight. "We were so euphoric, we forgot the magazine in the cafeteria. We went back to class, and about an hour later the principal's assistant called our names."

The accomplices dutifully trooped to the principal's office. They waited outside, exchanging looks, whispering. Sure, they were known troublemakers. But what had they done *today,* as a group, to warrant this visit to the big man? Nothing. Absolutely nothing.

"We were so naïve. We went in the office. The principal had this buzz cut. I'm sure he was doing his best to stay serious. And there in front of him on the desk was our magazine. The principal looked at us and said," Avidor lowers his voice, "'Boys, you've done a serious thing. You left this on a lunch tray and a cafeteria lady found it. You almost gave her a heart attack.' Talk about an epiphany."

The epiphany was that art, apart from being a mode of visual communication, could produce a reaction. *The cafeteria lady almost had a heart attack.* That was power.

When Avidor was a teen, his older brother worked as a journalist at the *East Village Other* in New York. The underground newspaper was famous for, among other things, its sex ads and the occasional publication of the comics special issue *Gothic Blimp Works,* which published the art of the best underground cartoonists of the day, like Robert Crumb and Spain Rodriguez.

The *East Village Other* had an office in the Lower East Side. "The cool thing about the office was the bathroom," Avidor remembers. "Because when Crumb and those cartoonists came through, they'd do frescoes in marker on the bathroom walls." The paper eventually decamped from the

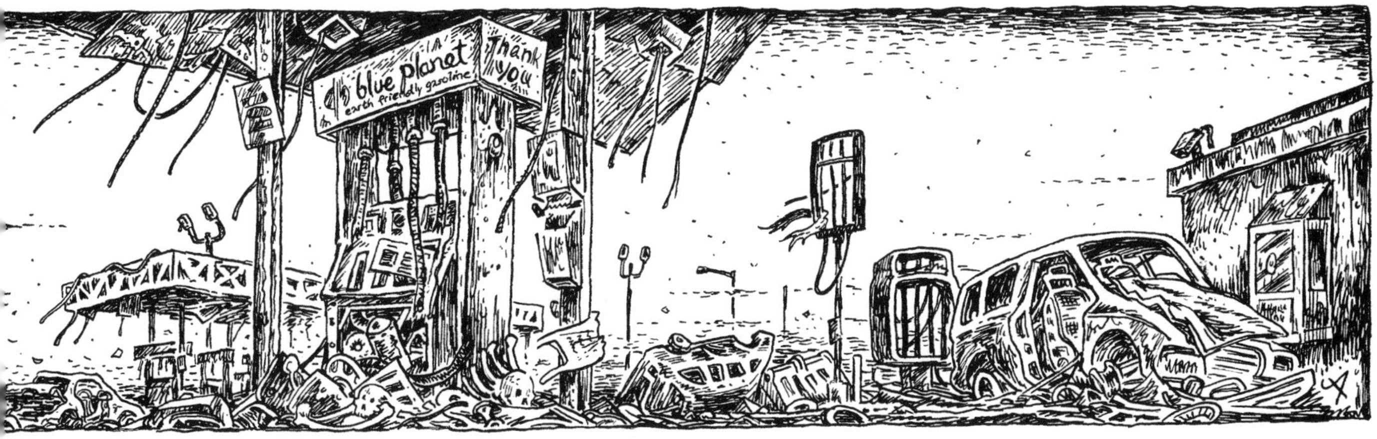
blue planet
earth friendly gasoline
Thank you

Bicyclopolis by Ken Avidor. © Ken Avidor

office, abandoning the bathroom art to the building manager and the roller brush. Gone forever.

But not Avidor's fascination with underground cartooning. In fact, he couldn't have been in a better place (New York City) or time (the 1970s) to start a career in cartooning. Underground magazines proliferated in the Big Apple of the seventies. Artistic careers develop from an admixture of talent, ambition, and happy accident. After graduating from the Parsons School of Design, Avidor snagged a plum illustration and cartooning job at *Screw*. The job actually paid him to create art—and for private consumption, not for mom's refrigerator magnet.

Screw was a porn magazine lorded over by publisher Al Goldstein, a larger-than-life figure who lived big and fell hard. Years later, the *Villager* and the *New York Times* would report his sordid decline from a Florida mansion to a flop in his in-laws' house. But in the seventies, Goldstein was the man; and his publication was creating jobs for artists, who designed *Screw*'s covers and ads. Avidor, then cartooning under the name Weiner, worked alongside artists Bruce Carleton, John Holmstrom, and Peter Bagge, all of whom launched careers from their work in the undergrounds.

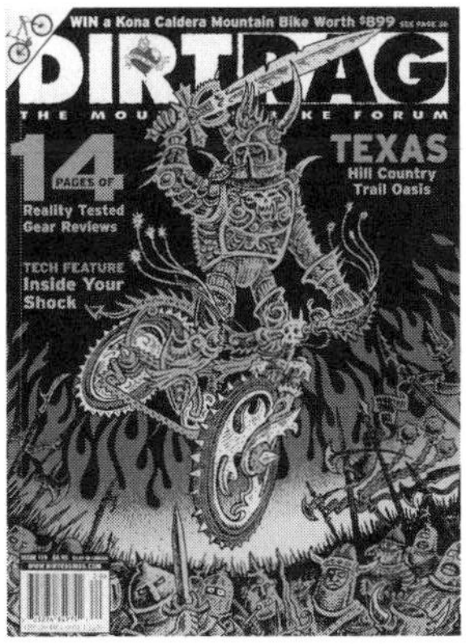
WIN a Kona Caldera Mountain Bike Worth $899
DIRT RAG
14 PAGES OF Reality Tested Gear Reviews
TEXAS Hill Country Trail Oasis
TECH FEATURE Inside Your Shock

Cover for *Dirt Rag* magazine by Ken Avidor. © 2006 Ken Avidor

During this period, Avidor also contributed to *Punk, Comical Funnies, Stop,* and *Weirdo.* With *Screw* alumnus Bagge, he published *The Wacky World of Ken Weiner and Peter Bagge* in the early eighties.

By the mid-eighties, escalating rental prices drove artists from New York City. Avidor and his wife participated in the exodus. On the advice of a friend, they moved to Minneapolis in 1986. Avidor describes the Minneapolis of that era as Bohemian. Lots of art, lots of music.

He mixed with the local cartooning community through shows at the now-defunct Rifle Sport Gallery, located near the current Block E in downtown Minneapolis. The gallery rubbed shoulders with Moby Dick's, a notorious bar that attracted a rough crowd and not a few urban legends. One of the legends placed a wall of sobriety medals, bestowed on Alcoholics Anonymous members, behind the bar.

In 1998, Avidor developed the environmental-themed strip "Sunny and Friends." But a year later, he found the creative muse that would possess him for the next four years, "Roadkill Bill." The strip expresses the anxieties of a squirrel, Roadkill Bill, unlucky enough to have tire tracks striped down his back. Bill evinces a lively dislike of rude motorists, traffic-clogged highways, environmental waste, and human stupidity. Car Busters Press published the collection in 2001.

> ART, APART FROM BEING A MODE OF VISUAL COMMUNICATION, COULD PRODUCE A REACTION. THE CAFETERIA LADY ALMOST HAD A HEART ATTACK. THAT WAS POWER.

The graphic novel *Bicyclopolis* is Avidor's latest obsession, a lushly drawn yet haunting vision of Minnesota in 2076. The book follows Flodge, a European emissary, as he bikes over the dry bed of Lake Superior and traverses the wastes of interior Minnesota en route to Bicyclopolis. In one image Flodge outruns a plastic grocery bag storm. In another he inspects a curious relic of American consumerism, a "Have a Nice Day" T-shirt.

In Avidor's post-industrial world, suburbanites live in a medieval kingdom. They scavenge in landfills and outrun mutants born from toxic waste exposure. Cars are arranged in rusty Stonehenge formations. Avidor has even included a religious cult, the descendants of Minnesota congressional representative Michele Bachmann, who pray for the return of suburbia.

Not one to shy from controversy, Avidor has channeled his skill with the pen into causes and courtrooms. He provided cover art for *False Witness: The Michele Bachmann Story,* a Minnesota comic written and penciled by Bill Prendergast, with finishes by Lupi, Daniel J. Olson, and Danno Klonowski. He also sketched the trial of Tom Petters, a businessman convicted of swindling investors out of billions.

Avidor himself has been the occasional subject of controversy, especially for his opposition to Public Rapid Transit legislation. But that's the life of a cartoonist. It's what Avidor learned in the principal's office back in 1963: Images have the power to create reactions. ■

ROADKILL BILL by KEN AVIDOR

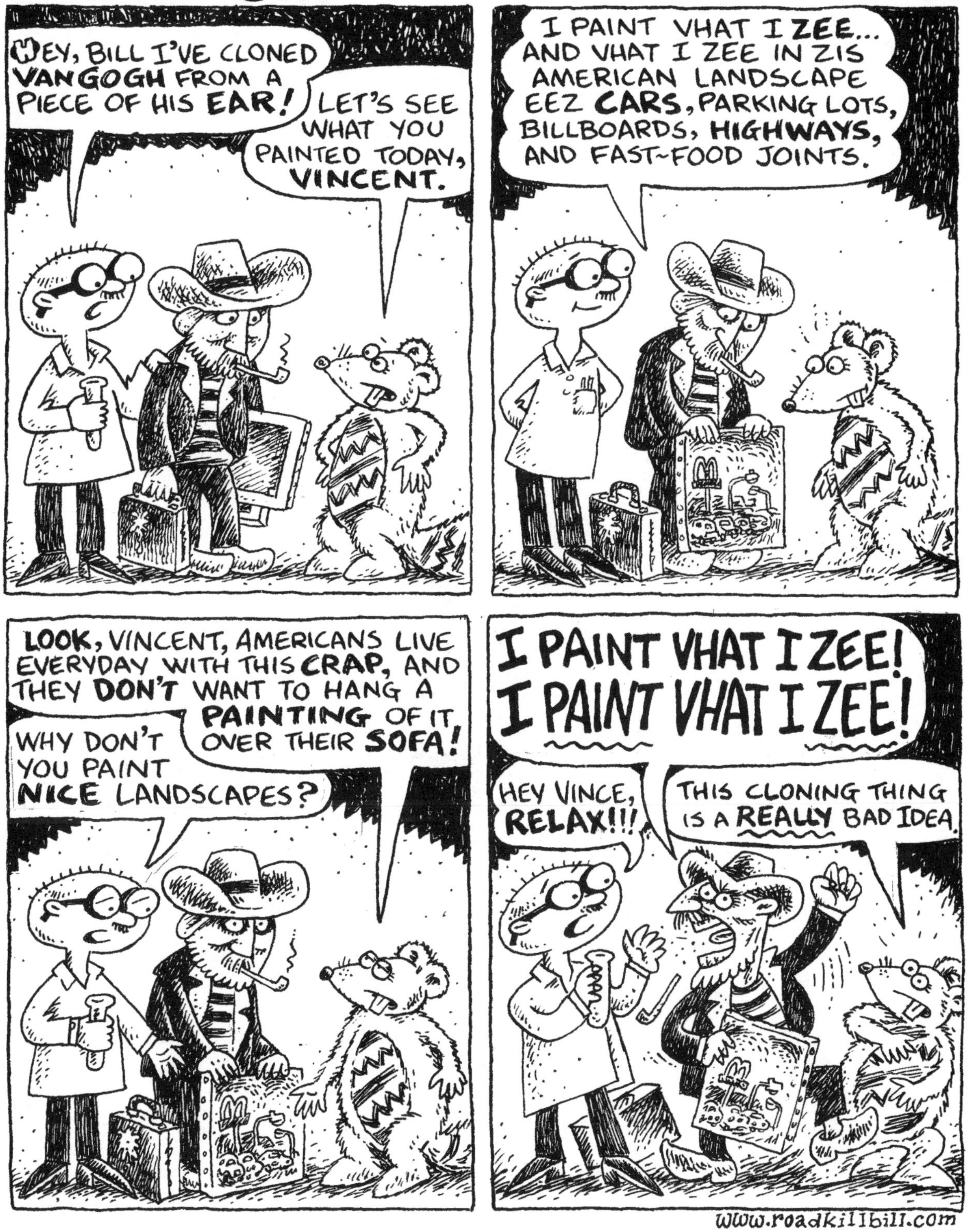
HEY, BILL I'VE CLONED VANGOGH FROM A PIECE OF HIS EAR!
LET'S SEE WHAT YOU PAINTED TODAY, VINCENT.
I PAINT VHAT I ZEE... AND VHAT I ZEE IN ZIS AMERICAN LANDSCAPE EEZ CARS, PARKING LOTS, BILLBOARDS, HIGHWAYS, AND FAST-FOOD JOINTS.
WHY DON'T YOU PAINT NICE LANDSCAPES?
LOOK, VINCENT, AMERICANS LIVE EVERYDAY WITH THIS CRAP, AND THEY DON'T WANT TO HANG A PAINTING OF IT OVER THEIR SOFA!
I PAINT VHAT I ZEE! I PAINT VHAT I ZEE!
HEY VINCE, RELAX!!!
THIS CLONING THING IS A REALLY BAD IDEA.
www.roadkillbill.com

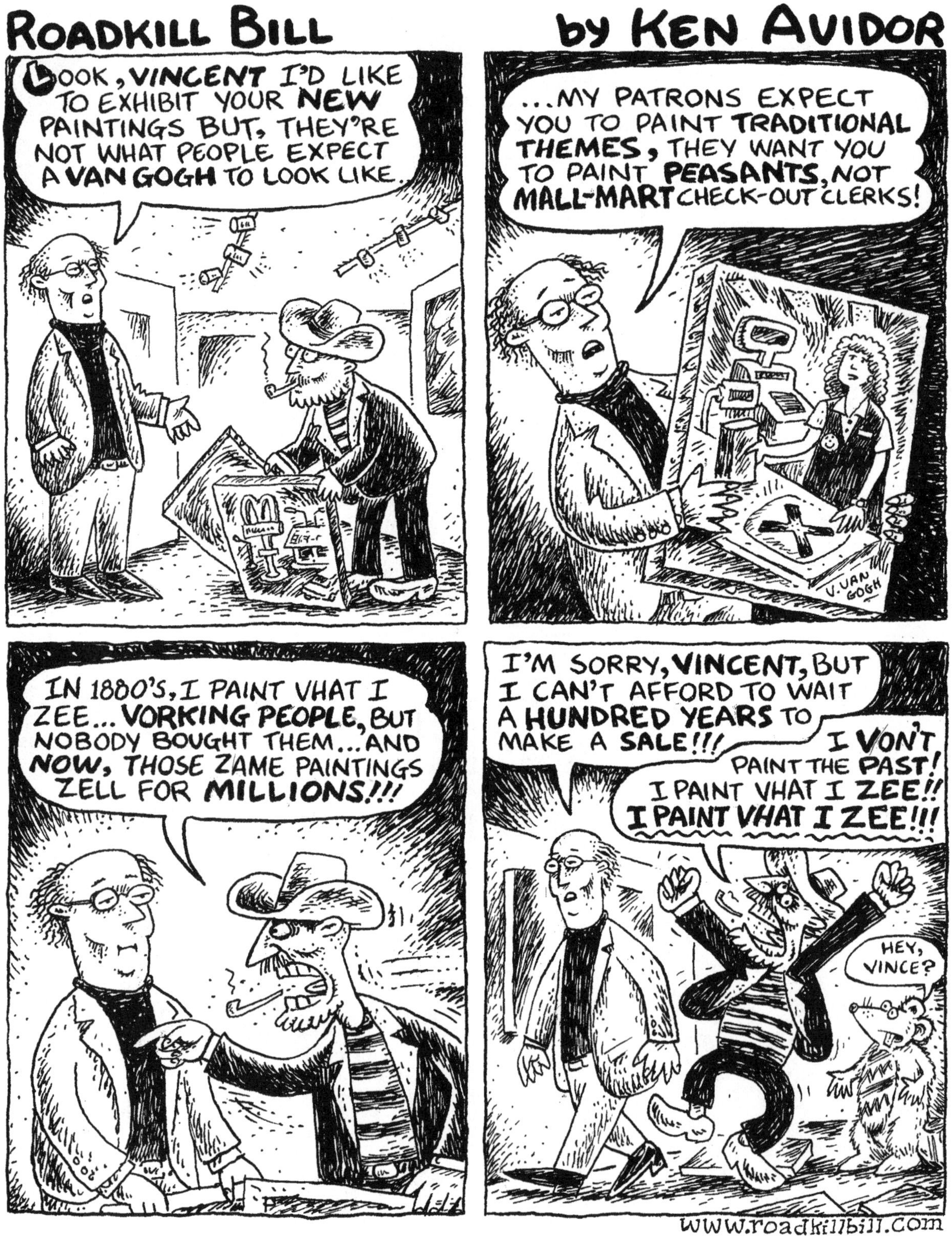
ROADKILL BILL
by KEN AVIDOR
LOOK, VINCENT I'D LIKE TO EXHIBIT YOUR NEW PAINTINGS BUT, THEY'RE NOT WHAT PEOPLE EXPECT A VAN GOGH TO LOOK LIKE...
...MY PATRONS EXPECT YOU TO PAINT TRADITIONAL THEMES, THEY WANT YOU TO PAINT PEASANTS, NOT MALL-MART CHECK-OUT CLERKS!
V. VAN GOGH
IN 1880'S, I PAINT VHAT I ZEE... VORKING PEOPLE, BUT NOBODY BOUGHT THEM... AND NOW, THOSE ZAME PAINTINGS ZELL FOR MILLIONS!!!
I'M SORRY, VINCENT, BUT I CAN'T AFFORD TO WAIT A HUNDRED YEARS TO MAKE A SALE!!!
I VON'T PAINT THE PAST! I PAINT VHAT I ZEE!! I PAINT VHAT I ZEE!!!
HEY, VINCE?
WWW.roadkillbill.com

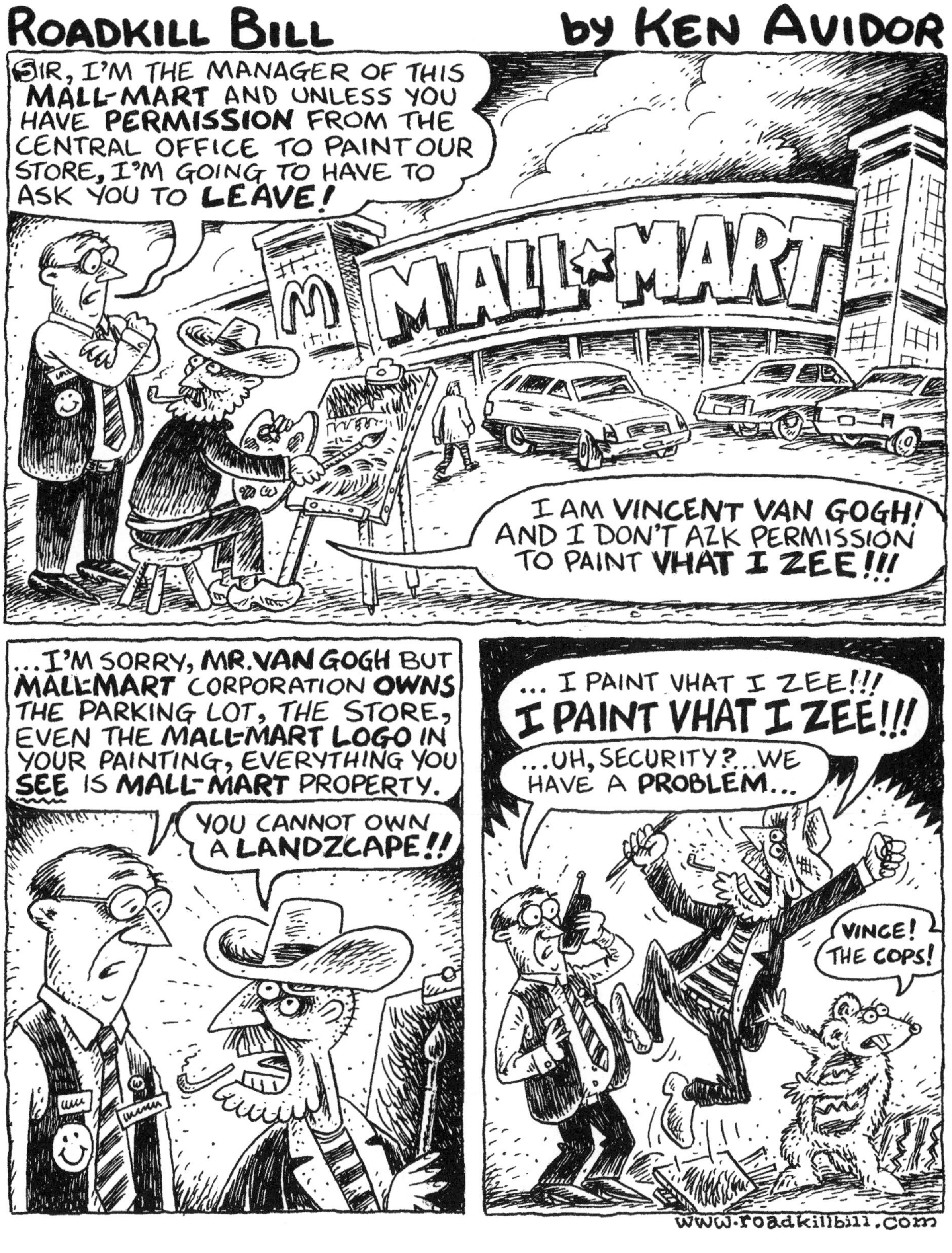
ROADKILL BILL
by KEN AVIDOR
SIR, I'M THE MANAGER OF THIS MALL-MART AND UNLESS YOU HAVE PERMISSION FROM THE CENTRAL OFFICE TO PAINT OUR STORE, I'M GOING TO HAVE TO ASK YOU TO LEAVE!
MALL★MART
I AM VINCENT VAN GOGH! AND I DON'T AZK PERMISSION TO PAINT VHAT I ZEE!!!
...I'M SORRY, MR. VAN GOGH BUT MALL-MART CORPORATION OWNS THE PARKING LOT, THE STORE, EVEN THE MALL-MART LOGO IN YOUR PAINTING, EVERYTHING YOU SEE IS MALL-MART PROPERTY.
YOU CANNOT OWN A LANDZCAPE!!
... I PAINT VHAT I ZEE!!!
I PAINT VHAT I ZEE!!!
...UH, SECURITY?...WE HAVE A PROBLEM...
VINCE! THE COPS!
www.roadkillbill.com

"Roadkill Bill" by Ken Avidor. © Ken Avidor

ROGER LOOTINE

Roger Lootine, the personality behind "Residue Comix," was biking to a meeting of the International Cartoonist Conspiracy. The ride wasn't far. Lootine rents an apartment in Northeast Minneapolis, and the Conspiracy hosts their monthly get-together-and-draw event at Diamonds, a coffee shop on Central Avenue in Northeast.

"But on the way, I ran into a group of bikers," Lootine remarks. "One of the girls had an SUV and the group was driving their bicycles to Buck Hill. It was such a sunny day." So, instead of drawing with the other cartoonists at the Conspiracy, Lootine heaved his bicycle onto the SUV and tore through the trails in Burnsville.

Artists are obsessed creatures, right? They obsess about their art, like van Gogh with his letters to Theo, or Monet putting off his mourning to capture his wife's death in oils.

But sometimes the artist's obsession is a toss-up. Lootine stands at a crossroads, with a long night of drawing down one path and the open road down the other. "I've never been so healthy in my life," says Lootine of his marathon bike rides. Not coincidentally, when he does sit down to draw, he draws bikes, cyclists, and the confirmed predator of both, the SUV.

Born in 1970, Lootine grew up with two older brothers and a sister in Palatine, Illinois. His older brothers were the physical, roughhousing members of the family; Lootine was the "scrawny kid with glasses. I always ended up in the hospital. I got stuck in the eye once. And there were these other health issues, so it was like, 'All right, Roger, you got to sit still for a couple months to recuperate.'" And if he had to sit still, he might as well do something. What he did was draw.

The kid with glasses planted himself in front of the TV with a pad of paper and a pencil. "This was before VCRs. If I needed to draw a hand, I'd sit in front of *Looney Tunes* and wait for a certain hand position to come on." Bugs, Daffy, or Yosemite Sam would pose, and Lootine would furiously copy. He taught himself to draw watching *Looney Tunes* and reading "Peanuts" strips.

As a student at the University of Illinois, Lootine drew one-panel political cartoons for the *Daily Illini*. "Then a spot opened up in the weekly arts section. So I started whipping off these weekly comics," he says. Unlike the political cartoons, Lootine's weekly comics didn't seek to educate or inform; they were pure entertainment. "I'd been trying to make a statement with the political cartoons, which no one read. But people actually read the weeklies, so they became my focus."

When Lootine moved to Minnesota, he took a job at Art Instruction Schools in Minneapolis. "You've probably seen the magazine ads for the school. Draw Tippy the Turtle, or draw the Pirate?" he says. Students would mail in assignments, and Lootine would grade them.

"With a lot of the early lessons, students worked on specific drawings. I'd place an overlay on their work. The overlay showed how the drawing could improve," says Lootine, who spent eleven years grading assignments. "In later lessons, I'd draw directly on the student's work. *The head should line up with the knee here. These parts need to line up.* I'd give it a grade, enter it in the computer, and send it on its way."

While working at Art Instruction Schools, Lootine developed a weekly strip for *Pulse of the Twin Cities*. And what a strip it was. "Residue Comix" traded on bodily functions, gross humor, naughtiness, and the kind of rants that would have made Tippy blanch a greener shade of pale.

Among "Residue's" joint-smoking, bong-toting, sex-obsessed population are Chump the chimpanzee, Crunchy the cockroach, and Alf the dog. Box-Cutter Willy, an evil-looking Mickey Mouse, and Crusader Sam, a dog whose patriotism extends to bombing foreign lands, make memorable cameos. The characters get high, ride bikes, offer the finger to rude motorists, sneer at political correctness, masturbate, and watch TV, which rules in "Residue" land.

LOOTINE'S COMICS HAVE A TENDENCY TO HIT THE ROAD AND KEEP ON GOING.

Like their creator, Lootine's comics have a tendency to hit the road and keep on going. One issue of "Residue Comix" hitched a ride to Joliet State Prison in Illinois. An inmate wrote Lootine a fan letter. "I was transferred to this rat hole three weeks ago from a downstate prison," writes the inmate, who goes on to mention that his jailors had refused him access to books. "So I've been sitting in this cell, twiddling my thumbs. Till yesterday, when someone laid a copy of 'Residue' #5 on me. I was laughing so hard that the pigs thought I'd been smokin' a doobie & took me for a drug test!"

Lootine has since moved on from the weekly strip and the job at Art Instruction Schools. "I burned out on art a couple years ago. Cartooning was a treadmill. I had a full-time job in cartooning and I had the strip. I didn't have time for anything else," he says.

Now he rides his bike and draws comics for bicycle magazines like *Urban Velo*. He's trying to recalibrate his relationship to comics, to pull back from full-throttled commitment to something more balanced. "I have a love/hate thing with cartooning. When I start a project, everything else falls to the side. I don't eat well. I don't exercise. My phone gets lost in a pile." But would he ever give up cartooning? Nope, Lootine says. "What else would I do?" ∎

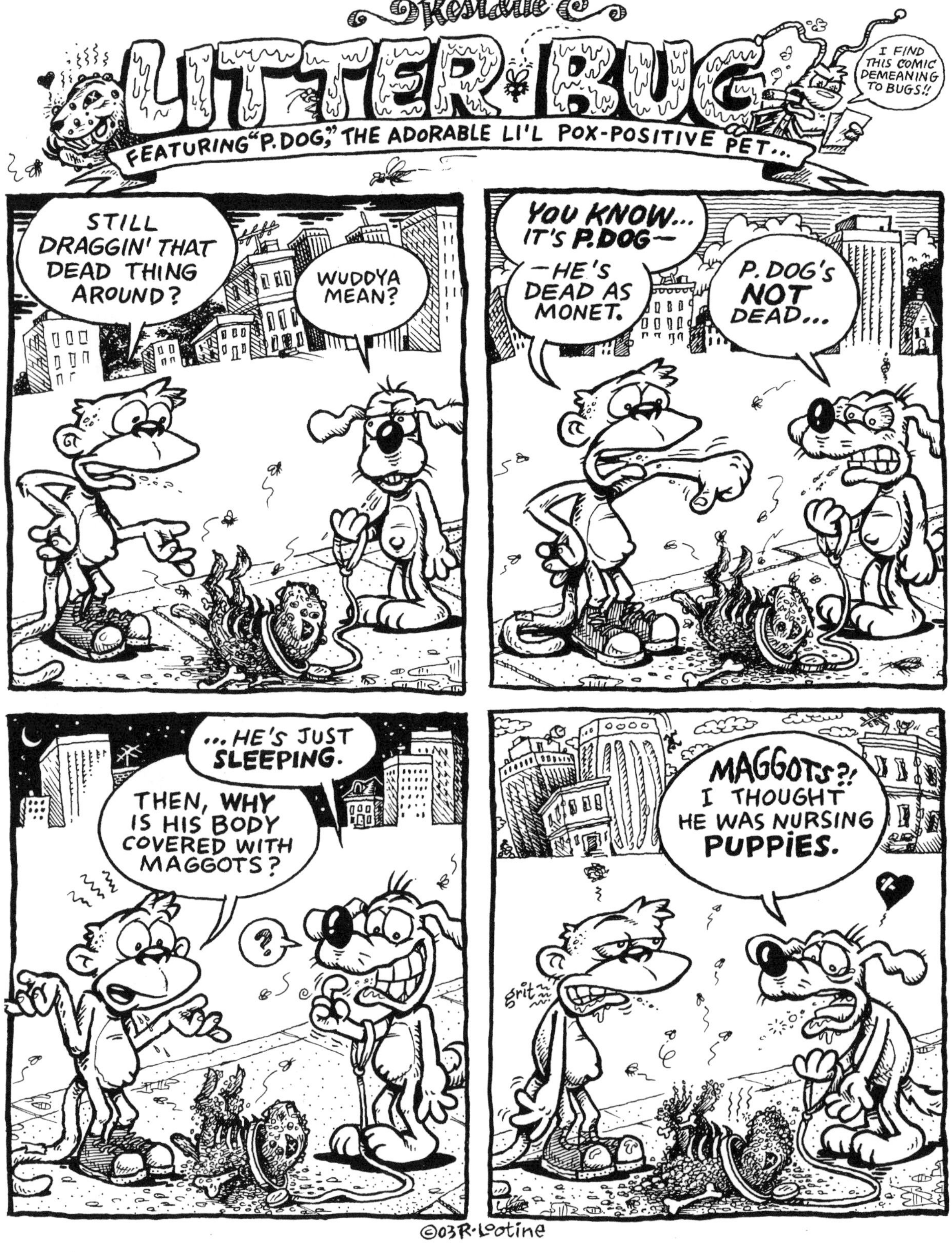
Residue tm
LITTER BUG
I FIND THIS COMIC DEMEANING TO BUGS!!
FEATURING "P.DOG," THE ADORABLE LI'L POX-POSITIVE PET...
STILL DRAGGIN' THAT DEAD THING AROUND?
WUDDYA MEAN?
YOU KNOW... IT'S P.DOG—
—HE'S DEAD AS MONET.
P.DOG'S NOT DEAD...
...HE'S JUST SLEEPING.
THEN, WHY IS HIS BODY COVERED WITH MAGGOTS?
?
MAGGOTS?! I THOUGHT HE WAS NURSING PUPPIES.
grit
©03R.Lootine

"Residue Comix" by Roger Lootine. © Roger Lootine

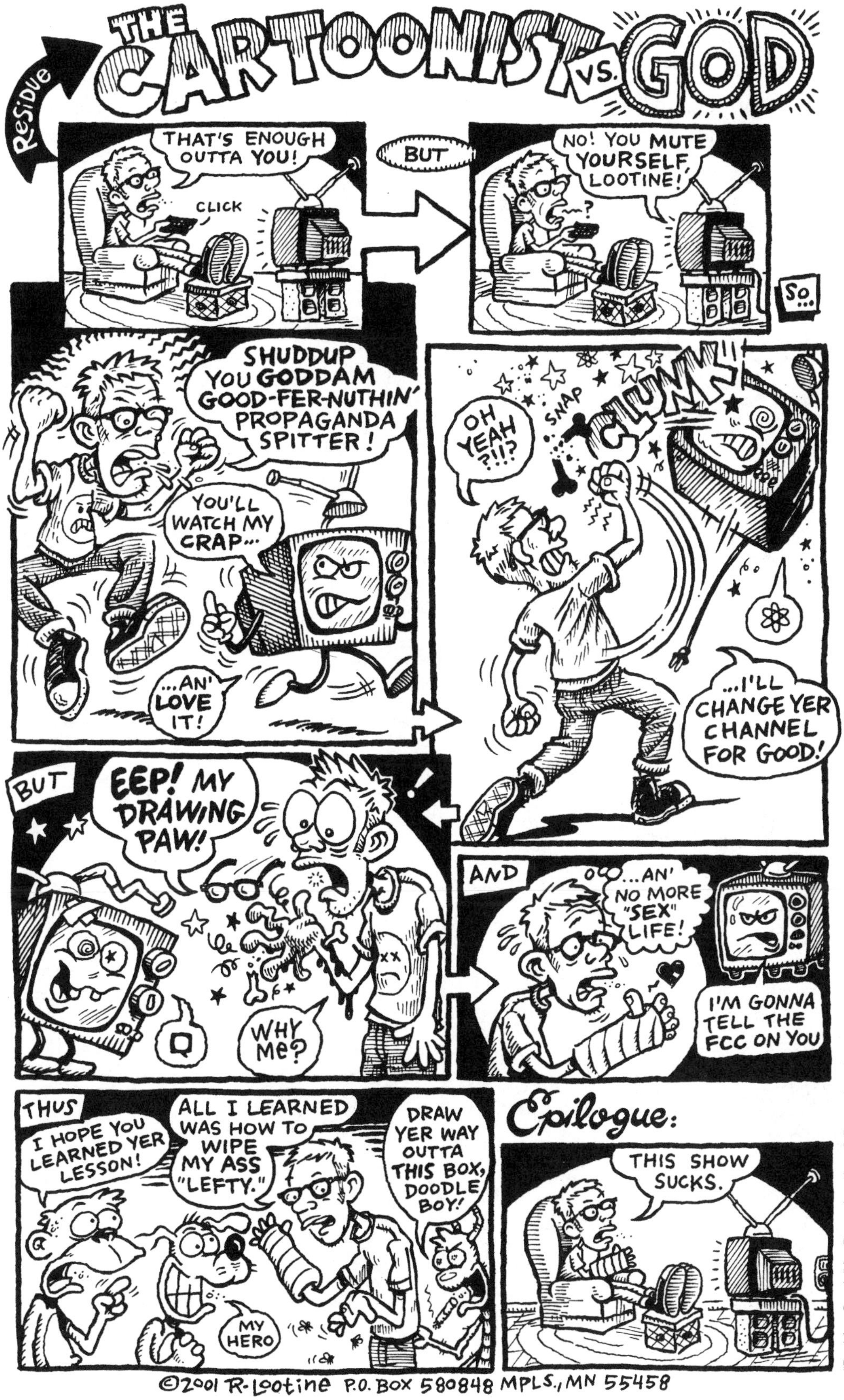
RESIDUE
THE CARTOONIST VS. GOD
THAT'S ENOUGH OUTTA YOU!
CLICK
BUT
NO! YOU MUTE YOURSELF, LOOTINE!
?
SO...
SHUDDUP YOU GODDAM GOOD-FER-NUTHIN' PROPAGANDA SPITTER!
YOU'LL WATCH MY CRAP...
...AN' LOVE IT!
OH YEAH ?!!?
SNAP
CLUNK!!
...I'LL CHANGE YER CHANNEL FOR GOOD!
BUT
EEP! MY DRAWING PAW!
WHY ME?
AND
...AN' NO MORE "SEX" LIFE!
I'M GONNA TELL THE FCC ON YOU
THUS
I HOPE YOU LEARNED YER LESSON!
ALL I LEARNED WAS HOW TO WIPE MY ASS "LEFTY."
DRAW YER WAY OUTTA THIS BOX, DOODLE BOY!
MY HERO
Epilogue:
THIS SHOW SUCKS.
©2001 R-Lootine P.O. BOX 580848 MPLS., MN 55458

"Residue Comix" by Roger Lootine. © Roger Lootine

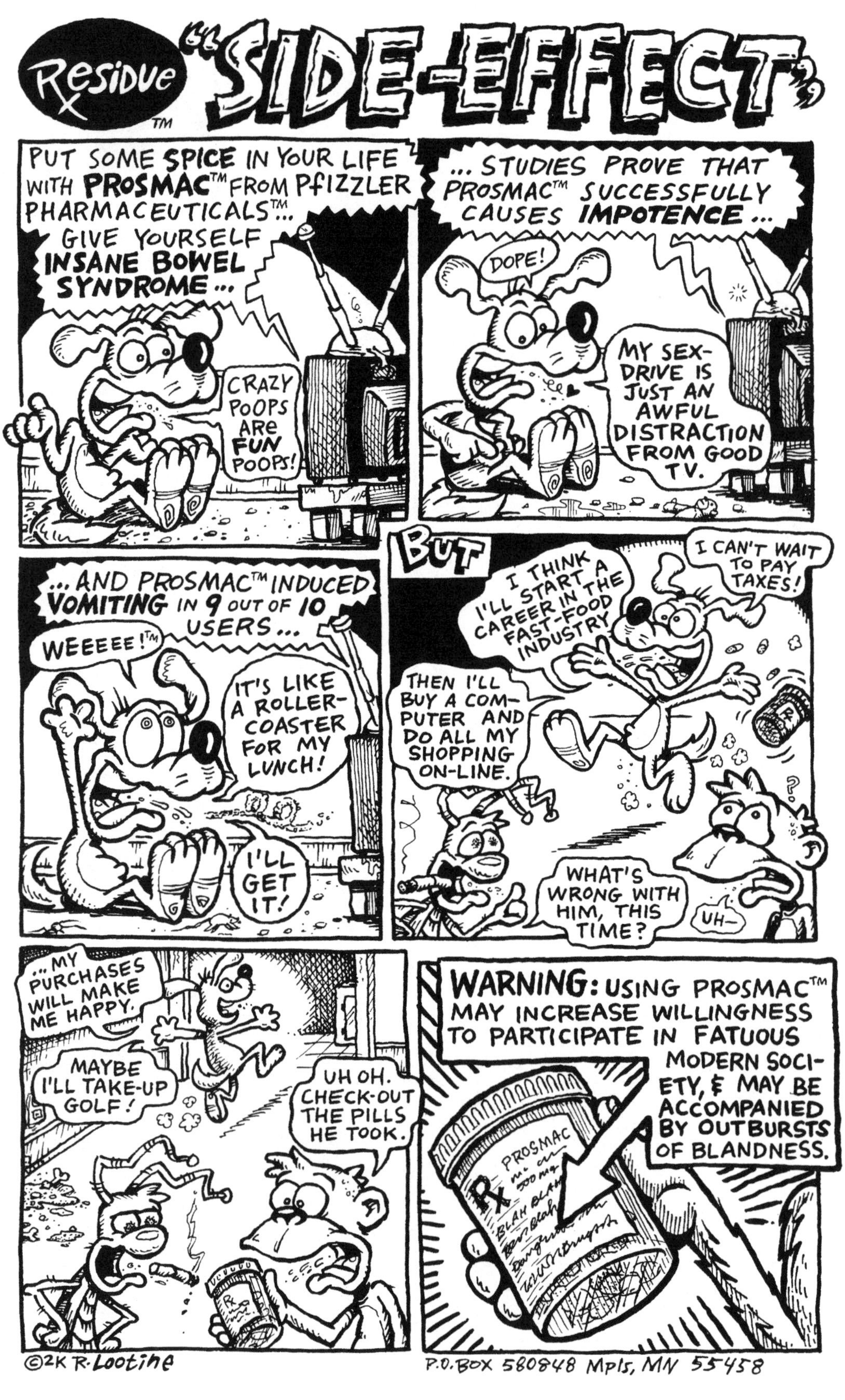
Residue ℞ TM
"SIDE-EFFECT"
PUT SOME SPICE IN YOUR LIFE WITH PROSMAC™ FROM Pfizzler PHARMACEUTICALS™...
GIVE YOURSELF INSANE BOWEL SYNDROME...
CRAZY POOPS ARE FUN POOPS!
...STUDIES PROVE THAT PROSMAC™ SUCCESSFULLY CAUSES IMPOTENCE...
DOPE!
MY SEX-DRIVE IS JUST AN AWFUL DISTRACTION FROM GOOD TV.
...AND PROSMAC™ INDUCED VOMITING IN 9 OUT OF 10 USERS...
WEEEEE!™
IT'S LIKE A ROLLER-COASTER FOR MY LUNCH!
I'LL GET IT!
BUT
I THINK I'LL START A CAREER IN THE FAST-FOOD INDUSTRY
I CAN'T WAIT TO PAY TAXES!
THEN I'LL BUY A COMPUTER AND DO ALL MY SHOPPING ON-LINE.
WHAT'S WRONG WITH HIM, THIS TIME?
UH—
...MY PURCHASES WILL MAKE ME HAPPY.
MAYBE I'LL TAKE-UP GOLF!
UH OH. CHECK-OUT THE PILLS HE TOOK.
WARNING: USING PROSMAC™ MAY INCREASE WILLINGNESS TO PARTICIPATE IN FATUOUS MODERN SOCIETY, & MAY BE ACCOMPANIED BY OUTBURSTS OF BLANDNESS.
PROSMAC
BLAH BLAH
©2K R. Lootine
P.O. BOX 580848 Mpls, MN 55458

"Residue Comix" by Roger Lootine. © Roger Lootine

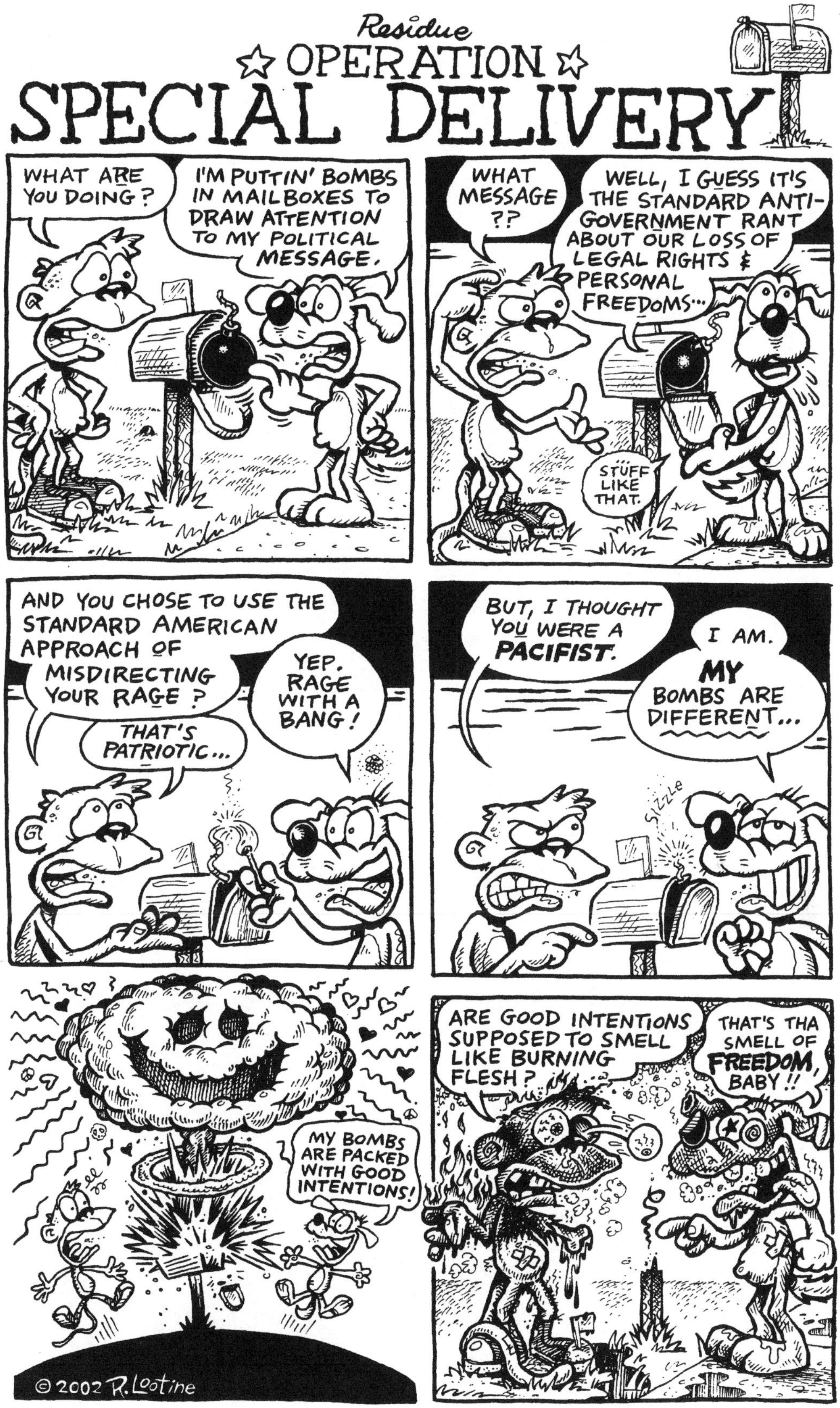
Residue
OPERATION
SPECIAL DELIVERY
WHAT ARE YOU DOING?
I'M PUTTIN' BOMBS IN MAILBOXES TO DRAW ATTENTION TO MY POLITICAL MESSAGE.
WHAT MESSAGE ??
WELL, I GUESS IT'S THE STANDARD ANTI-GOVERNMENT RANT ABOUT OUR LOSS OF LEGAL RIGHTS & PERSONAL FREEDOMS...
STUFF LIKE THAT.
AND YOU CHOSE TO USE THE STANDARD AMERICAN APPROACH OF MISDIRECTING YOUR RAGE ?
THAT'S PATRIOTIC...
YEP. RAGE WITH A BANG!
BUT, I THOUGHT YOU WERE A PACIFIST.
I AM. MY BOMBS ARE DIFFERENT...
SIZZLE
MY BOMBS ARE PACKED WITH GOOD INTENTIONS!
© 2002 R. Lootine
ARE GOOD INTENTIONS SUPPOSED TO SMELL LIKE BURNING FLESH?
THAT'S THA SMELL OF FREEDOM, BABY!!

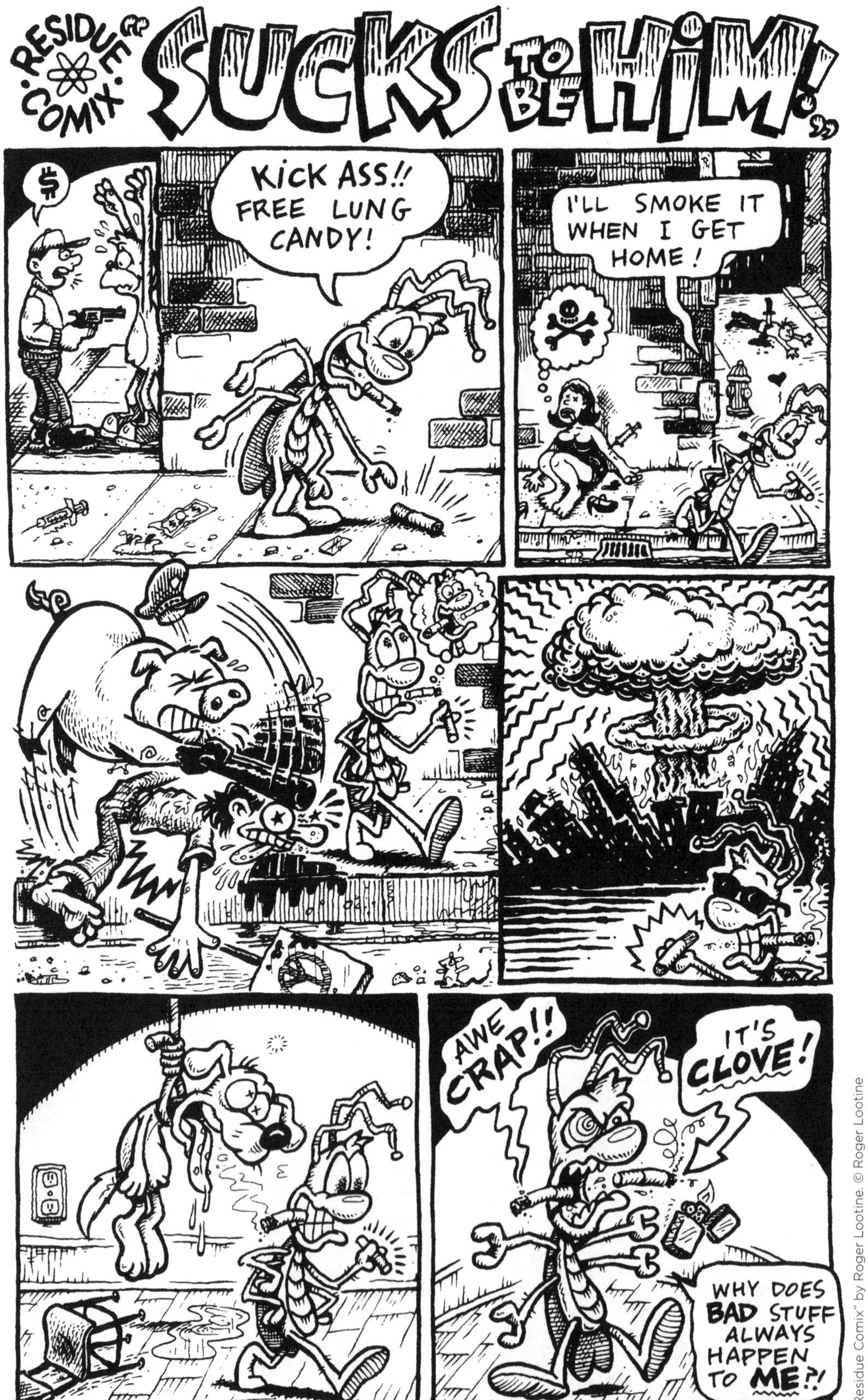
RESIDUE COMIX
SUCKS TO BE HIM!
$
KICK ASS!! FREE LUNG CANDY!
I'LL SMOKE IT WHEN I GET HOME!
AWE CRAP!!
IT'S CLOVE!
WHY DOES BAD STUFF ALWAYS HAPPEN TO ME?!
©2K R. Lootine P.O. BOX 580848 MPLS, MN 55458
"Residue Comix" by Roger Lootine. © Roger Lootine

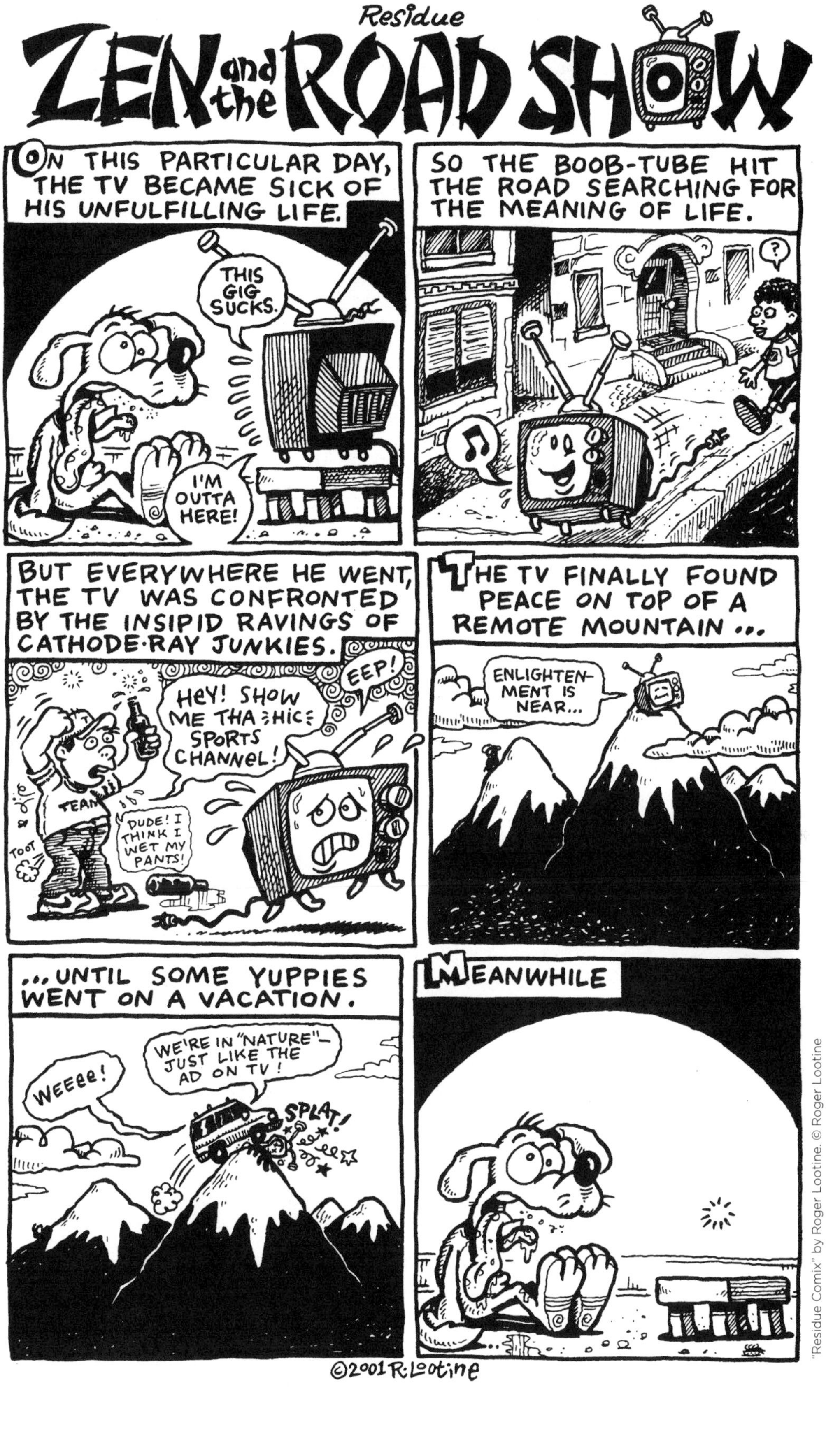
Residue
ZEN and the ROAD SHOW
ON THIS PARTICULAR DAY, THE TV BECAME SICK OF HIS UNFULFILLING LIFE.
THIS GIG SUCKS.
I'M OUTTA HERE!
SO THE BOOB-TUBE HIT THE ROAD SEARCHING FOR THE MEANING OF LIFE.
?
♫
BUT EVERYWHERE HE WENT, THE TV WAS CONFRONTED BY THE INSIPID RAVINGS OF CATHODE-RAY JUNKIES.
HEY! SHOW ME THA HIC SPORTS CHANNEL!
EEP!
TEAM
TOOT
DUDE! I THINK I WET MY PANTS!
THE TV FINALLY FOUND PEACE ON TOP OF A REMOTE MOUNTAIN ...
ENLIGHTEN-MENT IS NEAR...
... UNTIL SOME YUPPIES WENT ON A VACATION.
WEEEE!
WE'RE IN "NATURE"— JUST LIKE THE AD ON TV!
SPLAT!
MEANWHILE
©2001 R. Lootine

Choate Rosemary Hall is a boarding school in Wallingford, Connecticut. Andy Singer's parents sent him to Choate because they worried his public high school in California would introduce him to the "wrong element." But the wrong element always seems to be a step ahead of well-meaning parents. It was waiting for Singer at the boarding school entrance, swaying, slurring jokes, and offering a joint and beer bottle by way of a secret handshake.

Okay, so it didn't actually happen like that, but it might have, had Singer illustrated his wide-eyed initiation to boarding school culture. If anything, he says, boarding school provided an even better education than public school in the *high* life.

Choate also introduced Singer to secret identities. Legally, boarding school couldn't interfere in students' private lives, and yet their rules dictated what students could and could not do in and out of class. "As a result, students tended to lead double lives, just so they could break the rules," says Singer. And as long as the secret lives remained secret, school administrators turned a blind eye.

Double lives. Secrets. All in all, a great training ground for politicians and for cartoonists, whose job is to decode the schism between what a word means and what an image conveys. Much like the split between a person's intentions and actual deeds.

In "No Exit," Singer's long-running comic strip, he exploits these levels of meaning. For him, a carbon footprint is a patriotic stars-and-stripes foot stamping Mother Earth into the dust. *Public transit* refers to commuters astride a multi-bike. And the phrase "money buys freedom" represents the lifestyle of the rich and famous, whose homes are gated and guarded like maximum-security prisons.

A New York native, Singer attended Cornell University and then moved to California to follow his own version of the Hollywood dream. He wanted to be a cartoonist of some type or other. At the time, photocopiers were propelling a revolution in 'zines and 'zinesters.

"Technology always drives the kind of comics that get made," says Singer. "In the eighties you had these self-serve photocopy places, which were fairly cheap and good quality." Prior to that, cartoonists had relied on ditto machines, which were messy and lacked good resolution, or offset printing, which entailed large and expensive print runs, to reproduce art for mass consumption. Then Kodak and Xerox came out with copiers that provided good reproduction and nice solids, and at a price most self-publishers could afford.

"The idea with a 'zine was to make something in pen and ink that you could reproduce and send to friends," says Singer, who in the 1980s and

’90s worked for a couple of self-serve copy centers, including the California chain Copymat. “The one I worked for used to be owned by Scientologists. There were just boxes and boxes of *Dianetics* books stacked in the basement.”

Though Singer never found his calling in Scientology, he did find an outlet for his growing skill with the photocopy machine. He self-published his cartoons in a ’zine, *The Andrew B. Singer Coffee Table Book*. In the meantime, he snatched up the work of other ’zinesters, like Seth Tobacman, the punk artist behind *You Don’t Have To Fuck People Over To Survive* and *World War 3 Illustrated*.

In 1991, Singer swapped the Bohemian lifestyle of a struggling ’zinester for a steady gig at the *Daily Californian*, the University of Berkeley student paper and the paper for the city of Berkeley. Every semester, the *Daily Californian* held elections for cartoonists and columnists. In the winter of 1991, Singer threw his name in the ring.

“The paper had this enormous bulletin board. You’d take fifteen samples of your proposed column or cartoon, put them on the board, and then the employees would vote on them,” Singer says. “I drew a bunch of cartoons and won.” Singer’s daily panel cartoons, initially titled “It’s Not Funny” and later renamed “No Exit,” ran at the *Daily Californian* for nine and a half years.

With his wife, Singer moved to Minnesota in 2001 and brought “No Exit” with him. For a year and a half, ending in 2004, his panels appeared daily in the *St. Paul Pioneer Press*, at a time when papers were beginning to feel the crunch of competition. “The Internet and craigslist hammered news-

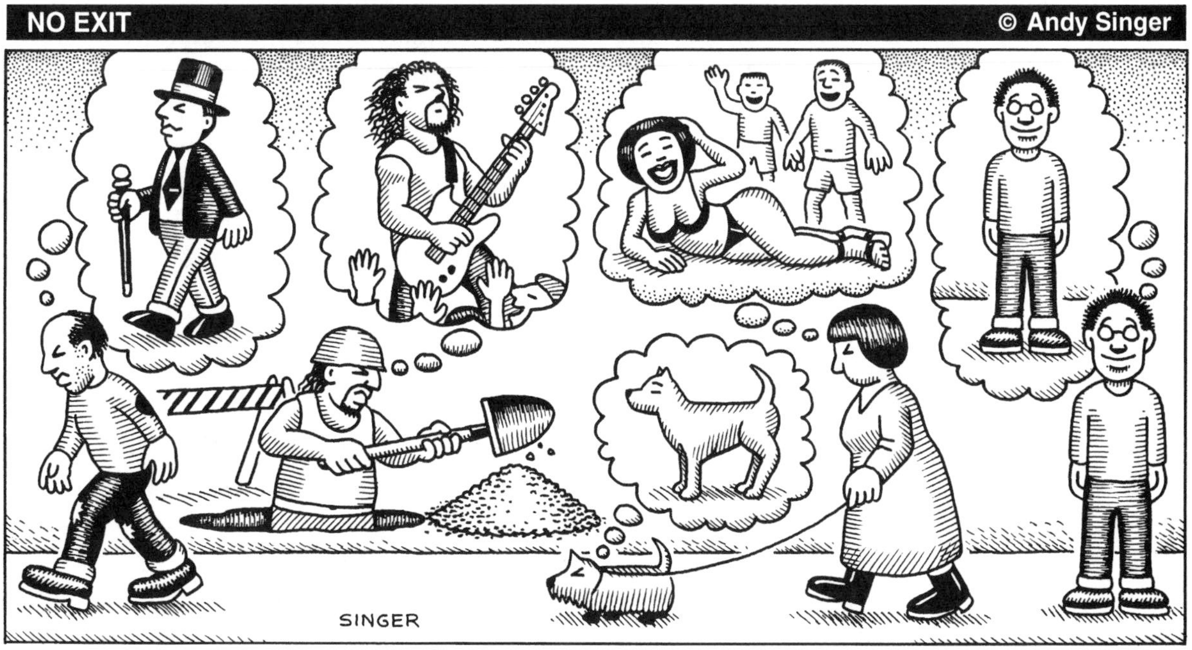
NO EXIT
© Andy Singer
SINGER

“No Exit” by Andy Singer. © Andy Singer

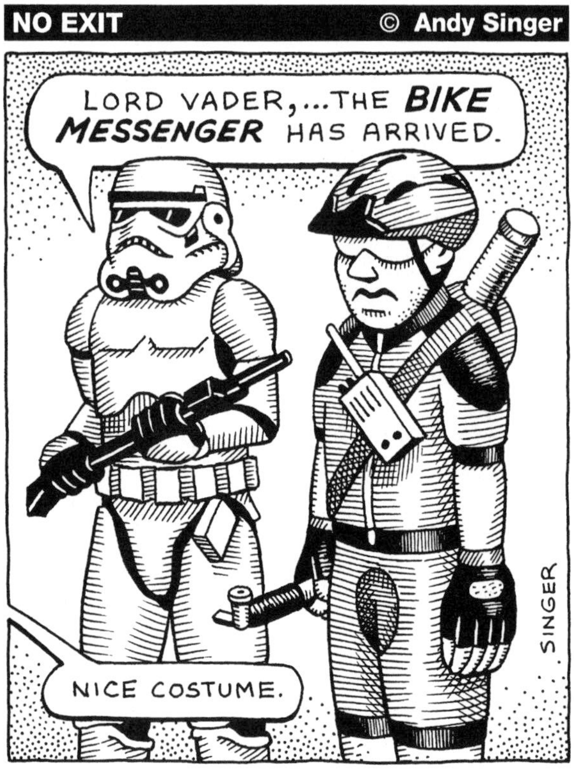
NO EXIT
© Andy Singer
LORD VADER,...THE BIKE MESSENGER HAS ARRIVED.
NICE COSTUME.
SINGER
"No Exit" by Andy Singer. © Andy Singer

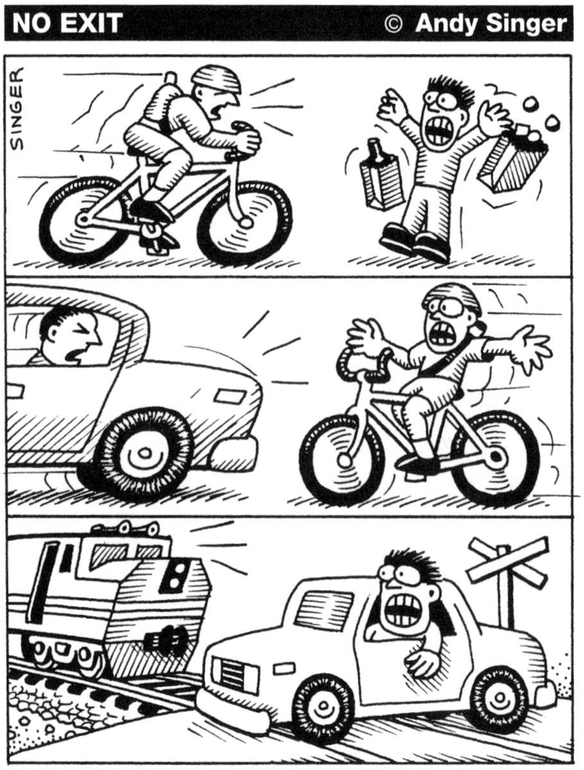
NO EXIT
© Andy Singer
SINGER
"No Exit" by Andy Singer. © Andy Singer

papers. They took away the classified ads, which had literally paid for the paper," says Singer. As a result, cartoonists were getting less and less for their comic strips, or not getting work at all.

"I was paid twenty dollars a week at the *Pioneer Press*. That's barely four dollars a comic. But I was having fun because my comic ran in a mainstream venue. Most of the papers I publish in are little alt weeklies. With those, you're already preaching to the choir," he says.

Publishing comics in a major newspaper means the chance to interact with a diverse audience and to raise a reader's hackles every now and again. Singer welcomed the sporadic letter to the editor condemning his comics.

But editors don't always share their cartoonists' renegade spirit. They have the advertisers and next week's paycheck to think of. Some of Singer's cartoons never made it past his editor.

"I did a split panel cartoon that said 'chick flick' in a panel that showed a couple embracing with flowers and 'dick flick' in a panel that showed a car going off a cliff and people shooting out of it. My editor said, 'We can't say the word *dick*,'" says Singer, and that was the end of that. Still, he was always grateful to his *Pioneer Press* editor, who, unlike many in the industry, chose to work with an independent cartoonist rather than buy a comics package put together by King Features or Tribune Media Service.

"The syndicates these days, it's like going to a fast food drive-thru," says Singer. "'Okay, I'll have a number three and a number five with extra fries,

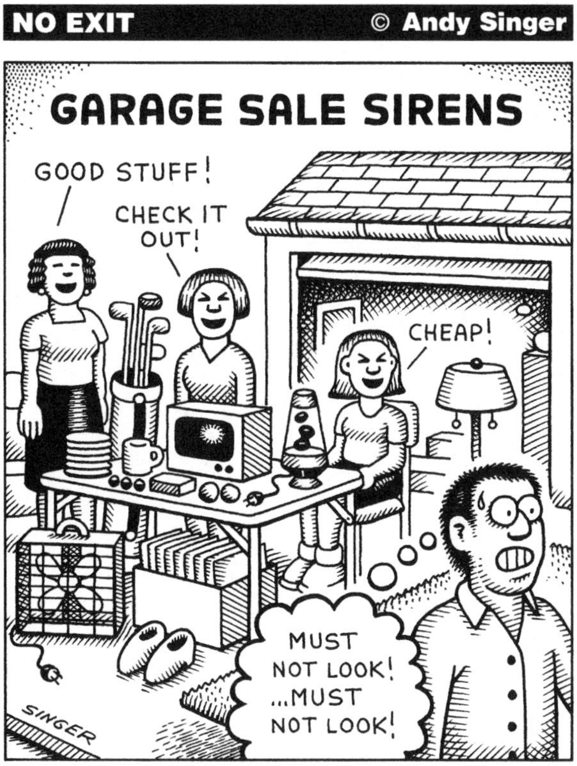
NO EXIT © Andy Singer
GARAGE SALE SIRENS
GOOD STUFF!
CHECK IT OUT!
CHEAP!
MUST NOT LOOK! ...MUST NOT LOOK!
SINGER

"No Exit" by Andy Singer. © Andy Singer

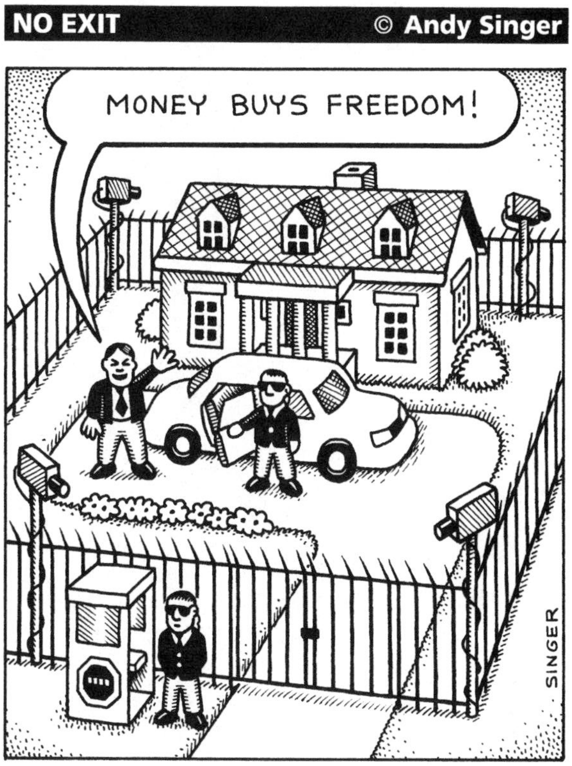
NO EXIT © Andy Singer
MONEY BUYS FREEDOM!
SINGER

"No Exit" by Andy Singer. © Andy Singer

and can you supersize that?' The syndicate packages the art in the right format. You just slap it in your paper and you don't even have to proof it."

To compete, Singer and other cartoonists have learned to self-syndicate, e-mailing art to editors directly. "No Exit" currently runs in the *Eugene Weekly, Salt Lake City Weekly, Athens News,* the *Bay Monthly,* and *Funny Times,* among other publications. A number of "No Exit" cartoons are collected in *Attitude Featuring Andy Singer: No Exit,* published by NBM Publishing.

Singer has also found success in reprints. Online comic banks (CartoonStock, PoliticalCartoons.com) sell reprint rights to educational publishers, governmental organizations, nonprofits, and corporate clients for a variety of uses, ranging from textbooks and manuals to PowerPoint presentations. His comics have found a new audience and a second life on the Internet and in a multilingual global market, "because cartoons can convey information in a verbal-visual shorthand that's unmatched by any other medium," he says. "And if they're just images, you can even communicate across language barriers."

But the words are half the fun of Singer's "No Exit" comics, especially when he is at his double-dealing best. He sets up the expectation—a three-panel sequence that shows a scruffy sad sack who, by virtue of a whisky bottle in panel two, discovers booze nirvana by panel three—only to subvert the expectation with the caption: "Poor Man's Prozac." ■

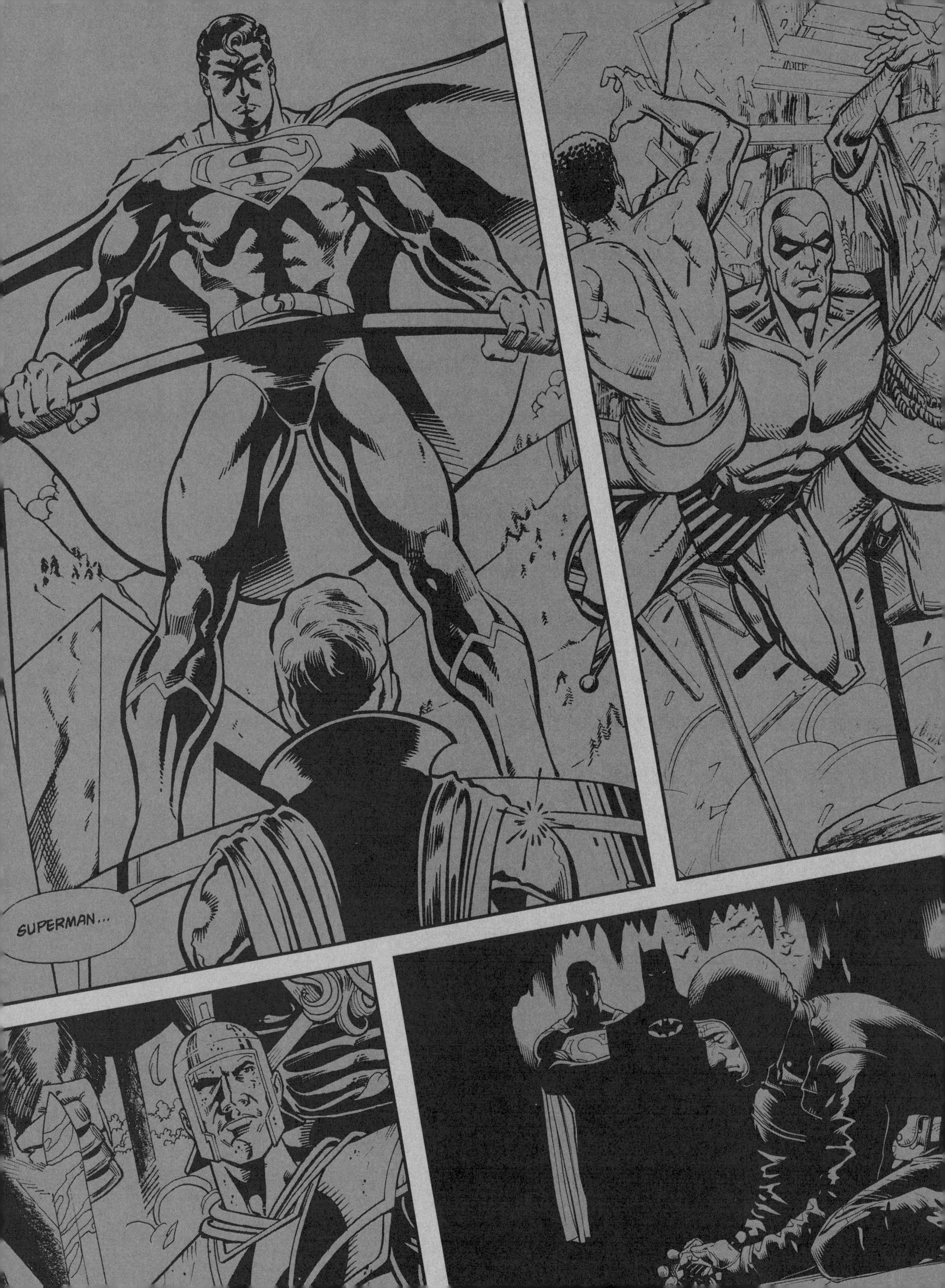
SUPERMAN...

THE SUPERMAN LEGACY

Comic Book Artists in Minnesota

Superman arrived in the nick of time. Bad guys were roaming Metropolis—crooked businessmen, swindlers, wife beaters, drunks—drowning good folk in a tide of misery that never seemed to ebb. Someone had to sweep the evildoers off the street and into the hoosegow. But who? Corrupt politicians? The police force, with their hand in gangland's back pocket? No, just the last son of Krypton. He heard the call for help and answered it.

Meantime, in Franklin Delano Roosevelt's America, Lost Men picked up the pieces of their lives, still shattered nearly a decade after the stock market crash of October 1929. The jobless waited in breadlines, looking for handouts, feeling sorry for the state of their shoes and their clothes, but shoes and clothes needed money.

FDR's New Deal had been clipping along since 1933, creating jobs, shoring banks, boosting the destitute, and offering a measure of hope where there was little to be had. Then 1937 hit with a thump. Economic progress didn't just pause; it tottered backwards. The Great Depression roared back and shook a nation that had assumed too much, too soon. It would take more than a New Deal to yank America out of its misery.

Jerry Siegel and Joe Shuster were a couple of Cleveland teens during the Depression, looking to crack the comic strip market. That's where the money was in the 1930s. If you wanted to draw comics, you drew for the papers. But editor after editor turned down the Siegel-Shuster story of a super-powered champion of the oppressed.

Then, as sometimes happens, luck stepped in for Siegel and Shuster. Sheldon Mayer, an artist employed by publisher M.C. Gaines, lifted their story, "Superman," out of the reject pile. He forwarded the strip to editor Vincent Sullivan, who was pulling together material for a new book. The boys would have to reformat their strip, but the story had something. Superman debuted in June 1938, on the cover of *Action Comics* No. 1. The superhero comic book was born.

Superman caught on with readers, who craved a hero bigger than their problems and the Great Depression. He possessed alien powers, good looks, and a sterling moral code that often put him in danger, but always in the cause of righting wrongs and defending humanity. He was the man in control, while many of his readers' lives felt so totally out of control.

By 1939, Superman had his own title, and Siegel and Shuster had the long-awaited strip. With both a comic book and a comic strip to draw, Shuster, the artist in the team, fell behind. Minnesotan Wayne Boring was called in to ghost under Shuster.

"Boring's style helped define the Superman of the 1940s and '50s," says David Mruz, comics historian and organizer of some of the Twin Cities' early comic book conventions. "When Boring first started, he tried to maintain Siegel and Shuster's style. But gradually he created his own."

Boring's work went uncredited until 1942, when *Superman*'s publisher, National Comics (later DC Comics), hired him as a staff artist. He is now considered one of the greatest artists to ever work on the title. His Superman was powerful and commanding, shooting through the air with steely precision and possessing a jaw as formidable as a granite block.

> SUPERMAN CAUGHT ON WITH READERS, WHO CRAVED A HERO BIGGER THAN THEIR PROBLEMS AND THE GREAT DEPRESSION.

Coincidentally, Boring's successor was also a Minnesotan. Curt Swan was born in 1920, fifteen years after Boring, in Willmar. During World War II, he worked as a cartoonist for the armed services paper *Stars and Stripes*. That experience led to a job with National Comics at the end of the war and, after a succession of other books, to work on *Superman; Superman's Pal, Jimmy Olsen; Superman's Girl Friend, Lois Lane;* and *Adventure Comics*.

Swan's tenure on *Superman* during the 1960s and '70s was as significant as Boring's had been earlier, if not more so, says Mruz. "Swan created the definitive Superman, and by definitive, I mean his version of Superman is the version everyone else followed." Swan's sleek and muscular Man of Tomorrow inspired the 1978 movie starring Christopher Reeve.

Siegel and Shuster's success with *Superman* in 1938 introduced a flood of superhero comics. Over the next few years, Batman, Captain America, and Wonder Woman joined the battle against wrongdoers. In 1940, Captain Marvel appeared in *Whiz Comics* No. 2.

Captain Marvel was the alter ego of boy reporter Billy Batson, who merely had to utter "Shazam!" to transform into a scarlet-clad, super-powered being. This new superhero was the invention of Fawcett Comics, a subsidiary of Fawcett Publications. The company's founder, Wilford Hamilton "Captain Billy" Fawcett—a veteran of World War I who, like Swan, had learned publishing while working for *Stars and Stripes*—started the business in 1919 in Robbinsdale, Minnesota, publishing magazines and bawdy humor (*Captain Billy's Whiz Bang*).

In the 1930s, Fawcett Publications relocated to New York. A number of artists moved with the company. One was Charles Clarence Beck, a native of Zumbrota, Minnesota. C. C. Beck originated the look of Captain Marvel and stayed with the title for thirteen years, a period defined by huge success—at one point *Captain Marvel* outsold *Superman*—and legal entanglements. National Comics sued Fawcett over copyright infringement. Captain Marvel, they said, was a Superman rip-off. National won in 1952.

"YOU CAN'T BE A PAINTER WITHOUT RECOGNIZING THE INFLUENCE OF VAN GOGH. AND YOU CAN'T BE A CARTOONIST WITHOUT RECOGNIZING THE INFLUENCE OF WALLY WOOD."

America entered World War II at the end of 1941. GIs shipped overseas and took their comics with them. Superheroes reigned during these years, but after the war, comic book readers hankered for something new. What they got were war, horror, and science fiction comics. And Entertaining Comics, presided over by Bill Gaines, gave them the best of the best: *Two-Fisted Tales*, *Frontline Combat*, *Weird Fantasy*, *Weird Science*, *The Vault of Horror*, and *The Crypt of Terror*.

EC rose to prominence on the talent of its writers and artists. Even in this gifted crowd, Wally Wood stood out. The son of a lumberman, Wood was born June 17, 1927, in Menahga, Minnesota, but spent his childhood moving between Minnesota, Wisconsin, and Michigan because of his father's timbering jobs. At six, Wood dreamed of a magic pencil that allowed him to draw anything his imagination conceived. Many years later, he pointed to this dream as his calling card to destiny.

"Wood is basically the van Gogh of cartooning. He was as talented, influential, and tormented as van Gogh, with the same mental struggles. Both men committed suicide," says comics historian Mruz. "You can't be a painter without recognizing the influence of van Gogh. And you can't be a cartoonist without recognizing the influence of Wally Wood."

Wood is best remembered for his work with *Mad Magazine* and other EC titles, in particular EC's line of science fiction, fantasy, and horror comics, which were cited by Dr. Fredric Wertham in his 1954 expose *Seduction of the Innocent*. Comic books were suddenly under fire, responsible for corrupting America's youth and inciting everything from promiscuity and drunkenness to violence and homosexuality.

To sidestep governmental oversight and further loss of sales, publishers formed a self-censoring body. From now on, comics would have to be submitted to the Comics Code Authority for approval. No more sex, violence, or challenges to authority. No more horror. No more EC. All that survived of Bill Gaines's empire was *Mad*.

In *Seduction of the Innocent,* Wertham blasted comics for their corruptive influence. Children, he assumed, were comics' mainstay audience, but in fact comics have always attracted a mixed readership. This assumption persists today and was behind a series of lawsuits that henpecked retailers, publishers, and creators throughout the 1980s and '90s. However, these challenges also gave shape to the Comic Book Legal Defense Fund.

The CBLDF started in 1986 with the Friendly Frank's case. Cops raided Frank Mangiaracina's comic book store in Lansing, Illinois, appropriating books they considered obscene. Among the confiscated titles was *Omaha the Cat Dancer,* a comic drawn and scripted by Minnesota couple Reed Waller and Kate Worley.

In Minneapolis, Greg Ketter got wind of the raid and was concerned. He had a bookstore, DreamHaven, and he sold comics that weren't always intended for young eyes. Along with Denis Kitchen, publisher of *Omaha the Cat Dancer,* Ketter rallied the comic book community. Comic book artists donated art for auction. Fans sent money. Ketter personally raised thousands of dollars to found the CBLDF, whose mission from the outset was to provide legal counsel and funds to the lawsuits' targets—and to educate the public about comics.

"We were trying to make the statement that comics are not just for kids. The comics confiscated in the Friendly Frank's case were clearly labeled for adults," says Ketter, also a publisher (the adult comic *XXXenophile* with Phil Foglio and collections of *Leonard and Larry,* a strip created by California cartoonist Tim Barela).

Over its lifetime, the comic book industry has weathered a number of changes. It grew into and survived the Great Depression and now in the twenty-first century finds itself once more navigating another economic downturn. Through it all, however, the industry and its art have managed to thrive and evolve.

Minnesota continues to plays its role too, providing a home to comic book artists (probably more than ever, given the option of telecommuting in the digital age) and a setting for adventure plots. If you look closely, you can find the Metrodome, the Foshay Tower, and the Triple Rock Club appearing in comics created by Minnesota artists. And if you thought Minnesota was rid of *Superman* artists, think again. Dan Jurgens and Doug Mahnke have both taken up the legacy of Boring and Swan, adding their individual stamps to the most recognizable superhero on earth. ∎

TERRY BEATTY

As 2008 came to a close, Terry Beatty rifled through folders, sorting old newspaper clippings and articles relating to his comics career. There were pieces from his hometown paper, the *Muscatine Journal,* announcing his first *Batman* gig, and interviews relating to his long-term creative partnership with writer Max Allan Collins and their leggy, pistol-packing private eye series *Ms. Tree.* "I had to prove who I was," the artist says. Was Beatty having an identity crisis? No, just a red-tape day with the U.S. government. "I had to prove to the government that I am who I say I am to get a passport for my honeymoon." Beatty was getting married in a couple months.

In person, the cartoonist sports natty attire and dark-rimmed glasses. He wears sideburns and a soul patch. Most any darn night you can find him camped at Lee's Liquor Lounge soaking up the latest rockabilly or roots country band. He's big into music. "That's another thing I love about the Twin Cities. There's some amazing music going on," he says. "It's a good thing I didn't grow up here. Because if I'd grown up in the Twin Cities, I would've been so distracted by all the music, movies, and art I would never have gotten anything done."

Beatty was born in 1958 in Muscatine, Iowa, "a little river town where there's not a whole lot to do. So there's a certain amount of creating your own entertainment," says Beatty, who moved to Minneapolis in his forties. His father taught junior high English. His mother loved art. A good combo for a boy destined to make a career in comics.

But first he had to be introduced to comics. His brothers took care of that. This was the so-called Silver Age of comics, roughly 1956 to 1970, and Beatty's brothers papered their bedroom floors with the good stuff.

"It was prime time for comic books because you had Jack Kirby on *Fantastic Four* and *Thor* and Steve Ditko doing *Doctor Strange* and *Spider-Man,*" says Beatty. "You had a terrific bunch of talent at DC Comics then, Joe Kubert and Carmine Infantino; and they still published those *80-Page Giants* with reprints of the Golden Age stuff."

"WE . . . HAD FUN WITH MS. TREE AS A CHARACTER BECAUSE SHE'S JUST FLAT-OUT NUTS AND WAY TOO TRIGGER-HAPPY."

The trigger for Beatty's career in comics was an issue of *Green Lantern.* Artist Gil Kane had drawn himself into a panel, "and suddenly it clicked for me. I realized, *Oh, yeah, somebody must draw these things,*" says Beatty, who decided one day *he* would be the guy drawing comics. Living in his small town, he was excited to see, in the letters section of a comic book, the name of another fan also from Muscatine.

"I showed the fan letter to my father, and he said, 'Oh, I know who that is. He was a student of mine,'" says Beatty. The fan was Max Allan Collins, ten years older than Beatty and already a published crime novelist, teaching

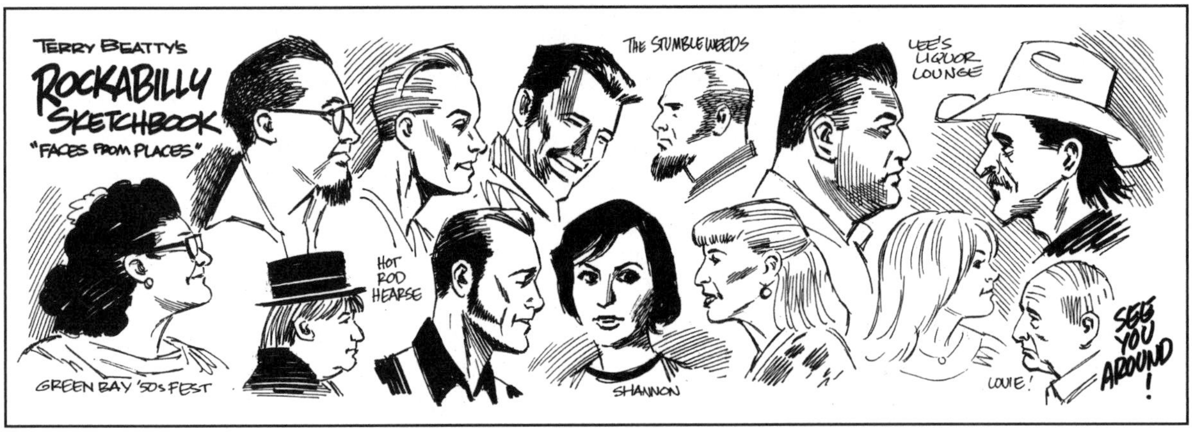
TERRY BEATTY'S
ROCKABILLY SKETCHBOOK
"FACES FROM PLACES"
THE STUMBLEWEEDS
LEE'S LIQUOR LOUNGE
HOT ROD HEARSE
GREEN BAY '50s FEST
SHANNON
LOUIE!
SEE YOU AROUND!

"Rockabilly Sketchbook" by Terry Beatty from *Big Funny*. © 2009 Terry Beatty

adult ed classes at the junior college. Beatty had to meet him. He enrolled in Collins's film studies class, "which pretty much involved going to the local mall theater, seeing the latest movie, and then stopping at the Pizza Hut afterward to discuss it."

Despite the age difference, Beatty and Collins struck up a friendship. They talked comics. They attended comic book conventions. They had a silent understanding that when Beatty, a budding cartoonist, got good enough at his art, maybe they would do a strip together.

Collins was a mover and shaker. He had big dreams and bigger talent, and he knew how to network. He was a lifelong "Dick Tracy" fan, and through connections, some luck, and perseverance, he nabbed a job writing the strip when creator Chester Gould retired. That helped when Collins and Beatty pitched a revamp of Harold Gray's "Little Orphan Annie" to the Tribune Media Syndicate. Unfortunately, they were beat to the punch by cartoonist Leonard Starr.

Undeterred, the writer-artist combo from Muscatine put together a sample comics page and distributed it to penny shoppers around the country. "We needed a dozen clients to have the project pay for itself," says Beatty. "We got six."

Beatty and Collins went ahead with the project anyway. Their weekly comics page consisted of a number of strips, all in different styles. The *Chicago Reader* decided to print only one, "Mike Mist," but the exposure from that strip led to a call from Dean Mullaney, who was starting Eclipse Comics and needed material.

Mullaney called Collins and, as Beatty recalls it, said, "'I'm starting this magazine and I'd like to run a detective feature. Would you like to do something?' Collins made up *Ms. Tree* on the phone." That was 1981.

Ms. Tree would run twelve years under various publishers—Eclipse Comics, Aardvark-Vanaheim, Renegade Press, and DC Comics. Ms. Tree is Michael Tree, wife of another Michael Tree, who is murdered on their honeymoon, leaving his widow a detective agency and a taste for vengeance. Ms. Tree wields a SIG P225 9mm. Not one to take a punch and run, she dispenses justice with iron will, steely intelligence, and bullets.

"We thought it would be much more interesting to have a female detective. The tough-guy male character had been done to death," says Beatty, who calls Ms. Tree "Mike Hammer in a dress." Nothing was too sacred or profane for the series creators or their heroine. "We did abortion clinic bombings. We did gay bashing. We did serial killers. And also had fun with Ms. Tree as a character because she's just flat-out nuts and way too trigger-happy."

Beatty and Collins dealt with Ms. Tree's mental state in the context of the story. The artist recalls the thought process leading up to Ms. Tree's institutionalization. "Okay, so she's a terrible role model. So, let's say she's crazy. Let's send her to the mental hospital and have her come out nice and happy." Ms. Tree returns to the world a better person, until she comes off her meds. Then it's back to business.

The two friends have also collaborated on the comic book series *Wild Dog* and *Johnny Dynamite*. Collins scripted the graphic novel *Road to Perdition,* which was later turned into a movie starring Tom Hanks, while Beatty upped his profile with an eleven-year run inking *Batman*.

Cover art by Terry Beatty for *Johnny Dynamite* (AiT/Planet Lar), a graphic novel by Max Allan Collins and Terry Beatty. © 2003 Max Allan Collins and Terry Beatty.

"I'd heard DC Comics was starting a series based on the animated *Batman* cartoons," says Beatty, whose sole intention was to get his foot in the door at the merchandising end, designing lunch boxes and poster art. But to hedge his bets, he also sent his portfolio to the series editor. "I knew Rick Burchett currently had the inking job on the *Batman* series. He was a friend. I didn't want to take his job. But I thought, *He's got to take a vacation sometime. Maybe they'll need an artist to do fill-in issues.*"

As chance would have it, Burchett decided to take a six-month hiatus from *Batman* to work on *Superman Adventures*. Beatty slipped into the inking job. Six months later, Burchett came back to *Batman,* but as penciller. Beatty spent more than a decade inking a succession of titles tied to the *Batman* animated shows. The last was *Batman Strikes!* with Minneapolis cartoonist Christopher Jones.

"Chris and I had known each other for years through the convention circuit and had talked about how we'd like to work together," says Beatty.

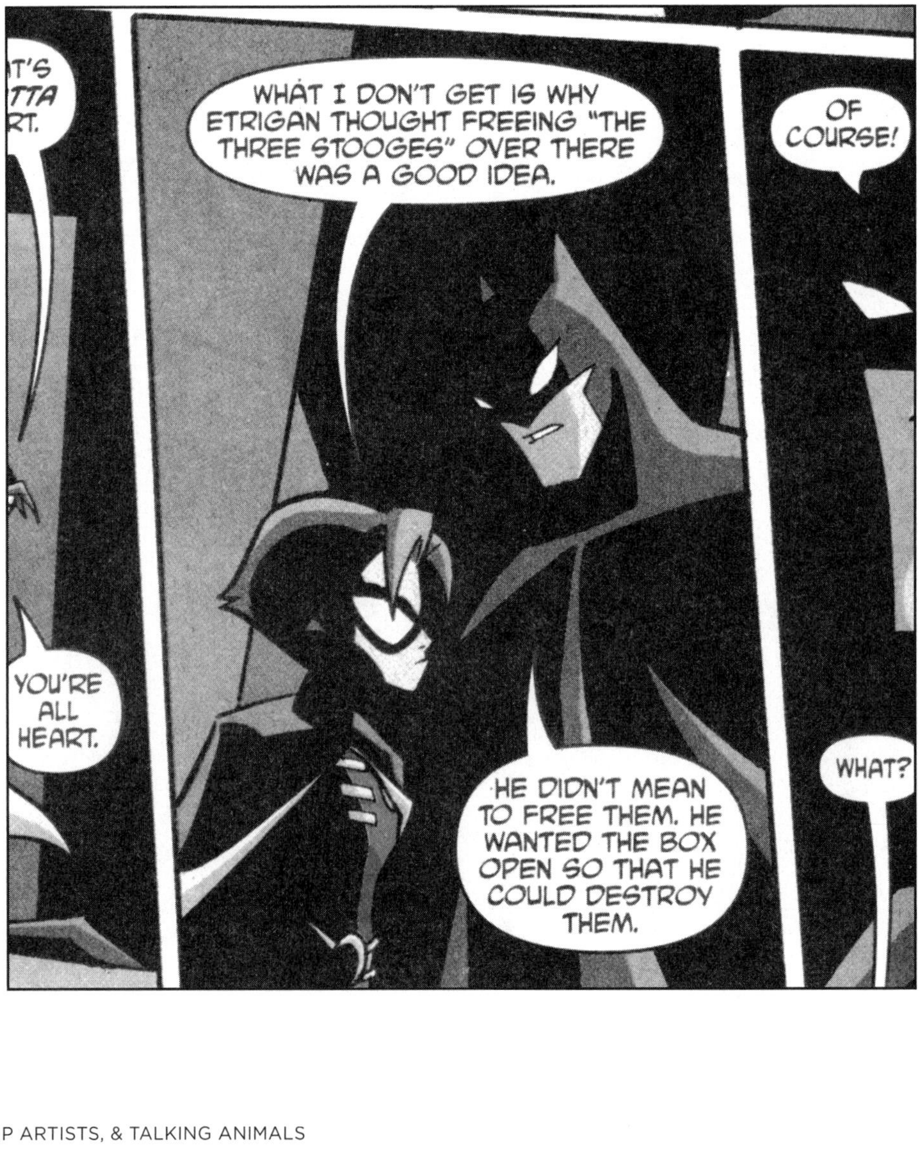
YOU'RE ALL HEART.
WHAT I DON'T GET IS WHY ETRIGAN THOUGHT FREEING "THE THREE STOOGES" OVER THERE WAS A GOOD IDEA.
HE DIDN'T MEAN TO FREE THEM. HE WANTED THE BOX OPEN SO THAT HE COULD DESTROY THEM.
OF COURSE!
WHAT?

Batman Strikes! No. 50 (DC Comics). Pencils by Christopher Jones; inks by Terry Beatty. © 2008 DC Comics

"When Joan Hilty [the editor] was putting the art team together for *Batman Strikes!,* she chose us, not knowing we lived ten miles apart."

Batman Strikes! had Beatty inking Jones's pencils. The trick to being a good inker, says Beatty, "is to not screw up what the penciller has done. Because I've been the penciller and seen my work inked" for the good and the bad. "The history of comic books is filled with wonderful pencillers whose work has been wrecked by bad inkers. On the other hand, you have some really wonderful combinations."

The Beatty-Jones partnership worked. "As an inker, I'm always happiest when I work with a good penciller," says Beatty. "Chris really puts a lot of thought into what he does. He's not one of those guys who draws a script by numbers. He thoroughly examines the scripts to figure out the best way to draw the story." Their collaboration lasted through 2008 and issue No. 50, when *Batman Strikes!* was cancelled to make room for a new animated series and a new comic book.

Beatty and Collins are still working together. They have joined forces on a *Road to Perdition* sequel, *Return to Perdition,* and have plans to bring their pistol-happy *Ms. Tree* out of retirement. Occasionally, you can find a Beatty cover on *Scary Monsters Magazine* and Beatty the artist at kit-building conventions, selling his sculpts of circus sideshow performers and retro pinups.

When asked about his best moment in comics, Beatty remembers a page he inked for a Batman/Superman graphic novel scripted by Paul Dini. The book won an Eisner Award for Best Graphic Novel in 1998.

"I was sitting at my drawing board, inking a page that had Batman, Superman, the Joker, Lex Luthor, and Harley Quinn on it," says Beatty. "And I just started to laugh because I realized: Here I am getting paid to do what I would do for fun. What I *did* for fun when I was eight years old. You can't beat that." ■

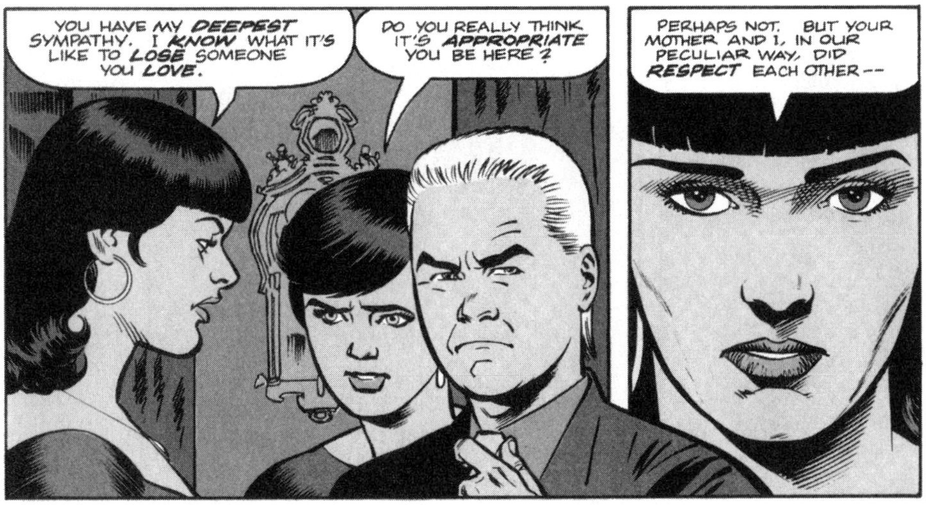
YOU HAVE MY DEEPEST SYMPATHY. I KNOW WHAT IT'S LIKE TO LOSE SOMEONE YOU LOVE.
DO YOU REALLY THINK IT'S APPROPRIATE YOU BE HERE?
PERHAPS NOT. BUT YOUR MOTHER AND I, IN OUR PECULIAR WAY, DID RESPECT EACH OTHER--

Ms. Tree Quarterly No. 1 (DC Comics). Script by Max Allan Collins; art by Terry Beatty. © 1990 Max Allan Collins and Terry Beatty

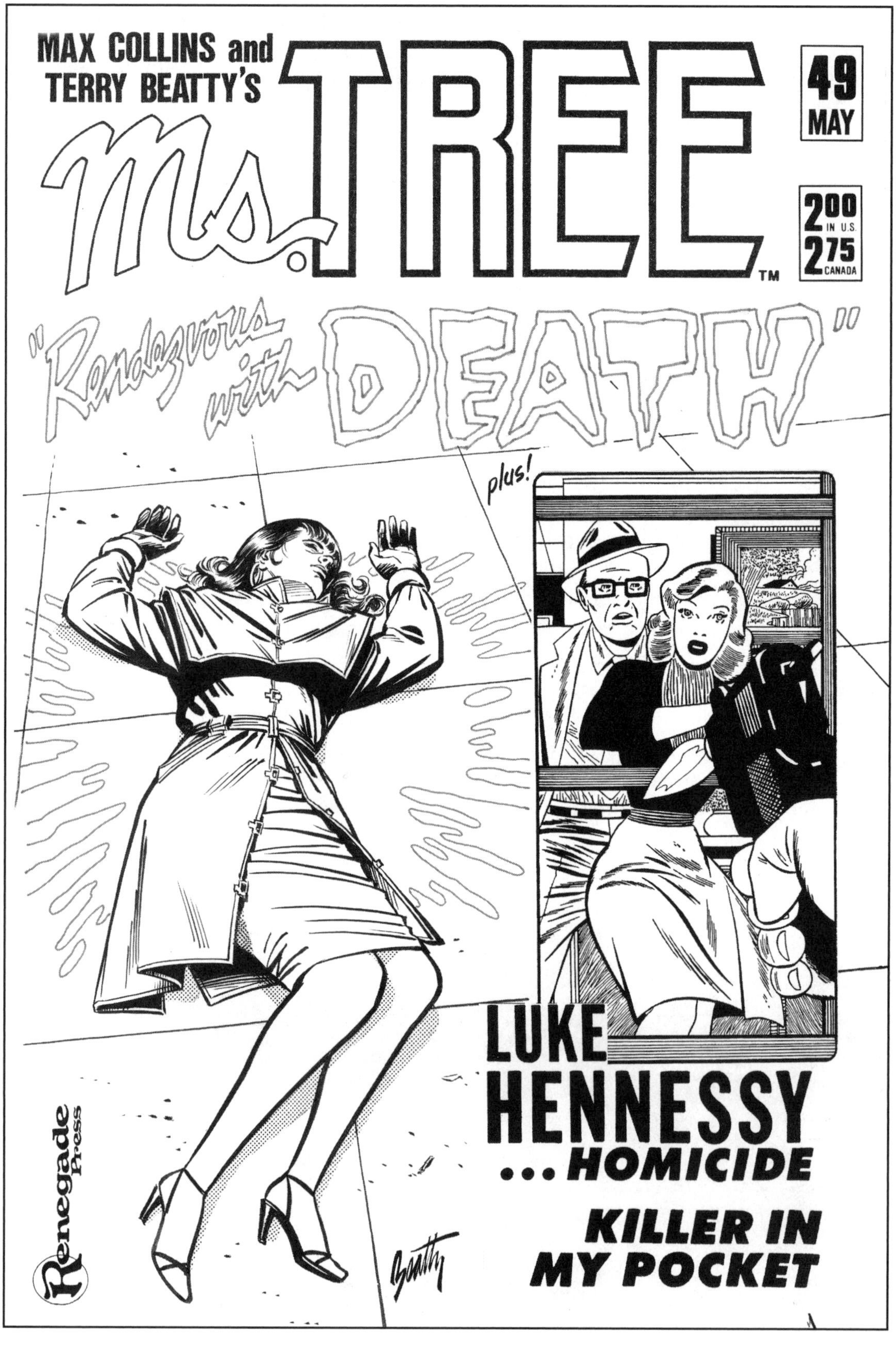
MAX COLLINS and
TERRY BEATTY'S
Ms. TREE
TM
49
MAY
2.00 IN U.S.
2.75 CANADA
"Rendezvous with DEATH"
plus!
LUKE HENNESSY
...HOMICIDE
KILLER IN MY POCKET
Renegade Press
Beatty

Cover for *Ms. Tree* No. 49 (Renegade Press) by Terry Beatty. © 1989 Max Allan Collins and Terry Beatty

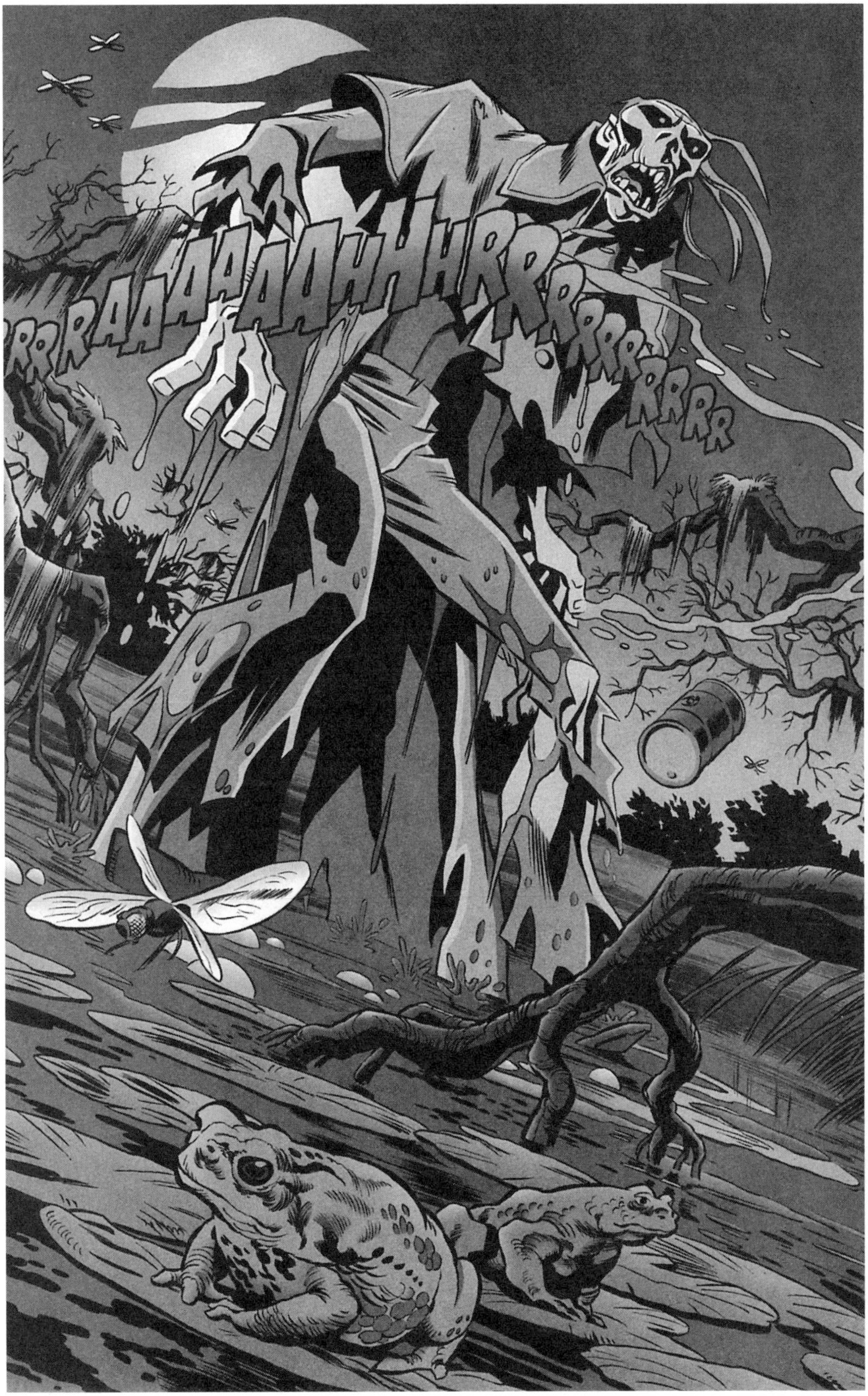
RRRRAAAAAAAHHHRRRRRRRRRRRR

Batman Strikes! No. 19 (DC Comics). Pencils by Christopher Jones; inks by Terry Beatty. © 2006 DC Comics

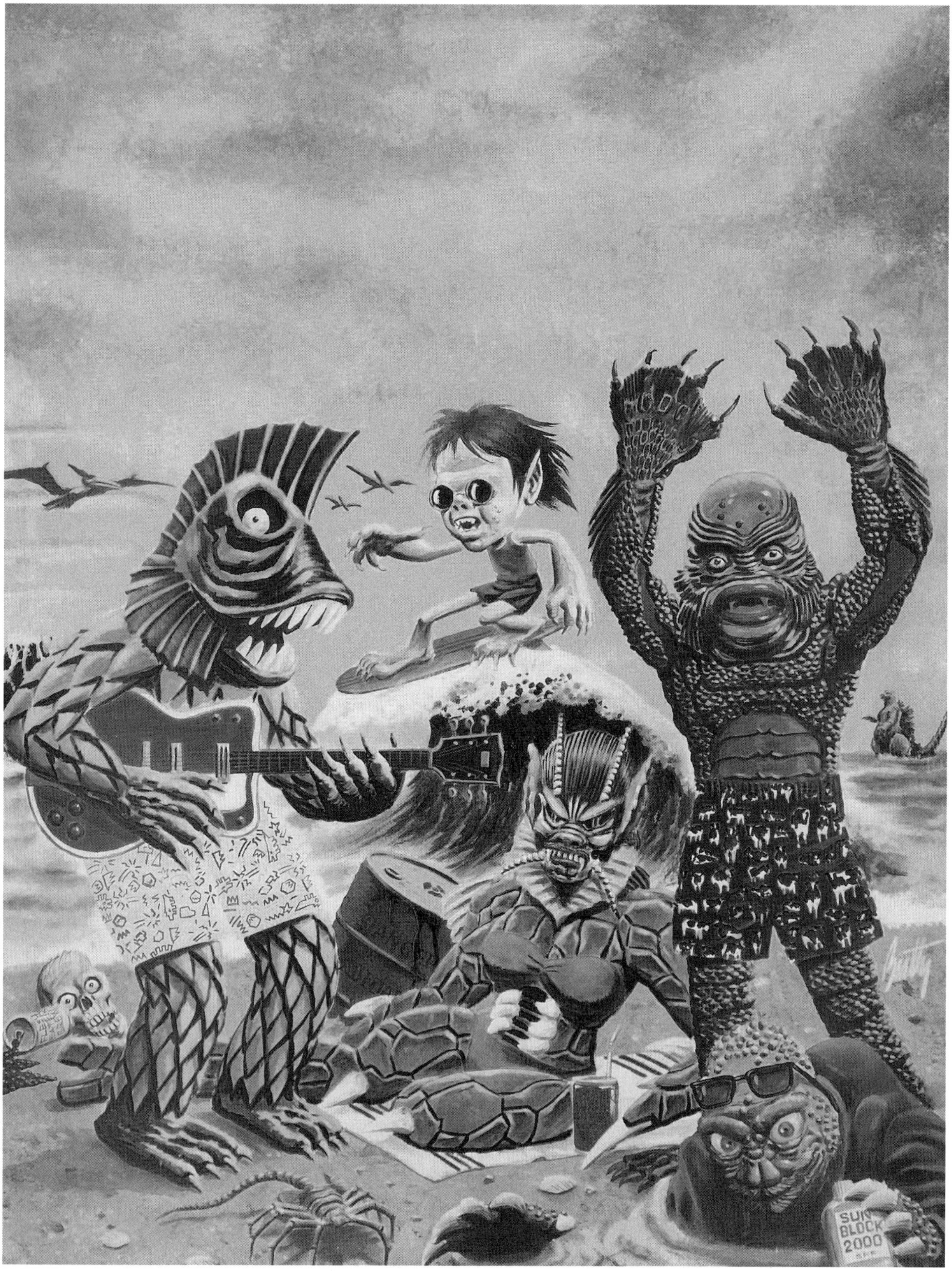
SUN
BLOCK
2000

Cover for *Scary Monsters: Monster Memories 2008* by Terry Beatty. © 2008 Terry Beatty

You don't make it in comics without discipline. No one's looking over your shoulder to see if you're keeping your end of the bargain: translating the writer's script into page layouts and knocking off pages at a rate that ensures you'll make the printing deadline. The publisher has to trust you to get the work done. "But some artists are total flakes," says Doug Mahnke. He has been an artist, specifically a comic book artist, for the past thirty years. "Trust me on that."

"I'LL NEVER GET BETTER AT WHAT I DO IF I DON'T ACCEPT THE FACT THAT I HAVE A LOT OF WORK AHEAD OF ME."

Mahnke didn't always have discipline. Art came easy to him. Too easy. He could dash off a drawing and still have time for a game of baseball or football. He loved sports. "Athletics kept me from being the two-headed kid in class," says Mahnke, who was born in Arizona but spent his early school years in Kansas. "Because when you collect comics, you're always the odd kid in school. Comics give you this extremely narrow focus, and they just consume you." He could've dumped his monthly comics habit, gone legit, but he had a dream to fulfill.

"My first desire was not to be a comic book artist but to be a superhero. When I was in first grade, I became the character Soap Man," says Mahnke. "I got two plastic bottles and filled them with soap, then I duct-taped them to my wrists. I had a cape, everything I needed to be a superhero. But I couldn't find a whole lot of villains in my neighborhood."

By ninth grade, Mahnke and his parents were living in Burnsville, Minnesota. The artist credits an art teacher at Metcalf Junior High School with "giving me the tools to grow as an artist for the rest of my life." One day, as Mahnke was drawing a human figure, his art teacher came over. "The legs are too short," she told him.

"Like a lot of kids who are used to their families telling them how good they are, I said, 'No, they're not,'" says Mahnke. "But she said, 'Yes, they are.' She could tell I was mad." The teacher grabbed art books off the shelf and opened them to drawings of human figures. "I looked at the proportions in the books and compared them to the proportions in my drawing, and I thought, *You know what? She's right.* Absolutely from that point on, I was indifferent to whether I was good or bad at art. I thought, *I'll never get better at what I do if I don't accept the fact that I have a lot of work ahead of me.*"

Despite an early fascination with superheroes, Mahnke never considered a career in comics. He was working at an amusement park as a T-shirt artist, and engaged to be married, when he stumbled upon a life-changing article. The article detailed the ascent of a well-known comic book artist, John Byrne, and, more pertinently, Byrne's six-figure income. "This was in the late eighties, when things were really ramping up in comics, and people were making big money. I'm thinking, *I could use that kind of money.* But I hadn't drawn comics in years." Not since he was a kid.

That didn't matter. Mahnke put together a portfolio of comic book art. He mailed his work to every art director at every comics publisher on his list, not knowing enough about the industry to realize artists don't usually submit work to art directors. However, by a strange twist of fate, the art director at Dark Horse Comics didn't toss his misdirected portfolio. He filed it in a cabinet, where John Arcudi, an up-and-coming writer, discovered it.

"I DON'T KNOW WHAT'S GOING TO HAPPEN IN THIS INDUSTRY. I GOT NO GUARANTEES. BUT I WANT TO ALWAYS BE RELEVANT. I CAN'T EVER BE AFRAID TO CHANGE WHAT I DO AND GROW AS A COMIC BOOK ARTIST."

Arcudi and Mahnke teamed up on the comic book series *Homicide* and again on *The Mask,* which many people remember from the 1994 movie starring Jim Carrey. Arcudi and Mahnke's run on *The Mask* began in 1989 with the character of Stanley Ipkiss, a neurotic milquetoast who turns into a madcap super-being when he dons the green mask. Writer and artist stayed with the Dark Horse series through the mid-nineties, a span that documents, in the pages of *The Mask Returns* and *The Mask Strikes Back,* Mahnke's significant growth as an artist, an evolution he's continued

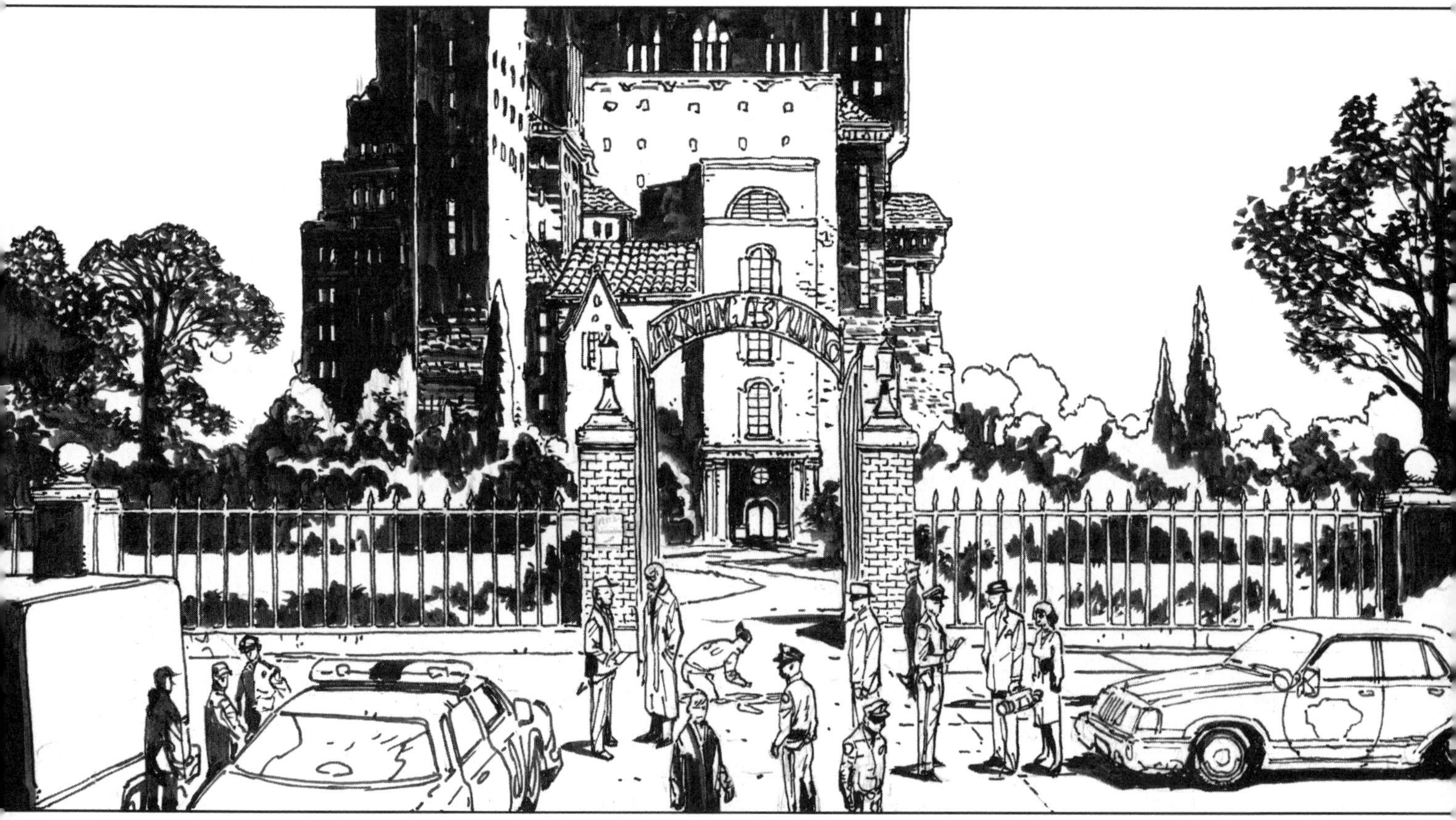
ARKHAM ASYLUM

Batman: The Man Who Laughs (DC Comics). Pencils by Doug Mahnke. © 2008 DC Comics at DC Comics, working on such titles as *Major Bummer, Black Adam: The Dark Age, Storm Watch: Post Human Division, JLA, Batman, Seven Soldiers of Victory: Frankenstein, Superman Beyond,* and *Final Crisis.*

"My art has changed so much because I made a commitment to change," says Mahnke. Early on, he sat down with his wife and hashed out his future in comics, a notoriously up-and-down business even in the good years. A series can take off or fail to launch. Editors move to rival publishers or are fired. The economy does a nosedive.

"I told my wife, 'I don't know what's going to happen in this industry. I got no guarantees. But I want to always be relevant. I can't ever be afraid to change what I do and grow as a comic book artist,'" Mahnke remembers saying.

And if Mahnke didn't start out with discipline, he grew into it, combining artistic skill with hard work and professionalism. "Doug can get an insane amount of work done if he has to," says Patrick Gleason, a fellow comic book artist with whom Mahnke shares a studio in Forest Lake, Minnesota. "His work ethic is extraordinary." So extraordinary that after receiving a concussion in an auto accident, rather than going to the hospital, Mahnke sat down at his drawing table. Why?

"I had a deadline the next day. I promised the editor I'd get the work done," Mahnke says. "I can't even tell you what was going through my mind at that point. I didn't sleep. I just sat there drawing. My eyesight was messed up. Everything was goofy, but I got the work done." ∎

Black Adam: The Dark Age No. 2 (DC Comics). Pencils by Doug Mahnke; inks by Christian Alamy. © 2007 DC Comics

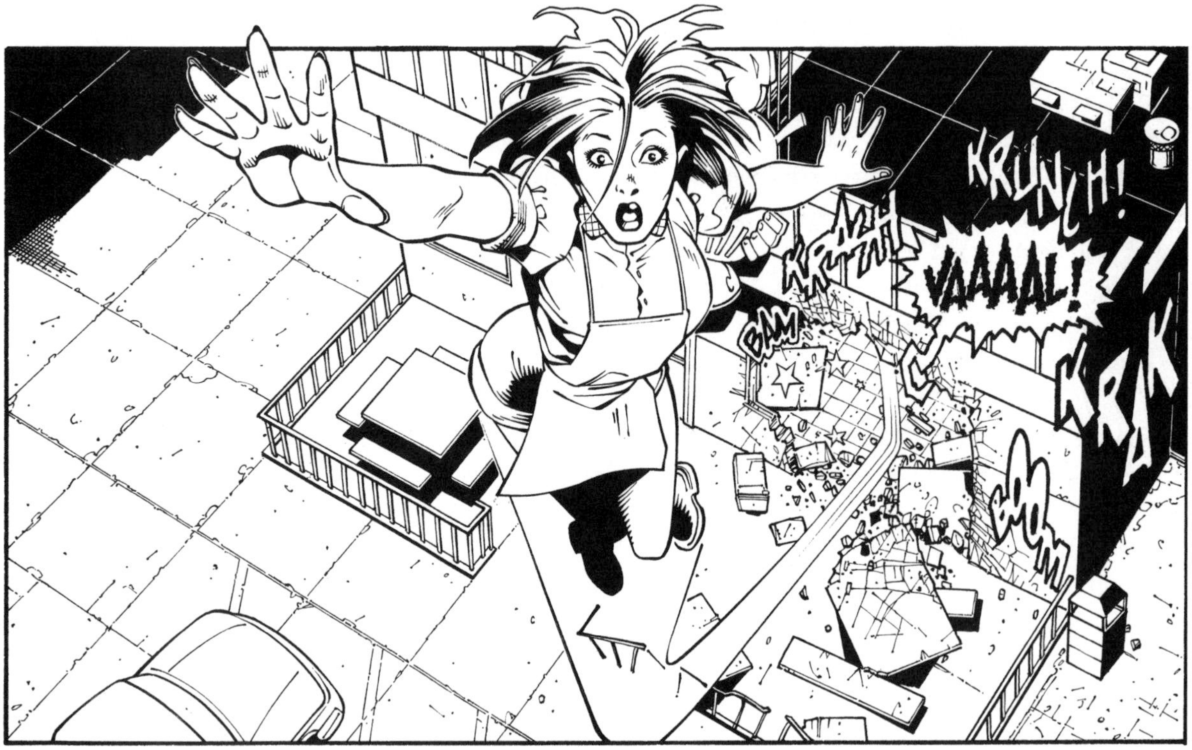
KRUNCH!
VAAAL!
BAM
KRAK

Major Bummer No. 6 (DC Comics). Script by John Arcudi; pencils by Doug Mahnke; inks by Tom Nguyen. © 1998 John Arcudi and Doug Mahnke

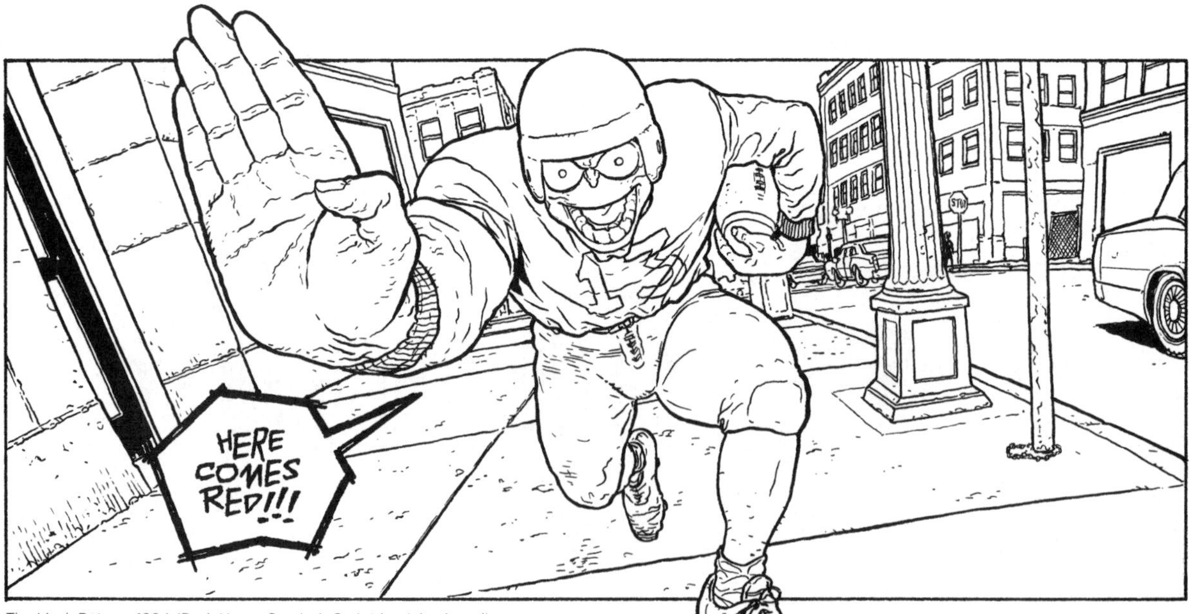
HERE COMES RED!!!

The Mask Returns 1994 (Dark Horse Comics). Script by John Arcudi; pencils by Doug Mahnke. © 1994 Dark Horse Comics

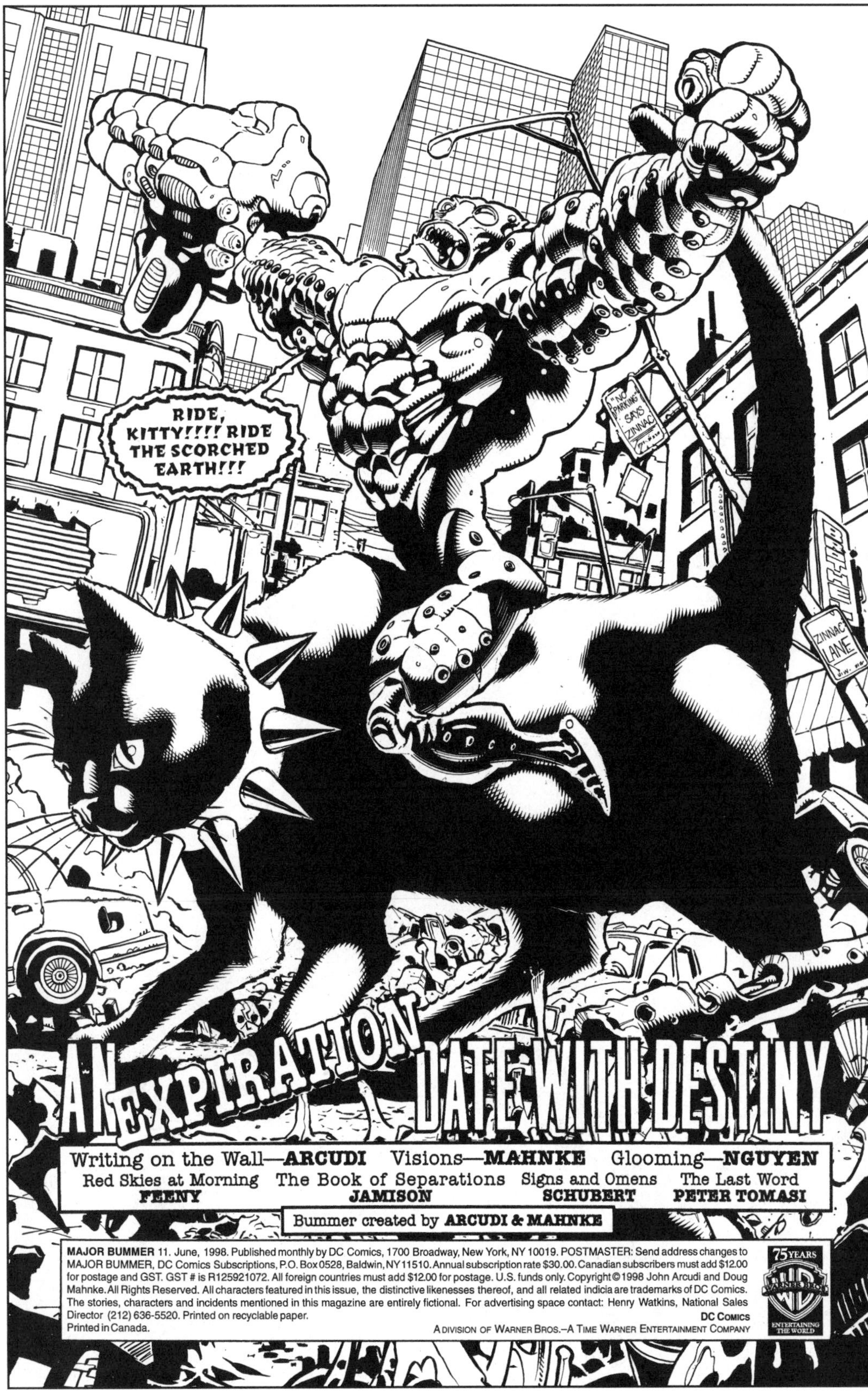
RIDE, KITTY!!!! RIDE THE SCORCHED EARTH!!!
"NO PARKING" SAYS ZINNAC
ZINNAC LANE
AN EXPIRATION DATE WITH DESTINY
Writing on the Wall—**ARCUDI** Visions—**MAHNKE** Glooming—**NGUYEN**
Red Skies at Morning **FEENY** The Book of Separations **JAMISON** Signs and Omens **SCHUBERT** The Last Word **PETER TOMASI**
Bummer created by **ARCUDI & MAHNKE**
MAJOR BUMMER 11. June, 1998. Published monthly by DC Comics, 1700 Broadway, New York, NY 10019. POSTMASTER: Send address changes to MAJOR BUMMER, DC Comics Subscriptions, P.O. Box 0528, Baldwin, NY 11510. Annual subscription rate $30.00. Canadian subscribers must add $12.00 for postage and GST. GST # is R125921072. All foreign countries must add $12.00 for postage. U.S. funds only. Copyright © 1998 John Arcudi and Doug Mahnke. All Rights Reserved. All characters featured in this issue, the distinctive likenesses thereof, and all related indicia are trademarks of DC Comics. The stories, characters and incidents mentioned in this magazine are entirely fictional. For advertising space contact: Henry Watkins, National Sales Director (212) 636-5520. Printed on recyclable paper.
Printed in Canada.
DC COMICS
A DIVISION OF WARNER BROS.–A TIME WARNER ENTERTAINMENT COMPANY
75 YEARS WARNER BROS. ENTERTAINING THE WORLD

Major Bummer No. 11 (DC Comics). Script by John Arcudi; art by Doug Mahnke. © 1998 John Arcudi and Doug Mahnke

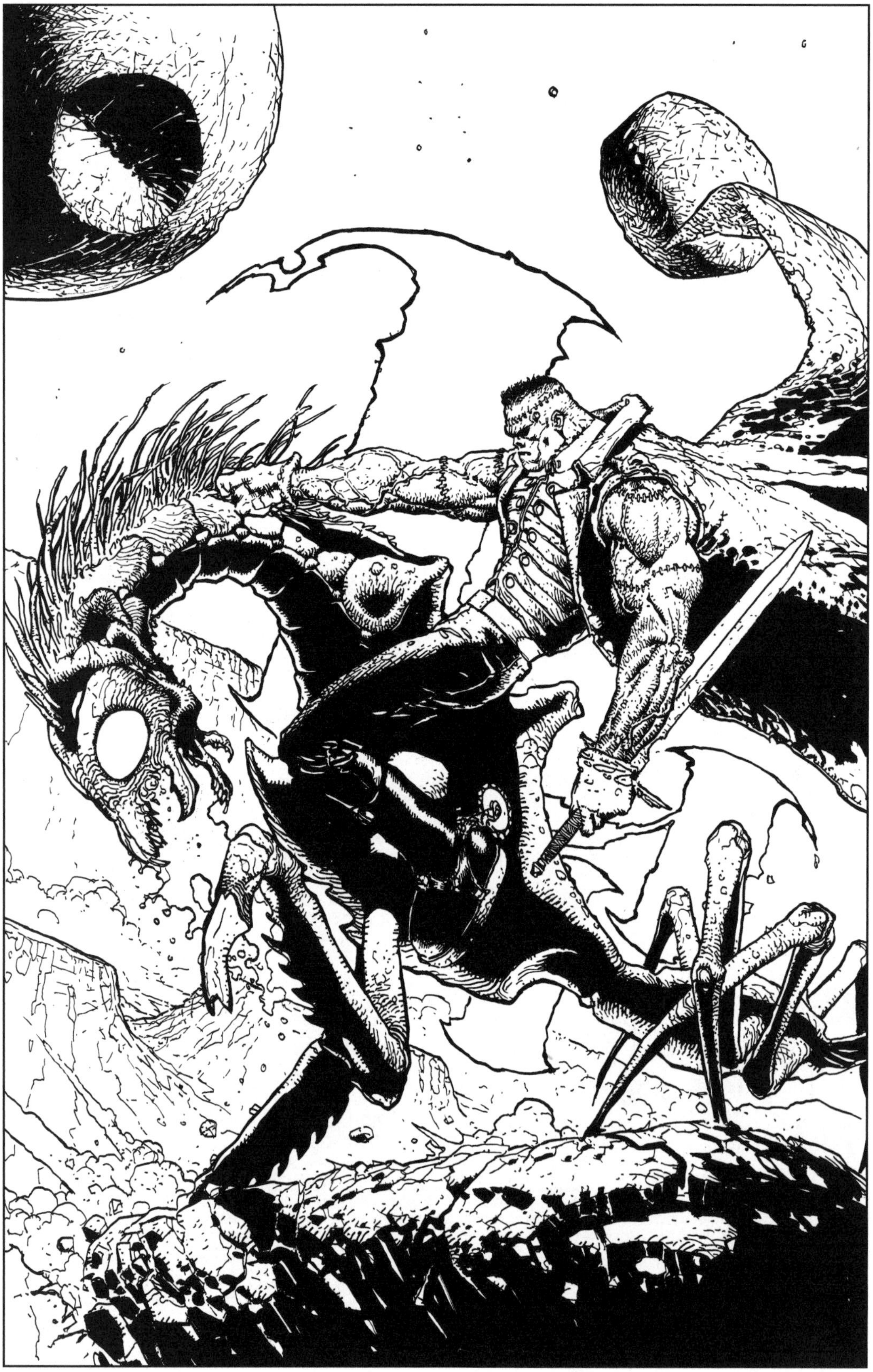

Seven Soldiers: Frankenstein No. 2 (DC Comics). Pencils by Doug Mahnke. © 2006 DC Comics

PATRICK GLEASON

No one knows comic book artist Patrick Gleason like Doug Mahnke.

"I'll tell you a story," Mahnke promises, planting himself on a couch in the artist studio he shares with Gleason in Forest Lake, Minnesota. His tone is reminiscent, turning back the clock more than ten years to the day they met. "It's one of my favorite stories about Pat. It says so much about him, about how he's an oddball in a good way. Pat had this friend Matt, who was a wannabe guy."

Matt wanted to be a comic book artist. Lucky for Matt that Doug Mahnke, a comic book artist, lived in Forest Lake, where Matt was employed at a pizza shop. Mahnke was an honest-to-goodness, working comic book artist, a penciller and inker for DC Comics, the home base of Superman and Batman, Flash and the Green Lantern. And Mahnke was living right there in Matt's quiet, rural town.

Matt hooked up with Mahnke. He asked to apprentice under the veteran, show him some of his art, get feedback—that kind of thing. "Only Matt never gave me anything to critique. He'd come to our meetings with maybe three sketches. I finally got wise to him," says Mahnke. "'You're drawing these sketches an hour before you meet with me. I can tell,' I told Matt. 'Don't do this to me again. Because you're wasting my time and you're wasting your time. Don't talk to me again unless you have something to show me.'"

One day Matt brought this friend, Patrick Gleason, to the meeting at Pulp Fiction, a book and comics store in Forest Lake that has since closed. Mahnke remembers the day. "I sat down, and I said, 'Okay, Matt, what do you got?' and again he basically had nothing. I was really disappointed. And I was sure Pat was going to be another Matt. So, I said to Pat," he pitches his voice to a menacing growl, "'Whaddya got?'"

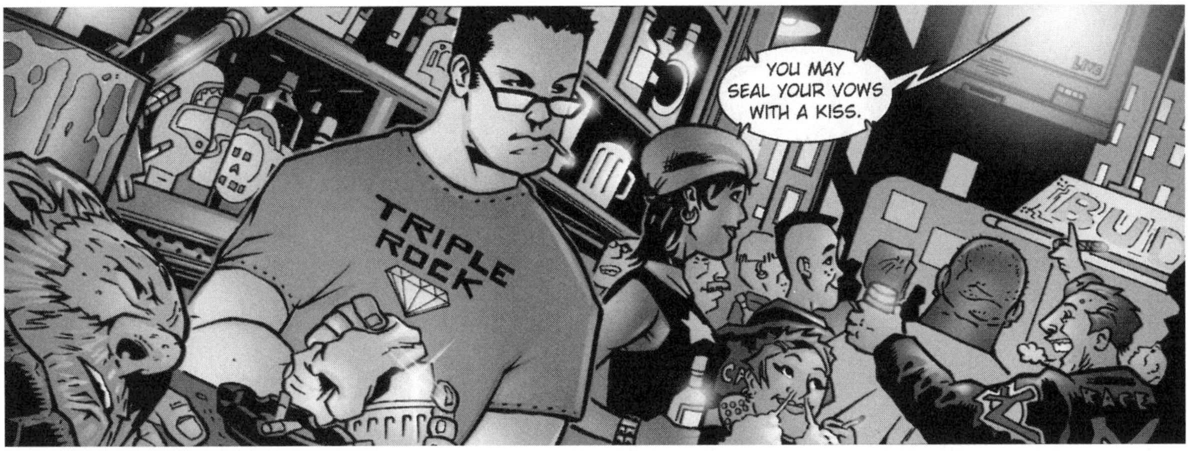
YOU MAY SEAL YOUR VOWS WITH A KISS.
TRIPLE ROCK

Noble Causes, Vol. 1: In Sickness And In Health (Image Comics). Script by Jay Faerber; pencils by Patrick Gleason. © 2003 Jay Faerber

The nineteen-year-old Gleason reached into a paper sack and pulled out a stack of comics thick as a phone book. "Pat had done more work at that age than a lot of professionals," says Mahnke. "He wasn't an inker yet. He'd finish his drawings with a Sharpie in a crude fashion. But I could see the obvious talent, the playfulness, the storytelling. He just had to be directed. I looked at Matt and said, 'Matt, this is the difference between somebody who wants to do something and somebody who *will* do something.'"

On the way to the parking lot, Mahnke slipped his number to Gleason and said, "Pat, you'll work in comics. I promise. Call me if you want."

The meeting with Mahnke changed Gleason's life. Maybe he would've gotten into comics by himself, but then maybe not. Gleason points out that Mahnke was the first person "who told me when my art wasn't good—in not always flattering terms." The feedback helped shape Gleason's art, and made the difference between Gleason being a mediocre wannabe artist living in rural Minnesota and a fresh new face on the comics scene.

If there are fairy tale stories in comics, Gleason lived one. His first assignment with a major publisher was huge: He—this fresh-faced kid from

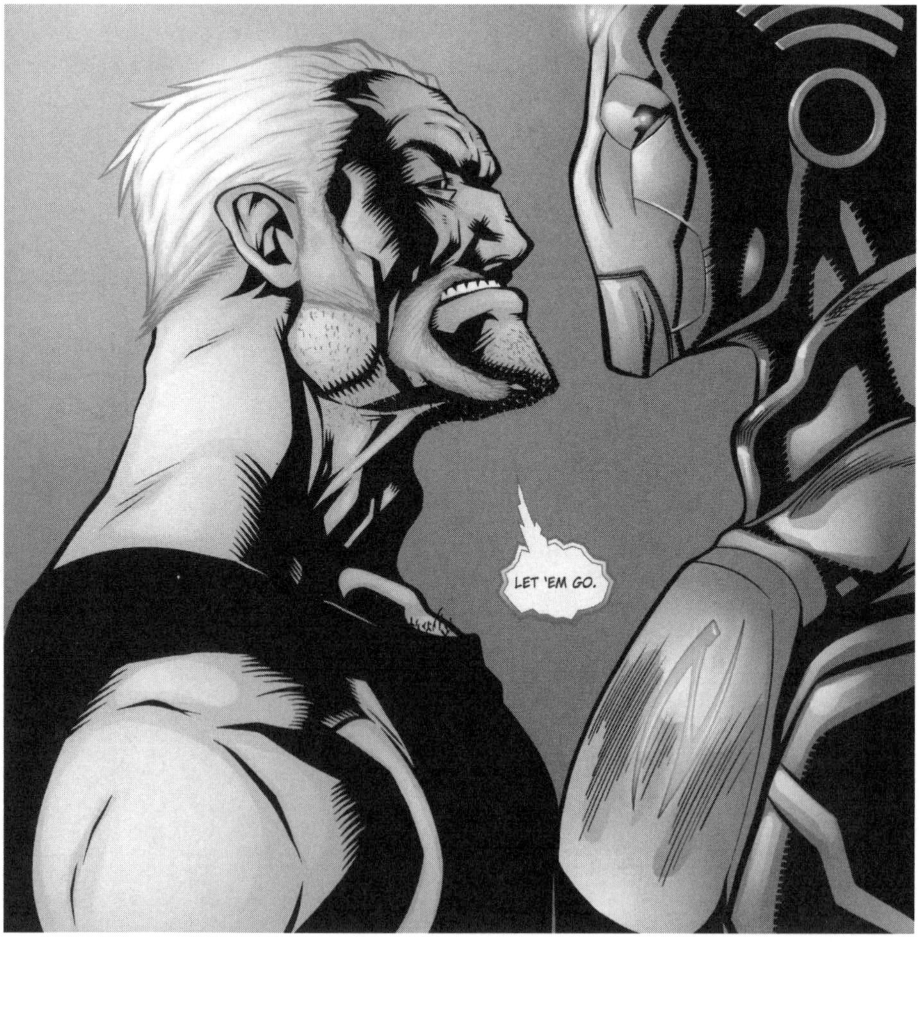
LET 'EM GO.

Noble Causes, Vol. 1: In Sickness And In Health (Image Comics). Script by Jay Faerber; pencils by Patrick Gleason. © 2003 Jay Faerber

Minnesota—was going to be penciling an *X-Men* spin-off. So, it was only a spin-off, but it was still an *X-Men* spin-off.

Of course, as in every fairy tale, there's also a twist. Gleason got a call about a month into the project. His editor had been fired. And, well, Gleason didn't have to worry about getting those pages done because he was off the book. Bye.

It looked like Gleason's career in comics was going to take a little longer getting started than he hoped. Fortunately, Mahnke needed an assistant and Gleason had time. He spent the next two years working alongside Mahnke. "Being Doug's assistant was the best job," says Gleason. For one thing, he got paid to hone his craft. For another, "Doug would get these huge comp boxes from the publisher. I'd go home with armloads of free comics."

During the apprenticeship, Gleason continued to send feelers into the comic book community and was eventually tapped to pencil back-up issues for *Noble Causes,* a series written by Jay Faerber and published by Image Comics. When the principal artist moved off the project, Faerber asked Gleason to take on lead pencil duties.

One job led to another. Gleason worked on DC properties *Hawkman: Secret Files* and *Aquaman.* Then, in 2005, Gleason snagged a primo job. He became lead penciller on *Green Lantern Corps,* a spin-off from the Green Lantern universe, which follows the exploits of a group of intergalactic space cops.

"I'd been drawing weird, underwater stuff for *Aquaman,* people floating around in water. So the transition to *Green Lantern Corps* was easy because now I was drawing weird outer-space stuff and people floating around in space," says Gleason, who continues to draw *Green Lantern Corps* for DC.

Back in Forest Lake, Gleason and Mahnke have shifted from protégé and mentor to peers. They share a second-story studio in a commercial block downtown. Gleason says the arrangement is ideal for guys employed in a famously solitary profession. He observes, "When you're working against a deadline, which you do a lot in comics, it's nice to have someone there in the trenches with you. Someone who's going through the same thing you're going through." ∎

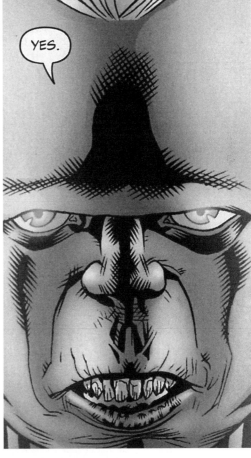

Green Lantern Corps: Sins of the Star Sapphire (DC Comics). Pencils by Patrick Gleason. © 2009 DC Comics

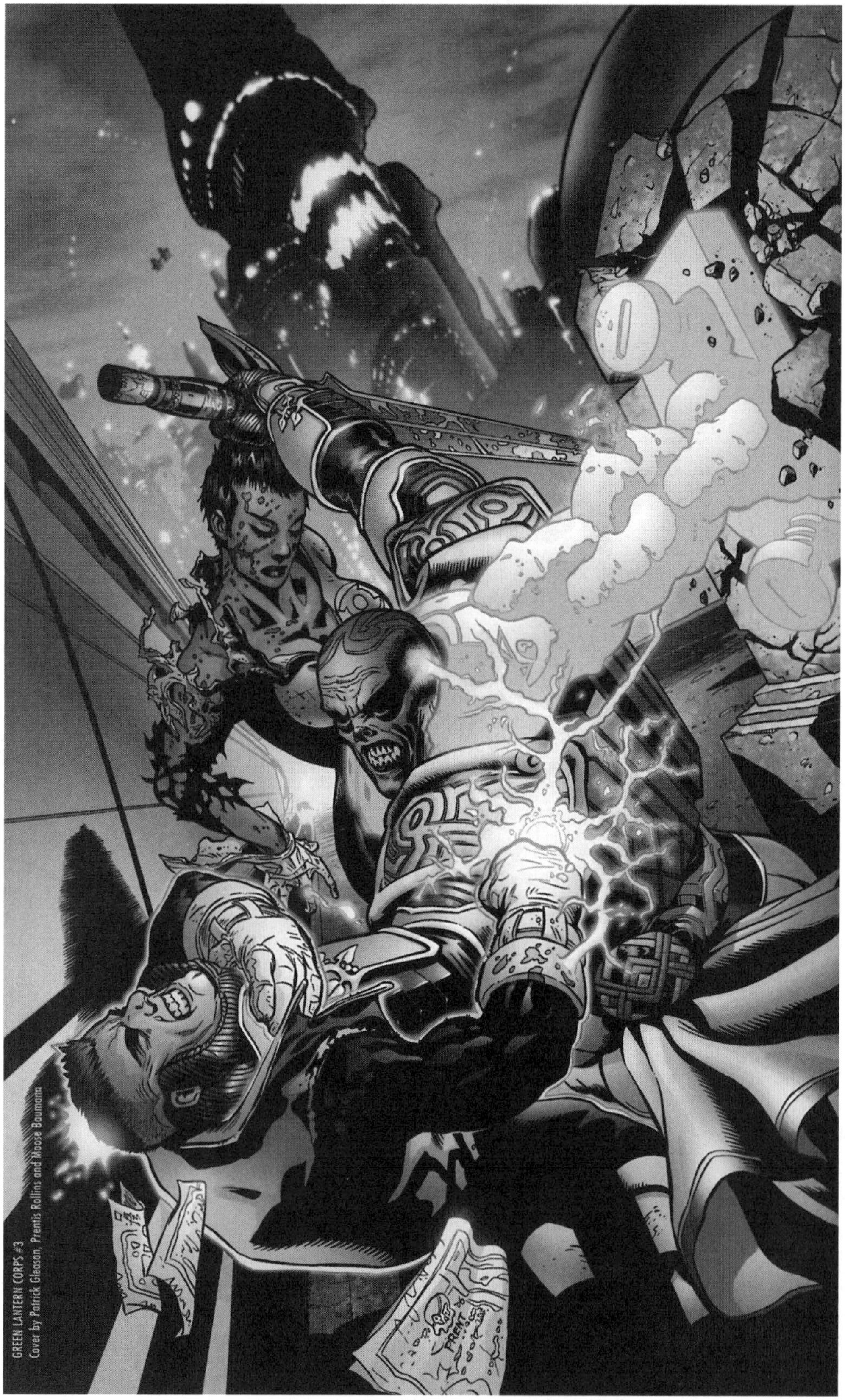
GREEN LANTERN CORPS #3
Cover by Patrick Gleason, Prentis Rollins and Moose Baumann

Green Lantern Corps No. 3: To Be a Lantern (DC Comics). Pencils by Patrick Gleason. © 2007 DC Comics

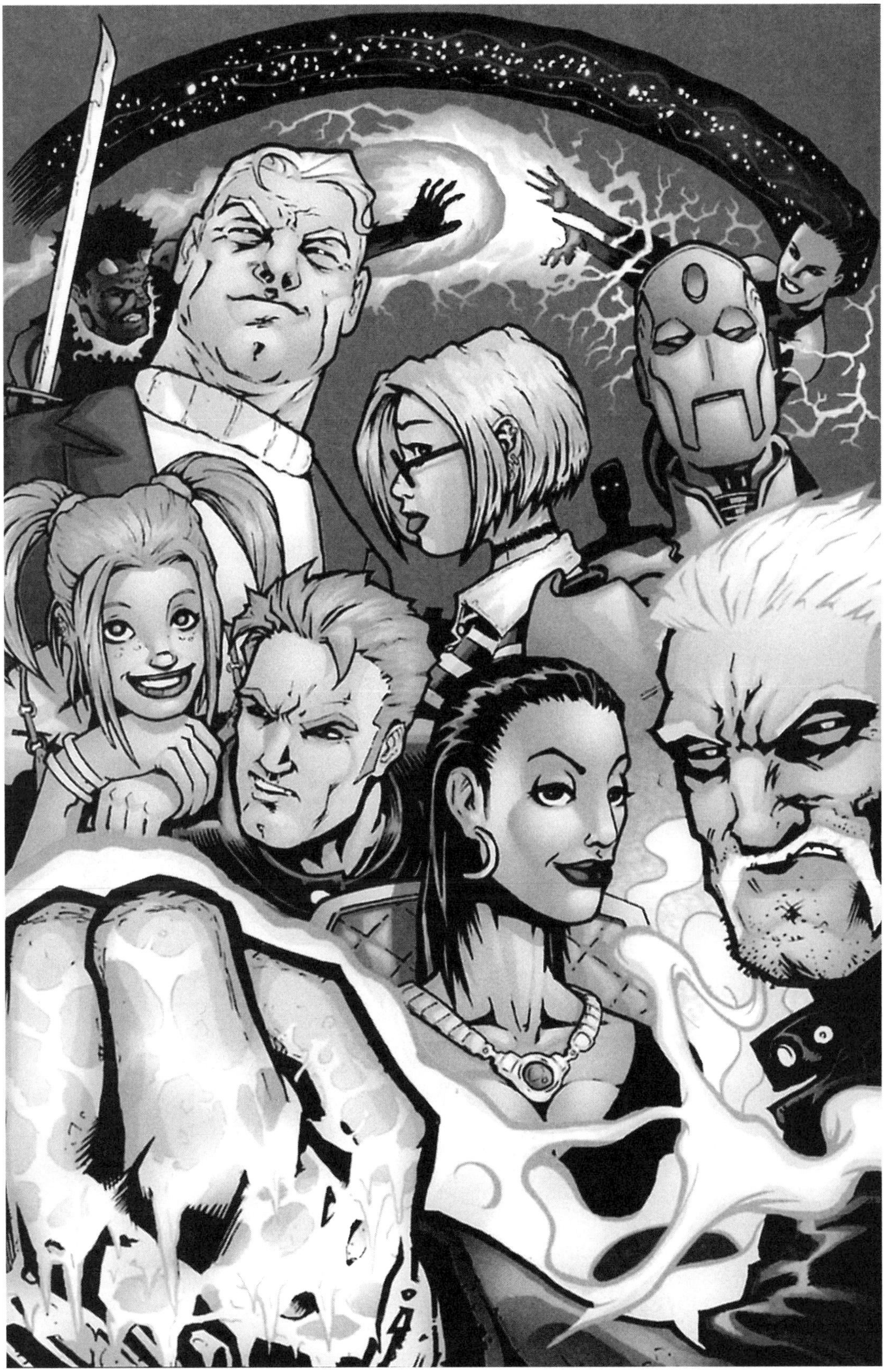

Noble Causes, Vol. 1: In Sickness And In Health (Image Comics). Script by Jay Faerber; pencils by Patrick Gleason. © 2003 Jay Faerber

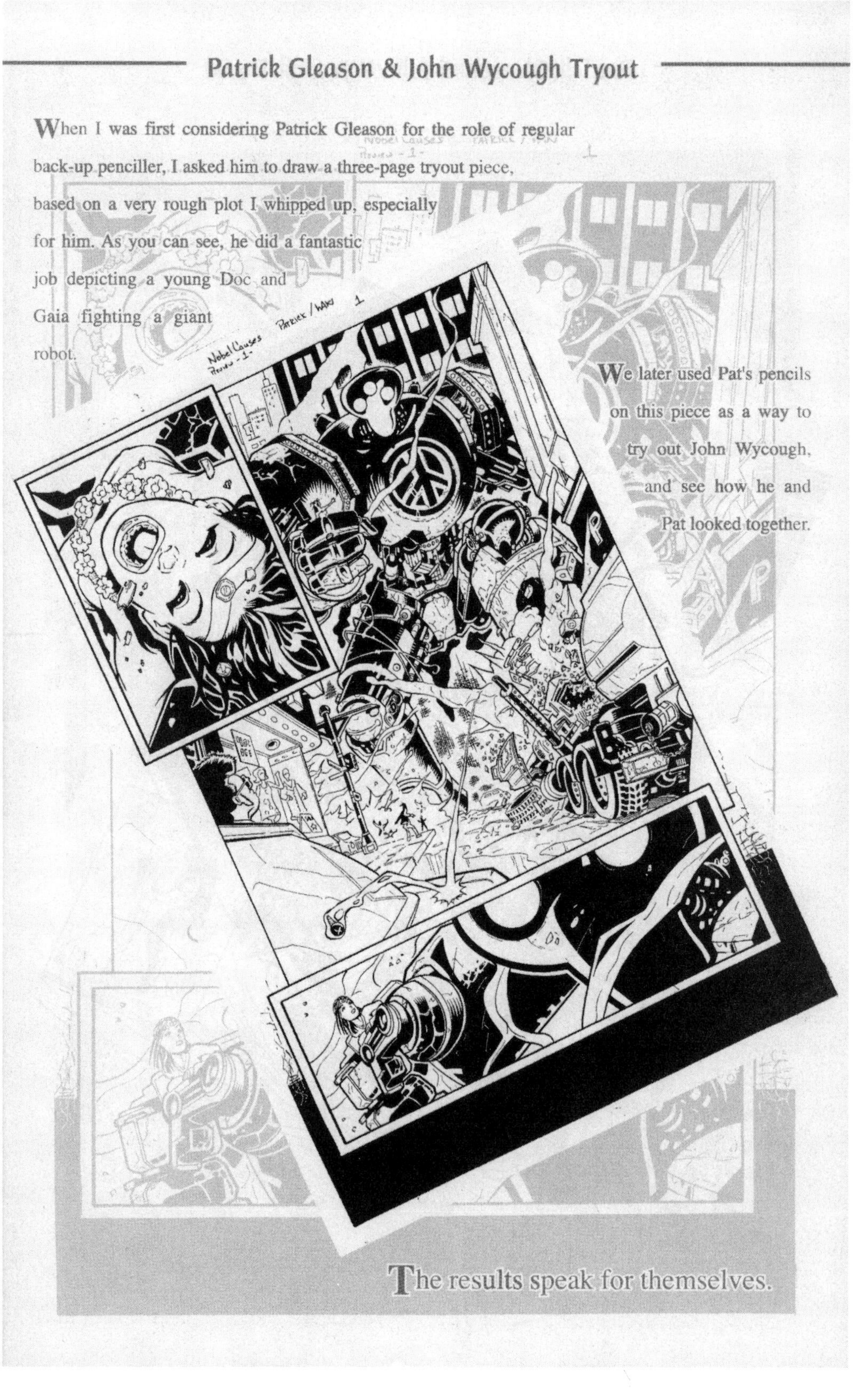

Patrick Gleason & John Wycough Tryout

When I was first considering Patrick Gleason for the role of regular back-up penciller, I asked him to draw a three-page tryout piece, based on a very rough plot I whipped up, especially for him. As you can see, he did a fantastic job depicting a young Doc and Gaia fighting a giant robot.

We later used Pat's pencils on this piece as a way to try out John Wycough, and see how he and Pat looked together.

The results speak for themselves.

Noble Causes, Vol. 1: In Sickness And In Health (Image Comics). Script by Jay Faerber; pencils by Patrick Gleason. © 2003 Jay Faerber

PETER GROSS

Peter Gross had been working in comics for over twenty years when he and London-based writer Mike Carey put out their new series, *The Unwritten,* in 2009. The pair had developed the series top to bottom. The process took months of phone chats, e-mails, meet-ups at conventions, and finally the pitch to Vertigo. This wasn't the first series Gross and Carey had pitched. But it was the one they cared most about.

"I'm getting old enough now that I don't have tons of projects left in me," says Gross. Both he and Carey are in their fifties. "And when I looked at doing another book, I wanted it to be something special, something that had meaning outside comics."

Vertigo liked the pitch. It was a go. So in May 2009, in the deep muck of an economic recession, Gross and Carey unveiled the first issue of *The Unwritten* and crossed their fingers.

"We'd been hearing all this great stuff from the people at Vertigo," says Gross. "The executives, the marketing people, they were saying it was one of the best first issues they'd ever read."

But what would the comic-buying public think? At the moment, with unemployment hovering near ten percent, bankruptcies, foreclosures, and a catastrophic national debt occupying news headlines, the general public was more inclined to salt away spare dimes than plunk them down for a comic. Timing is everything in comics. But then, so is a well-told story.

Born in St. Cloud, Minnesota, Gross self-published his first comic series, the black-and-white *Empire Lanes,* in Duluth in the mid-1980s. "That was at the end of the black-and-white boom, when everyone was trying to self-publish something after the success of the *Teenage Mutant Ninja Turtles,*" says Gross, who now lives in Minneapolis.

The *Teenage Mutant Ninja Turtles* series was a publishing phenomenon. The creators, Kevin Eastman and Peter Laird, proved to other comic book writers and artists that you didn't need a publisher to sell your book. You could print, publish, and distribute a comic by yourself, then sit back while the profits rolled in. The first issue of Gross's fantasy epic appeared in December 1986, by which time the market had already begun to sag under the glut of self-published black and whites. Still, *Empire Lanes* No. 1 sold a respectable 30,000 copies.

> "EVERYONE CALLS VERTIGO THE HBO OF COMICS BECAUSE VERTIGO PUTS STORY BEFORE EVERYTHING ELSE."

Even as the black-and-white market toppled, Gross shifted to contract work with Marvel, Dark Horse, and DC Comics. DC, in particular the imprint Vertigo, has been Gross's mainstay since 1991.

"Everyone calls Vertigo the HBO of comics because Vertigo puts story before everything else," says Gross. DC handles the superhero stories.

Vertigo handles adult titles, a vague label that covers everything from *100 Bullets* and *Y: The Last Man* to *Fables* and *Sandman.*

At first, Gross did a lot of inking for DC. He inked pages for *Doctor Fate.* "When that got canceled," he says, "I ended up on *Books of Magic,* which was a spin-off from a Neil Gaiman miniseries, basically a Harry Potter story. Everybody says Neil invented Harry Potter before *Harry Potter.* What Neil says is that he and J. K. Rowling stole from the same sources."

Books of Magic introduces readers to Tim Hunter, an English boy in big glasses who's told that he is the next great sorcerer. Vertigo brought Gross on to ink. But soon he was penciling the series, and then both scripting and penciling.

Gross's next project for Vertigo was another Gaiman spin-off. Gaiman is a British writer famed for the comic book series *Sandman,* which began in the late 1980s and was instrumental in establishing the Vertigo imprint at DC. The spin-off was *Lucifer,* which borrowed a recurring character from *Sandman,* Lucifer, a.k.a. Satan, and built a story around the handsome figurehead of hell. Carey scripted the series, which lasted seventy-five issues and wrapped up in 2006.

"EVERYBODY SAYS NEIL INVENTED HARRY POTTER BEFORE HARRY POTTER. WHAT NEIL SAYS IS THAT HE AND J. K. ROWLING STOLE FROM THE SAME SOURCES."

"Mike and I share a certain approach to story, and we mesh well. We got to a point on *Lucifer* where I could anticipate what he was going to do and he could anticipate what I was going to do," says Gross. So when *Lucifer* ended, it was natural for the pair to want to reunite. They tossed around ideas. But nothing caught fire, until they conceived of another magical boy, along the lines of Tim Hunter from *Books of Magic* but not quite because he's a fictional confection even within the fictional world of the comic book.

The Unwritten narrates a story within a story. On one level, the series tells the story of Tommy Taylor, the boy wizard featured in a series of best-selling fantasy novels. On another, *The Unwritten* is about Tom Taylor, the son of the books' author, Wilson Taylor, and the inspiration for the fictional boy wizard.

"Tommy Taylor is the boy in the books, and Tom Taylor is the boy the books were named after. And when the story begins, Tom is an adult. He's a Z-list celebrity who makes a living going to conventions and signing his father's books," says Gross. "After the thirteenth *Tommy Taylor* book was published, Tom's father disappeared, taking his fortune with him and abandoning Tom, a young teenager, to grow up as the most famous boy on earth."

Fans naturally want to make the connection between Tommy the boy wizard and Tom the man at the convention table, a conceit that the adult Tom indulges with a politeness bordering on edgy annoyance. He despises the fans and their demented notions. He's a man, not a character from a book. Or is he? Events transpire that muddy the borders of real life and fiction.

Vertigo encouraged readers to pick up *The Unwritten* with a sweetheart deal; they sold issue one, a mammoth forty pages long, for one dollar. "I was discouraged that the retailers didn't order more," Gross says of the weeks leading up to the release. "I thought it would be ordered heavier, but then given the market and the economy, I could totally understand."

The Unwritten hit stands May 13. Gross in Minneapolis and Carey in London waited for news. They searched online review sites—good reviews. They checked retailer forum sites—*The Unwritten* was selling. Two weeks after the release date, Gross received a phone call from his editor. The first issue had sold out. A second print run was ordered, with the release date for issue two still a couple weeks away.

"It's a combination of good storytelling and good marketing," Gross says of the book's growing momentum. *The Unwritten* "got reviewed more than I expected and the reviews were more universally good than I expected, so it worked better than expected in a lot of ways," the artist says. Much better. Vertigo renewed the series, and in 2010 *The Unwritten* garnered three Eisner Award nominations, for Best Single Issue, Best Continuous Series, and Best New Series. ∎

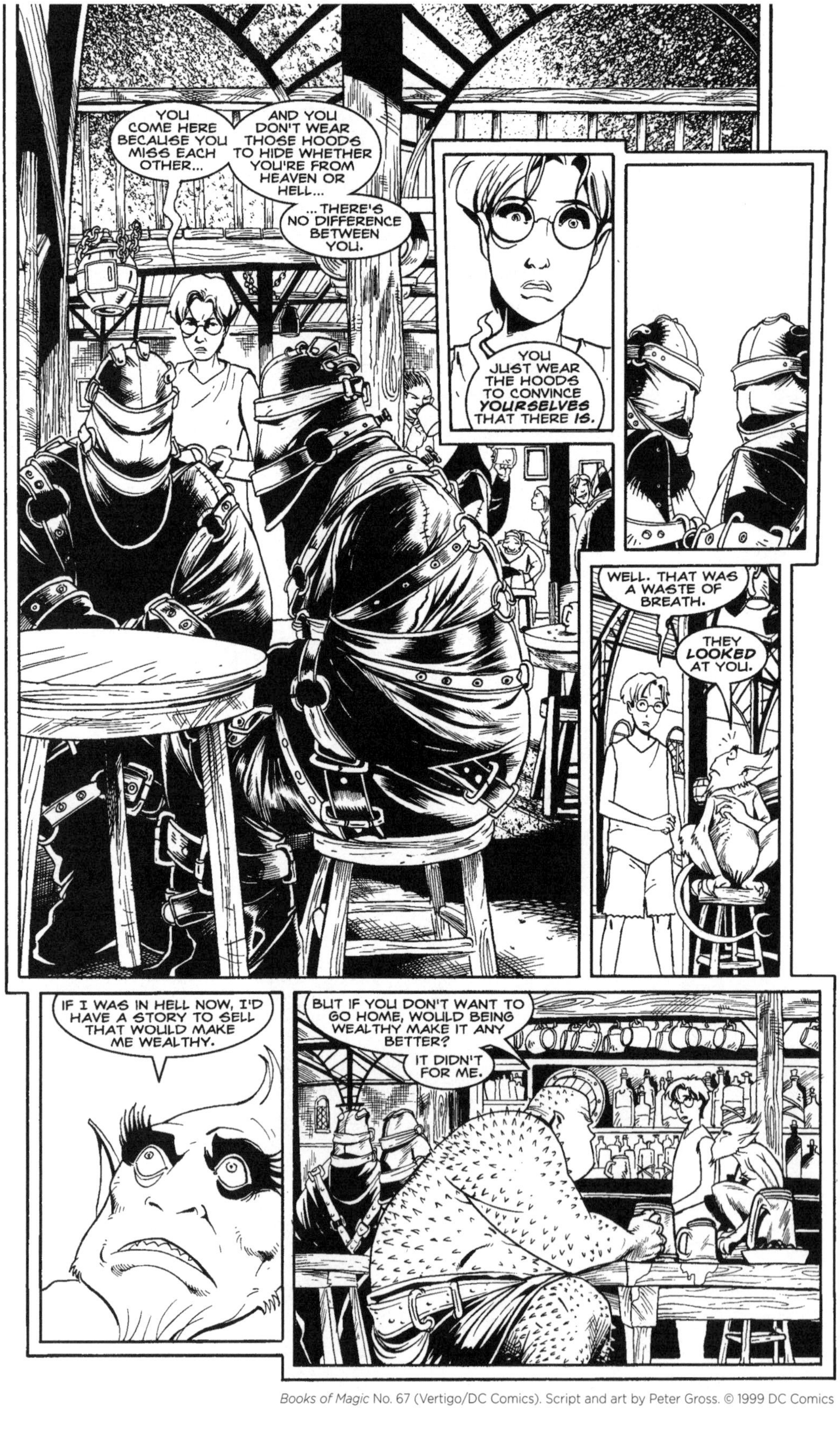
YOU COME HERE BECAUSE YOU MISS EACH OTHER...
AND YOU DON'T WEAR THOSE HOODS TO HIDE WHETHER YOU'RE FROM HEAVEN OR HELL...
...THERE'S NO DIFFERENCE BETWEEN YOU.
YOU JUST WEAR THE HOODS TO CONVINCE YOURSELVES THAT THERE IS.
WELL. THAT WAS A WASTE OF BREATH.
THEY LOOKED AT YOU.
IF I WAS IN HELL NOW, I'D HAVE A STORY TO SELL THAT WOULD MAKE ME WEALTHY.
BUT IF YOU DON'T WANT TO GO HOME, WOULD BEING WEALTHY MAKE IT ANY BETTER?
IT DIDN'T FOR ME.

Books of Magic No. 67 (Vertigo/DC Comics). Script and art by Peter Gross. © 1999 DC Comics

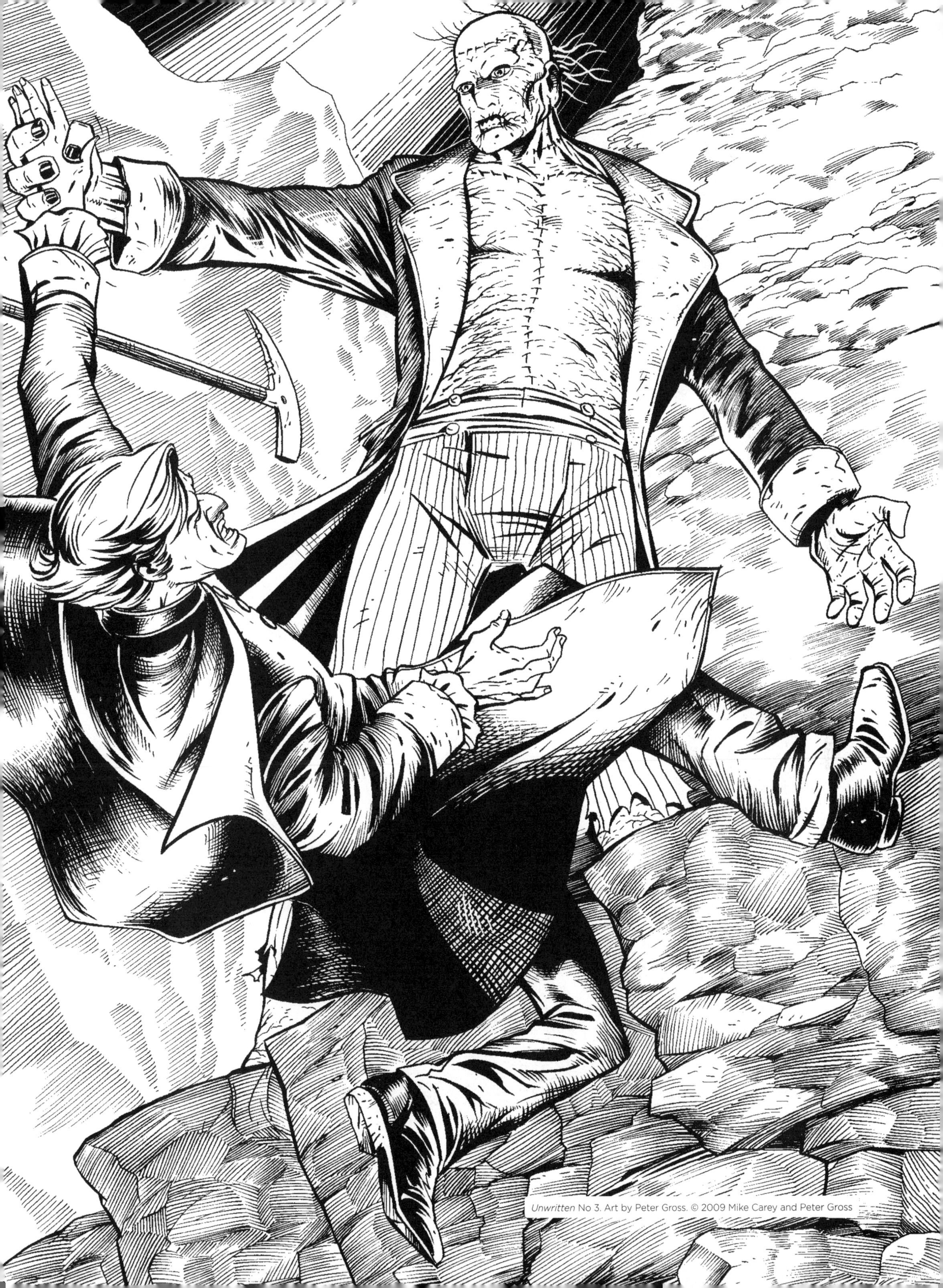

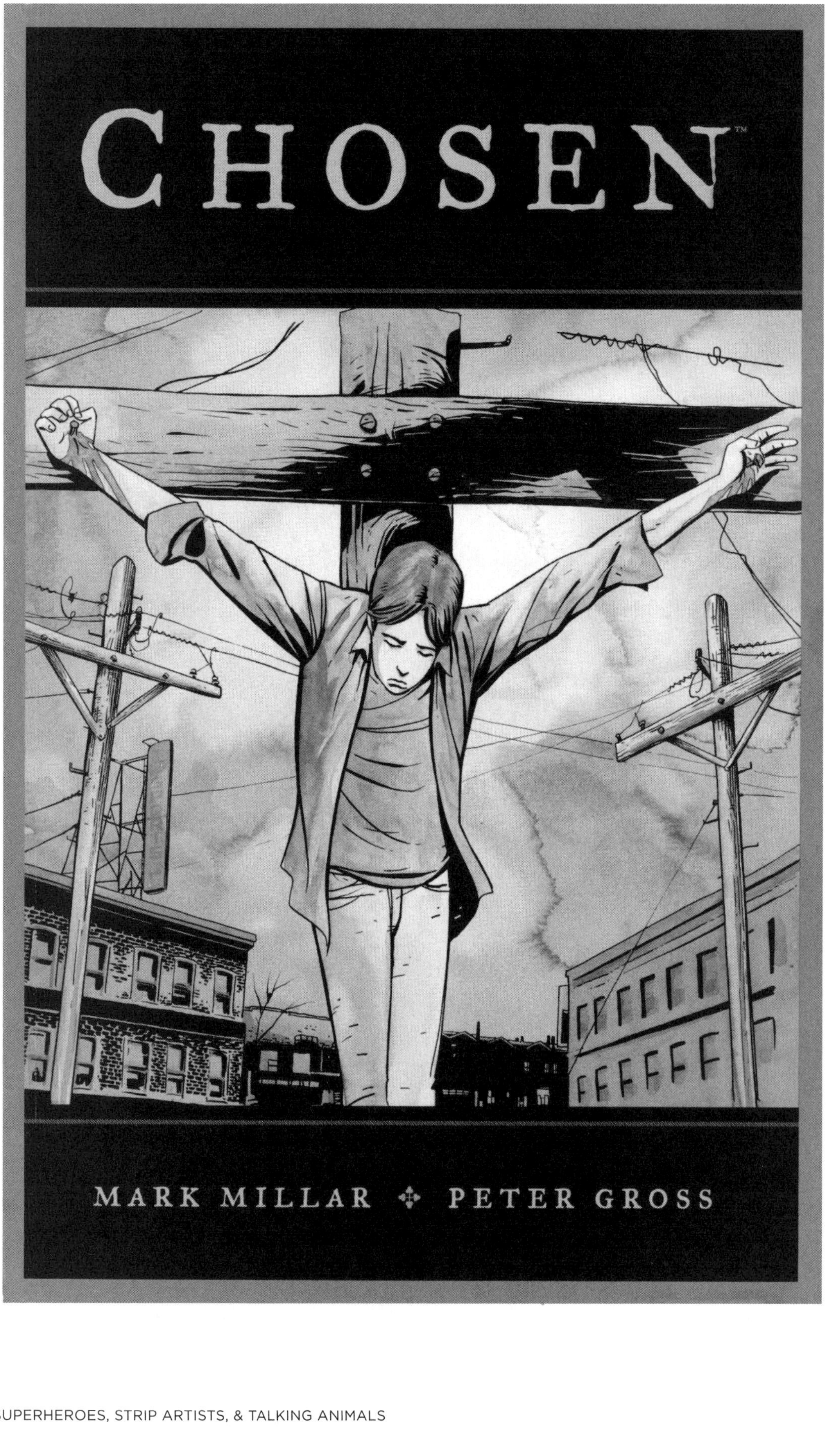
CHOSEN™
MARK MILLAR ✣ PETER GROSS

Chosen (Image Comics). Script by Mark Millar; art by Peter Gross. © 2005 Mark Millar and Peter Gross

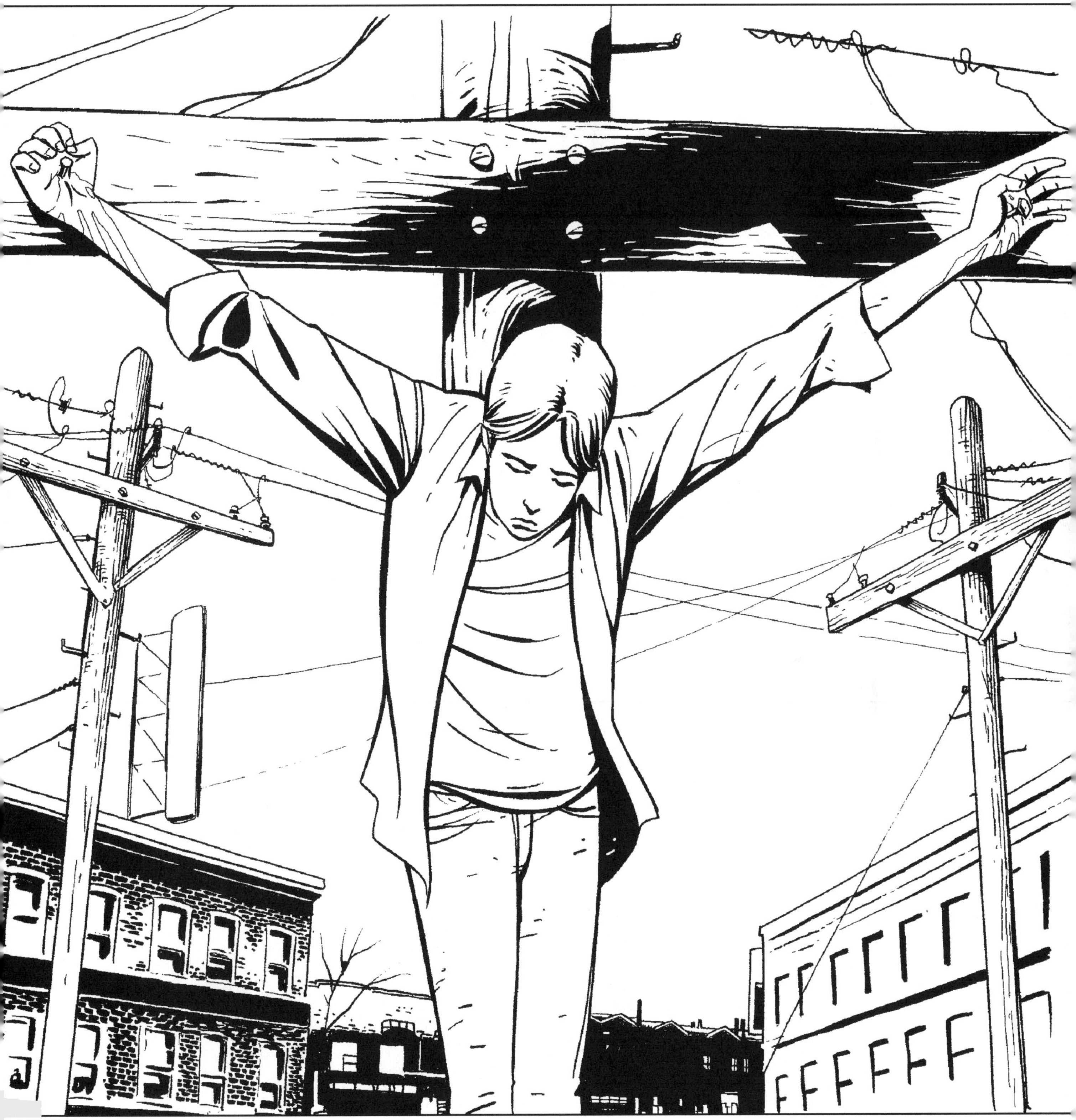

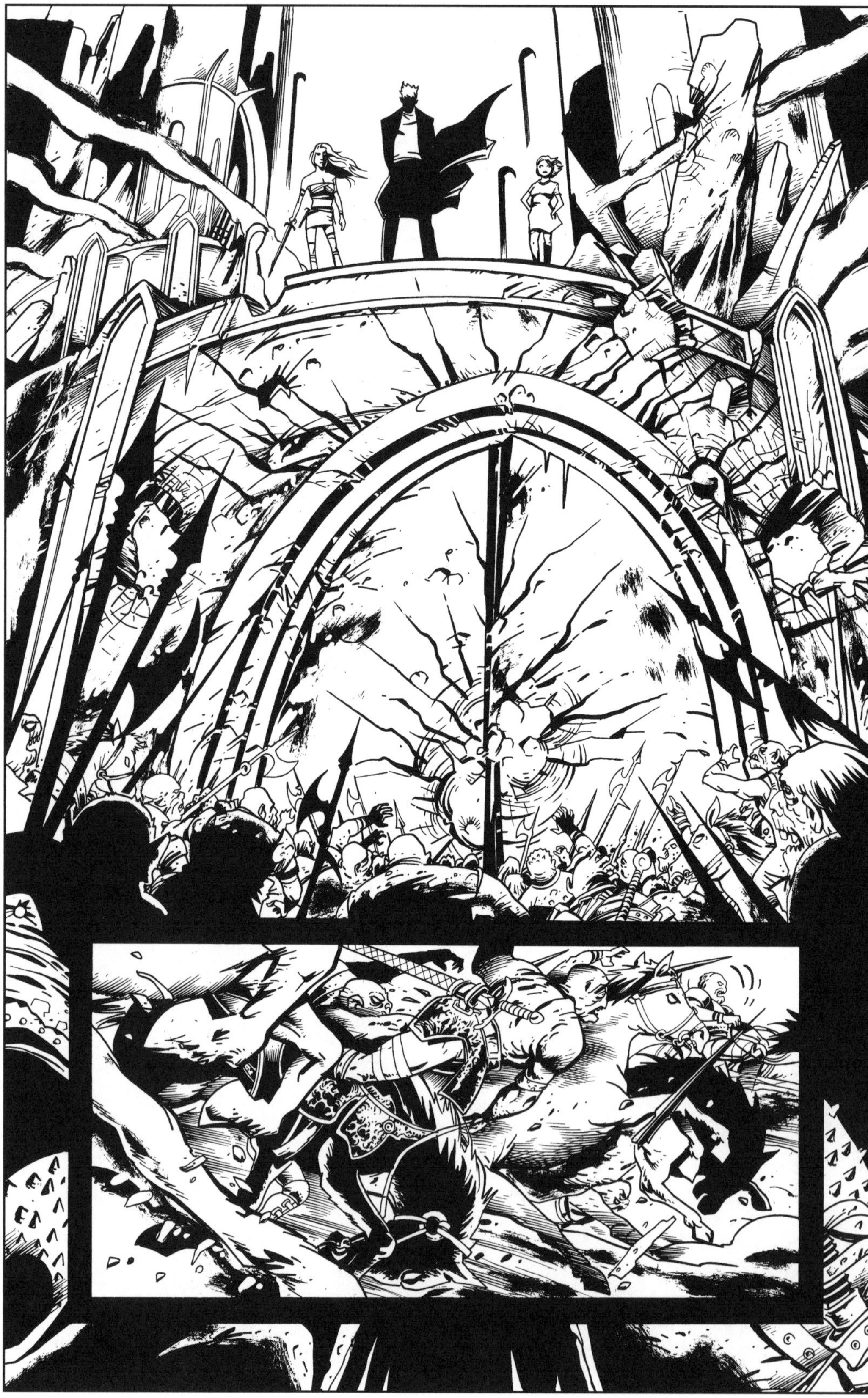

Lucifer No. 65 (Vertigo/DC Comics). Art by Peter Gross and Ryan Kelly. © 2005 DC Comics

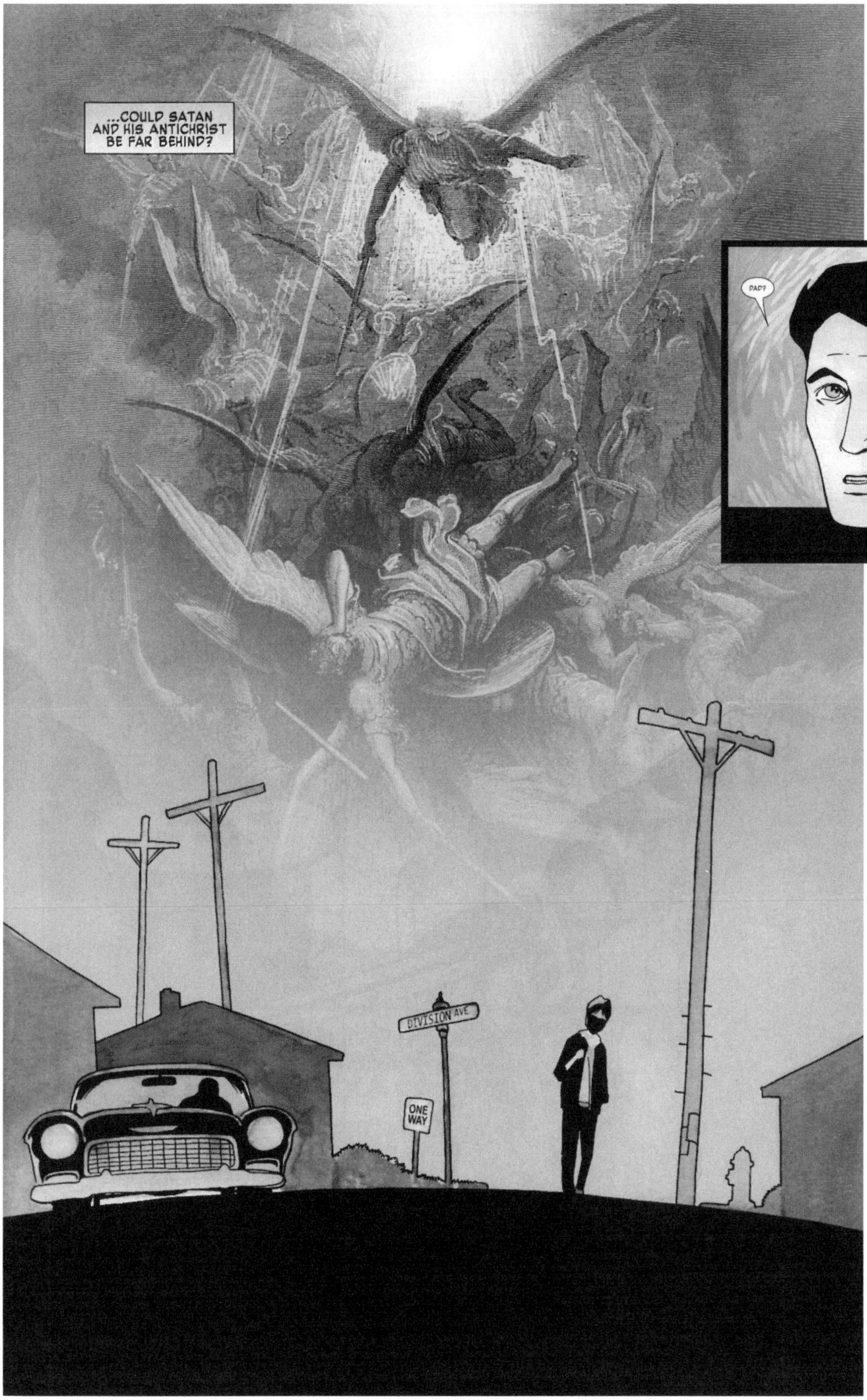
...COULD SATAN AND HIS ANTICHRIST BE FAR BEHIND?
DIVISION AVE
ONE WAY

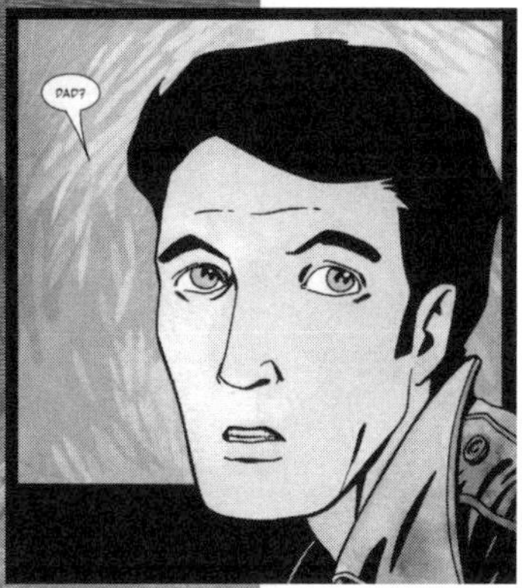
DAD?

Chosen (Image Comics). Script by Mark Millar; art by Peter Gross. © 2005 Mark Millar and Peter Gross

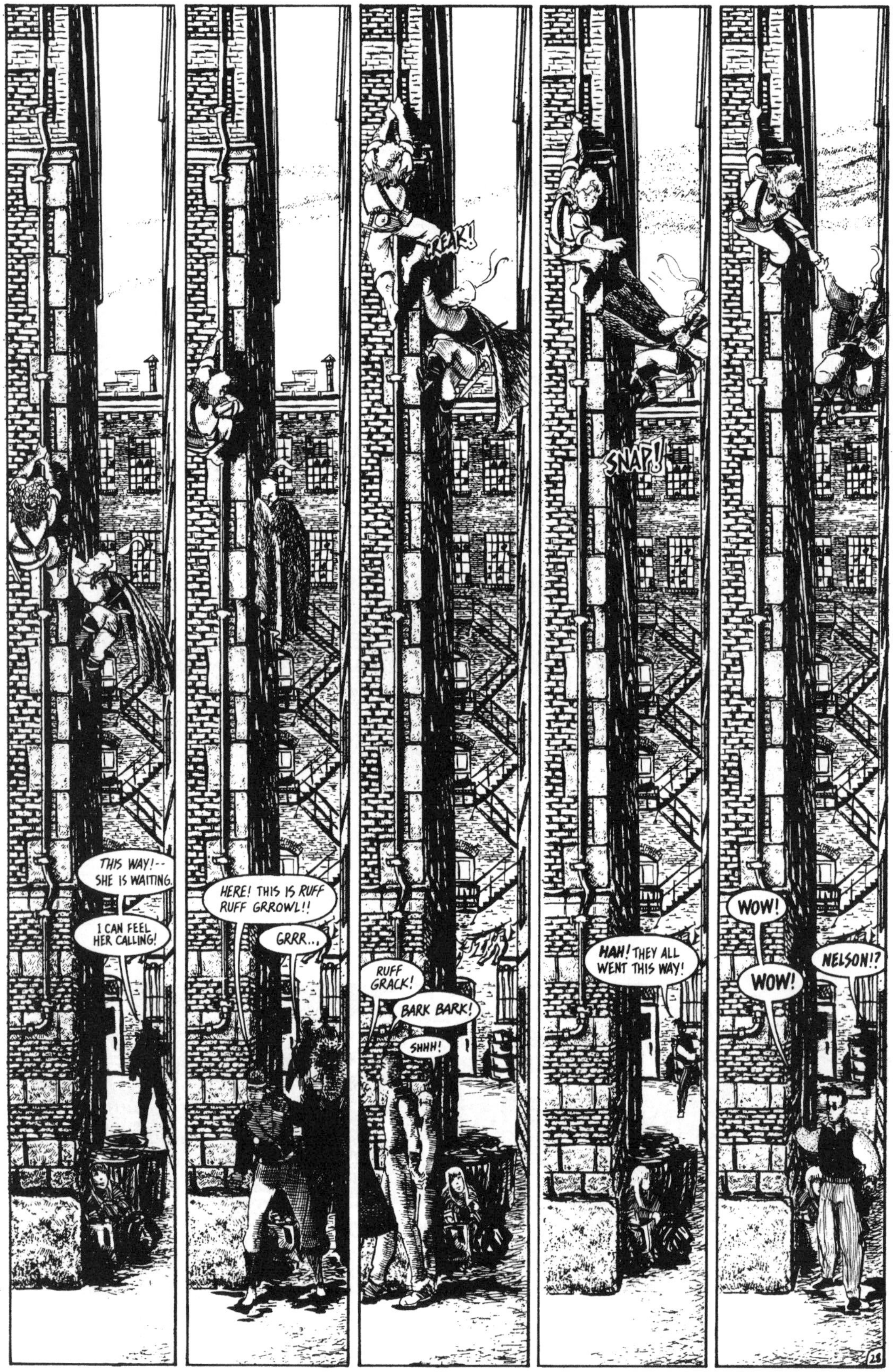
THIS WAY!-- SHE IS WAITING.
I CAN FEEL HER CALLING!
HERE! THIS IS RUFF RUFF GRROWL!!
GRRR...
CREAK!
RUFF GRACK!
BARK BARK!
SHHH!
SNAP!
HAH! THEY ALL WENT THIS WAY!
WOW!
WOW!
NELSON!?

Empire Lanes No. 2 by Peter Gross. © 1987 Peter Gross

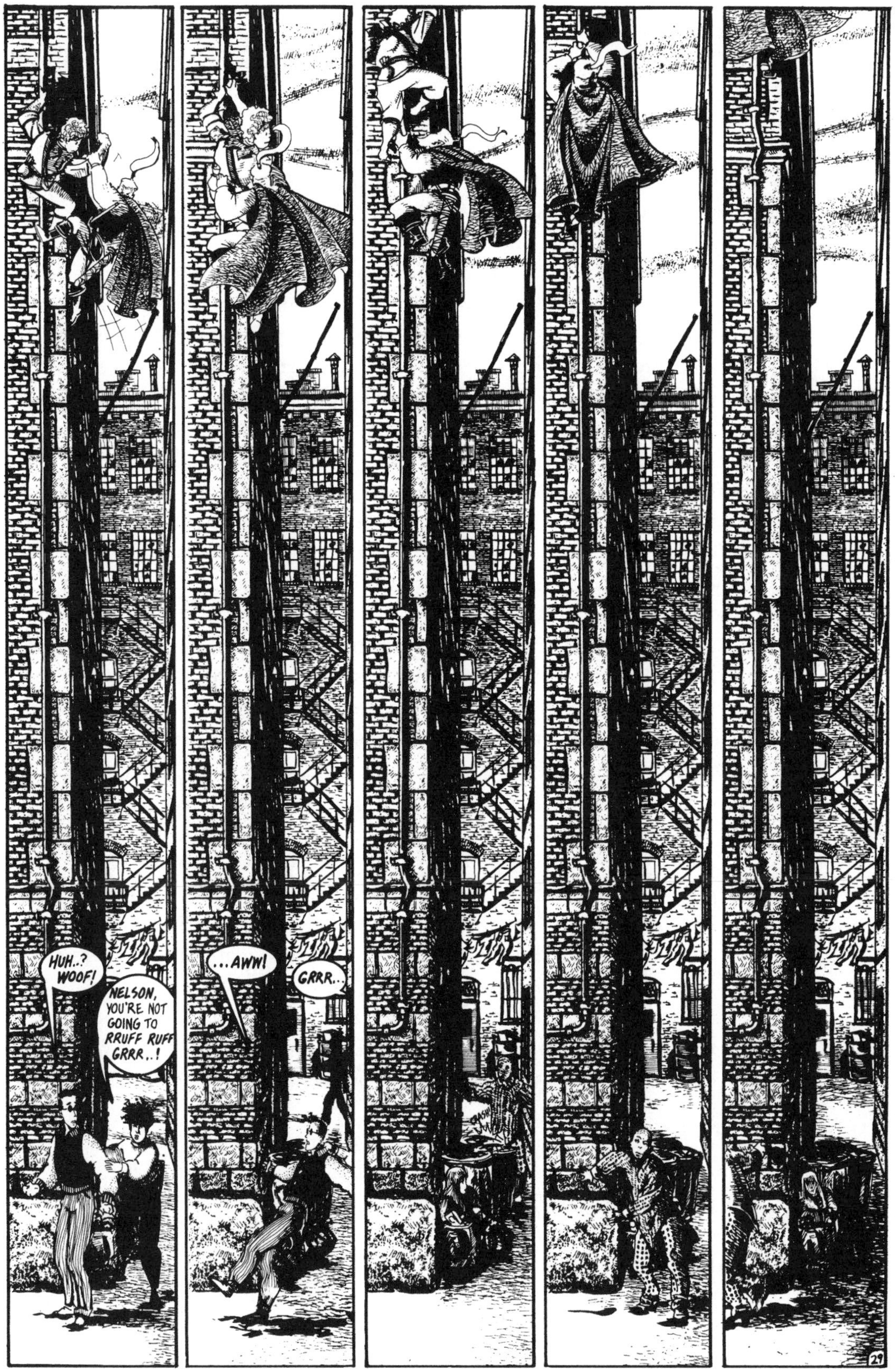
HUH..? WOOF!
NELSON, YOU'RE NOT GOING TO RRUFF RUFF GRRR..!
...AWW!
GRRR...
CRASH!
29

Empire Lanes No. 2 by Peter Gross. © 1987 Peter Gross

Dan Jurgens lives on a quiet street in a Minneapolis suburb. Weekday mornings, his neighbors pack into hybrid cars, SUVs, and sedans and commute to the Twin Cities for work. Like them, Jurgens's workday begins early, but unlike them, he pads downstairs to a studio off the front entry, clicks on the light, falls into a chair, and gets down to business.

"'Oh, I didn't know that you were a cartoonist,'" Jurgens recalls people saying to him. "'We thought you stayed home and your wife supported you.' It's not like that anymore. Now comics have gotten to a point where they're part of contemporary popular culture. There's more awareness. People realize, 'Oh yeah, you can make a living making comics.'"

Jurgens has made a living from comic books since 1982. He's made a living drawing and writing comics in Minnesota just as long. "Back when I started, I was a community of one," he says. "There were guys doing indie comics in Minnesota, but I was the only one doing anything for Marvel or DC." Others had tried to work for the mainstream comics publishers while living in Minnesota, but they advised Jurgens against it. It couldn't be done, they told him in the 1980s.

Jurgens was born in Ortonville on the Minnesota–South Dakota border in 1959. His father owned a hardware store on the town's main street. "It was your classic small-town Midwest upbringing," he says. In 1977, Jurgens graduated from Ortonville High School. He moved to the Twin Cities and attended the Minneapolis College of Art and Design two decades before the college inaugurated its comic art degree program. He majored in design with a minor in illustration.

"When you're getting an education like that, you look for different applications. With graphic design, I could work for a design firm or an ad agency," he says. "Comics was something that always interested me. I knew I wanted to pursue it. But I didn't know if it would work out as a career, and if it didn't that would be fine."

In 1981, Jurgens, a senior at MCAD, attended a local comics convention and met DC artist and writer Mike Grell. He showed Grell his portfolio, and in a matter of months Jurgens too was working at DC, drawing the monthly series *Warlord*, which Grell scripted.

Young artists often ask Jurgens for advice on landing a job in comics. "What I tell them is as true today as it was when I started. The vast majority of people assume they're ready when in truth they're not. Because if you show up in the right place with the right tools in your toolbox—in other words, the right art, the right style—you'll get a shot."

Jurgens's shot with Grell was a major coup. Right out of the gate, he was drawing a monthly series and doing it from his home in Minnesota. "DC took a chance with me. But by that time, you had Federal Express and overnight delivery," which made it possible for Jurgens to overnight his pages to New York.

From 1984 to 1985, Jurgens worked on a twelve-issue maxi-series, *Sun Devils,* with writer Gerry Conway. "After six issues, Gerry's workload was such that they needed someone else to write. Gerry knew I had an interest in writing, so he said, 'Do you want to write it? You know more about these characters than anyone else we're going to find,'" Jurgens remembers. And another door opened.

"'OH, I DIDN'T KNOW THAT YOU WERE A CARTOONIST. WE THOUGHT YOU STAYED HOME AND YOUR WIFE SUPPORTED YOU.'"

With four years of penciling work and a year of writing behind him, Jurgens approached DC with a pitch for a series. This time, however, he didn't want to revamp someone else's character. He wanted to create his own. Jurgens's superhero series *Booster Gold* first appeared in February 1986. More notable, however, is that Booster is still around years later, appearing and reappearing in DC series and single issues.

"We've all created characters," Jurgens says. Comic book creators are always inventing fresh superheroes and villains to populate the DC and Marvel universes. "But the characters come out and then you never see them again. For whatever reason they don't click. But twenty-five years later, Booster Gold is still viable, perhaps more viable now than he ever was." Booster, like the Twins' Joe Mauer or Lance Armstrong, is a star for today's celebrity-hungry marketplace. He excels at his job and is not afraid to parlay his prowess into multi-million-dollar endorsements.

Booster Gold is Michael Jon Carter, a college football player and star athlete living in twenty-fifth-century Gotham City. When Carter gets caught up in a scandal, he loses everything. He is kicked off the team and thrown out of school. Still licking his wounds, he takes a job as a night watchman at the Metropolis Space Museum. One of the exhibits is a time machine. Carter, with nothing left for him in his own time, uses the machine to travel to the twentieth century, where with his future-age technology he becomes the superhero Booster Gold.

Jurgens came up with the idea for Booster Gold watching the 1984 Olympics. "I was watching a diving event, and one of the divers already had his endorsements lined up. That meant that as soon as he won a gold medal, he already had an endorsement deal waiting," Jurgens says. "Booster's a guy who's going to cash in on being a superhero. If he's about to capture a plane that's diving into the city, he'll call News 11 and say, 'Hey, I'm going to be there. Make sure you get it on film.'"

Booster pursues product endorsements the way other superheroes pursue supervillains. He's the face of ads, promotional giveaways, and blatant self-promotion. He'll do his job and nab the baddies, but at the end of the day he appreciates seeing his picture on the evening news.

Jurgens wrote and drew *Booster Gold* for two years, after which he transitioned to *Superman,* also as writer and penciller. Jerry Siegel and Joe Shuster introduced *Superman* to a Depression-era America in 1938. Jurgens came to the title fifty years later and stayed with it well into the 1990s. The artist felt a personal connection with the title character. "Superman as Clark Kent grew up on a small farm in Smallville, Kansas. I grew up in a small town, Ortonville, in Minnesota. So, there's a resonance. I have that small-town resonance with Superman."

Work on *Superman* led to one of the highlights of Jurgens's career and one of the big events in nineties comics. Jurgens, along with three other writers, editor Mike Carlin, and a crew of artists, brought about *The Death of Superman* in 1992. Killing off Superman had been a running joke with the creative team for years. Finally, someone said, "Let's do it," and the idea took form.

"With *The Death of Superman,* what intrigued all of us was not so much telling the death of Superman, but writing about a world *without* a Superman. You'd be able to address the question, what does Superman mean to America in a fictional sense?" says Jurgens, who was tapped to write and draw the issue in which Superman dies, not at the hands of Lex Luthor or Brainiac, his most cerebral opponents, but after a knockdown, drag-out fight with Doomsday, a purely physical villain.

The creative team knew the storyline would attract readers. They anticipated a sales blip. But what they got was a sales explosion. *The Death of Superman* story arc, told through four separate, interrelated comics every month (*Superman, The Adventures of Superman, Action Comics,* and *Superman: The Man of Steel),* brought people into comic stores who hadn't read comics in years. Television news programs reported on the fictional death of Superman. Columnists weighed in. Jurgens and his fellow creatives were flooded with interview requests.

Through all the media hubbub, Jurgens still had to wake up every morning, flip on the light, and sit down to draw the next issue. "No one had any idea what we would be propelled into. That we'd end up with a story that's still in print in one fashion or another fifteen, going on twenty, years later. You can't plan for it. You can't hope for it," says Jurgens.

In 2007, Jurgens returned to drawing, and later writing and drawing, *Booster Gold* as a monthly series. He also worked on *Spider-Man* and *Thor* for Marvel Comics.

"Honestly, when I first started in comics, I was thinking, *I'll do this for a couple years, then I'll go out and get a real job,*" says Jurgens. Many cartoonists do that. They invest a dozen or more years in comics and then move on to something else. Jurgens has invested thirty years. "Comics are a fun way to make a living, and I think I'm pretty good at it. I enjoy doing it. You add all that together, and I don't really know what else I would do." ■

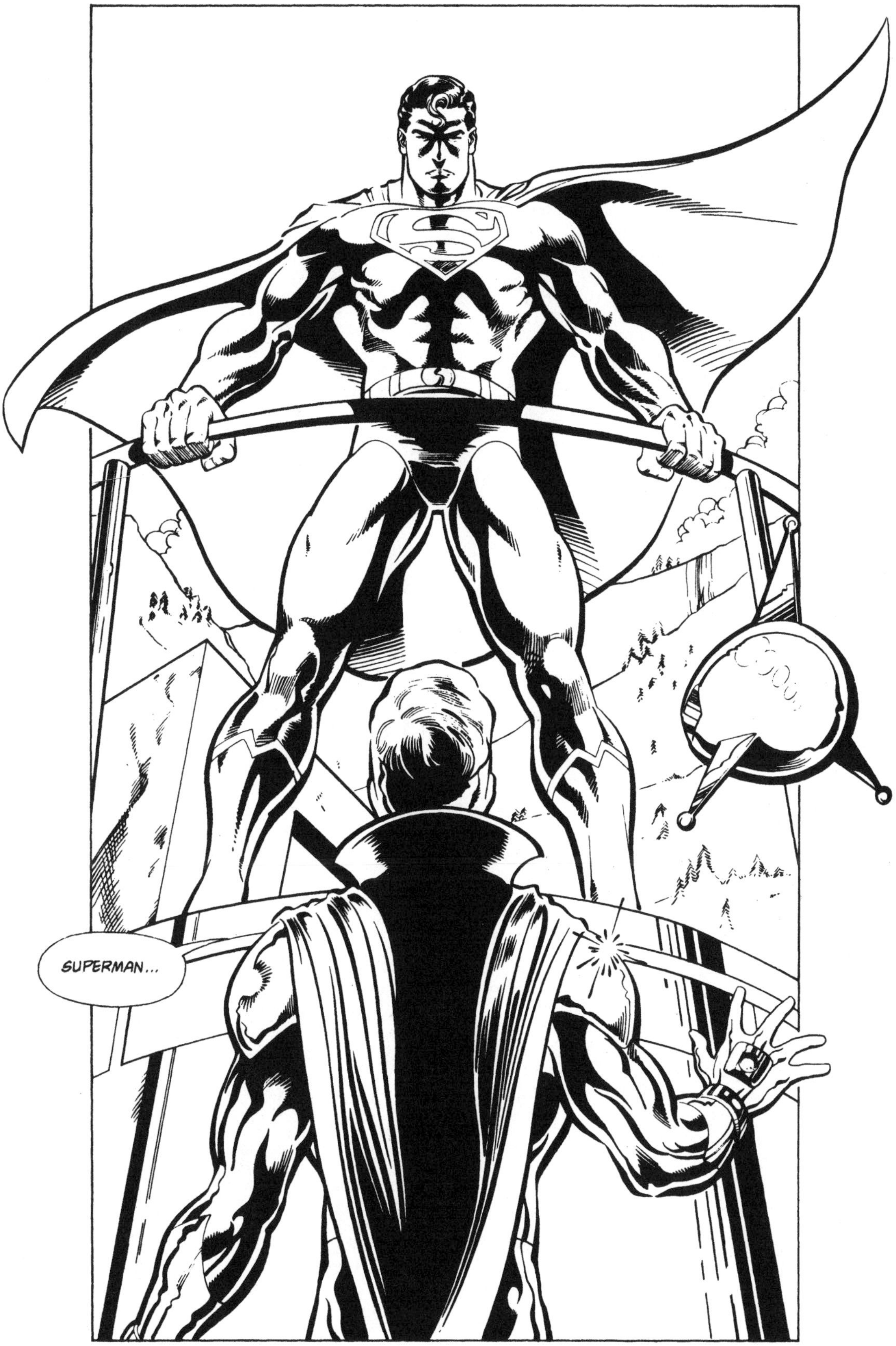
SUPERMAN...

Showcase Presents: Booster Gold Vol. 1 (DC Comics), the collected *Booster Gold* comics from the 1980s, by Dan Jurgens.

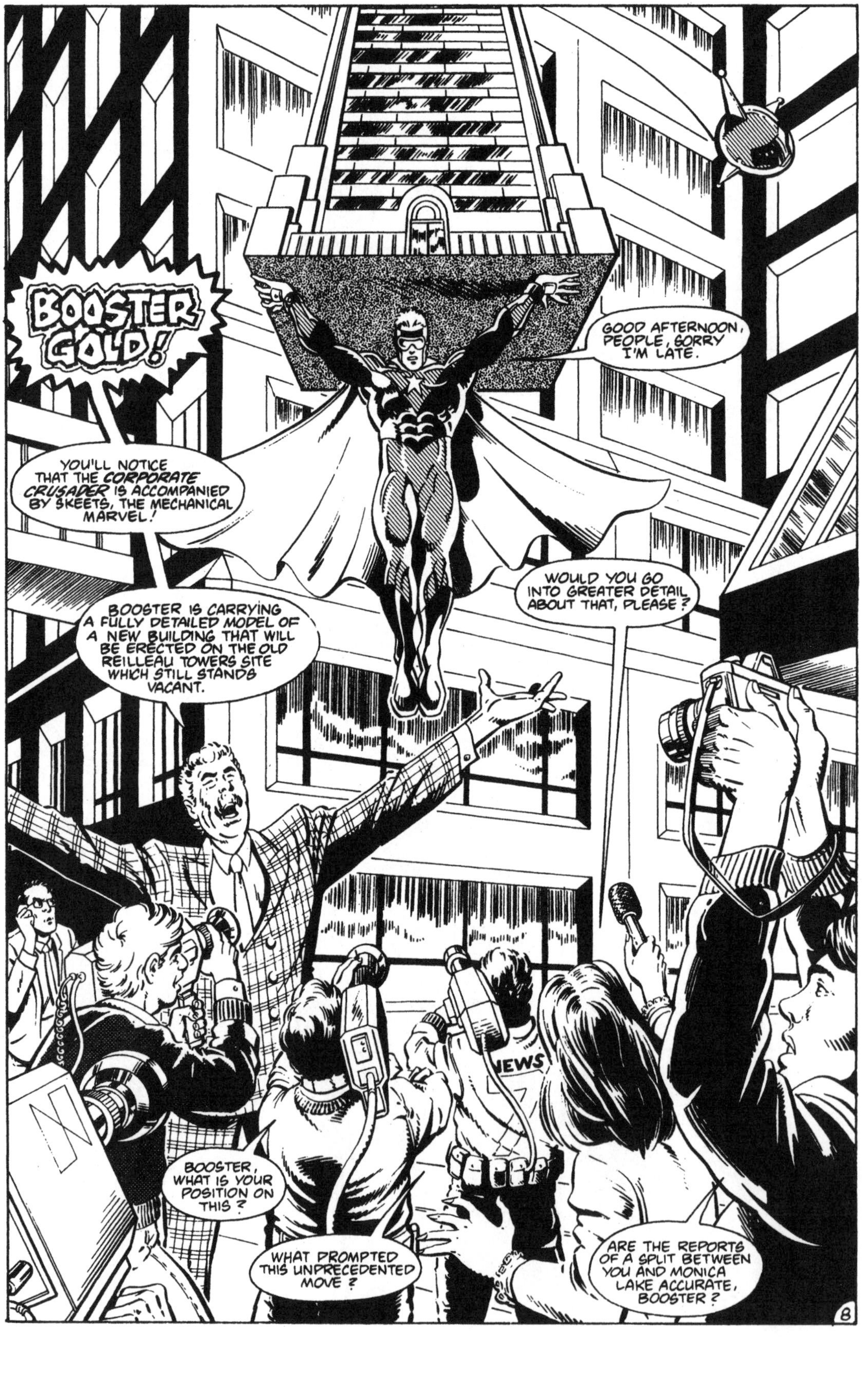
BOOSTER GOLD!
YOU'LL NOTICE THAT THE *CORPORATE CRUSADER* IS ACCOMPANIED BY SKEETS, THE MECHANICAL MARVEL!
GOOD AFTERNOON, PEOPLE, SORRY I'M LATE.
BOOSTER IS CARRYING A FULLY DETAILED MODEL OF A NEW BUILDING THAT WILL BE ERECTED ON THE OLD REILLEAU TOWERS SITE WHICH STILL STANDS VACANT.
WOULD YOU GO INTO GREATER DETAIL ABOUT THAT, PLEASE?
NEWS
BOOSTER, WHAT IS YOUR POSITION ON THIS?
WHAT PROMPTED THIS UNPRECEDENTED MOVE?
ARE THE REPORTS OF A SPLIT BETWEEN YOU AND MONICA LAKE ACCURATE, BOOSTER?
8
Showcase Presents: Booster Gold Vol. 1 (DC Comics), the collected *Booster Gold* comics from the 1980s, by Dan Jurgens. © 2008 DC Comics.

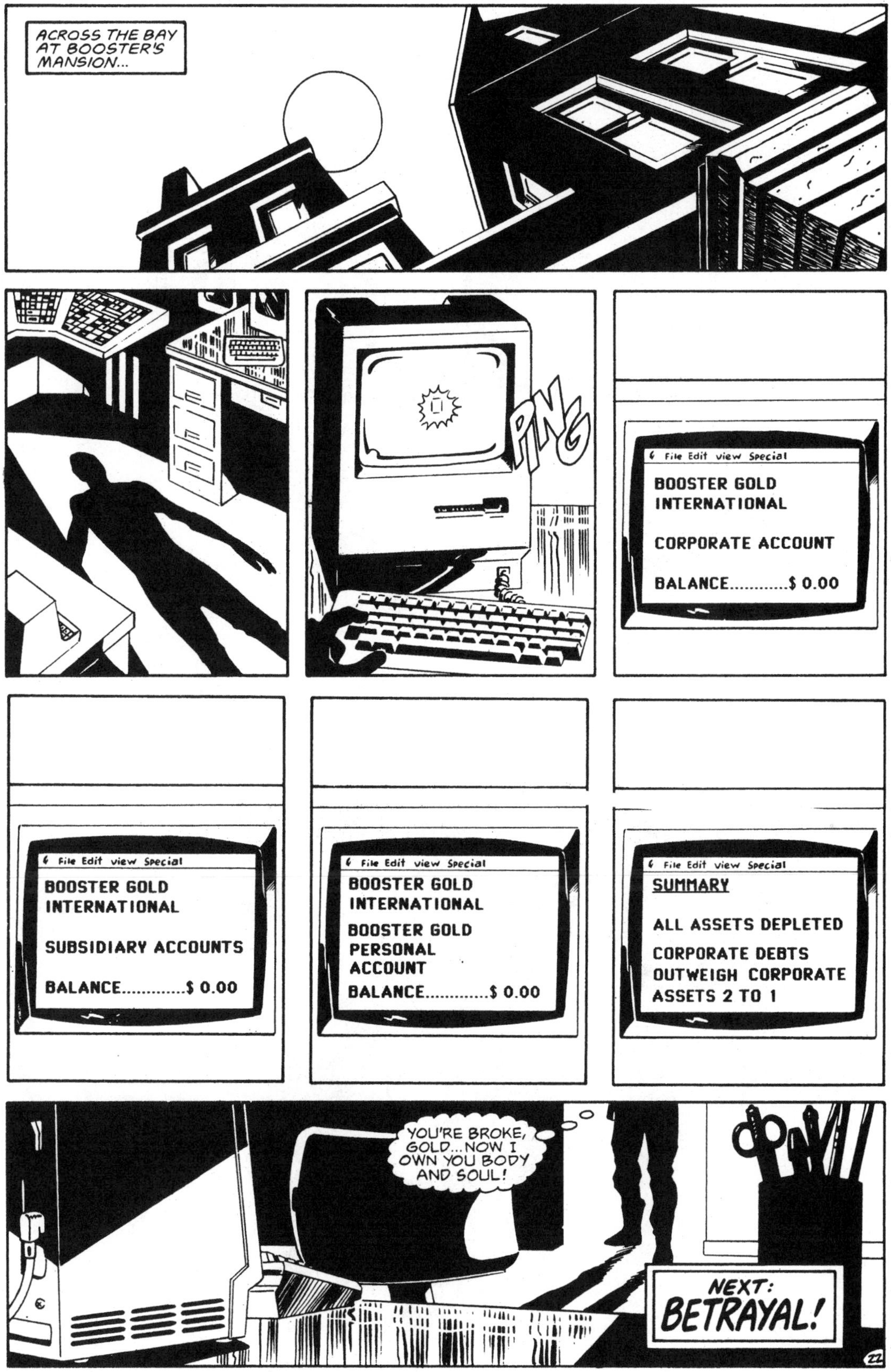
ACROSS THE BAY AT BOOSTER'S MANSION...
PING
File Edit view Special
BOOSTER GOLD INTERNATIONAL
CORPORATE ACCOUNT
BALANCE............$ 0.00
File Edit view Special
BOOSTER GOLD INTERNATIONAL
SUBSIDIARY ACCOUNTS
BALANCE.............$ 0.00
File Edit view Special
BOOSTER GOLD INTERNATIONAL
BOOSTER GOLD PERSONAL ACCOUNT
BALANCE.............$ 0.00
File Edit view Special
SUMMARY
ALL ASSETS DEPLETED
CORPORATE DEBTS OUTWEIGH CORPORATE ASSETS 2 TO 1
YOU'RE BROKE, GOLD...NOW I OWN YOU BODY AND SOUL!
NEXT: BETRAYAL!

Showcase Presents: Booster Gold Vol. 1 (DC Comics), the collected *Booster Gold* comics from the 1980s, by Dan Jurgens. © 2008 DC Comics.

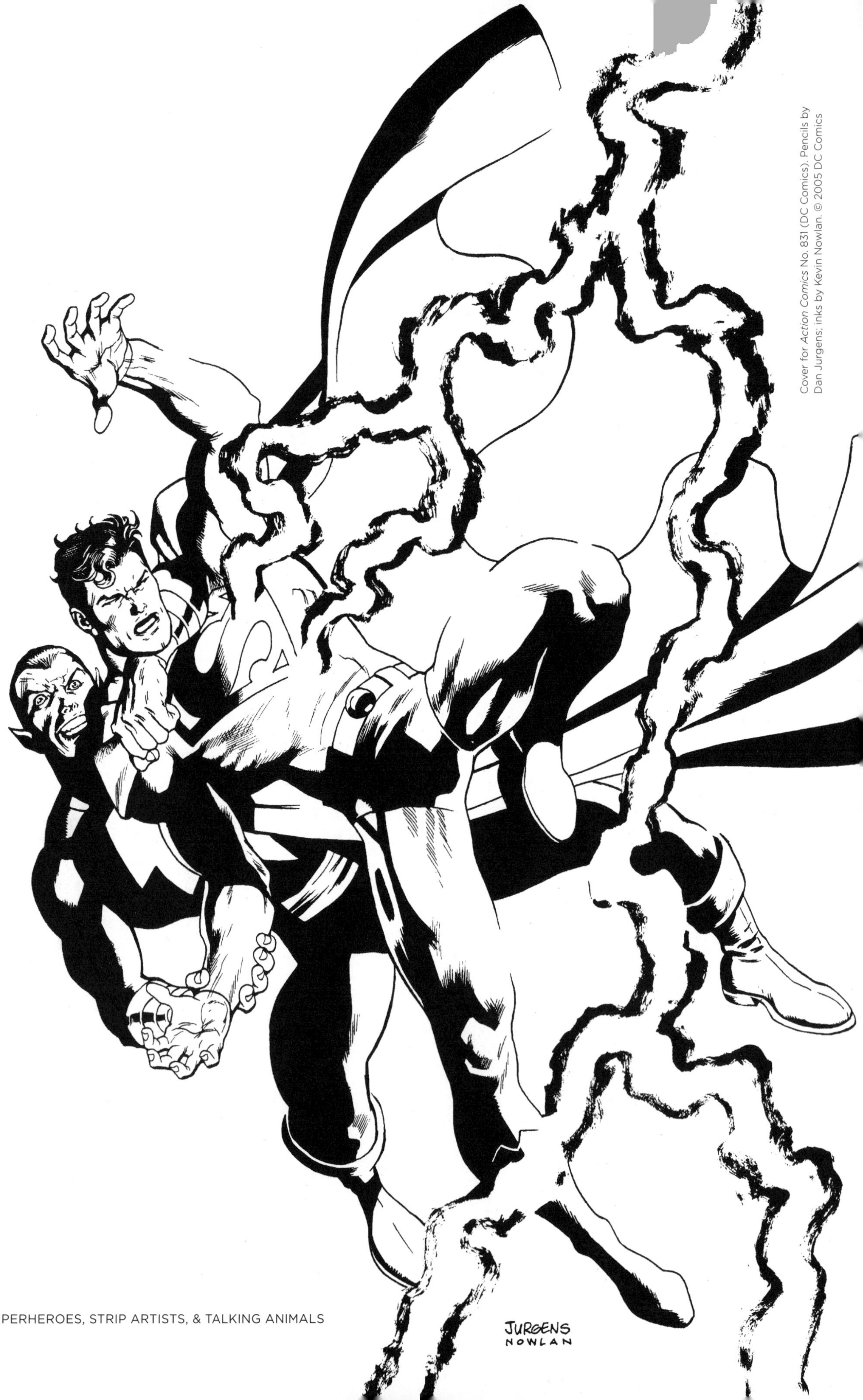
JURGENS
NOWLAN

Cover for *Action Comics* No. 831 (DC Comics). Pencils by Dan Jurgens; inks by Kevin Nowlan. © 2005 DC Comics

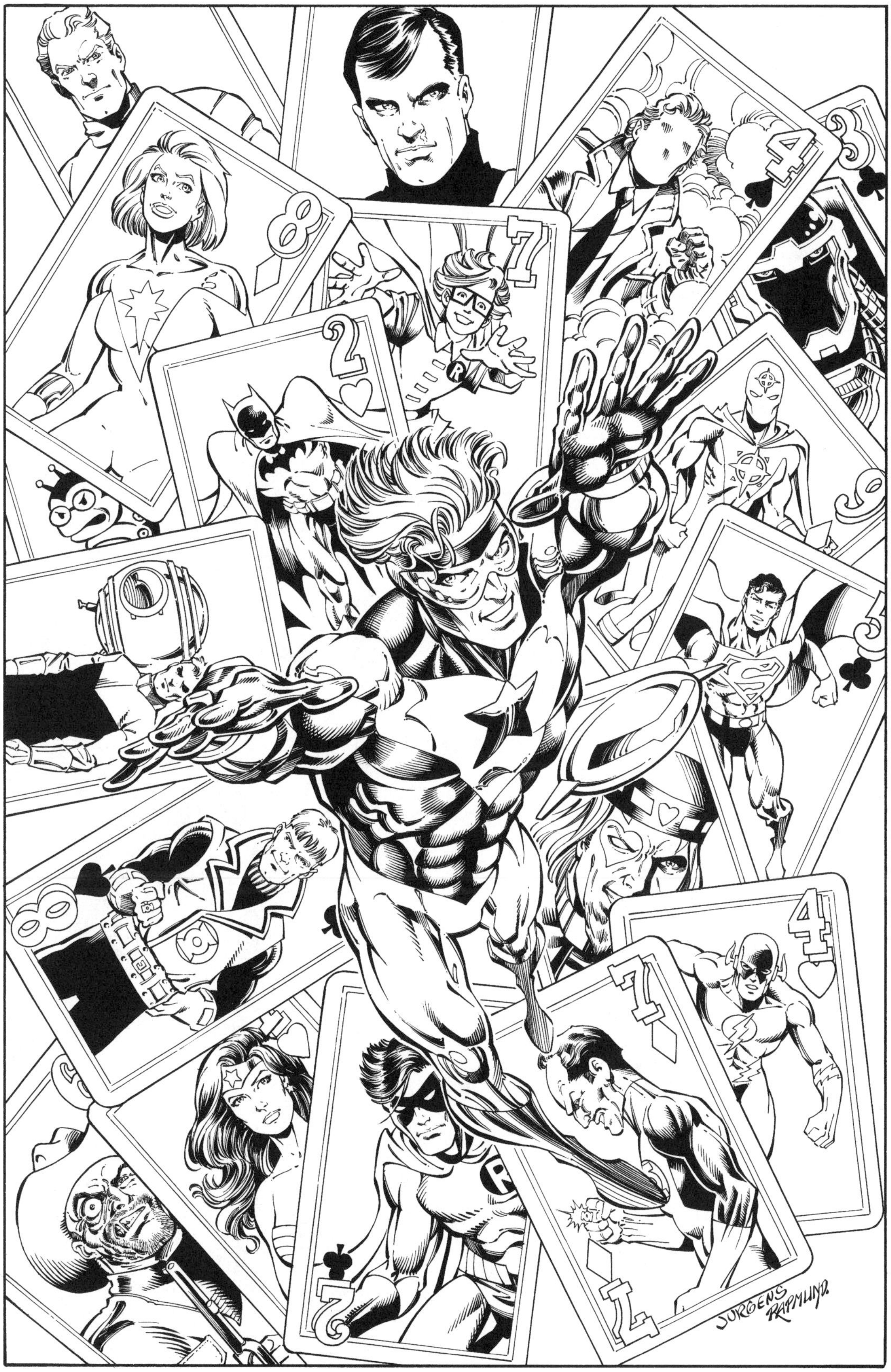
JURGENS
RAPMUND

Cover for *Booster Gold* No. 1 (DC Comics). Pencils by Dan Jurgens; inks by Norm Rapmund. © 2007 DC Comics

"When it comes to comics, I was a late bloomer," confides Ryan Kelly, comics artist, illustrator, oil painter, teacher, man with many hats, and jokester. According to one of Kelly's web postings, he resides in a yellow house built by a butcher in 1874. According to the same post, the house, located in St. Paul, is overflowing with ghosts. When asked to confirm or deny the presence of ghosts, the artist apologizes. "Yeah, I've got a sense of humor people don't always get."

Kelly was born in Minneapolis in 1976. Following the storyline of many artist bios, he recognized an affinity for the arts at an early age. He enrolled at the Minneapolis College of Art and Design and launched in a dozen directions at once. "I was taking drawing, painting, design, and comic book classes, but I wasn't bringing all those skills together. At that age, I was passing the time, not trying to make great art," says Kelly. "I was a slow learner on a big slow curve."

> "I WAS TAKING DRAWING, PAINTING, DESIGN, AND COMIC BOOK CLASSES, BUT I WASN'T BRINGING ALL THOSE SKILLS TOGETHER.... I WAS A SLOW LEARNER ON A BIG SLOW CURVE."

Kelly didn't know which direction to take his artistic career. Into a design office and a shirt and tie? Into the hardscrabble world of fine arts? Into comic books? One advantage of attending MCAD was the opportunity to be mentored by instructors and working professionals like Barbara Schulz and Peter Gross. After graduation, Gross hired Kelly as an intern and assistant on *Books of Magic* and *Lucifer,* monthly comics Gross was penciling for Vertigo.

When Kelly went to work for Gross, "Peter had already been drawing comics for fifteen years. He'd done everything—drawn his own comic and published it, drawn for small presses and mainstream comics. He was knowledgeable and willing to share that knowledge," Kelly says. The apprenticeship pushed Kelly to grow as an artist and to devote his energies to comics.

Some artists explode onto the scene. Others accumulate a solid body of work before they're *discovered*. Kelly classes himself among the latter category. "I was working in the background for a lot of years. I was twenty-eight and hadn't done anything really important, while there were all these twenty-two-year-old kids out there, getting full volumes of work published. Nothing really happened until I started drawing *Local*."

Published by Oni Press, *Local* leapfrogs through twelve American cities over as many years, following the heroine, Megan McKeenan, as she matures from grunge girl in issue one to a fleshed-out, experience-laden veteran of life in issue twelve. "Some of the sharpest slices of life the medium has ever seen," pens comic book writer Brian K. Vaughn in a blurb for *Local*. Sequential Tart, an online review site, calls the series "the coolest short film *never* shown on IFC or Sundance Channel."

In those years when Kelly was "working in the background," he drew *Giant Robot Warriors* for publisher AiT/Planet Lar. Not a blockbuster graphic novel by any means, but through a strange turn of events, *Giant Robot Warriors* would be the title to launch Kelly onto center stage.

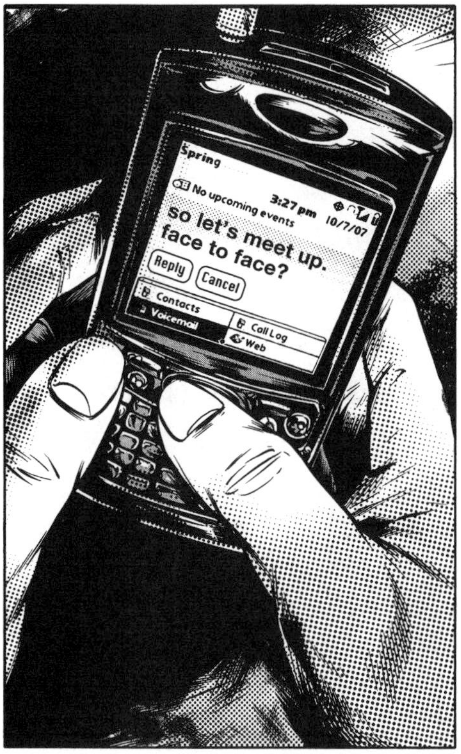
Spring
No upcoming events
3:27pm
10/7/07
so let's meet up.
face to face?
Reply
Cancel
Contacts
Voicemail
Call Log
Web

The New York Four (Minx/DC Comics). Script by Brian Wood; art by Ryan Kelly. © 2008 DC Comics

Brian Wood, a writer at AiT/Planet Lar, took note of Kelly's work and in 2005 asked him to collaborate on a new series, *Local,* a gritty, real-time narrative far removed from Kelly's fantasy work on *Books of Magic* and *Lucifer.* The partnership worked. "With *Local,* people started noticing my art. It was getting critical attention and positive reviews. Each issue, as it came out, was an event, which had never happened to me before." Kelly received his most localized attention for *Local* with issue two, "Polaroid Boyfriend," also called the Minneapolis issue. Writing in the afterword, the artist puts his quirky humor to use, swearing he can't remember drawing the issue, that it appeared fully formed on his doorstep. But, all the same, he does recall lobbying to have Minneapolis included in the series.

"I spent upwards of $500,000 in television and radio ads," writes Kelly. "Getting Minneapolis chosen was no doubt going to be a public relations nightmare and my team needed to grease the palms of the fat cats in charge. Bribes were taken. Deals were brokered. Lives were ruined." And, anyway, Wood liked the idea.

In issue two, Kelly draws on memory to illustrate a strip of Minneapolis along Lyndale Avenue circa 1995. The heroine, Megan, and the mysterious man with whom she shares Polaroid snapshots shudder outside Hum's Liquor and the Red Dragon restaurant. In another panel, the man chugs coffee from Spyhouse and then bolts upstairs to Megan's apartment, where Minneapolis signposts abound. Copies of *City Pages* litter a coffee table. Refrigerator art announces Dillinger Four playing at the Triple Rock. Megan shops at the Wedge, a neighborhood landmark, and works at Oar Folkjokeopus, a record store long since replaced by Treehouse Records.

Though Kelly wasn't going for photorealism with the cities he documented, he wanted to "make them appear like humans really inhabited those spaces and places. I was mostly accurate, but people would point out little mistakes, like putting an album by Low, which wasn't released until after 1995, in the window at Oar Folkjokeopus." Low, incidentally, has another comics connection; the group's bassist, Zak Sally, is a Minneapolis artist and creator of the graphic novel *Sammy the Mouse.*

Kelly and Wood have continued their creative partnership. They collaborated on the graphic novel *The New York Four* and have teamed up on issues of *Northlanders* and *DMZ* for DC Comics. Still, says Kelly, "Brian and I see *Local* as one of the most important things we've done because it came at a time when we were both growing as creative people and as individuals, both having kids for the first time. Brian wrote a good story, and that's what I care about. I'd rather work on a good story than one that pays a lot of money or, you know, gets me recognized as the one guy who draws zombie-pirate-ninja books really well." ■

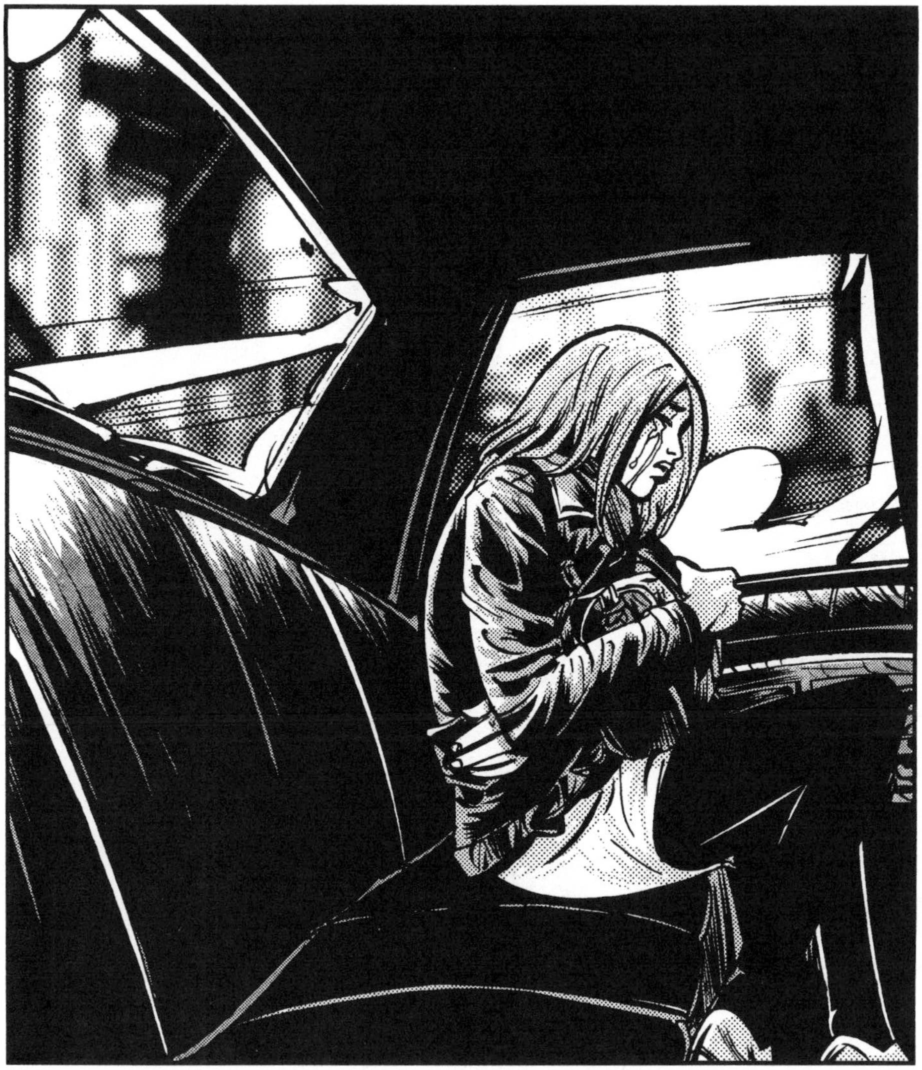

The New York Four (Minx/DC Comics). Script by Brian Wood; art by Ryan Kelly. © 2008 DC Comics

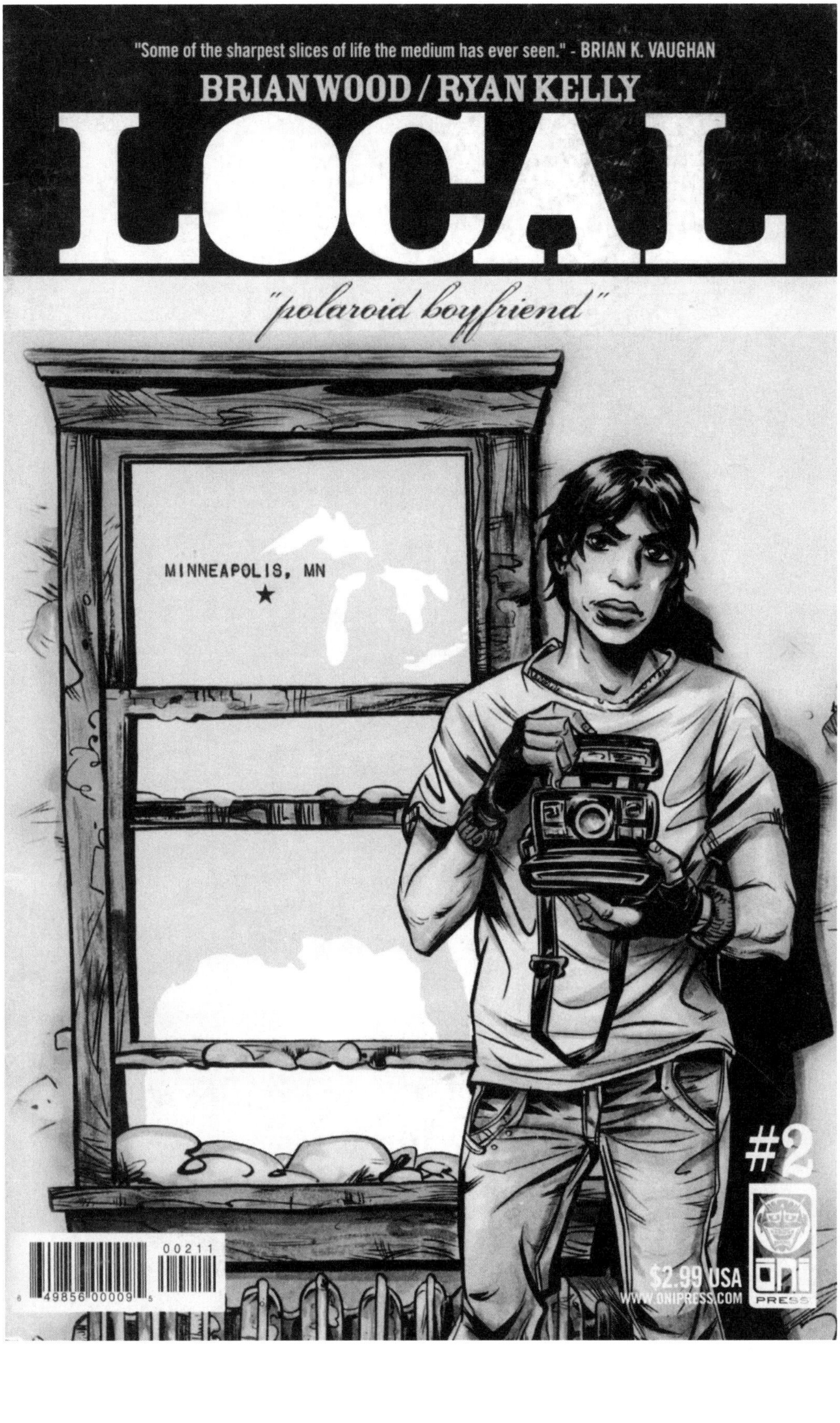
"Some of the sharpest slices of life the medium has ever seen." - BRIAN K. VAUGHAN
BRIAN WOOD / RYAN KELLY
LOCAL
"polaroid boyfriend"
MINNEAPOLIS, MN
#2
$2.99 USA
WWW.ONIPRESS.COM

Local No. 2 (Oni Press). Script by Brian Wood; art by Ryan Kelly. © 2005 Brian Wood and Ryan Kelly

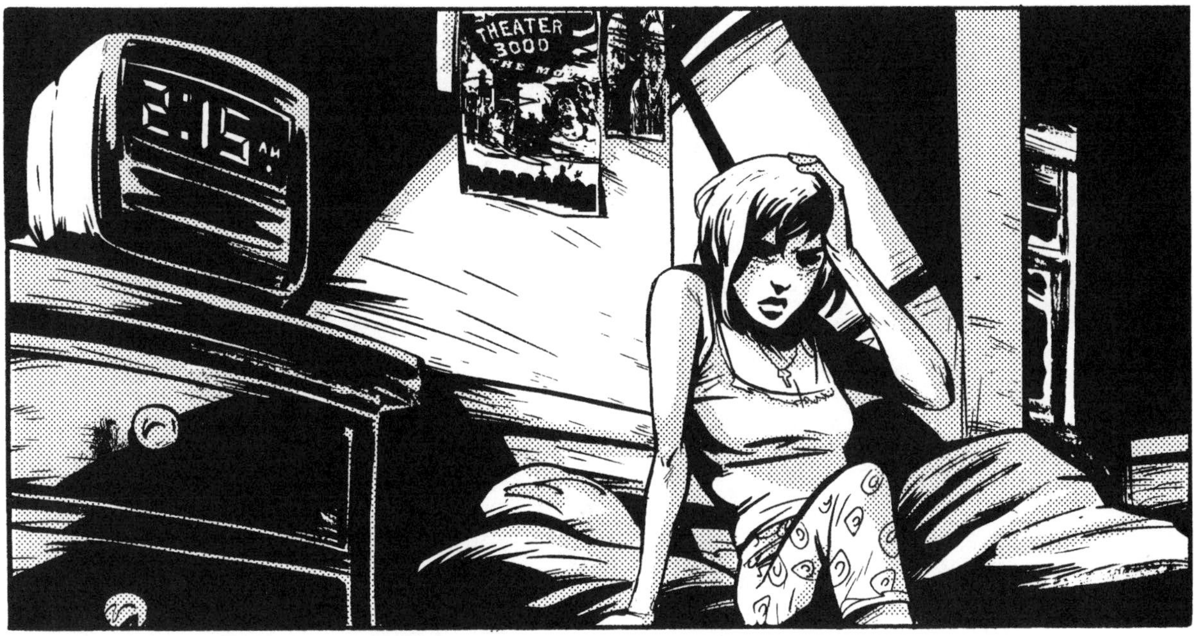
2:15 AM
THEATER 3000

Local No. 2 (Oni Press). Script by Brian Wood; art by Ryan Kelly. © 2005 Brian Wood and Ryan Kelly

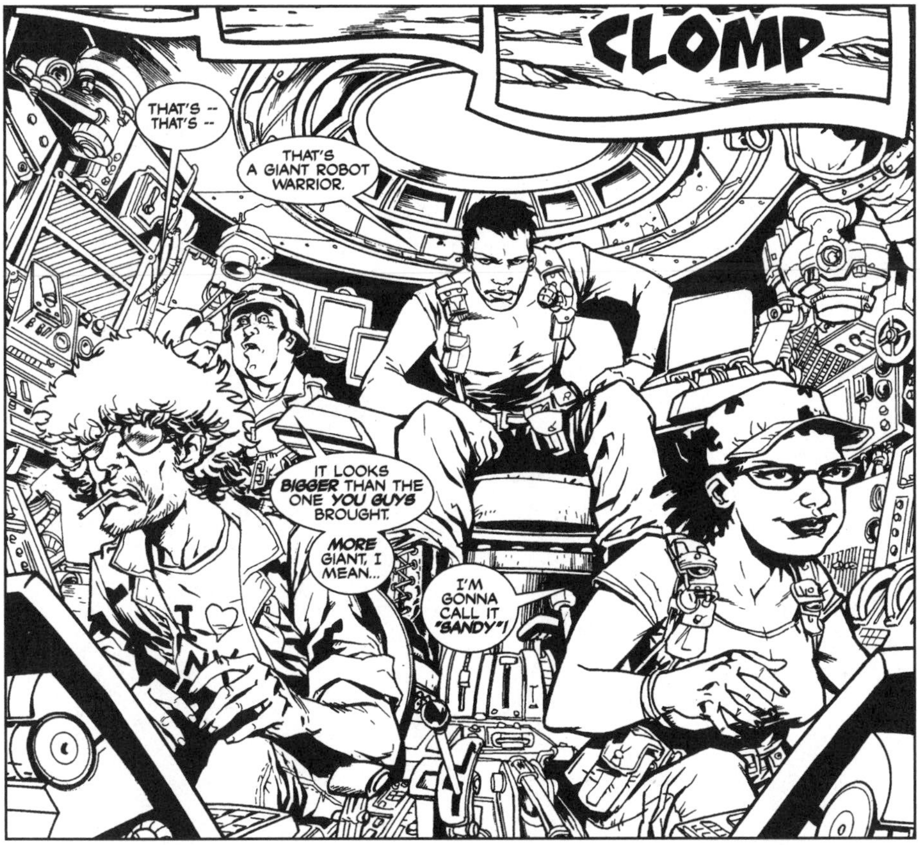
CLOMP
THAT'S -- THAT'S --
THAT'S A GIANT ROBOT WARRIOR.
IT LOOKS **BIGGER** THAN THE ONE ***YOU GUYS*** BROUGHT.
MORE GIANT, I MEAN...
I'M GONNA CALL IT ***"SANDY"***!

Giant Robot Warriors (AiT/Planet Lar). Script by Stuart Moore; art by Ryan Kelly. © 2004 Stuart Moore and Ryan Kelly

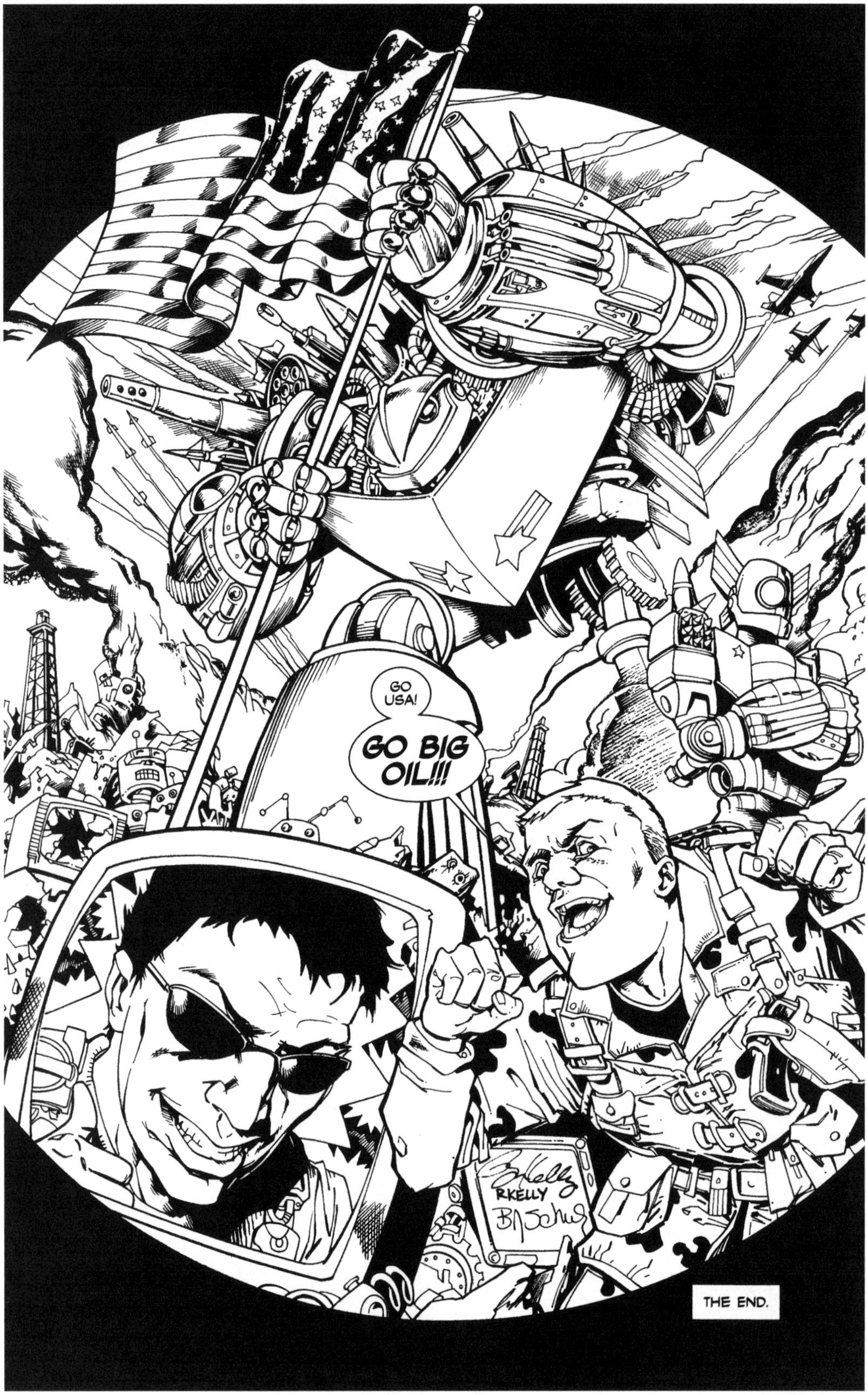
GO USA!
GO BIG OIL!!!
THE END.

Giant Robot Warriors (AiT/Planet Lar). Script by Stuart Moore; art by Ryan Kelly. © 2004 Stuart Moore and Ryan Kelly

GORDON PURCELL

In 2005, Gordon Purcell secured an all-expenses-paid trip to New York and a chance to win one million dollars. He'd correctly answered the phone screener's trivia questions, nailed the audition, and received the callback notice. He'd been selected to appear on *Who Wants to Be a Millionaire*.

Purcell, a Twin Cities comic book artist, had only two hours of sleep before the show taped. But he'd brought his trivia smarts with him, a list of "Phone a Friend" lifelines to help with the tough questions, and samples of his artwork: drawings of host Meredith Vieira, which he shared with her and the live audience. Vieira chatted with Purcell about comic books and asked a series of questions that increased in difficulty as the show progressed.

If Purcell had been drawing his TV moment, rather than living it, he would've offered a close-up of the contestant's staring eyes and the sweat dotting his upper lip—small beads drawn individually and painstakingly. Purcell is a detail man. When he draws the bridge of the starship U.S.S. *Enterprise*, you can bet he'll itemize every button, gizmo, and doodad. He whips out lifelike renderings of the *Star Trek* crew like nobody's business. But that's work; that's where Purcell has total control. On the set of *Who Wants to Be a Millionaire*, Vieira was in control and firing the questions like phaser blasts.

> FOR ALL HE KNEW, COMIC BOOK ARTISTS WERE JUST OLDER VERSIONS OF HIMSELF, UNPAID FANS BUT WITH MORE PENCILS.

Purcell walked away with $50,000 in prize money. His appearance aired in October. For two nights, the guy behind some of comics' most recognizable licensed properties came out from behind the drawing board and basked in the spotlight. That doesn't happen often in comics.

Comic book fans know the titles Purcell draws—*Star Trek, The X-Files, Young Indiana Jones, Beyond the Wall,* and *Phantom Chronicles*—but they don't know the artist on sight. They might be familiar with his name, but if they bumped into him at a comic book store they'd think, *One more fan getting his weekly fix.*

Born in Michigan in 1959, Purcell grew up in neighboring Wisconsin. As a child, he knew he wanted to pursue art, perhaps even comics. "But I had no idea how the comics business worked or even how you were paid to make comics," he says. For all he knew, comic book artists were just older versions of himself, unpaid fans but with more pencils. Purcell's answer came in the form of a book, Stan Lee's *Drawing Comics the Marvel Way*. "That's when I realized comics could be a career."

In 1977, Purcell began his first year at the University of Minnesota. His focus was on theater and visual arts. The theatrical studies would come in handy later, teaching the young comic book artist about set design, character design, costuming, and blocking. A theater course also sent Purcell to New York.

DC and Marvel had their headquarters in New York, and Purcell didn't see any reason why he shouldn't drop by and introduce himself. That bold move produced an interview at DC. Purcell, still a college senior, was invited to participate in a new talent program for the comic book publisher.

DC also gave the young cartoonist a one-off assignment. They asked him to work on a bonus book (a free comic stuffed inside another comic) that would be paired with the next issue of *Flash*. Purcell recalls the book's meaty plot: "The villain, Dr. Light, fights Little Boy Blue and The Blue Boys and shows just what an idiot he is when he's conquered by three kids."

Still trying to get his foot in the door, Purcell drew for a number of smaller publishers but never took his eyes off the heavyweights DC and Marvel. Finally, Marvel announced a call for applicants.

"They had ten thousand submissions for each category, both penciller and writer," says Purcell. "I was one of the finalists. But that showed me how many people want to break into Marvel and DC, and they only have so many jobs."

Finding work as a comic book artist, Purcell says, is like finding work as an actor. "You're always auditioning, and you're always getting rejected. As an actor, if you don't get a job you can always tell yourself, *I didn't get the part because I didn't look right or I reminded the director of her first husband.* But with artists, people look at whether you can draw or not. If your Batman looks like Batman, then you probably have some skill."

Slowly, Purcell built up his portfolio and, almost as important, his network of industry connections. Since the 1980s, he has penciled a number of books. But he's probably best known for his work on *Star Trek*.

Just as Hollywood adapts comic books to the silver screen, publishers adapt film and television properties to comic books. The *Star Trek* license has circulated among the comic book publishers: Gold Key, Marvel, DC, Malibu, and IDW, among others. And wherever the license has gone, Purcell has usually gone with it.

"In many ways, I was originally chosen to work on *Star Trek* because of the work I did on Dr. Light," says Purcell, referring to the bonus book that started his career. "I drew faces really well. So DC gave me another book. After that, they said, 'You draw faces well. That must mean you can draw *Star Trek.*'"

Purcell has worked on four *Star Trek* properties: the original *Star Trek, The Next Generation, Deep Space Nine,* and *Voyager.* Recently, he penciled *Star Trek: Year Four,* a series scripted by D. C. Fontana, a writer on the original TV series.

Being able to draw faces sounds like a bizarre segue to a new job, until you consider that one of Purcell's primary responsibilities with licensed work is to reproduce the look and feel of the original TV series or film property. In other words, Captain Picard better resemble Patrick Stewart and not some anonymous gent with a shiny scalp. But that's where Purcell stands out. He's an artist who does his research, which is a good thing because fans would know if he didn't. So would the actors.

"When Paramount Studios owned *Star Trek,* they first had their people approve the art. Then they passed my art on to the actors who had sign-off rights in their contracts," says Purcell. If an actor or a studio exec wanted a change, Purcell would have to make the change. But that was a rare occurrence.

A lot of comic book artists wouldn't want the added pressure of having to please studio execs and Hollywood actors. But Purcell's a devoted *Star Trek* fan, and he gets to do what most fans can't do. "I can draw William Shatner as a thirty-five-year-old Captain Kirk again, when he's thin and nice looking and fit," says Purcell. Not even Hollywood can do that. ■

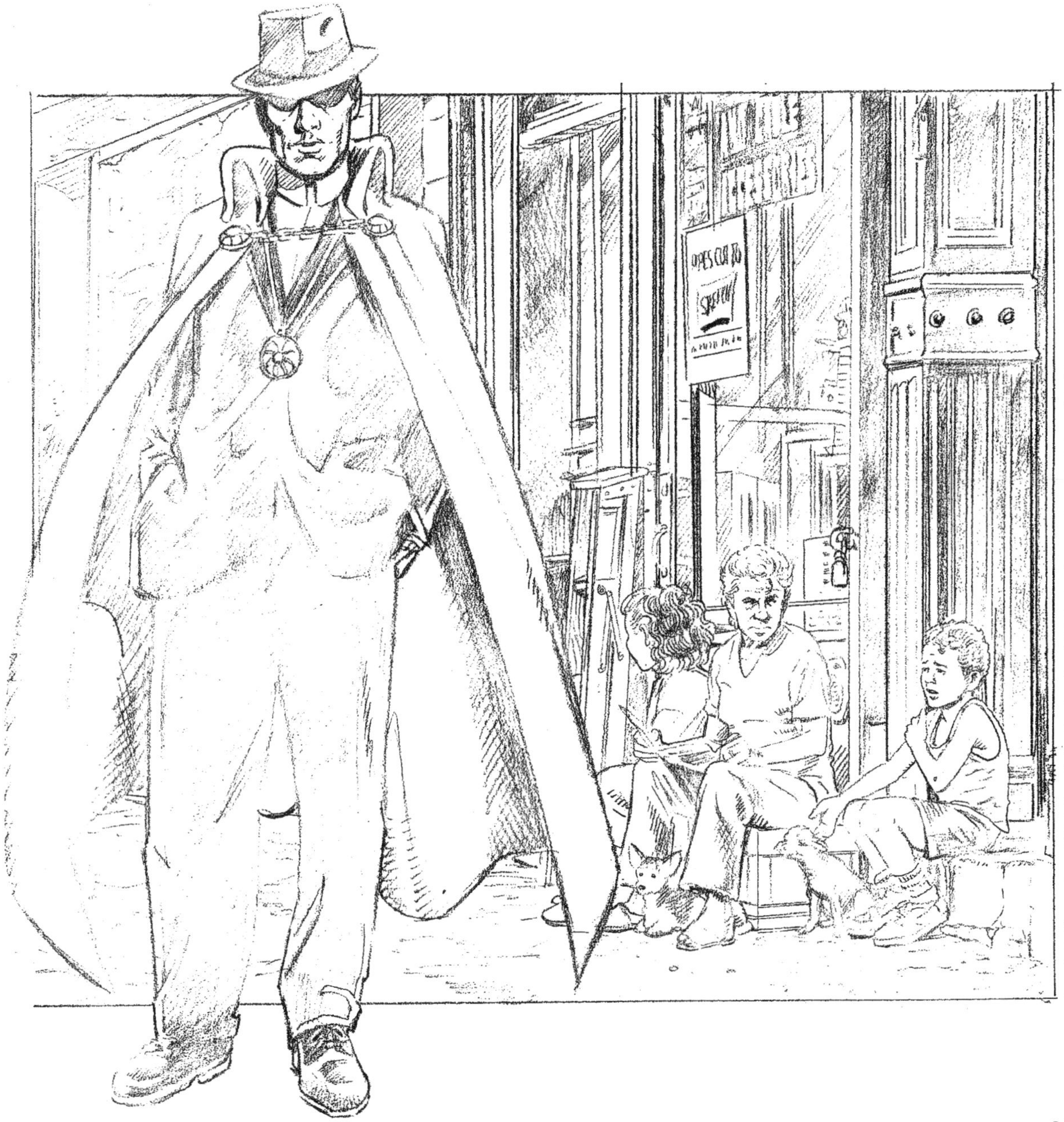

Star Trek: Generations (IDW). Pencils by Gordon Purcell; inks by Jerome Moore. © 1994 DC Comics and CBS

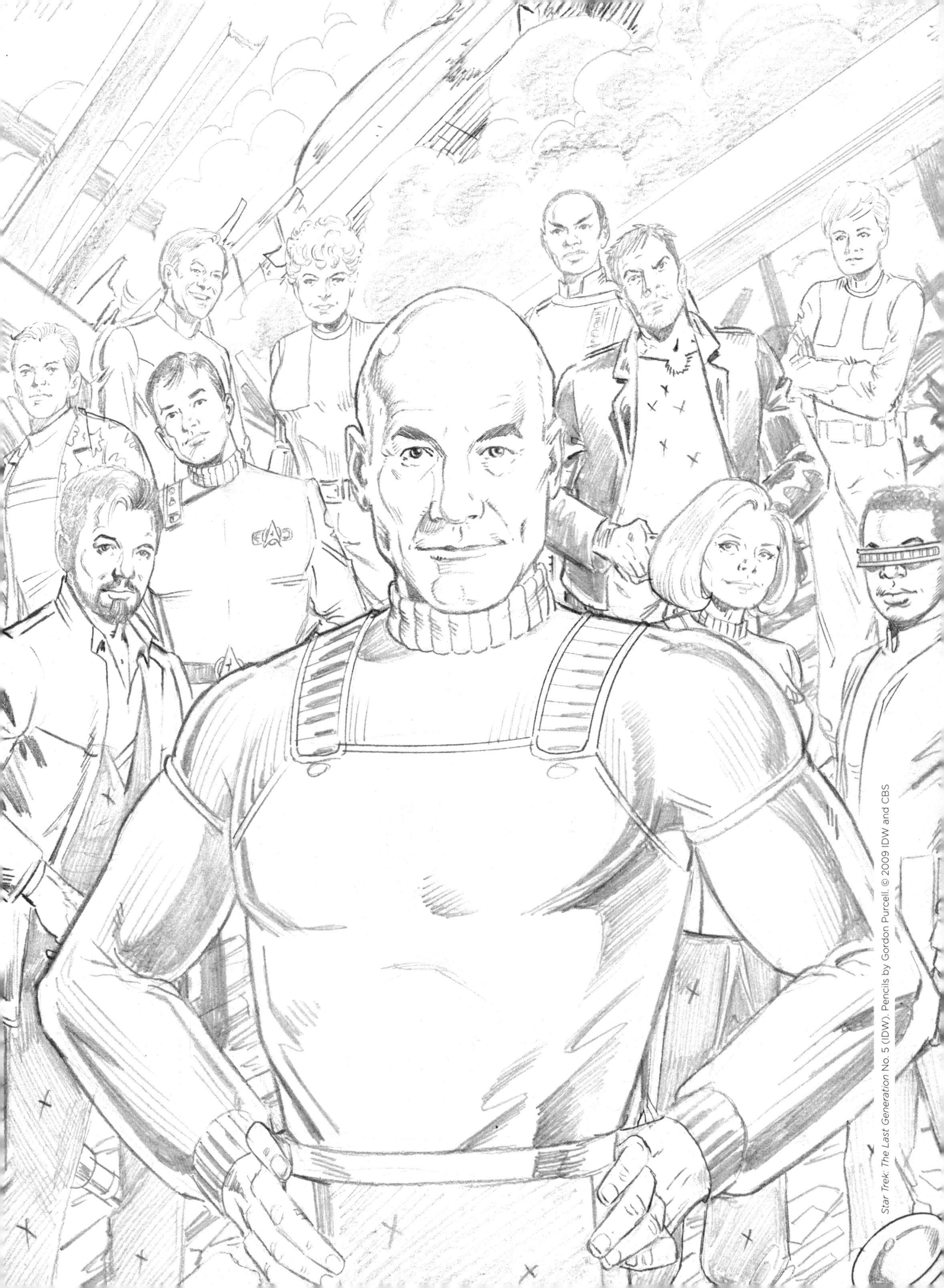

Star Trek: The Last Generation No. 5 (IDW), Pencils by Gordon Purcell. © 2009 IDW and CBS

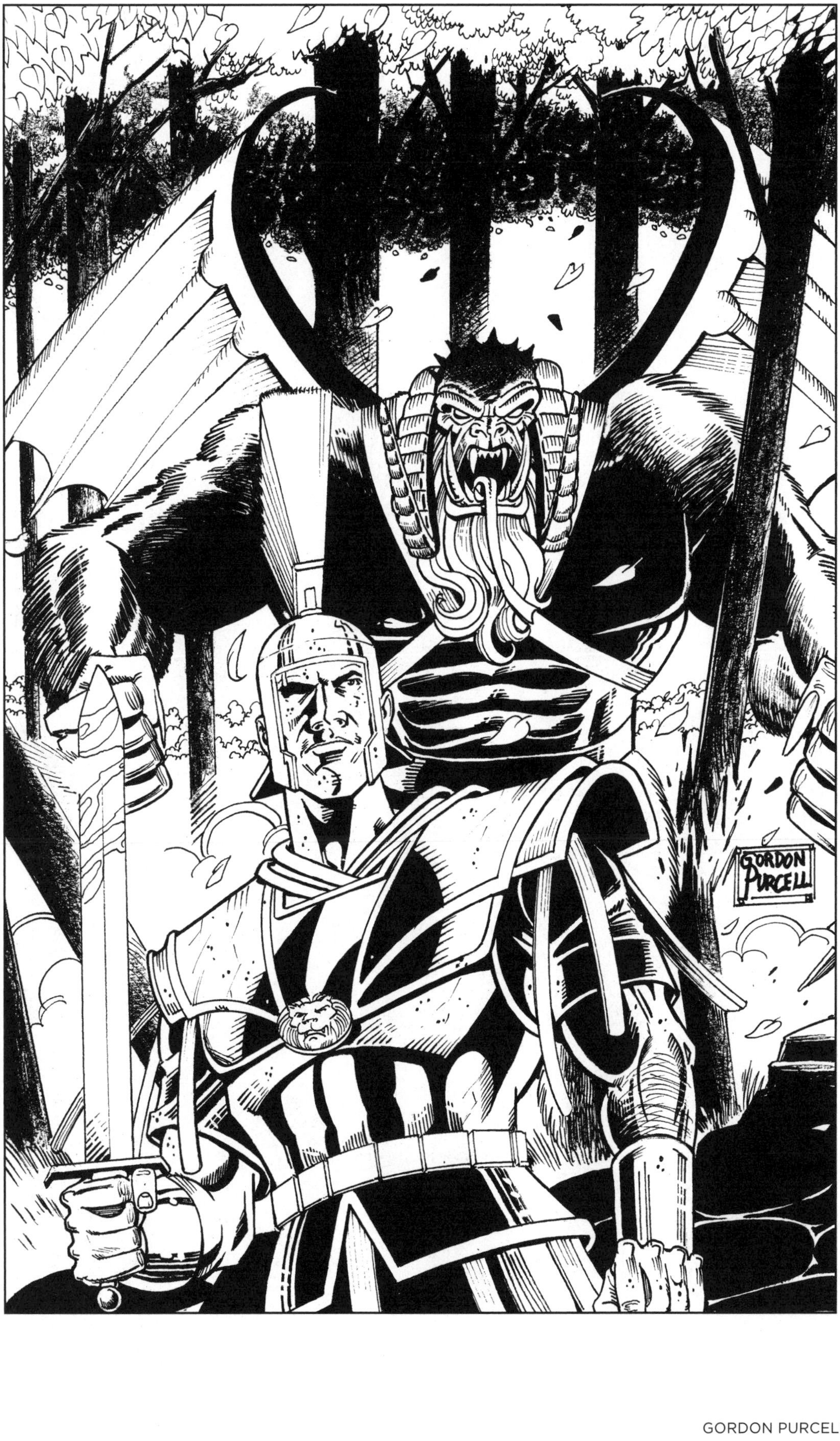
GORDON PURCELL

Cover for *Beyond the Wall* No. 1 (IDW). Art by Gordon Purcell. © 2009 IDW

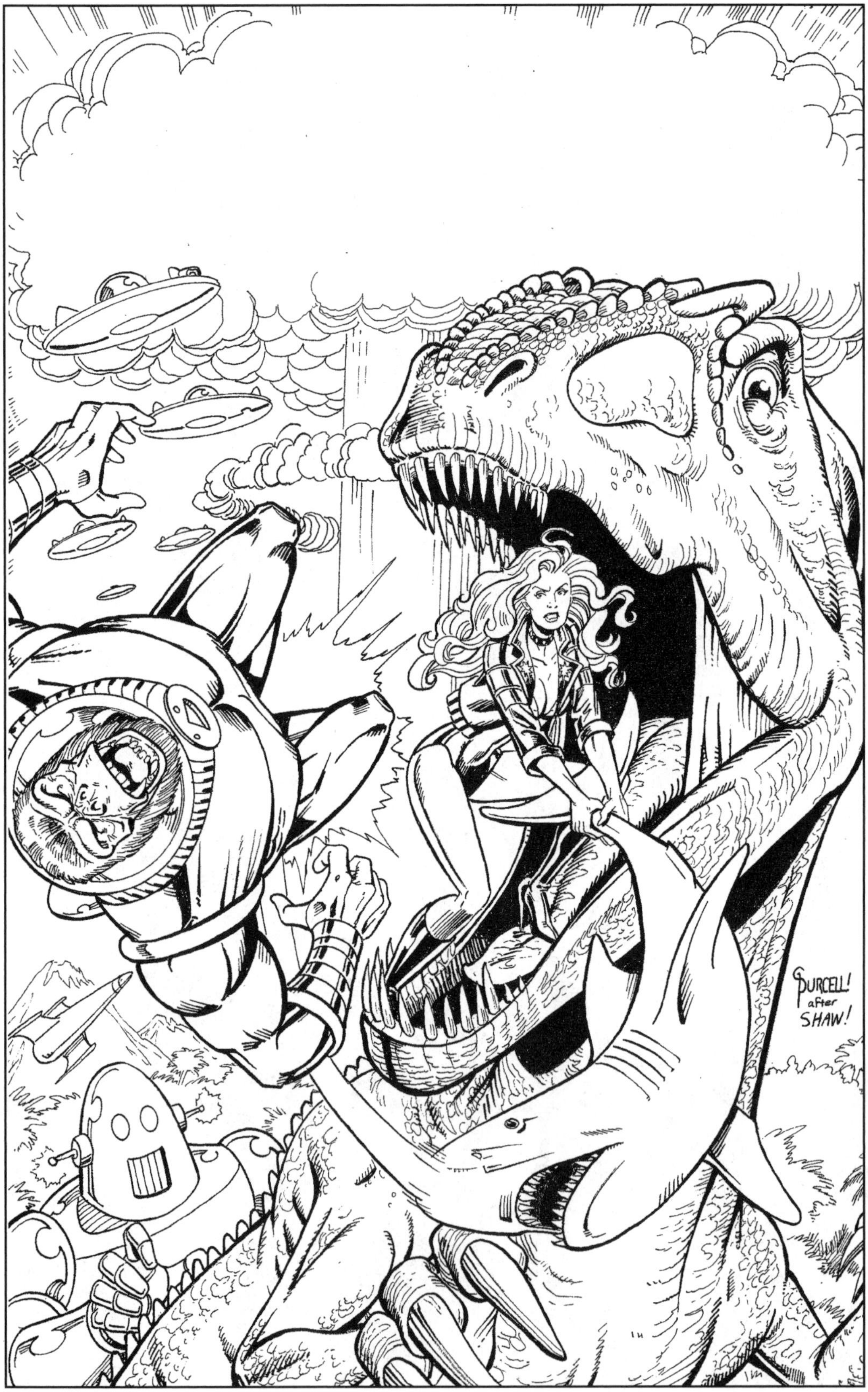
PURCELL!
after
SHAW!

Cover for *Flare* No. 31 (Heroic Publishing). Pencils and inks by Gordon Purcell. © 2005 Heroic Publishing, Inc.

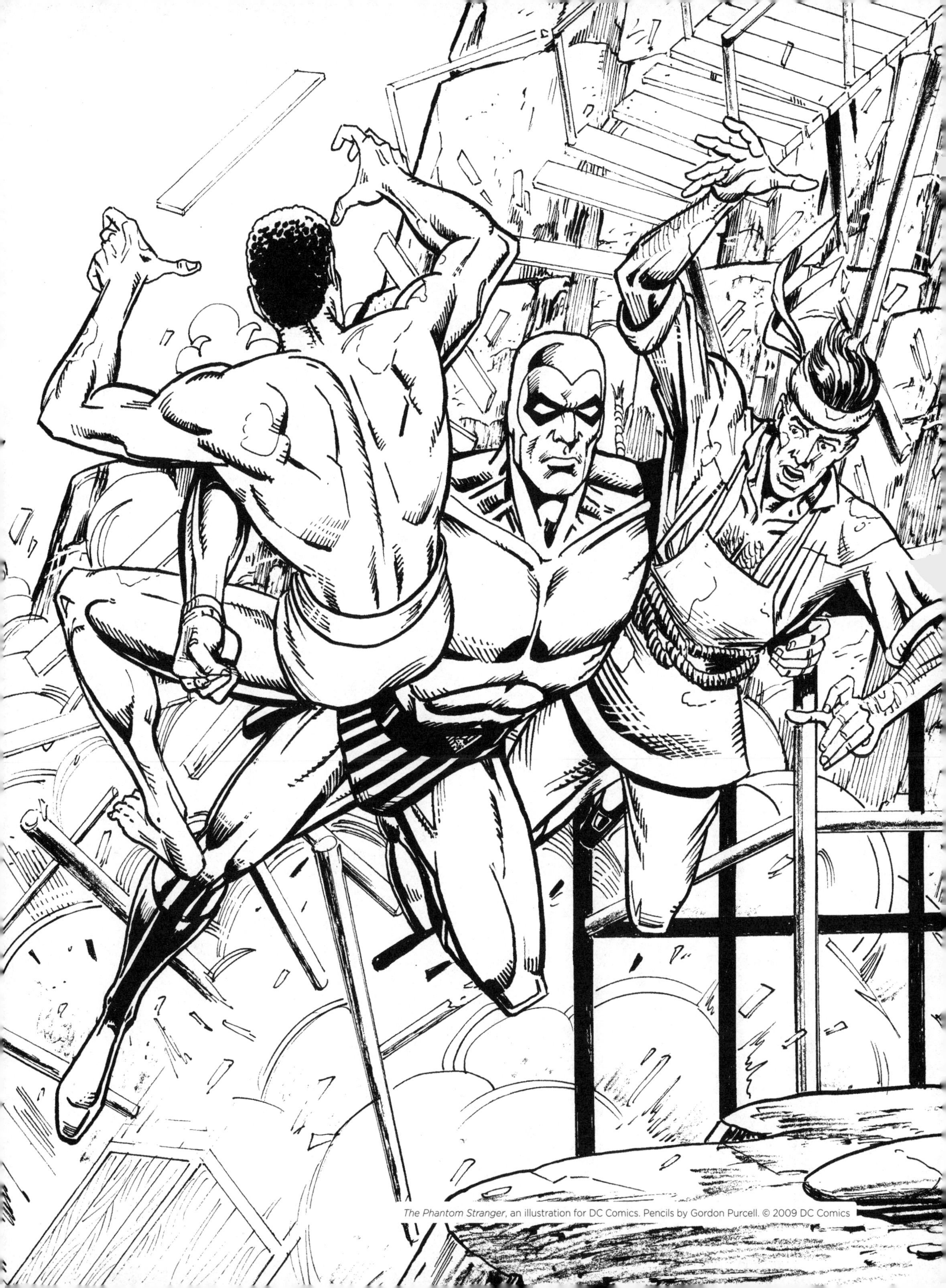

The Phantom Stranger, an illustration for DC Comics. Pencils by Gordon Purcell. © 2009 DC Comics

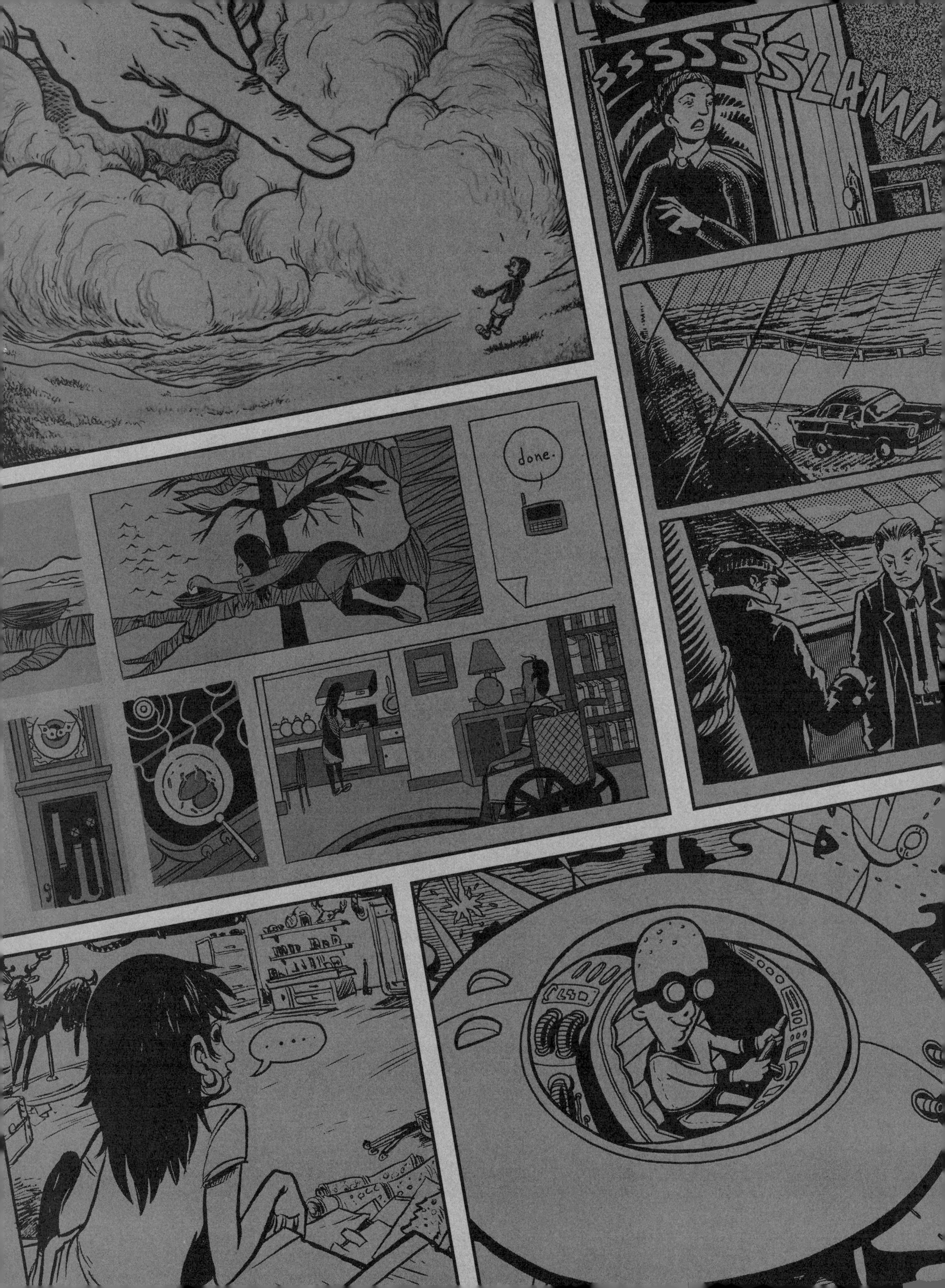
ssSSSSLAMM
done.

ALTERNATIVE UNDERGROUND

The Rise of Do-It-Yourselfers and Indie Presses

Underground has a seductive ring, exciting a jumble of images of cabals, secret missives, pot-stirring anarchists, garter belts, torn posters, indie labels, basement beer keg parties, and comix. And that's comix with an X, as in XXX and S-E-X. Time to turn down the lights and lock the door, baby.

Underground comix swaggered into the aftermath of the Comics Code, which had effectively snipped the thrill from between the pages of mainstream comics. Wertham's *Seduction of the Innocent* (1954) began the emasculation, which the publishers completed with the Code and its laundry list of no-nos. It was as if someone's blue-haired granny had co-opted the editorial desk. And this dame didn't hold with backtalk or unflattering depictions of authority. She sniffed at lusty babes, cleavage, Batman and Robin buddy-buddiness (because, Lord knows, there's something wrong with a man and boy kicking around in a cave), and anything having to do with horror and cheap thrills.

Comix gave the finger to the Code. But it took a while for the kids of the 1950s, who had seen their comics burned, spirited away by well-meaning parents, and codified, to grow up and become cartoonists in their own right. Their adulthood merged with the late 1960s, a period of social unrest and youthful idealism, embodied by hippie culture and civil disobedience. And if there was a place and time to be, it was San Francisco in 1968. Robert Crumb, whose father Chuck grew up on the family farm in southeast Minnesota, made comix history that year when he pushed a baby carriage filled with copies of his self-published *Zap Comix* through Haight-Ashbury. Crumb's art was outstanding and his success revolutionary because it galvanized his fellow cartoonists to push the fringes of their medium.

For Crumb and the other comix artists, no subject was so low or unseemly that it couldn't be elevated to art. Sex orgies. Masturbation. Free love. But if sexual fixation had been the extent of their revolution, the movement would have dissipated like a two-day hangover. Instead, comix flourished, nurtured by a freeing of limitations. With no one looking over their shoulders, no publisher dictating content, the artists tested the form. They drenched their comics in politics, hippiedom, rock music, and LSD. Anthologies featured groundbreaking talents: Crumb, S. Clay Wilson, and Spain Rodriguez.

Yet for all its liberated tone, comix tended to reduce women to slavering sexual playthings. In the early 1970s, women launched their own movement and their own anthologies with titles like *Wimmen's Comix* and *Tits & Clits*. Trina Robbins, Aline Kominsky, Lynda Barry, and Willy Mendes developed out of the women's comix movement.

> NO SUBJECT WAS SO LOW OR UNSEEMLY THAT IT COULDN'T BE ELEVATED TO ART. SEX ORGIES. MASTURBATION. FREE LOVE.

A second wave of underground comix arose in the mid-seventies, with a ratty, self-made aesthetic derived from punk music. New York City supported a number of alternative papers that published the work of these new cartoonists, among them Ken Weiner (Avidor), who, before moving to Minneapolis, contributed art to *Punk* and *Screw*.

This period also saw the development of nonreturnable direct market distribution in comic book retailing. Previously, retailers bought comics on consignment. Copies that didn't sell were returned to publishers for pulping. With direct marketing, retailers had to purchase comics outright and retain unsold issues for after-market collectible sales. This move coincided with the end of drug- and department-store spin racks featuring the latest comic book titles. Specialty comic book stores became the norm, which was an advantage because a specialty store could stock a variety of comics but a disadvantage too because comics were gradually receding from public view. Now you had to make a special trip to buy comics.

Even as the direct market system took hold, two young men were signaling a new era in self-published black-and-white comics. Kevin Eastman and Peter Laird self-published *Teenage Mutant Ninja Turtles* to enormous success. Cartoonists didn't need publishers to reach a mass audience. They could distribute a comic nationwide through the direct market system. Peter Gross, then living in Duluth, distributed the first issue of his black-and-white comic *Empire Lanes* in 1986.

Alternative comics took hold in the 1980s and '90s. Like their underground forebears, they sought an alternative to mainstream, typically superhero, comics. But unlike undergrounds, alternative comics were less interested in evincing a countercultural ethos than in promoting an array of individual styles and stories. Autobiography had gained a foothold with Harvey Pekar's *American Splendor* in 1976 and continued to pick up converts, who found fresh material in personal histories.

Dan Clowes, Chester Brown, and Pete Bagge invigorated comics with their technical brilliance and comic timing. In 1982, Fantagraphics began publishing Jaime and Gilbert Hernandez's groundbreaking *Love and Rockets*. Alternative publishers sprang up: Drawn and Quarterly, Top Shelf Productions, Dark Horse, and Eclipse. They filled gaps in comics publishing, putting money behind genre work and offbeat titles that didn't fit in the mainstream. (In Minnesota, Kevin Cannon, Zander Cannon, Will Dinski, Zak Sally, and Tim Sievert have all had work published through the alternative presses.)

In today's comics industry, the Internet provides what cartoonist and cartooning historian Scott McCloud calls the "infinite canvas" of the web. Liberated from the page, webcomics give readers the potential to scroll, follow the story and images through a series of clicks and hyperlinks, and watch animations. A new generation has emerged, cartoonists like Minnesota's Sarah Morean, who started out reading webcomics rather than print comics and developed her work among an online community of cartoonists.

Still, for all the wizardry of Internet technology, nothing compares to the sensual experience of holding a comic in your hand, turning the pages, and showcasing it on a dedicated shelf. Do-it-yourselfers, taking a cue from the underground, are printing their own comic books, minicomics, 'zines, and graphic novels at a cost that's in the reach even of an artistically inclined short-order cook or front-office receptionist. Their efforts run from a page to several hundred pages and take the shape of stapled pamphlets, hardbacks, trades, and framed art. Cartoonists like Marcus Almand, Christopher Brudlos, and Joseph Brudlos are combining the small-press and DIY ethic with a visual style derived from Japanese comics. Almand scripted *Razor Kid*. The Brudlos brothers write and draw the web and print comic *Alpha Shade*. Both series owe a debt to manga.

Underground comix brought sex out of the closet. Alternatives opened the door to anything-goes storytelling. So, what's obsessing Minnesota's newest crop of cartoonists? The usual: personal angst, superheroes, animals, a little naughty, a little nice, bicycles, big guns, the environment, and aw-shucks parodies of that noblest of archetypes, the cartoonist. ∎

BIG TIME ATTIC: ZANDER & KEVIN CANNON

The story of Northeast Minneapolis cartooning and illustration firm Big Time Attic hinges on coincidence, the coincidence of a school and a last name. In 1998, Kevin Cannon attended Iowa's Grinnell College as a freshman. He intended to study art, having built a reputation in his hometown, a first-ring suburb of Minneapolis, for portraiture and poster art made for high school teams. If Leonardo da Vinci had been born in Minnesota in the late twentieth century, he too probably would've found himself designing fundraising posters and business logos rather than the refectories of Catholic monasteries.

This is not to say that Kevin modeled his career after long-haired, long-bearded Italian painters. But as he entered college, he knew he wanted to be an illustrator and perhaps even—dare he presume?—an artist. So, naturally, he approached the school's paper, the *Scarlet & Black*. He could illustrate ads. He could illustrate mascots. He could illustrate illustrations. Whatever. Only this was 1998, the doorway to a new technological millennium, and thanks but no thanks, the *Scarlet & Black* would stick with photographs. Illustrations were so last century. But, hey, had Kevin ever considered drawing a cartoon strip?

So Kevin created the cartoon strip "Johnny Cavalier" for Grinnell's newspaper and ultimately scooped the Charles M. Schulz Award for college cartooning two years running. But first, to bone up on his *Scarlet & Black* predecessors, Kevin searched the newspaper archives. That search uncovered another Cannon who'd drawn strips for Grinnell, Zander Cannon. Zander had created "Booperman" during his tenure at the *Scarlet & Black*. He'd since graduated and moved to Minneapolis. On a whim, Kevin e-mailed the elder Cannon.

Zander Cannon was born in Boston in 1972. His father worked for United Airlines, so Zander's childhood was a patchwork of hometowns. He graduated from Smoky Hill High in Aurora, Colorado, and then attended Grinnell College, where he majored in English and devoted large chunks of time to theater.

"I started doing the comic strip 'Booperman' just for fun," says Zander. But the bug caught. He decided he liked drawing strips, even if he couldn't decide what type of strip he was drawing. "I had a character with glasses and a striped shirt in most of the strips. But I was trying out a different style every week. One week I'd draw a haunted house story, the next an adventure story."

Still in college, Zander began sending his portfolio to comics publishers. New England Comics was impressed enough to offer him a job drawing their comic book series *Chainsaw Vigilante*. Despite the suggestive title, the vigilante isn't a psychopathic killer à la *Texas Chainsaw Massacre*. Rather, he's an absurdist superhero whose main weapon of intimidation just happens to be a chainsaw. Zander divided his time between college studies and the various treatments of chainsaws in comic book storylines.

With *The Replacement God,* Zander moved from absurdist superheroes to Visigoths and dying gods. Zander created the series for Slave Labor Graphics. *The Replacement God* embroiders a fantasy as intricately patterned as a medieval tapestry. Knute, a castle drudge, is offered his freedom by King Ursus XLVI. But this regal show of magnanimity is withdrawn belatedly when the monarch realizes that Knute is in fact the Replacement God, the mortal designated to replace the dying God of the Dead and put an end to the Ursus monarchy. Thus ensues a cat-and-mouse intrigue, as Knute and newfound companion Anne (a gal with man problems) struggle to evade the king's Dread Expatriate Visigoth Death Horde and Fire Brigade.

IF LEONARDO DA VINCI HAD BEEN BORN IN MINNESOTA IN THE LATE TWENTIETH CENTURY, HE TOO PROBABLY WOULD'VE FOUND HIMSELF DESIGNING FUNDRAISING POSTERS AND BUSINESS LOGOS RATHER THAN THE REFECTORIES OF CATHOLIC MONASTERIES.

At its peak, *The Replacement God* sold 10,000 copies, a far cry from the millions of copies *Superman* sold in its prime but a solid number for a small independent title. Zander's career profile moved up a notch, and with the help of a connection or two, namely comic book artist Gene Ha, he found work on *Smax* and *Top Ten,* titles originated by comic book legend Alan Moore (*Watchmen, V for Vendetta, The League of Extraordinary Gentlemen*).

But what about the e-mail Kevin sent to Zander? Well, it led to an internship with Zander then. Finally, in 2004, the Cannons, along with interactive designer Shad Petosky (who has since co-founded interactive and animation firm PUNY Entertainment), established Big Time Attic.

The cartooning and illustration firm and its principals have designed a Wisconsin amusement park (with Petosky), illustrated teaching guides and posters, and collaborated with writer Jim Ottaviani on the graphic books *Bone Sharps, Cowboys and Thunder Lizards,* and *T-Minus: The Race to the Moon.* In 2009, they also brought out the educational graphic book *The Stuff of Life: A graphic guide to genetics and DNA* and developed a follow-up title.

In between contract deadlines for Big Time Attic, Zander has scripted *Top Ten Season 2* and *Star Trek: The Next Generation: Ghosts* for mainstream publishers and continued work on his graphic novel *Heck,* about a man who inherits a doorway to Dante's *Inferno.* Kevin also developed a graphic novel, *Far Arden,* posting pages to his website as he completed them.

Army Shanks plays the brawling protagonist of Kevin's adventure yarn. *Far Arden* takes place in an Antarctic that is unusually peopled by a circus strongman, an orphan dressed in fox, college coeds, a conniving professor, and an old flame with curves to build a dream on. Everyone wants the map to the mythical isle Far Arden and will do whatever it takes to acquire it. Top Shelf Productions published the graphic novel, which in 2010 clinched an Eisner nomination for Best Publication for Teens.

"There are three things you can be in comics," advises Zander. "You can be very fast, very good, or very easy to talk to. If you're any two of those things, you'll always have work. I've never met someone who's all three." Yet whatever the mix, the Cannons have managed to persevere in a competitive industry and create a business around their art. A business founded, initially, on the coincidence of a shared last name and a college in Iowa. ■

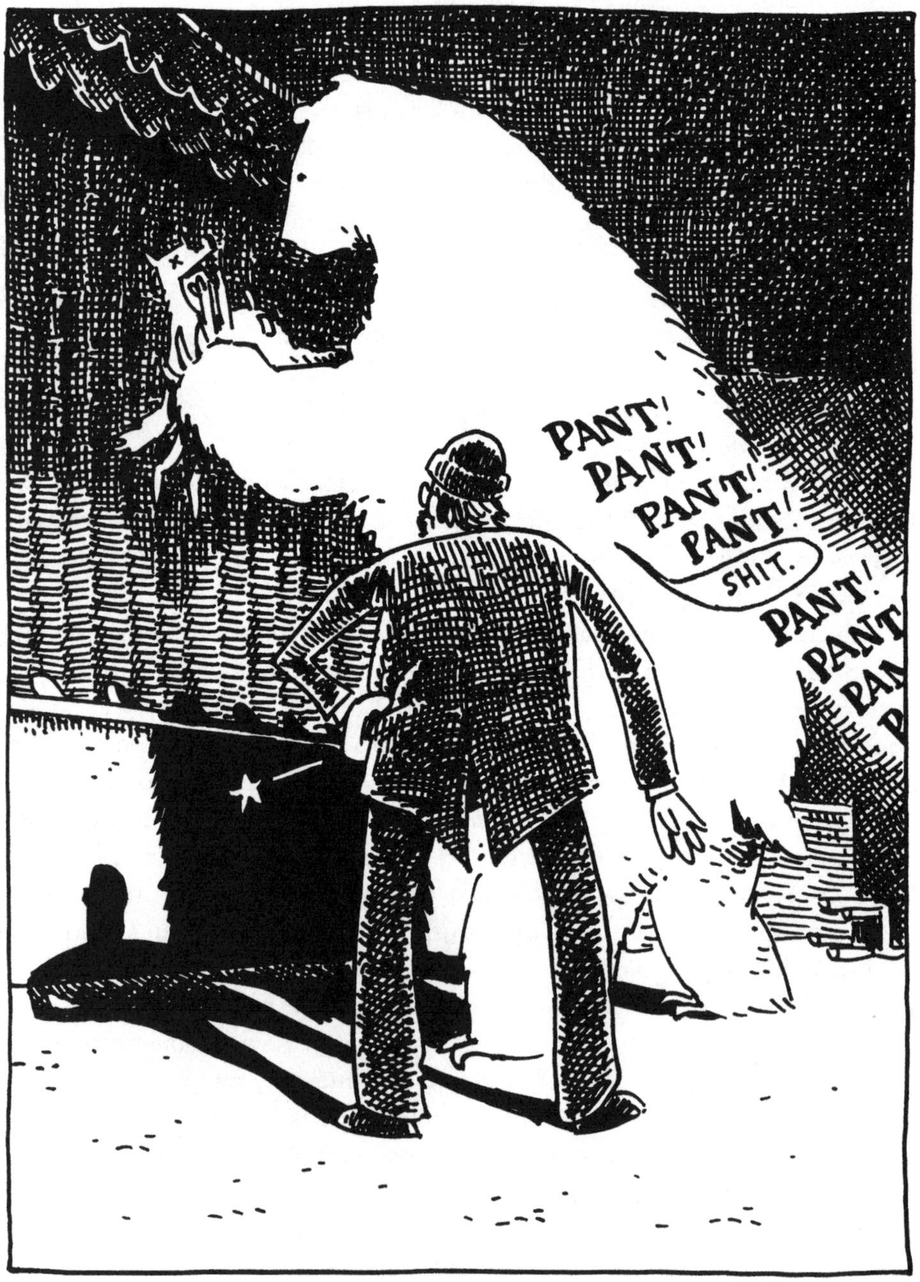
PANT! PANT! PANT! PANT!
SHIT.
PANT! PANT!

Far Arden (Top Shelf Productions) by Kevin Cannon. © 2009 Kevin Cannon

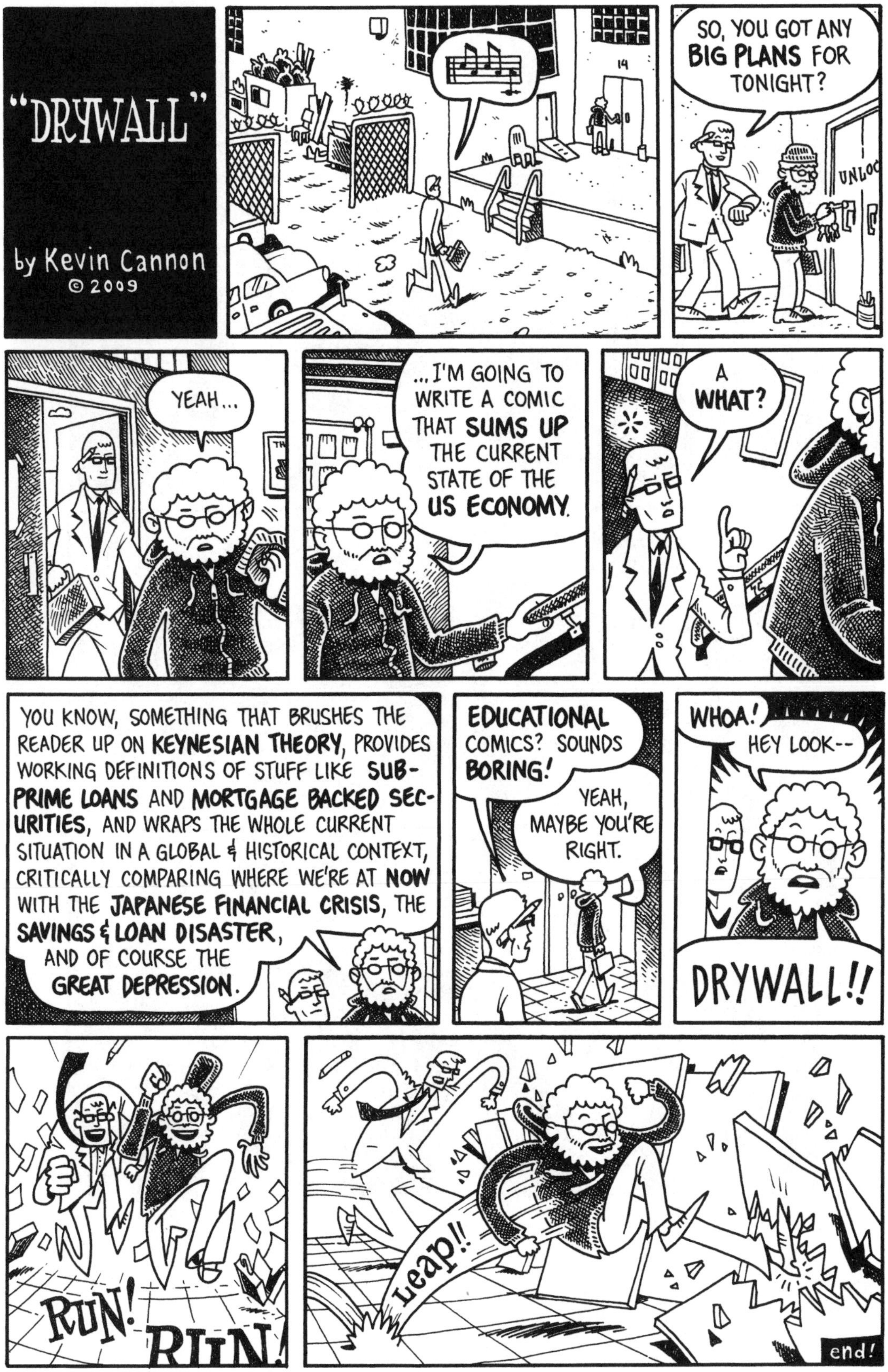
"DRYWALL"
by Kevin Cannon ©2009
SO, YOU GOT ANY BIG PLANS FOR TONIGHT?
UNLOC
YEAH...
...I'M GOING TO WRITE A COMIC THAT SUMS UP THE CURRENT STATE OF THE US ECONOMY.
A WHAT?
YOU KNOW, SOMETHING THAT BRUSHES THE READER UP ON KEYNESIAN THEORY, PROVIDES WORKING DEFINITIONS OF STUFF LIKE SUB-PRIME LOANS AND MORTGAGE BACKED SECURITIES, AND WRAPS THE WHOLE CURRENT SITUATION IN A GLOBAL & HISTORICAL CONTEXT, CRITICALLY COMPARING WHERE WE'RE AT NOW WITH THE JAPANESE FINANCIAL CRISIS, THE SAVINGS & LOAN DISASTER, AND OF COURSE THE GREAT DEPRESSION.
EDUCATIONAL COMICS? SOUNDS BORING!
YEAH, MAYBE YOU'RE RIGHT.
WHOA!
HEY LOOK--
DRYWALL!!
RUN! RUN!
LEAP!!
end!

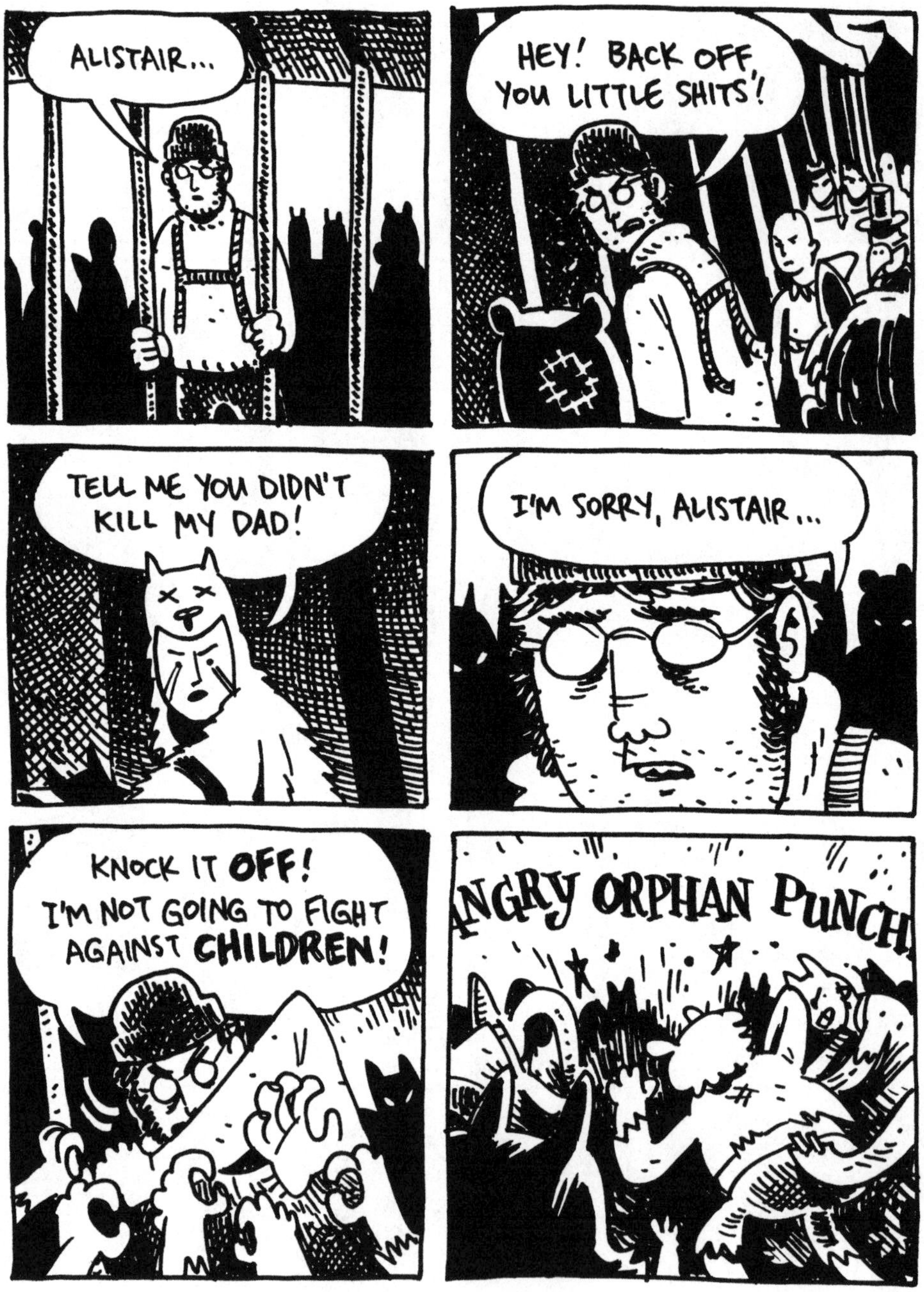
ALISTAIR...
HEY! BACK OFF YOU LITTLE SHITS!
TELL ME YOU DIDN'T KILL MY DAD!
I'M SORRY, ALISTAIR...
KNOCK IT OFF! I'M NOT GOING TO FIGHT AGAINST CHILDREN!
NGRY ORPHAN PUNCH

Far Arden (Top Shelf Productions) by Kevin Cannon. © 2009 Kevin Cannon

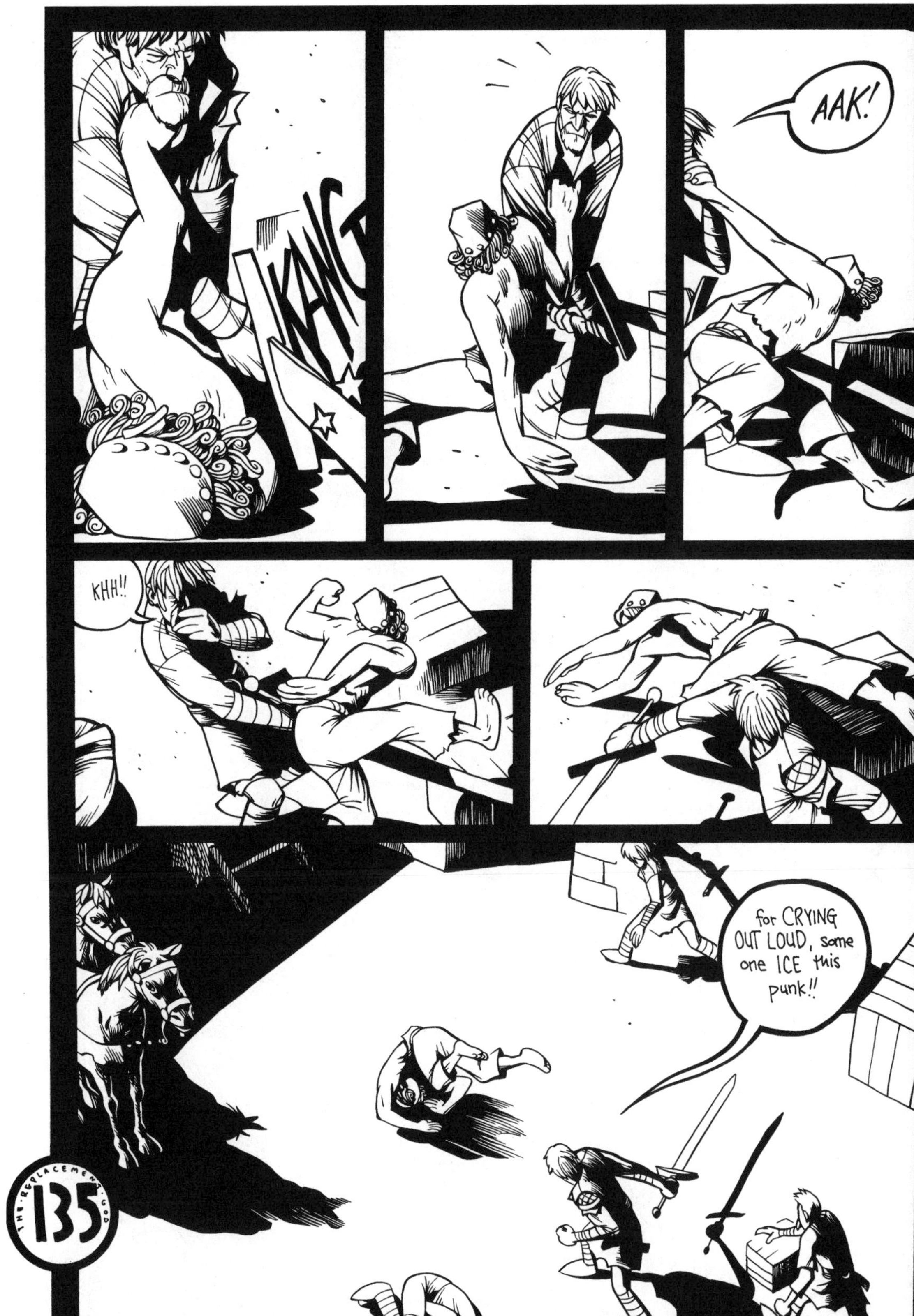
KANG
AAK!
KHH!!
for CRYING OUT LOUD, some one ICE this punk!!
THE·REPLACEMENT·GOD
135

The Replacement God (Handicraft Guild) by Zander Cannon. © 1998 Zander Cannon

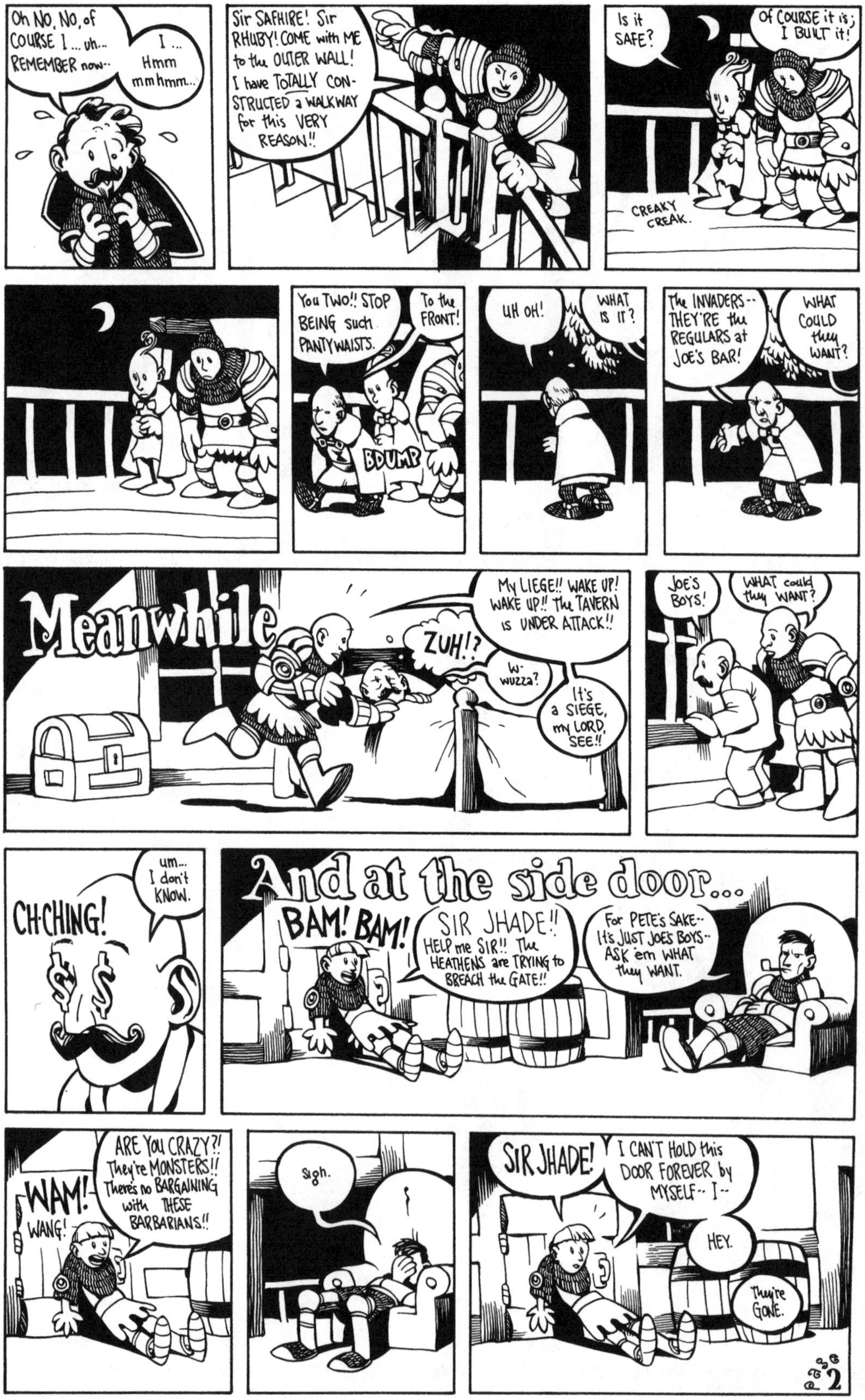
Oh NO, No, of COURSE I ... uh... REMEMBER now--
I ... Hmm mmhmm...
Sir SAFHIRE! Sir RHUBY! COME with ME to the OUTER WALL! I have TOTALLY CON-STRUCTED a WALKWAY for this VERY REASON!!
Is it SAFE?
Of COURSE it is; I BUILT it!
CREAKY CREAK.
You TWO!! STOP BEING such PANTYWAISTS.
To the FRONT!
BDUMP
UH OH!
WHAT IS IT?
The INVADERS-- THEY'RE the REGULARS at JOE'S BAR!
WHAT COULD they WANT?
Meanwhile
My LIEGE!! WAKE UP! WAKE UP!! the TAVERN is UNDER ATTACK!!
ZUH!?
W-wuzza?
It's a SIEGE, my LORD, SEE!!
JOE'S BOYS!
WHAT could they WANT?
CH-CHING!
um... I don't KNOW.
And at the side door...
BAM! BAM!
SIR JHADE!! HELP me SIR!! The HEATHENS are TRYING to BREACH the GATE!!
For PETE'S SAKE-- It's JUST JOE'S BOYS-- ASK 'em WHAT they WANT.
WAM!
WANG!
ARE YOU CRAZY?! They're MONSTERS!! There's no BARGAINING with THESE BARBARIANS!!
Sigh.
SIR JHADE!
I CAN'T HOLD this DOOR FOREVER by MYSELF-- I--
HEY.
They're GONE.
2

The Replacement God (Handicraft Guild) by Zander Cannon. © 1998 Zander Cannon

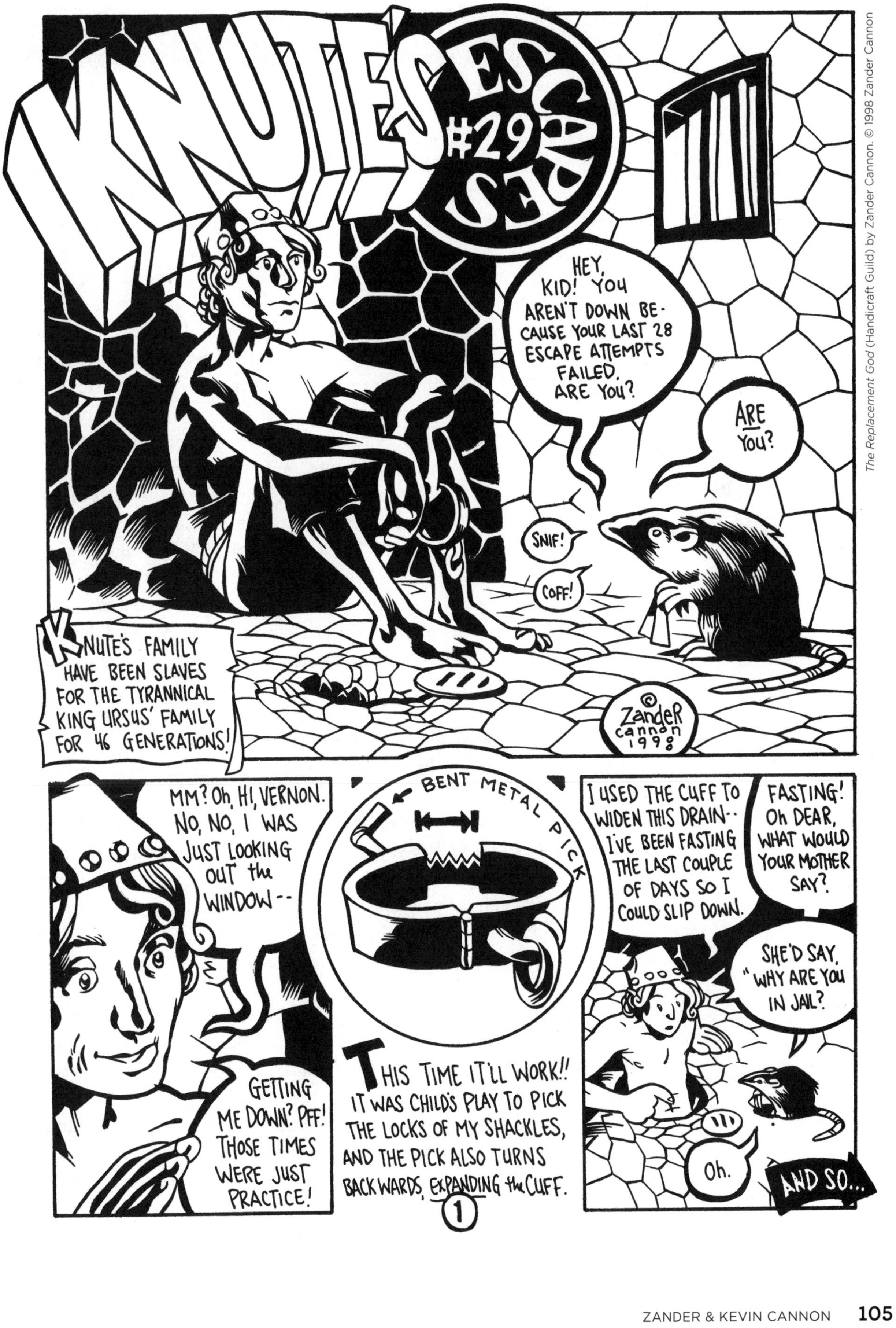
KNUTE'S ESCAPES #29
KNUTE'S FAMILY HAVE BEEN SLAVES FOR THE TYRANNICAL KING URSUS' FAMILY FOR 46 GENERATIONS!
HEY, KID! YOU AREN'T DOWN BE-CAUSE YOUR LAST 28 ESCAPE ATTEMPTS FAILED, ARE YOU?
ARE YOU?
SNIF!
COFF!
© ZANDER CANNON 1998
MM? Oh, HI, VERNON. NO, NO, I WAS JUST LOOKING OUT the WINDOW--
GETTING ME DOWN? PFF! THOSE TIMES WERE JUST PRACTICE!
BENT METAL PICK
THIS TIME IT'LL WORK!! IT WAS CHILD'S PLAY TO PICK THE LOCKS OF MY SHACKLES, AND THE PICK ALSO TURNS BACKWARDS, EXPANDING the CUFF.
1
I USED THE CUFF TO WIDEN THIS DRAIN-- I'VE BEEN FASTING THE LAST COUPLE OF DAYS SO I COULD SLIP DOWN.
FASTING! Oh DEAR, WHAT WOULD YOUR MOTHER SAY?
SHE'D SAY, "WHY ARE YOU IN JAIL?
Oh.
AND SO...

Tom Cruise is a Scientologist. John Travolta too. And Will Dinski is, well, he's not quite a Scientologist, but he did sit through their introductory personality test. In Dinski's minicomic *Are You Often Compulsive In Your Behavior?*, archived online at Dinski's website, the cartoonist recounts the day he stopped in at the Scientology reading room on Nicollet Mall in Minneapolis.

In the comic, the cartoon version of Dinski halts before a sandwich board that reads: FREE PERSONALITY TEST. It's midwinter. Snow clogs Nicollet Mall. Chaffing against the cold, Dinski does what many Minneapolitans have fantasized about but never had the courage to pursue: He rings through the door of the Scientology reading room. A man greets Dinski and sets him down with a 250-question personality test.

> "HONESTLY, IF I LIVED IN PORTLAND I WOULDN'T GET ANYTHING DONE. I'D BE GOING OUT WITH CARTOONISTS ALL THE TIME AND GOING TO PARTIES. I NEED TIME TO GET WORK DONE."

"Does it seem cold in here?" the cartoon version of Dinski asks his host. The man replies tersely, "The boiler's out." Frigid puffs of air tremble from Dinski's lips. He delves into question 45: *Do you often feel that people are looking at you or talking about you behind your back?* Dinski scans the room. In a corner, his host huddles with Scientology chums. Is it Dinski's imagination, or are they gossiping about him?

Later, the cartoon Dinski sits down with his test results. "It says here you're nervous. Do you feel nervous?" the Scientologist asks.

"Well," Dinski considers, his foot a blur of agitated motion, "anxious sometimes, I guess."

The real-life Dinski hails from Illinois. He moved to Minnesota to attend the Minneapolis College of Art and Design. A lot of out-of-state students transit through Minnesota while they pursue college educations. Dinski was one of those who chose to remain, a decision he mulls over in another minicomic, *The Midwestern Artist,* in which he examines the lives of F. Scott Fitzgerald and Charles Schulz, native Minnesotans who relocated to the coasts to pursue fortunes.

Cartoonists don't have to locate in big cities, but they often do. They also tend to go where publishers are. DC and Marvel are anchored in New York. Independent publishers are scattered across the United States, but no sizeable comics publishers have yet roosted in the Twin Cities.

Still, Dinski has a measured response for his decision to stay in Minneapolis. "Honestly, if I lived in Portland"—a noted comics hotbed—"I wouldn't get anything done. I'd be going out with cartoonists all the time and going to parties. I need time to get work done."

Dinski works a full-time job as a print production manager and squeezes in art time whenever he can. "I have a strict schedule. I get in two hours every night, for certain, with a night off every week. It's like working two jobs, only one doesn't pay very well." The pace is brutal, but cartooning is a hard-won skill built up like an Olympian's endurance. "If you stop drawing," he says, "you get rusty."

Dinski's style is smoothly formal. The formality derives, in large part, from the grid structure he uses. "I started using the grid so I could pace the words and pictures, and decide which came first and which came second." In *Cool, Beautiful and Irreplaceable,* text and image occupy side-by-side panels. Dinski controls the story with a tip of the balance, increasing text or expanding an image when necessary.

Cool, Beautiful and Irreplaceable is longer than most of Dinski's work. The compact graphic novel introduces the reader to Dr. Fingers, plastic surgeon to the stars, and his celebrity clientele. Dinski's story questions surface realities because none of the characters can live up to their celebrity billing. They are a mass of flaws. Enter Dr. Fingers. He nips and tucks the sags with alacrity. But as to the damaged psyches, well, that's out of his hands. Top Shelf Productions published Dinski's book as *Fingerprints* in 2010.

In the virtual world, Dinski commands an online audience with a steady stream of minicomics (scanned as webcomics) and pages from his serialized graphic novel *Covered in Confusion.* Minicomics fit Dinski's schedule. They can run anywhere from one page to several. But they also suit his talent for sketching brief moments of encounter, some drawn directly from the cartoonist's own experiences.

In *Routine,* another Dinski minicomic, a family man goes through the motions of living. The man arises, eats breakfast, kisses his wife, and heads into the morning commute. He is the personification of complacent middle age, all the way to the last panel, when Dinski throws his curve ball. The friendly routinized man, the homey husband, the neighbor everyone likes, erupts from a gun shop grinning manically and sporting a Bernard Goetz zeal for civilian vigilantism. Happily, Dinski didn't need to consult personal experience for *Routine.* He left that to his imagination. ∎

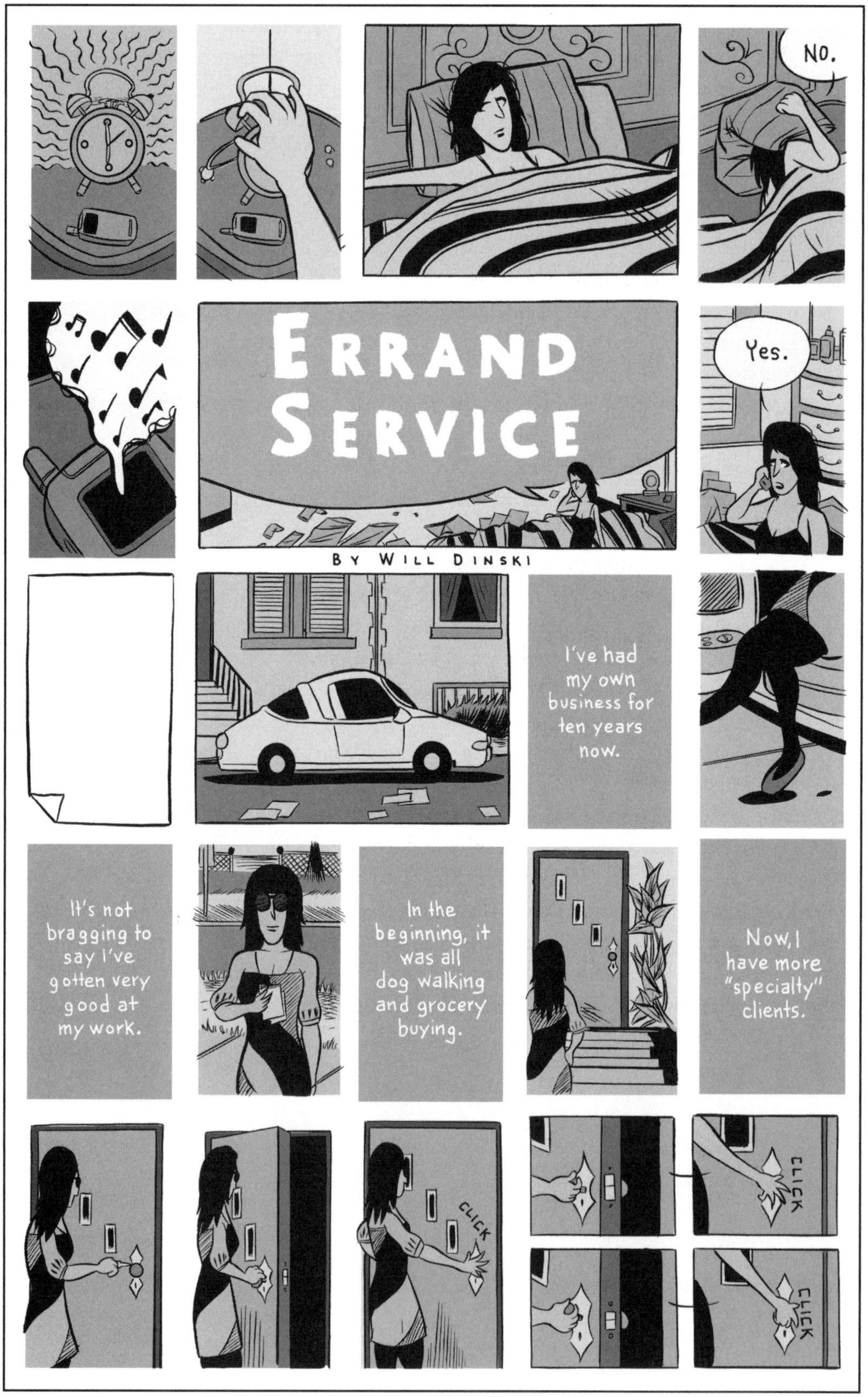
No.
ERRAND SERVICE
BY WILL DINSKI
Yes.
I've had my own business for ten years now.
It's not bragging to say I've gotten very good at my work.
In the beginning, it was all dog walking and grocery buying.
Now, I have more "specialty" clients.
CLICK
CLICK
CLICK

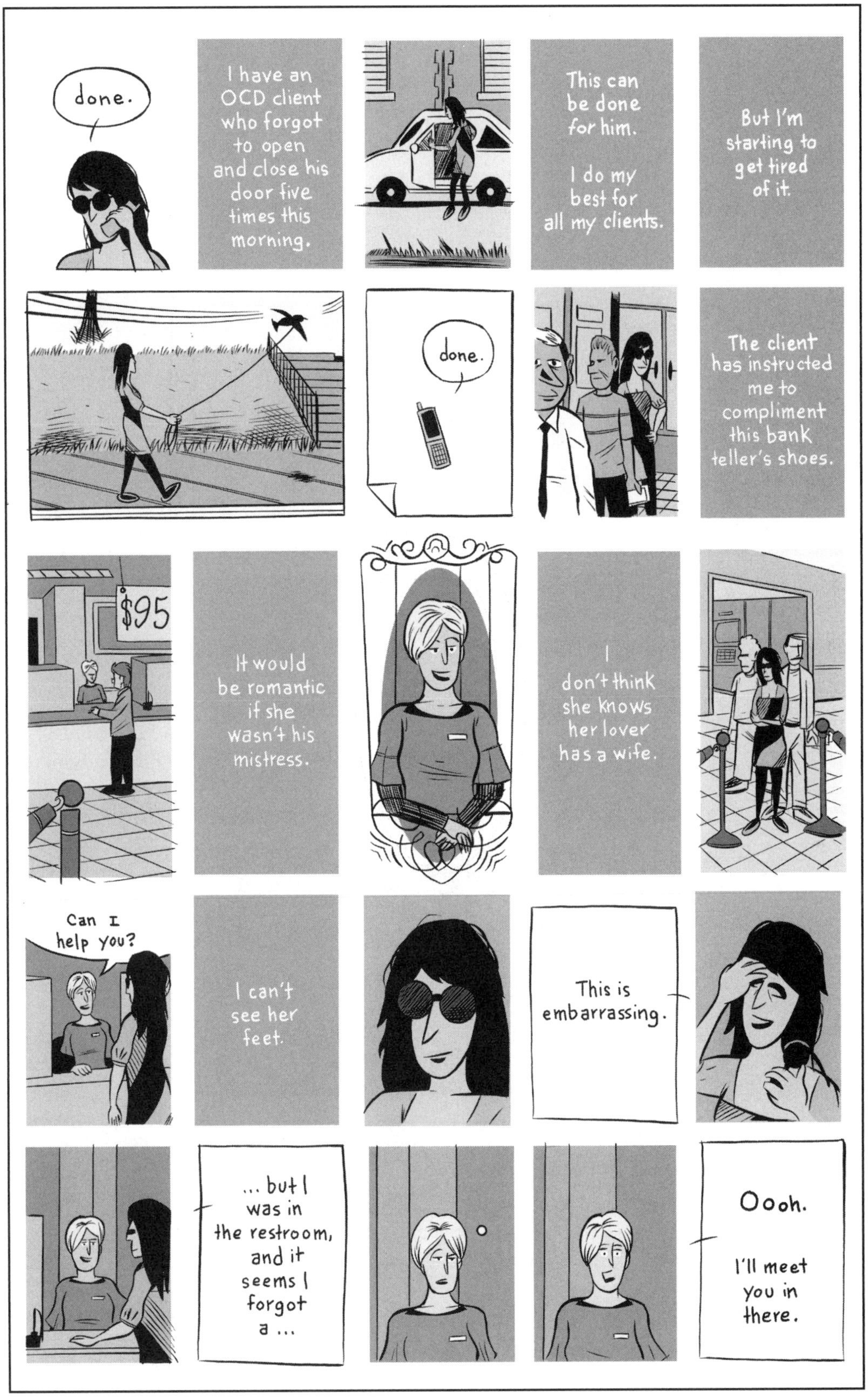
done.
I have an OCD client who forgot to open and close his door five times this morning.
This can be done for him.
I do my best for all my clients.
But I'm starting to get tired of it.
done.
The client has instructed me to compliment this bank teller's shoes.
$95
It would be romantic if she wasn't his mistress.
I don't think she knows her lover has a wife.
Can I help you?
I can't see her feet.
This is embarrassing.
... but I was in the restroom, and it seems I forgot a ...
Oooh.
I'll meet you in there.

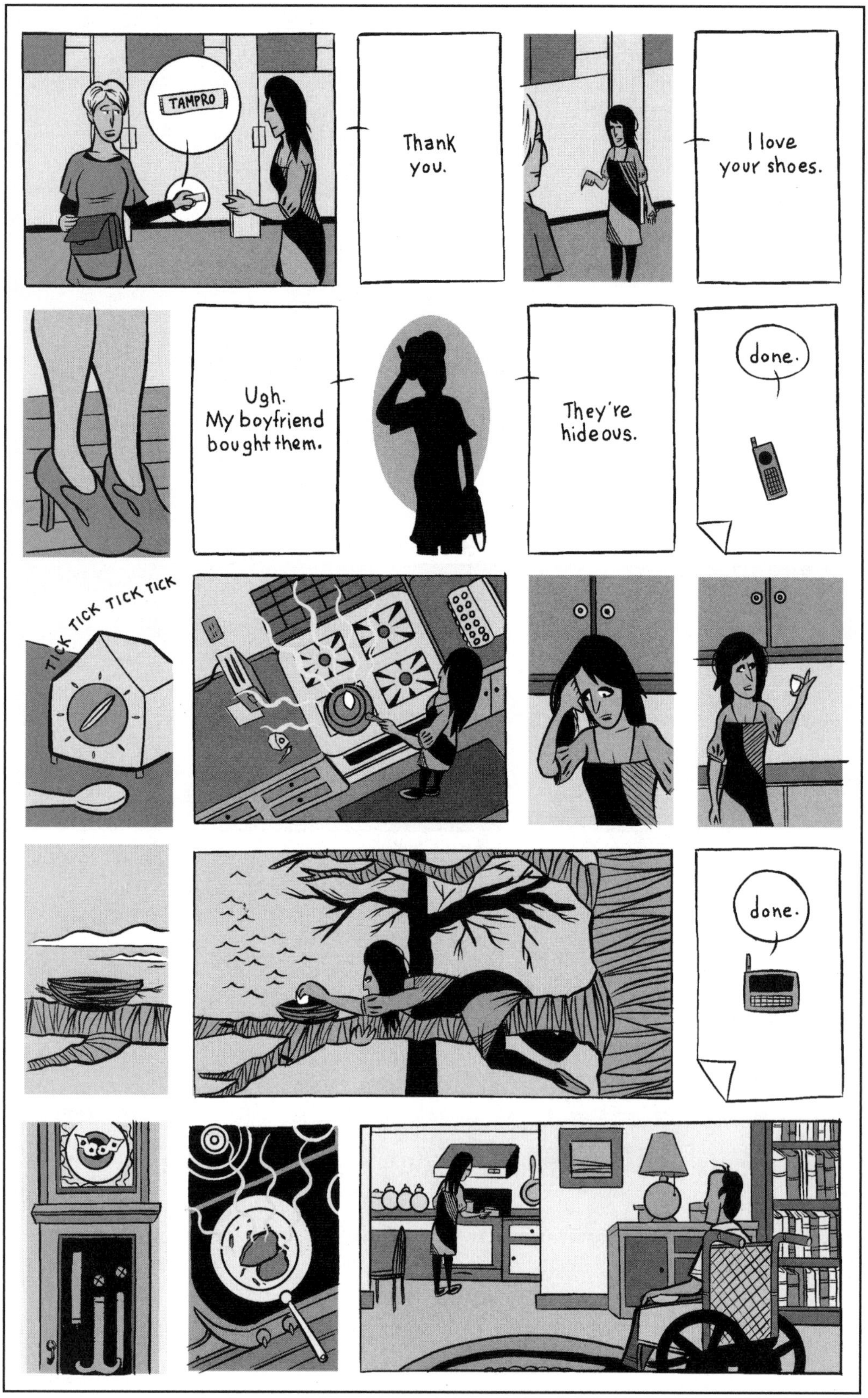
TAMPRO
Thank you.
I love your shoes.
Ugh. My boyfriend bought them.
They're hideous.
done.
TICK TICK TICK TICK
done.

"Errand Service" by Will Dinski. © 2008 Will Dinski

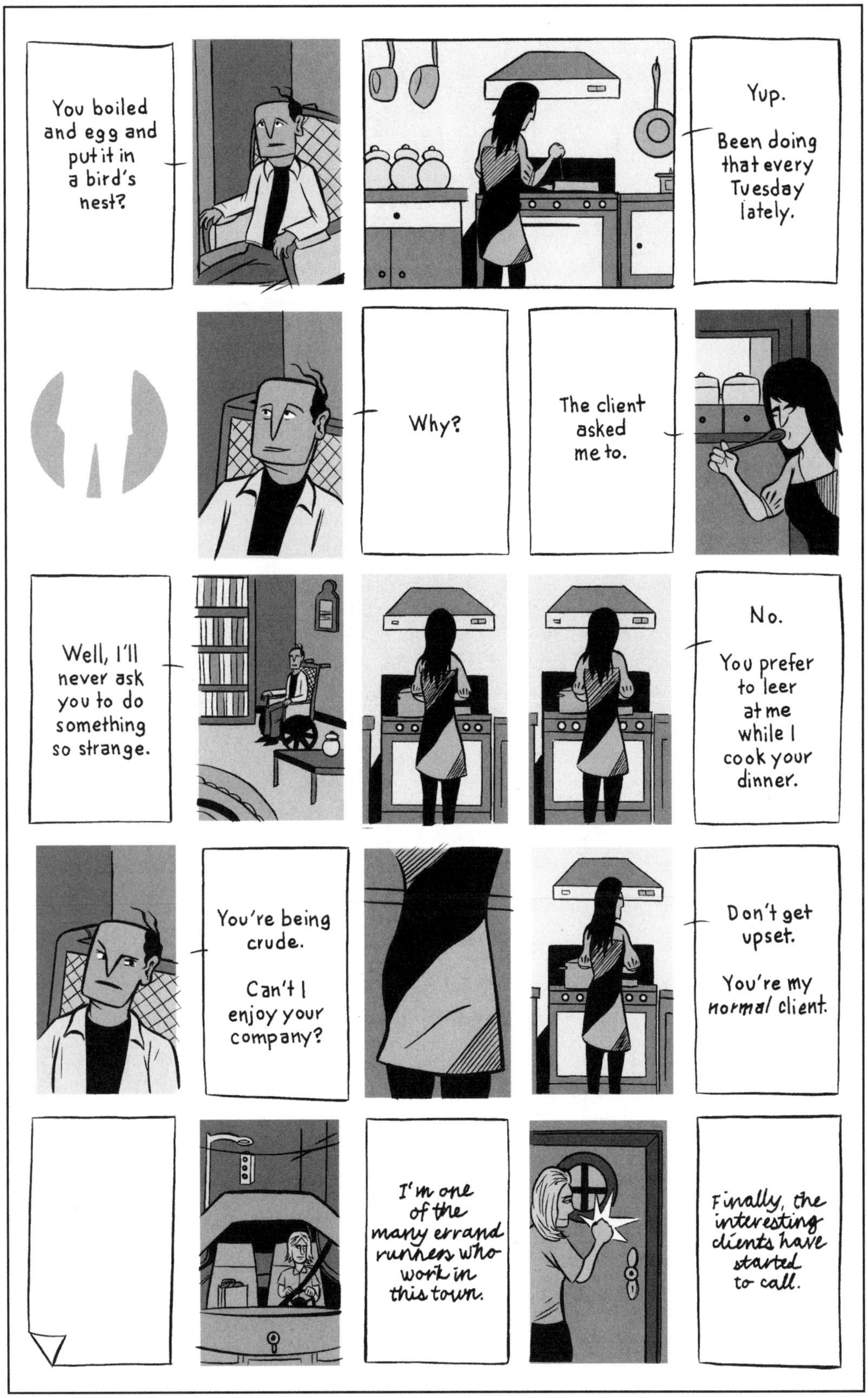
You boiled and egg and put it in a bird's nest?
Yup.
Been doing that every Tuesday lately.
Why?
The client asked me to.
Well, I'll never ask you to do something so strange.
No.
You prefer to leer at me while I cook your dinner.
You're being crude.
Can't I enjoy your company?
Don't get upset.
You're my *normal* client.
I'm one of the many errand runners who work in this town.
Finally, the interesting clients have started to call.

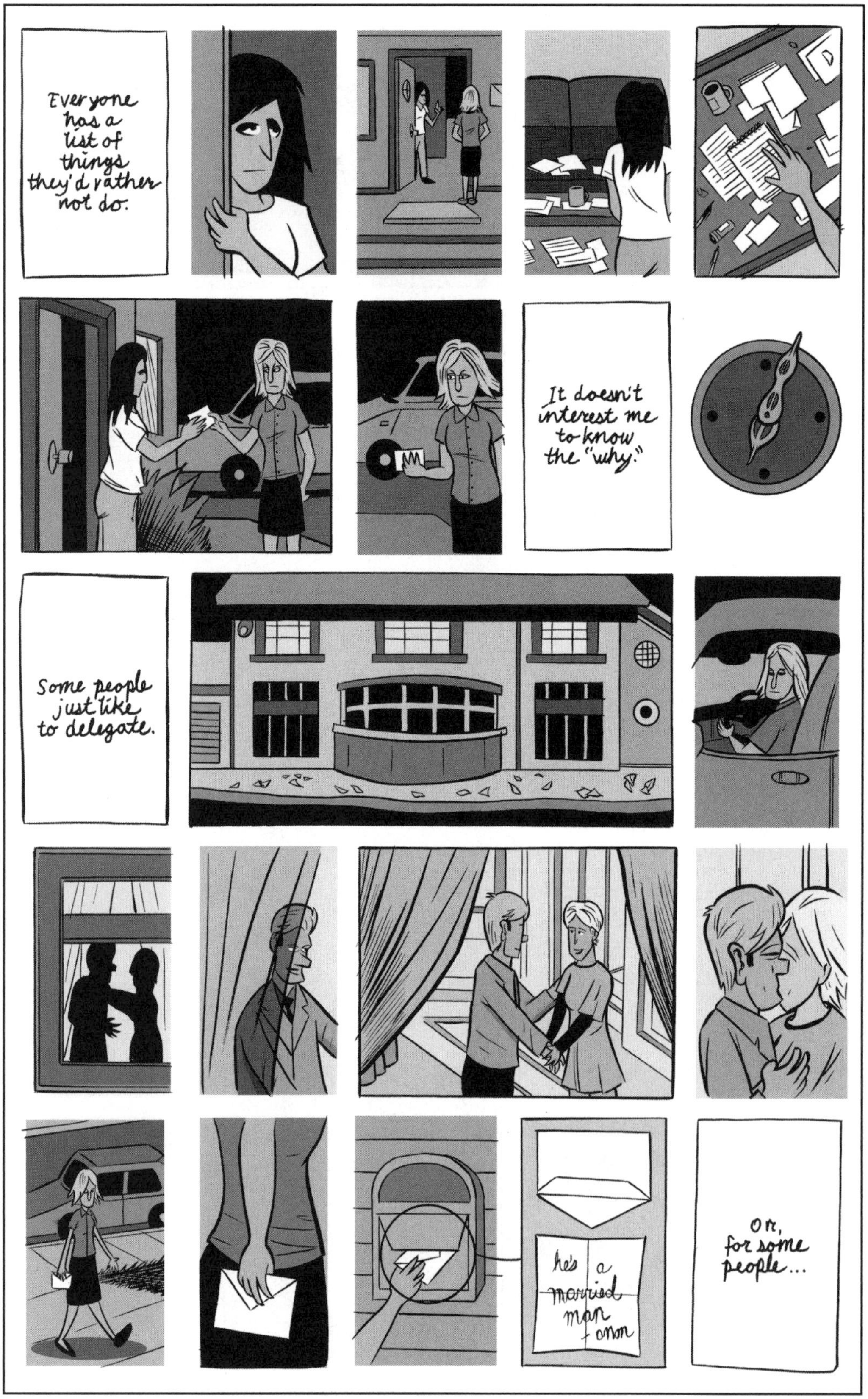
Everyone has a list of things they'd rather not do.
It doesn't interest me to know the "why."
Some people just like to delegate.
he's a married man anon
Or, for some people...

"Errand Service" by Will Dinski. © 2008 Will Dinski

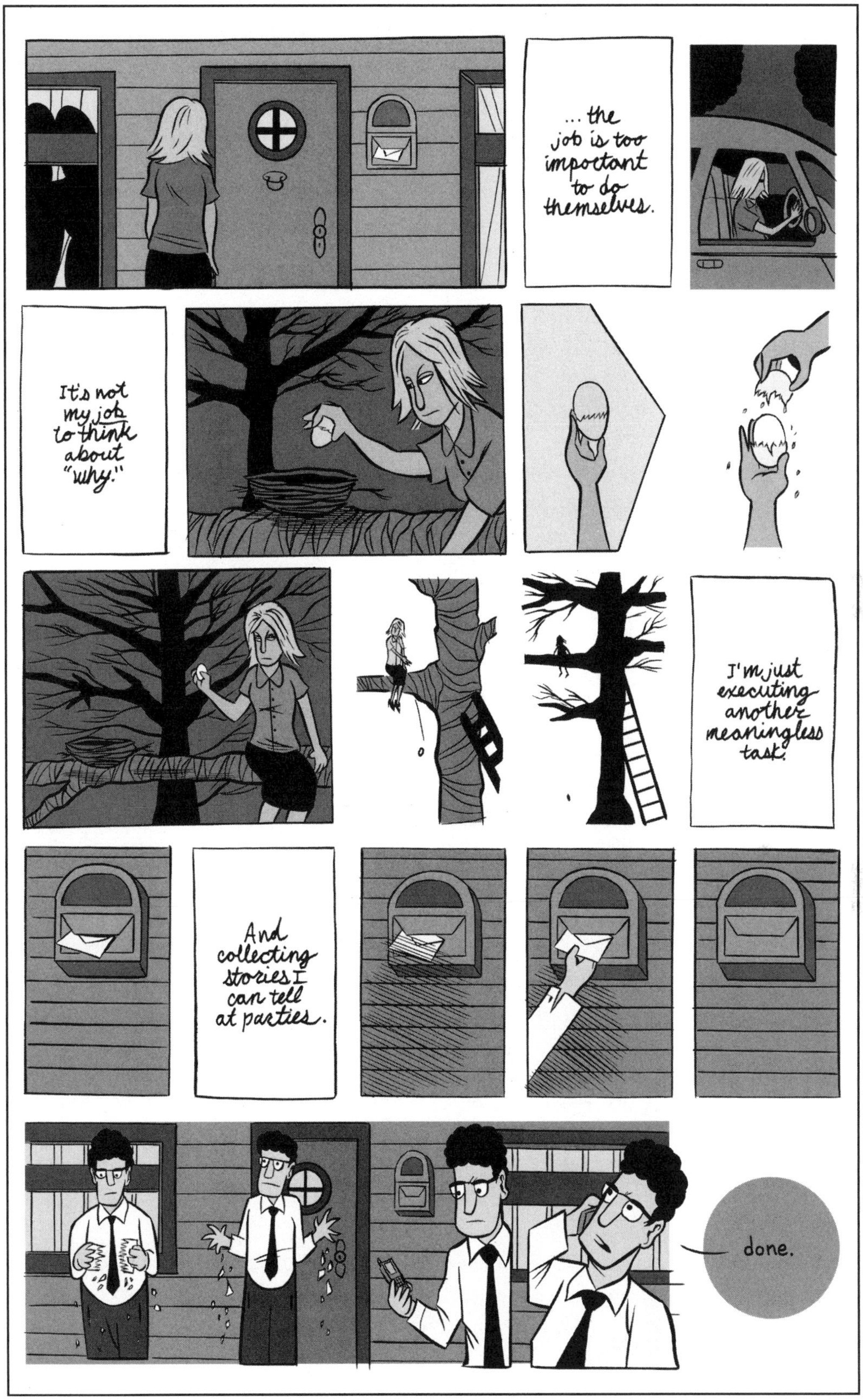
... the job is too important to do themselves.
It's not my job to think about "why."
I'm just executing another meaningless task.
And collecting stories I can tell at parties.
done.

CHRISTOPHER JONES & MELISSA KAERCHER

Christopher Jones and Melissa Kaercher have the social bug encoded in their genes. They help organize large events, like the mammoth annual Twin Cities science fiction and fantasy convention CONvergence, and more modest get-togethers, like themed movie nights exploring the work of famous film directors. They go where people go, and people go to them.

Folk wisdom holds that two such outsized personalities cannot collaborate on the same project with any hope of retaining a modicum of sanity. Folk wisdom is not perfect. Neither are the superheroes who populate Jones and Kaercher's *Dr. Blink: Superhero Shrink,* a series that examines the hang-ups, complexes, and idiosyncrasies of the world's superheroic population.

Jones pencils and inks and Kaercher letters and colors the series co-created with writer John Kovalic, creator of the comic book series *Dork Tower.* The trio gets along just fine, as creative super-entities go. Each contributes his or her part to the neurotically tangled life stories that trip the reader's funny bone and tax Dr. Blink's expertise as psychoanalyst to superheroes.

Dr. Blink: Superhero Shrink, published by Dork Storm Press, reveals (or revels in?) the fragile emotions of the larger-than-life superheroes flinging themselves and their problems onto the doctor's couch. Among his patients: the last man of an obliterated race, suffering from survivor's guilt; an airborne hero afraid of heights; and a telepath who won't let the doctor get a thought in edgewise because she already knows what he's thinking.

The existence of *Dr. Blink* owes a debt, in part, to a mother with pluck and a small Minnesota newspaper. When Jones was ten, his mother conveyed him to the offices of the *Owatonna People's Press.* She knew her son had talent and just assumed the paper would have a job for him.

"The very nice but somewhat baffled receptionist directed us to a staff writer who was also a comics fan," Jones says. "I showed him my artwork and told him I wanted to write a superhero comic." The journalist could have sent mom and son on their way. Instead, he talked to the editor, who let the ten-year-old draw a full-page superhero strip, *Mr. Muscle,* for the paper's weekly insert.

The job taught Jones how to tell a story with words and images and how to meet a deadline, even if he did cut it close a few times. *Mr. Muscle* ended after fifty-one weeks. A short run but long enough to persuade Jones to stick with his art.

Kaercher, Jones's future collaborator, grew up in the Twin Cities dreaming of computers. Her dad bought her computers but drew the line at gaming software. If she wanted games, she would have to design them herself. She did. She developed a crude *Star Wars* game, in which fighter pilots attacked enemies with a hail of commas.

Kaercher's savvy led to jobs in website development, useful for paying tuition at the University of Minnesota. And quite unexpectedly, her skills also laid a foundation for her later work in comics.

By 2003, the creator of *Mr. Muscle* had worked his way into mainstream comics. Jones slipped into a contract job at DC Comics and then built on the opportunity. He had also met Kaercher through a shared interest in science fiction and fantasy conventions.

At yet another science fiction convention, Jones encountered Kovalic, a transplanted Brit living in Madison, Wisconsin. Kovalic was a game designer and comic book writer and artist. Jones approached Kovalic and somewhat offhandedly suggested, "If you ever want to work on something together—a superhero parody or something—just let me know."

Two weeks later, Kovalic phoned. "I've got an idea," he told Jones.

The idea was *Dr. Blink*. Originally, Jones penciled, inked, lettered, and colored Kovalic's scripts. Then Jones got one of those calls that every comic book artist dreams of: DC wanted him to pencil their new Batman series, *Batman Strikes!* Great. But that meant he had less time for *Dr. Blink*. Kaercher was summoned into the fold.

"Artists used to letter and color comics by hand. Now a lot of them use computers," says Kaercher, giving a shorthand explanation for why someone like her—a self-described computer geek—could find work in comics. These days, cartoonists scan original pencil drawings into computers and use programs like Adobe Illustrator and Photoshop to finish the pages.

Kaercher's lettering and coloring work on *Dr. Blink* led to more jobs. "In comics, people come in wanting to pencil or write. Those are the big jobs everyone wants," she says. "Very few come in saying, 'I want to be a letterer or a colorist.'" Kaercher colored *Femme Noir* for writer Christopher Mills and penciller Joe Staton. Capstone Press, a Minnesota textbook publisher, also hired her to work on their nonfiction graphic history series.

In 2007, Kovalic, Jones, and Kaercher collected their work on *Dr. Blink* in the trade paperback *Id. Ego. SUPEREGO! Dr. Blink* came about because Jones made an offhand comment to Kovalic. Kaercher entered into the picture through a contact. The series evolved. The collaborators finished the series, wrapped up, then moved on to other projects that cropped up, expectedly or unexpectedly. Hardly a career trajectory that would pass muster with a high school guidance counselor. But it worked for them.

"You get asked, 'How do you break into the comics industry?'" says Jones, who had his break at ten. "Really, there's no consistent way to break in. What happens is you get your foot in the door somewhere, then all these weird connections start to happen. A writer you know gets a job and asks to work with you. A publisher remembers your name. One project leads to another. It's different for everybody." ■

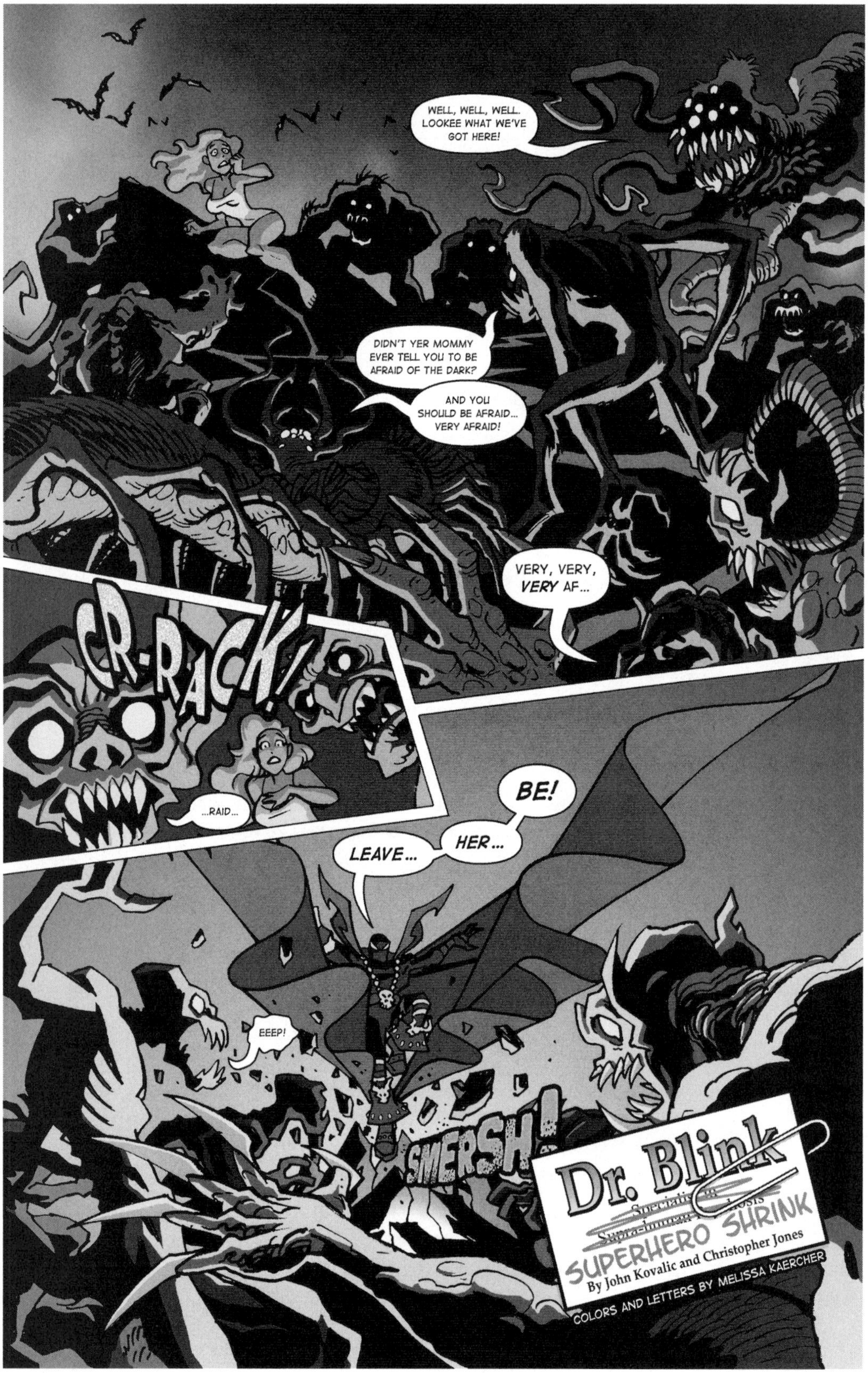
WELL, WELL, WELL. LOOKEE WHAT WE'VE GOT HERE!
DIDN'T YER MOMMY EVER TELL YOU TO BE AFRAID OF THE DARK?
AND YOU SHOULD BE AFRAID... VERY AFRAID!
VERY, VERY, *VERY* AF...
CR-RACK!
...RAID...
LEAVE...
HER...
BE!
EEEP!
SMERSH!
Dr. Blink
SUPERHERO SHRINK
By John Kovalic and Christopher Jones
COLORS AND LETTERS BY MELISSA KAERCHER

Dr. Blink: Superhero Shrink No. 3. Script by John Kovalic; line art by Christopher Jones; colors and letters by Melissa Kaercher. © 2006 Dork Storm Press, John Kovalic, Christopher Jones, and Melissa Kaercher

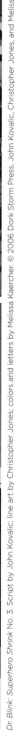

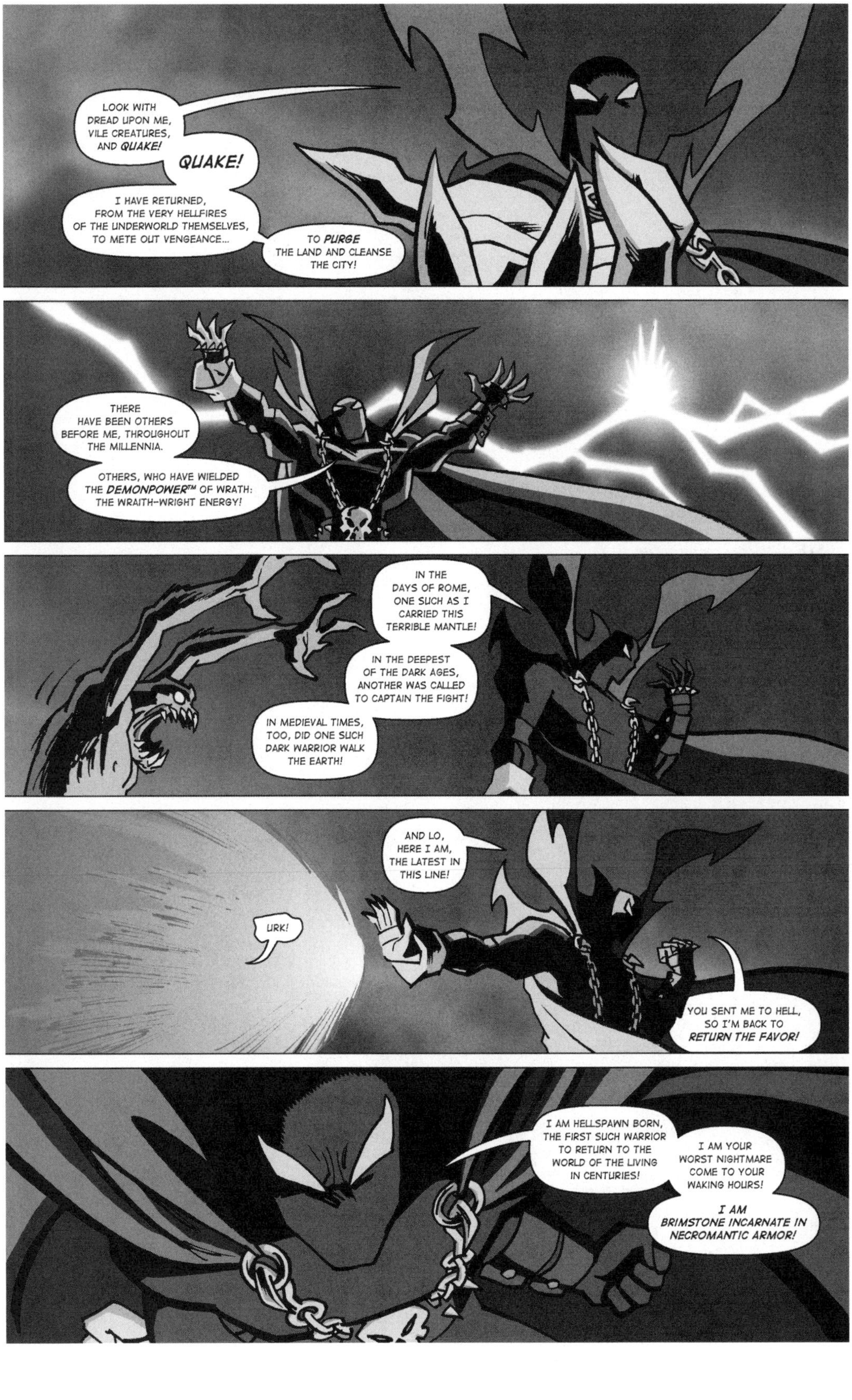
LOOK WITH DREAD UPON ME, VILE CREATURES, AND *QUAKE!*
QUAKE!
I HAVE RETURNED, FROM THE VERY HELLFIRES OF THE UNDERWORLD THEMSELVES, TO METE OUT VENGEANCE...
TO *PURGE* THE LAND AND CLEANSE THE CITY!
THERE HAVE BEEN OTHERS BEFORE ME, THROUGHOUT THE MILLENNIA.
OTHERS, WHO HAVE WIELDED THE *DEMONPOWER™* OF WRATH: THE WRAITH-WRIGHT ENERGY!
IN THE DAYS OF ROME, ONE SUCH AS I CARRIED THIS TERRIBLE MANTLE!
IN THE DEEPEST OF THE DARK AGES, ANOTHER WAS CALLED TO CAPTAIN THE FIGHT!
IN MEDIEVAL TIMES, TOO, DID ONE SUCH DARK WARRIOR WALK THE EARTH!
AND LO, HERE I AM, THE LATEST IN THIS LINE!
URK!
YOU SENT ME TO HELL, SO I'M BACK TO *RETURN THE FAVOR!*
I AM HELLSPAWN BORN, THE FIRST SUCH WARRIOR TO RETURN TO THE WORLD OF THE LIVING IN CENTURIES!
I AM YOUR WORST NIGHTMARE COME TO YOUR WAKING HOURS!
I AM BRIMSTONE INCARNATE IN NECROMANTIC ARMOR!

Dr. Blink: Superhero Shrink No. 3. Script by John Kovalic; line art by Christopher Jones; colors and letters by Melissa Kaercher. © 2006 Dork Storm Press, John Kovalic, Christopher Jones, and Melissa Kaercher

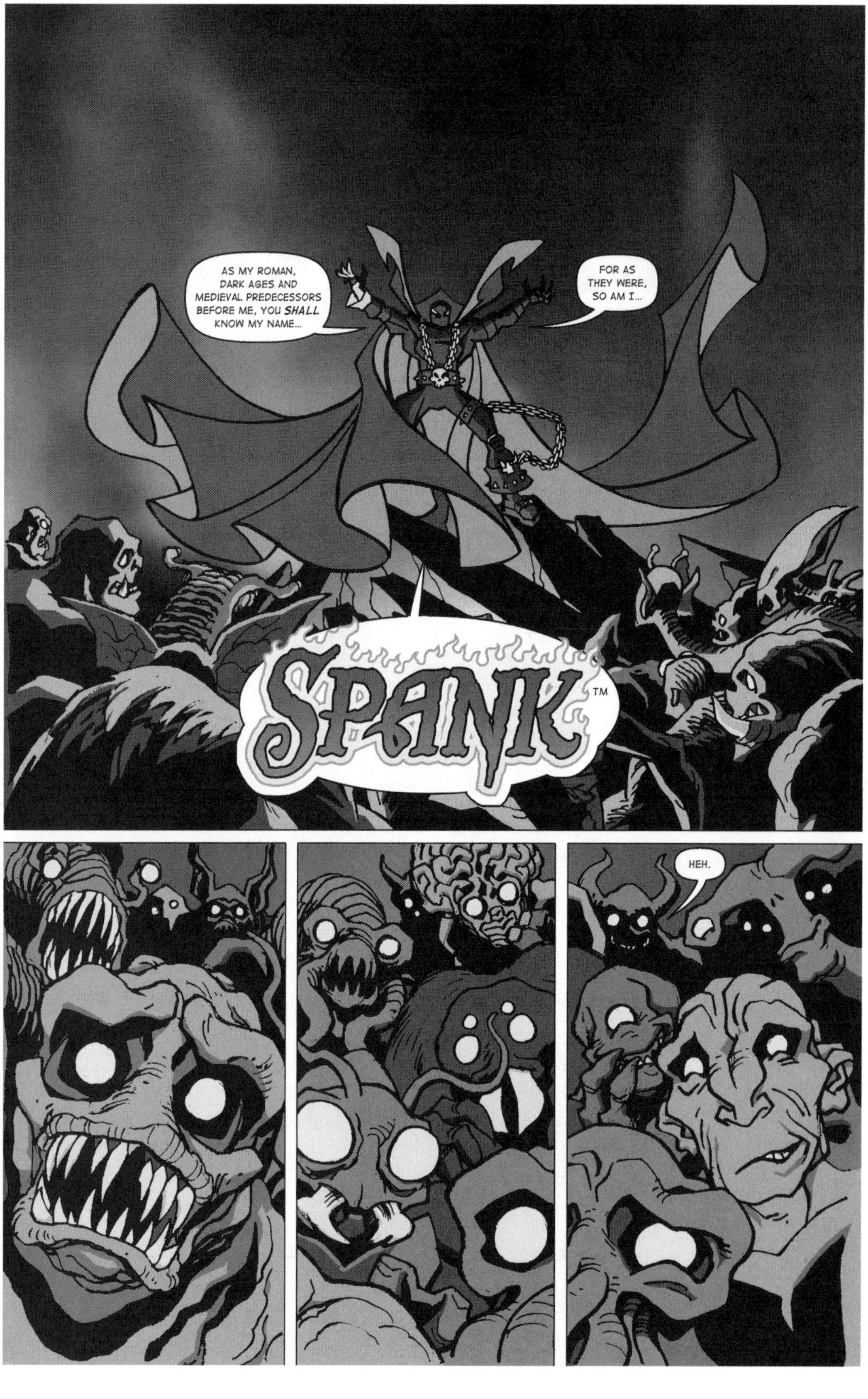
AS MY ROMAN, DARK AGES AND MEDIEVAL PREDECESSORS BEFORE ME, YOU *SHALL* KNOW MY NAME...
FOR AS THEY WERE, SO AM I...
SPANK™
HEH.

Dr. Blink: Superhero Shrink No. 3. Script by John Kovalic; line art by Christopher Jones; colors and letters by Melissa Kaercher. © 2006 Dork Storm Press, John Kovalic, Christopher Jones, and Melissa Kaercher

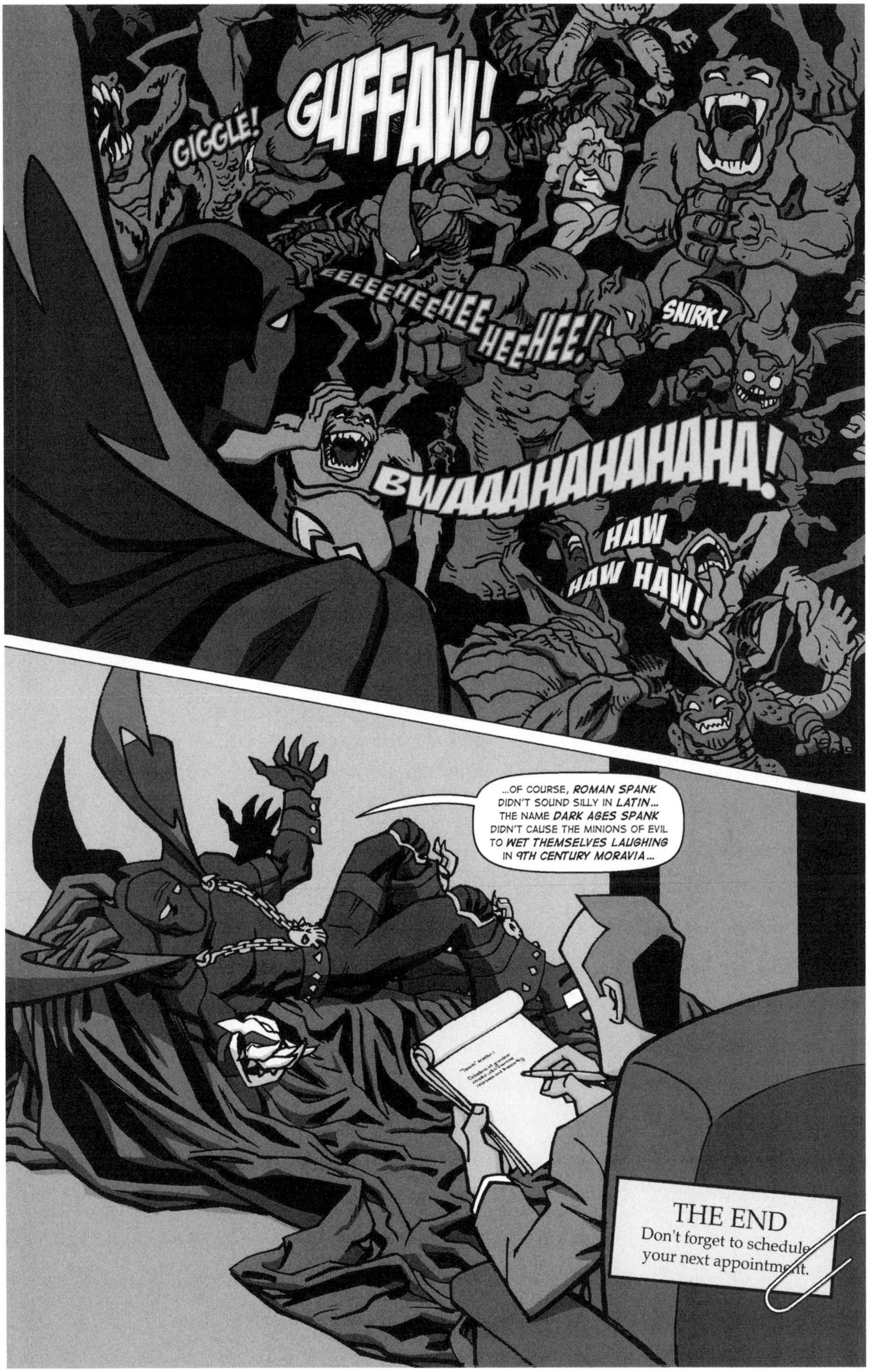
GIGGLE!
GUFFAW!
EEEEEHEEHEE HEEHEE!
SNIRK!
BWAAAHAHAHAHA!
HAW HAW HAW!
...OF COURSE, ROMAN SPANK DIDN'T SOUND SILLY IN LATIN... THE NAME DARK AGES SPANK DIDN'T CAUSE THE MINIONS OF EVIL TO WET THEMSELVES LAUGHING IN 9TH CENTURY MORAVIA...
THE END
Don't forget to schedule your next appointment.

Dr. Blink: Superhero Shrink No. 3. Script by John Kovalic; line art by Christopher Jones; colors and letters by Melissa Kaercher. © 2006 Dork Storm Press, John Kovalic, Christopher Jones, and Melissa Kaercher

Barbara Schulz can't tell you the number of times people have asked, "Are you related to Charles Schulz?" Yes, she and the creator of "Peanuts" share a last name, Minnesota, and an interest in comics. But, no, they are not related.

It's hard to avoid the Charles Schulz reference when you're a comic art instructor at the Minneapolis College of Art and Design, as Barb Schulz is. Or if you number among the millions who grew up reading "Peanuts" and now find yourself employing the strip as a common reference point. *Looks like Pigpen cleaned this house. Good grief.*

Barb harbors a special affinity for Snoopy, who began his cartoon life like any old dog. He caught balls, chased after Charlie Brown, and stole sweets. If he talked at all, he barked. But gradually, as the strip matured, thought balloons began to puff over Snoopy's head. The beagle became self-aware. He had opinions, bore grudges, and, like self-aware mutts everywhere, wool-gathered. Snoopy was at his dreamiest when atop his dog house, a type-writer before him, cranking out the next great American novel.

"Snoopy always seemed to begin his books with something like, 'It was a dark and stormy night and a shot rang out,'" says Barb. "I told myself that one of these days I was going to use that line in a comic."

Barbara Schulz was born in Superior, Wisconsin, the city that with Duluth, Minnesota, constitutes the Twin Ports on Lake Superior. Schulz's entry into comics came, as is so often the case, through older brothers. She had three of them, "so comic books were everywhere. They'd bring home horror and science fiction comics. There was always something to read on my brothers' floors," she says. The oldest brother, top dog in the sibling hierarchy,

THE OLDEST BROTHER, TOP DOG IN THE SIBLING HIERARCHY, SEALED HIS COMICS IN A LOCKED CLOSET.

sealed his comics in a locked closet. "There's no greater challenge for a five-year-old than to get into a locked closet." Schulz and her two brothers got around the lock by taking the door off its hinges.

As a teenager in the 1980s, Schulz took a job at Collector's Connection in Duluth. She wanted to be a cartoonist, and what better way to focus on the craft and meet local craftspeople than to work at a comic book store? Schulz got to know all the comic book store stereotypes. The investor-collectors who finger every issue looking for the Holy Grail of comics. The connoisseurs who are able to list every writer-artist team ever attached to *Iron Man*. And the practitioners, the true-blue comic book professionals. This was the category Schulz favored.

Schulz's boss introduced her to Peter Gross, a Collector's Connection regular and a comic book artist. "I was lucky to meet somebody in Duluth who actually wanted to do comics," she says. Duluth had an arty reputation, but the artists tended to flock to the fine arts. Gross was in his twenties and self-publishing a black-and-white comic. "Peter hired me to help with the edits. At first I was only working for him in an office capacity, but that led to me working on the actual art."

Gross's and Schulz's creative paths continued to intersect. When Gross found work at Marvel and DC Comics/Vertigo, he brought in Schulz to do fill-ins on backgrounds and to ink. In the late 1990s, both artists were among the original instructors hired to build the comic art program at the Minneapolis College of Art and Design. Schulz continues to teach at MCAD and has been instrumental in bringing in Minnesota's cartooning talent (Terry Beatty, Zak Sally, and Vincent Stall) as instructors.

The age-old saw of art professors is that they never have enough time for their own work. There are always more papers to grade and more portfolios to critique. Schulz saw her artistic goals getting shoved aside by teaching duties. So, she took a tip from ceramics artists.

"Summer is the busy season for them. That's when they're driving to art festivals and selling pots," she explains. But they need to throw pots in order to sell them. They take care of that in the winter, their off season. "I do the same thing with my comics. I ink really well during the school year. But the big-brain work, the layouts and stories, I save for summer when I don't have classes."

Schulz has inked a number of comic book titles—*The Mask: The Hunt for Green October, From Heaven to Hell, Micronauts,* and *Hercules: The Twelve Labors*—and penciled *G.I. Joe: Battle Files.* Her minicomics come out in creative spurts. *Groundhog's Day* was inspired by a friend. Schulz began the mini in 1999 but set it aside, only returning to it in 2008 when she needed something for a comic art show at the Minnesota Museum of American Art in St. Paul.

Lately, she has funneled her creative energies into *Hitchhiker Vinaigrettes,* a coming-of-age narrative told through interconnected sketches. Then there's that Snoopy story that has been dogging her for years. In 2009, Schulz finally rolled up her sleeves and laid down a mini that offers a conspiratorial wink at her inadvertent namesake, Charles Schulz.

The Dark and Stormy Night derives its title from Snoopy's failed attempts at literary bestsellerdom. But, really, the Schulz comparison ends there. It's hard to imagine a "Peanuts" strip that encompasses wind-lashed palms, a shadowy rendezvous, and a dead body on the floor.

If ill health hadn't intervened, Charles Schulz would have been drawing till the day he died. That's how he wanted it. Barb Schulz understands his zeal. "When you think about it, I teach comics. I research comics. I draw comics," she says. "But I never get tired of comics." ∎

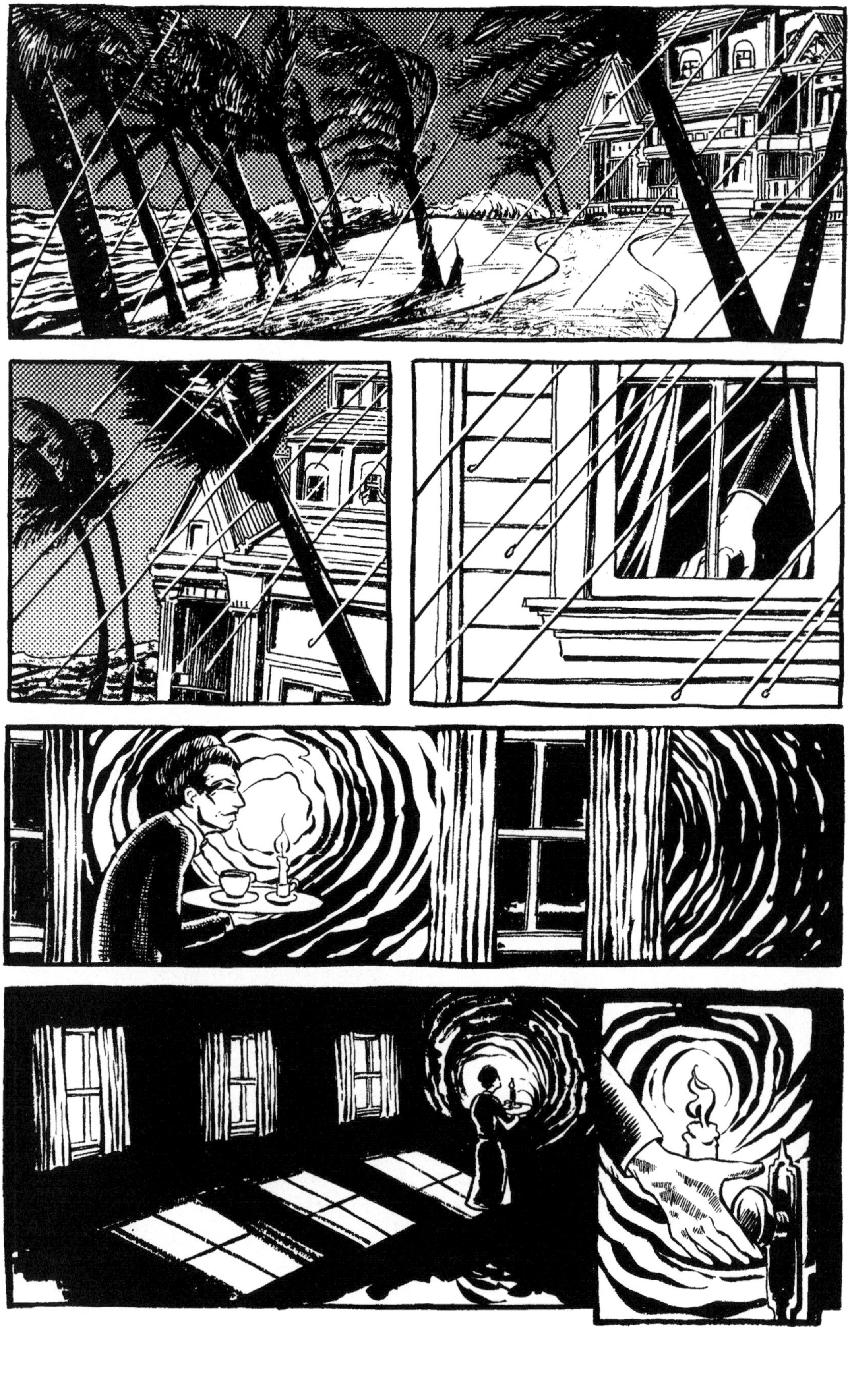

"Dark and Stormy Night" by Barbara Schulz. © 2009 Barbara Schulz

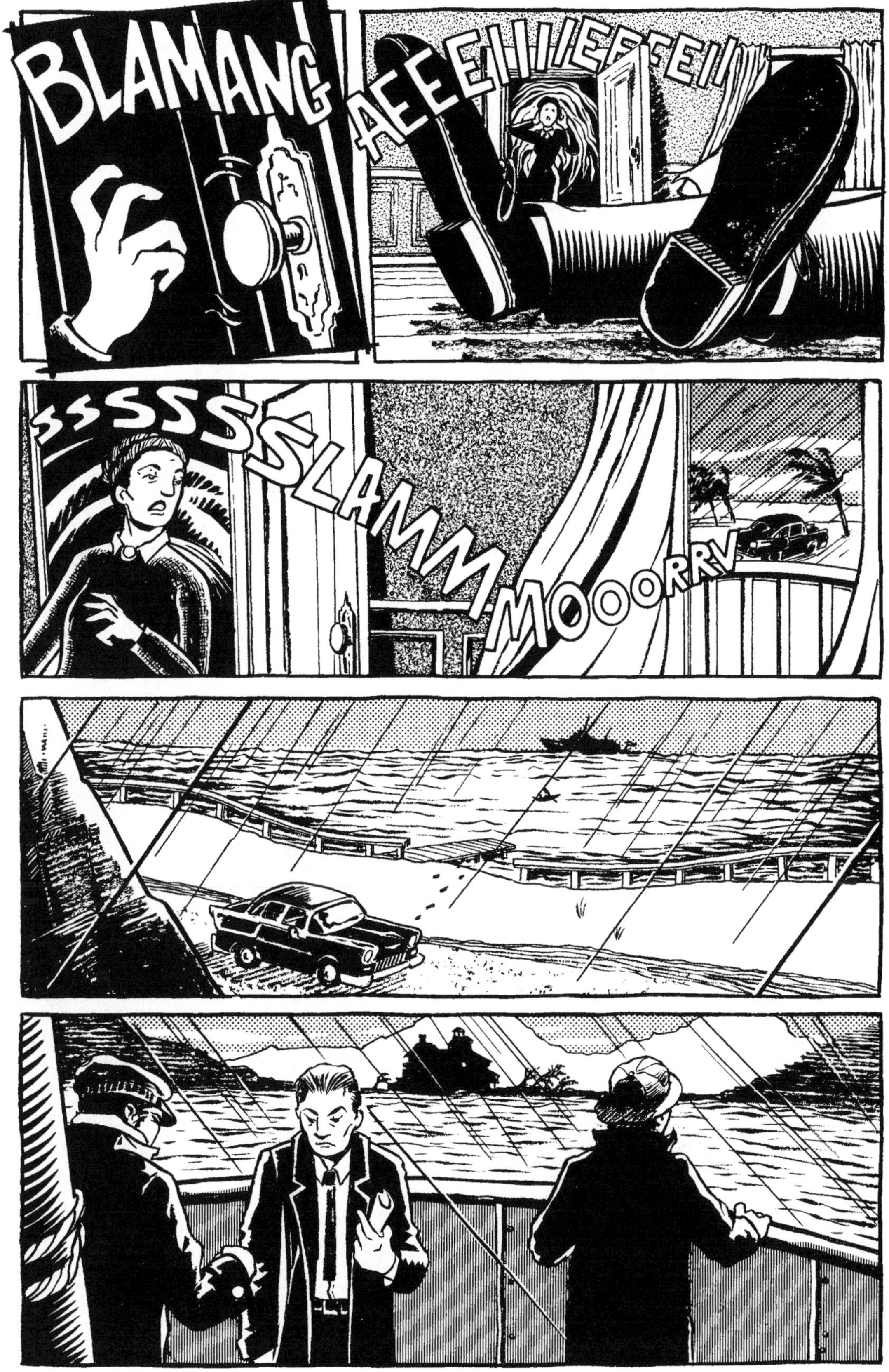
BLAMANG
AEEEIIIIEEEEII
SSSSSSLAMMMOOORRV

SUPERHEROES, STRIP ARTISTS, & TALKING ANIMALS

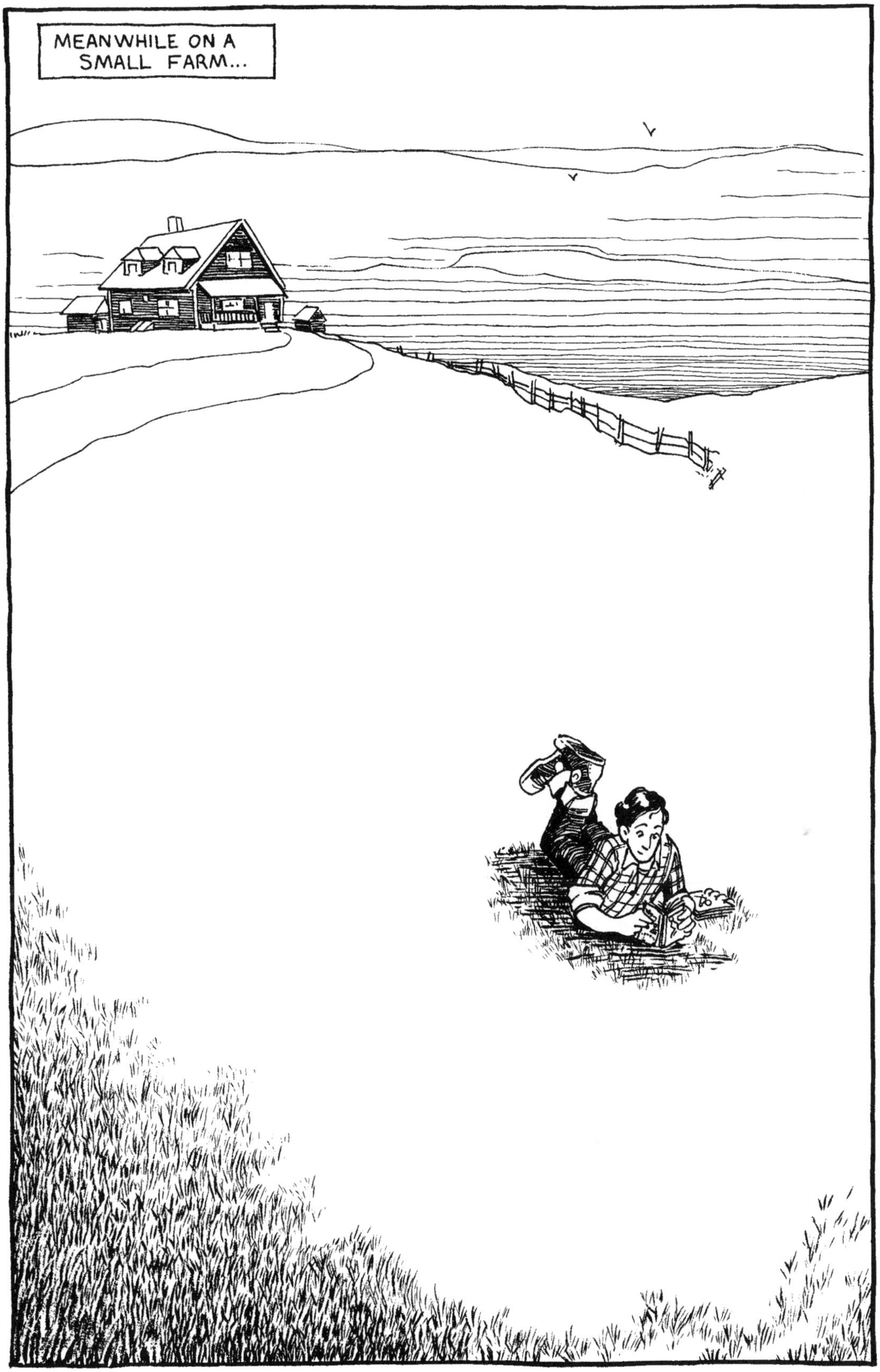
MEANWHILE ON A SMALL FARM...

ZAK SALLY

Zak Sally leases a studio space in an old warehouse in Northeast Minneapolis. Several decades ago this sprawling complex of drafty rooms and uneven floors housed packing crates and rumbled with the traffic of forklifts and brawny men shouting orders. The building is now re-constituted as artist studios and commercial space, a sign of changing times in Northeast, where blue-collar manufacturing has gentrified to bohemian industry: illustration and animation firms, art crawls, and exhibition openings.

Sally has selected a basement studio, not for the moody lighting afforded by half-size windows or the background ambiance of furnaces, but for the solidity of the concrete floor. He owns a fifty-year-old printing press that might crash through less stable flooring. Besides being a cartoonist, Sally is also a publisher, the founder of La Mano, which has published three volumes of Sally's own *Recidivist* series and a collection by John Porcellino, creator of *King-Cat Comics,* called *Diary of a Mosquito Abatement Man.*

As he sits as his desk, Sally, nearing forty, slim, bespectacled, flips on a lamp that throws a circle of light around him and not much else. Behind him, a smaller room radiates a chalky glow. This is the art room, where Sally hangs his work in progress, page after page detailing the maunderings of Sammy the Mouse and his cohorts in binge drinking, H. G. Feekes and Puppy. Feekes is a duck. Puppy is a puppy.

"*Sammy the Mouse* is probably the only comic I've done since I was fourteen that's meant to be enjoyed," says Sally, the first to call his previous series, *Recidivist,* serious stuff. A recidivist is someone who chronically relapses, typically to a life of crime. The reader doesn't come away from *Recidivist* with warm fuzzies. The short graphic stories reveal an artist testing the language of comics—panel transitions, scene changes, angles, shots, the interplay of word and image—and its ability to communicate impressions and feelings.

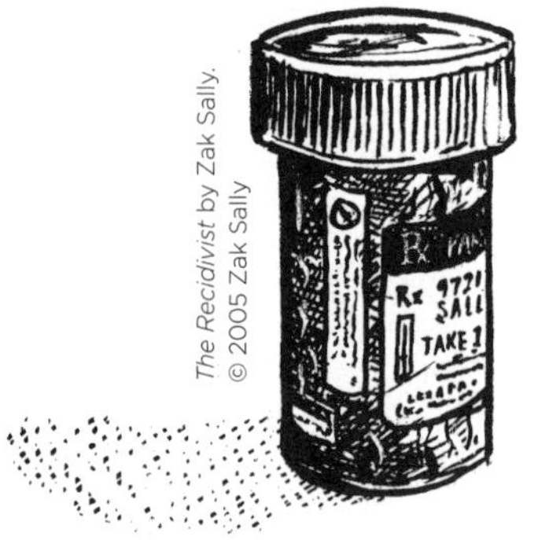
Rx
Rx 9771
SALL
TAKE 1

The Recidivist by Zak Sally.
© 2005 Zak Sally

In one story, a surgeon and team of nurses labor over the body of a patient who has misspent his life in substance abuse and hard living. "If this were an innocent animal," says the surgeon, "I would shed a tear and then put a bullet in its head." He then storms out, unwilling to squander his talents on a lost cause, someone who will hit the corner liquor store once he's released. The nurse continues the surgery alone, and in the convolutions of the patient's organs discovers a folded letter from the unconscious patient. In it he begs, "Please don't let me die."

"I'd worked myself into this lifelong pursuit of comics as a serious medium and as a serious means of expression," recounts Sally. "With the third issue of *Recidivist,* I felt I'd worked myself into a corner. I wanted to do a different kind of comic."

Sally thought hard about it and decided that comics were really good at telling stories, like cowboys around a campfire, or coeds in the student union boasting about last weekend. Free-flowing fiction. Sally's graphic novel *Sammy the Mouse,* the first volume of which was published by Fantagraphics in 2007, is 100-percent pure story-telling, no preservatives added. "*Sammy* is a talk-driven story that's practically slapstick," says the artist. Slapstick dosed with hallucinogens.

Sammy and friends exist in a world that is strangely subter-ranean. Bare bulbs light crooked walks, which are flanked by crooked buildings that cant drunkenly over streets. A giant beer bottle houses a liquor store and a giant baby encloses a bar. Sammy, Puppy, and Feekes stumble through this surreal world, driven by Feekes's desire to get tight.

The idea for *Sammy* came to Sally a decade ago "when I was drunk," says the cartoonist. That was during Sally's days as a bassist for the band Low. Low originated in Duluth, Minnesota, as did Sally, who was born there in 1971.

"My grandparents have these sixteen-millimeter films from when I was growing up. There's one of my sister's fifth birthday party. I was three. My sister gets these comic books for her birthday, and you see her put them aside. It was so creepy to see me in that film," says Sally, "because all of a sudden I'm like—you can just tell I'm not paying attention to anyone at the party anymore. All I can see are these comics. I head right for them."

When he was still a boy, Sally and his family moved to Bethesda, Mary-land. He spent hours at the local comics store, Big Planet Comics. "They had a back area for the dirty comics but also for those comics that didn't fit in with everything else," says Sally, referring to the alternative comics pro-duced by people like Bill Griffith, Gary Panter, and Harvey Pekar. "Basically, it was like if you went to the back area you were a porn hound or something."

Sally had heard about the Los Angeles brothers Gilbert and Jaime Her-nandez, whose series *Love and Rockets,* published by Fantagraphics, had rev-olutionized alternative comics. The Hernandez brothers' books were among those located in the back area, a section off-limits to teenaged Sally. But the guy at the counter knew him and let him through. Sally picked up issue No. 21 of *Love and Rockets* and the first issue of *Yummy Fur* by Chester Brown.

Reading those books, says Sally, "was like going to your first punk show. Everything I'd read before that was decimated."

After quitting the band, Sally settled in Minneapolis and devoted him-self to cartooning. He self-published *Recidivist,* then published *Sammy the Mouse,* volumes one and two, through the same publisher that had intro-duced him to the Hernandez brothers, Fantagraphics. If Sally needed further evidence that his life had come full circle, in 2008, he was asked to inter-view Jaime Hernandez for the annual Rain Taxi: Twin Cities Book Festival in Minneapolis. ∎

"BASICALLY, IT WAS LIKE IF YOU WENT TO THE BACK AREA YOU WERE A PORN HOUND OR SOMETHING."

Sammy the Mouse, Vol. 2 by Zak Sally. © 2008 Zak Sally.

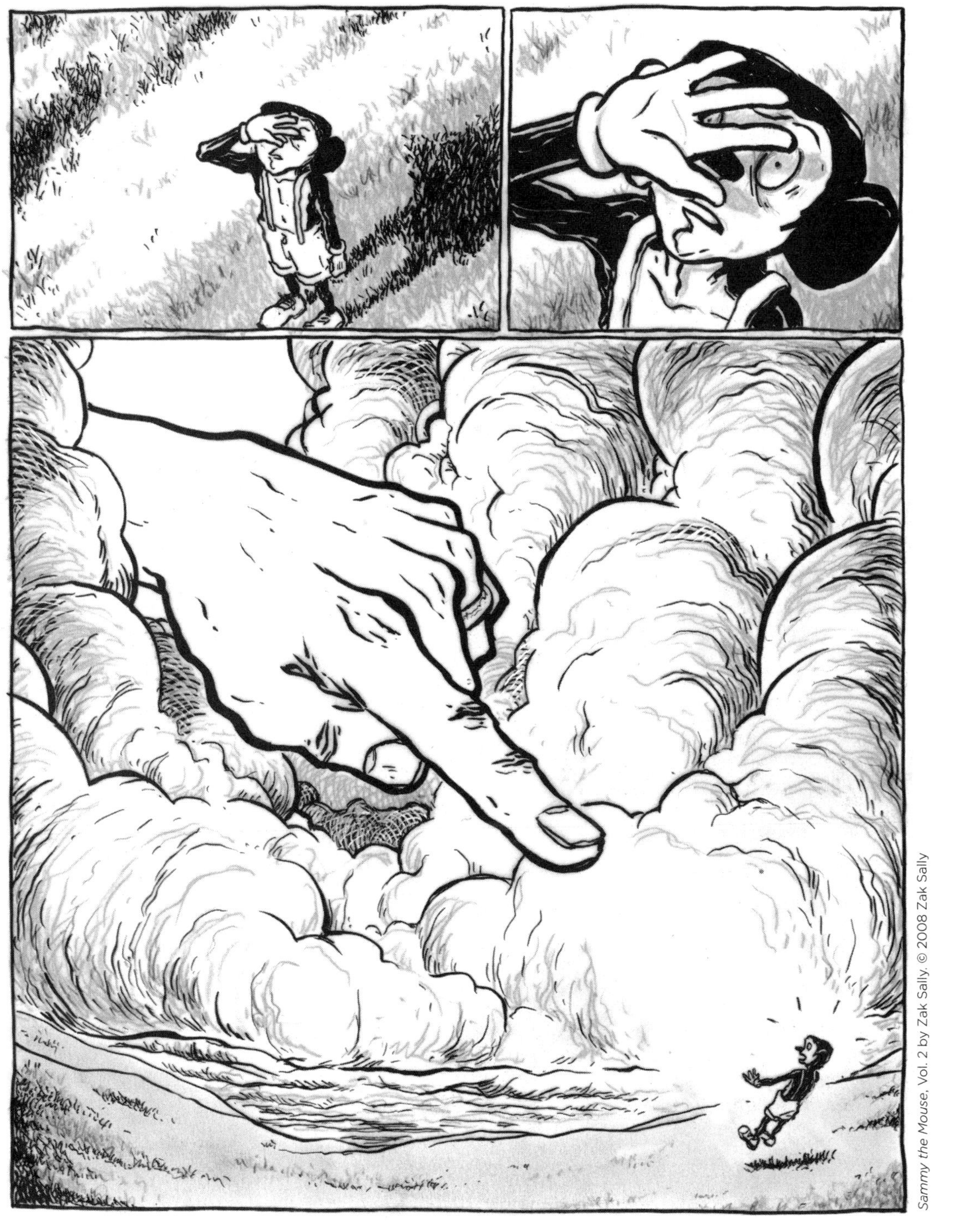

Sammy the Mouse, Vol. 2 by Zak Sally. © 2008 Zak Sally

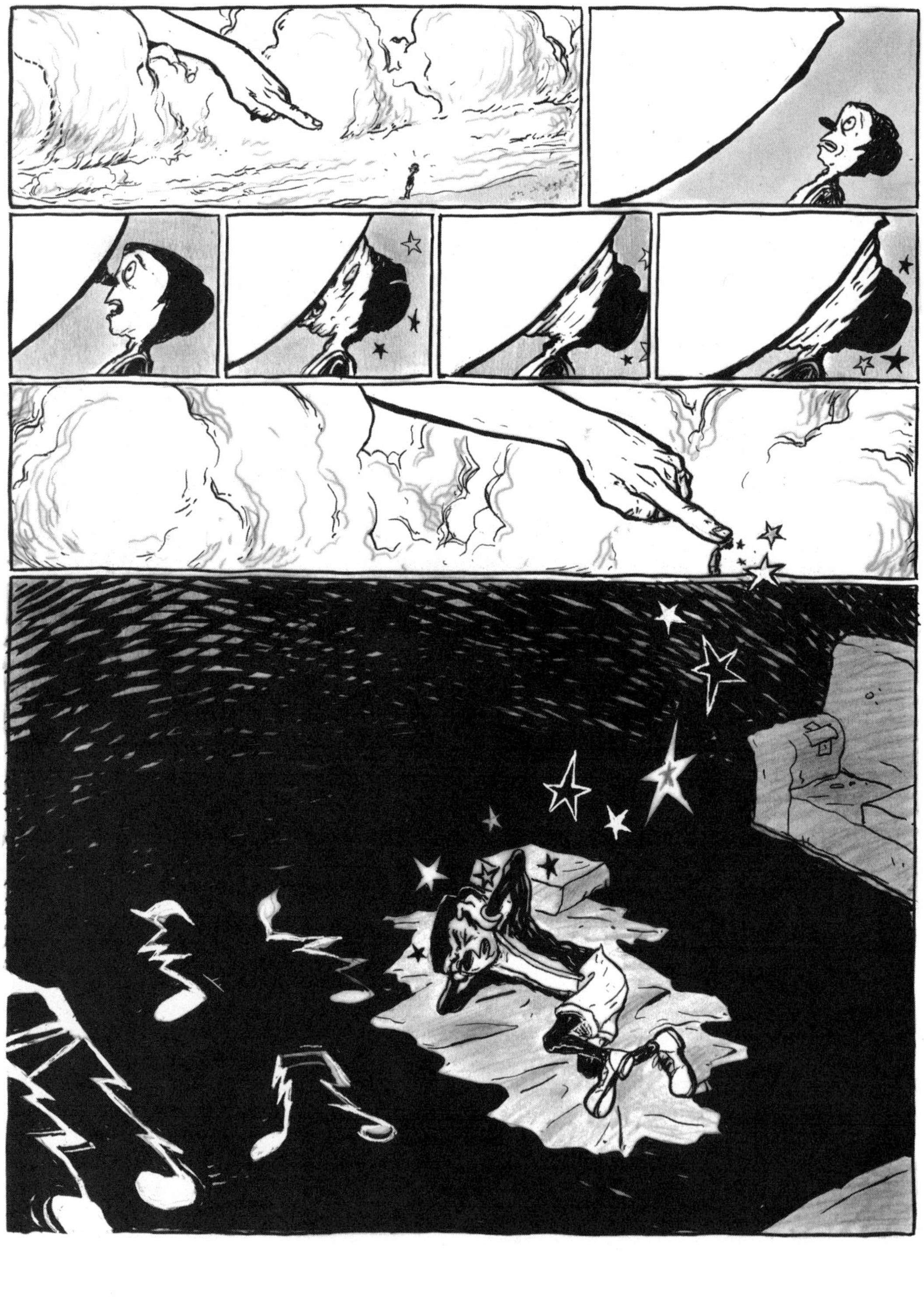

Sammy the Mouse, Vol. 2 by Zak Sally. © 2008 Zak Sally

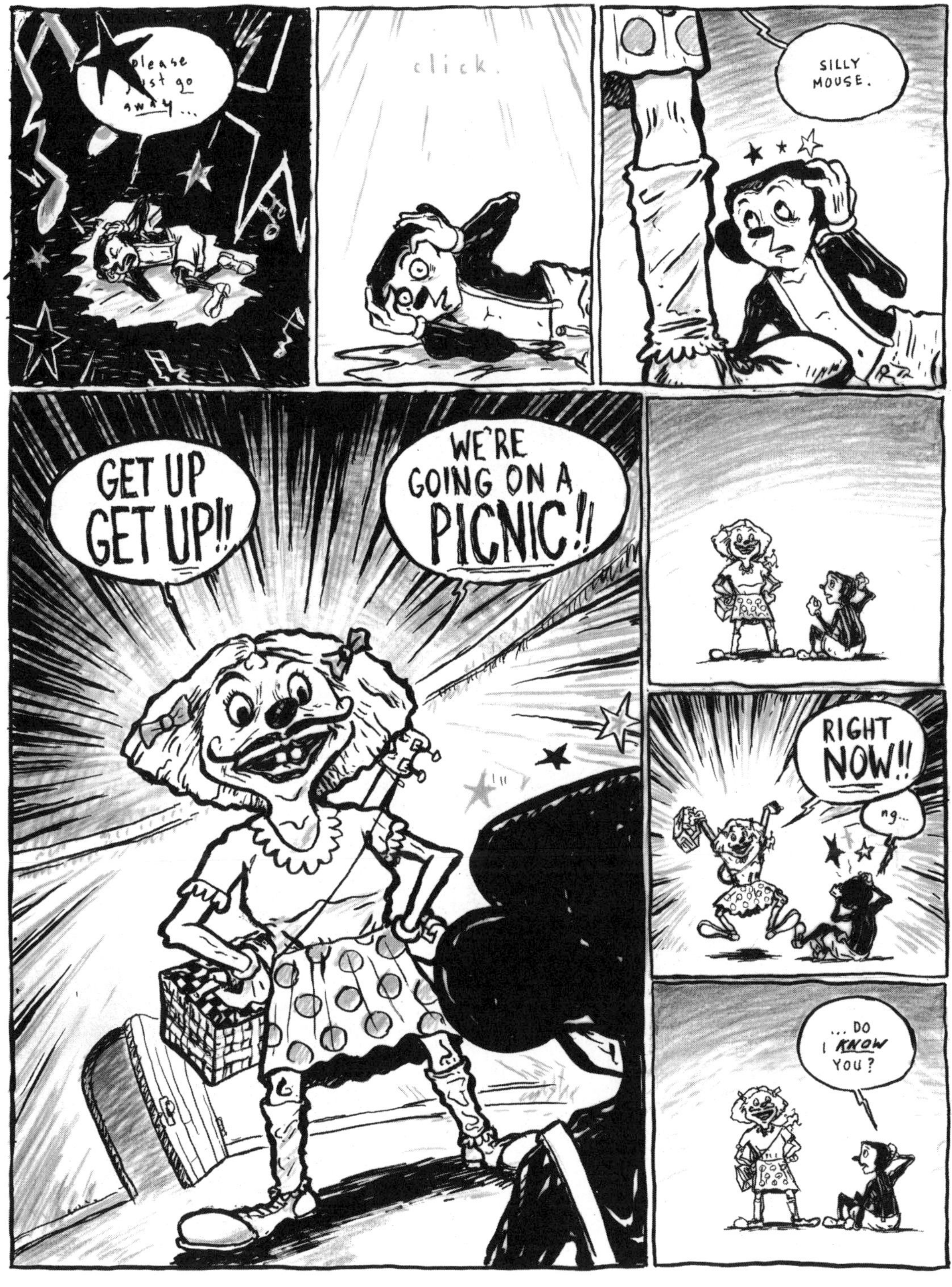
please just go away...
click.
SILLY MOUSE.
GET UP GET UP!!
WE'RE GOING ON A PICNIC!!
RIGHT NOW!!
ng...
...DO I KNOW YOU?

IS IT TIME TO KISS THIS GOODNIGHT
AND PUT IT TO BED?
ASK THE ANGELS. MAYBE THEY WILL KNOW.
TOO LATE.
WE'RE DONE HERE.
THE END.

The Recidivist by Zak Sally. © 2005 Zak Sally

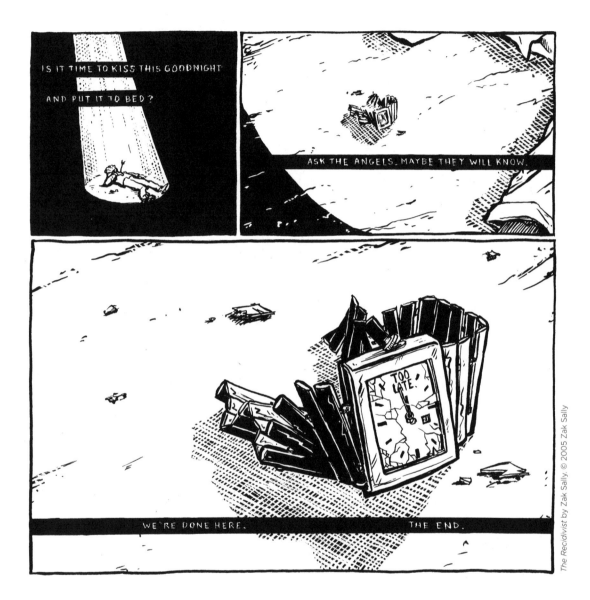

As a boy in the 1990s, Tim Sievert felt his world tilt. His hometown of Davenport, Iowa, was stable enough—not located over a fault line. That wasn't the cause of the disturbance. No, it was the comic books he had lugged home, *X-Men* and *Spider-Man,* whose over-the-top stories and adrenaline-charged art spilled out into the hazy afternoon, ramping up the color on everything and putting crazy notions in his head about radioactive spiders, mutants, and life-altering powers. School and homework just seemed so lame in comparison.

The Minneapolis College of Art and Design gave Sievert a place to try out his own superheroics, on paper at least. He muscled up some spandex-clad heroes and put them through their paces, doing whatever superheroes do when the artist drawing them is just learning his craft. Probably looking a little stiff and awkward as they soar to the rescue of the most recent target of supervillainy.

Sievert had decided he would devote himself to superhero comics. Then he met Vincent Stall, a Minneapolis comics artist and, at the time, MCAD professor. "Vince introduced me to the other side of comics," says Sievert of alternative comics. They offer an alternative to mainstream superhero comics, not just in style but in content. They can be absurdist fantasies, geek drama, memoir, anything.

Stall was Obi Wan leading his apprentice in the ways of the art form. Sievert was asked to trust his instincts, to find the stories that wanted to be told through him and that only he could tell. The plasticity of comics allows an artist to stretch the imagination. So, Stall urged, give the imagination some room.

Sievert had already developed a senior project and drawn a number of pages when his world shook again. But this time it was a major tremor. His mother died, and suddenly the project he had been working on no longer fit his experience.

"I was working on a story I didn't understand anymore," says Sievert. "So, I had to ask myself what kind of story did I understand well enough to tell? Well, I knew about someone dying. I could talk about that."

Sievert scrapped his senior project and started anew—the night before his last semester began. Students have a year to complete the senior project. Sievert finished *That Salty Air* in three and a half months.

That Salty Air is the story of Hugh, a fisherman, and his young wife, Maryanne, who lead an idyllic life by the sea. The sea is more than livelihood to Hugh; it's the benevolent force that molds his world. But that love turns to hatred when Hugh learns that his mother has drowned in the sea. How could the sea have turned against him? How could it have murdered? Wife, vocation, and future are cast aside as Hugh pursues his Ahab-like revenge.

"The last week of school I spent making photocopy versions of *That Salty Air* and sending it to Brett Warnock and Chris Staros at Top Shelf. I sent it expecting absolutely nothing," says Sievert, building up to the punch line. "A week and a half later, I get a call while I'm watching TV. 'Hi, this is Chris Staros from Top Shelf,' the person said. 'I liked your book. Can we talk about this?'"

When *That Salty Air* came out in 2008, Sievert blogged a lot and made the promotional rounds. He attended the local comic book conventions and did the usual stuff—circulated his name, autographed books, babysat.

Sometimes even a well-ordered convention can stray from the business at hand, as happened to Sievert and Brett Von Schlosser, his tablemate at FallCon. "Brett and I ended up babysitting these two kids," he says. "They were running around by themselves and ended up at our table. We were like, 'Why are you kids running around unchaperoned?' Their dad was off somewhere looking at comics. So, eventually we just said to the kids, 'Here, grab a chair and draw pictures. We'll sell them for you.'"

> "DRAWING COMICS IS HARD, FRUSTRATING WORK, BUT IT'S ALSO THE MOST GRATIFYING THING I'VE EVER EXPERIENCED."

After *That Salty Air* hit stores, Sievert took a break from comics. "But if you want to draw comics professionally, you have to get a book out every year," he says. "People take you more seriously when you have another book coming out. At a convention, the Top Shelf guys asked me, 'You got another book?' And I said, 'Maybe,' and they're like, 'Well, you better figure it out.'"

Sievert threw himself back into art with a series of webcomics for Top Shelf's online comics site, Top Shelf Comix. *The Intrepideers and the Brothers of Blood* is a comic fantasy in the mode of Dungeons and Dragons, based on Sievert's gaming group the Intrepideers.

"Drawing comics is hard, frustrating work," says Sievert. "But it's also the most gratifying thing I've ever experienced. When I finish a page of *The Intrepideers,* I tack it to my bulletin board, and I won't even go to bed. I'll sit there till two or three in the morning and just look at it." ■

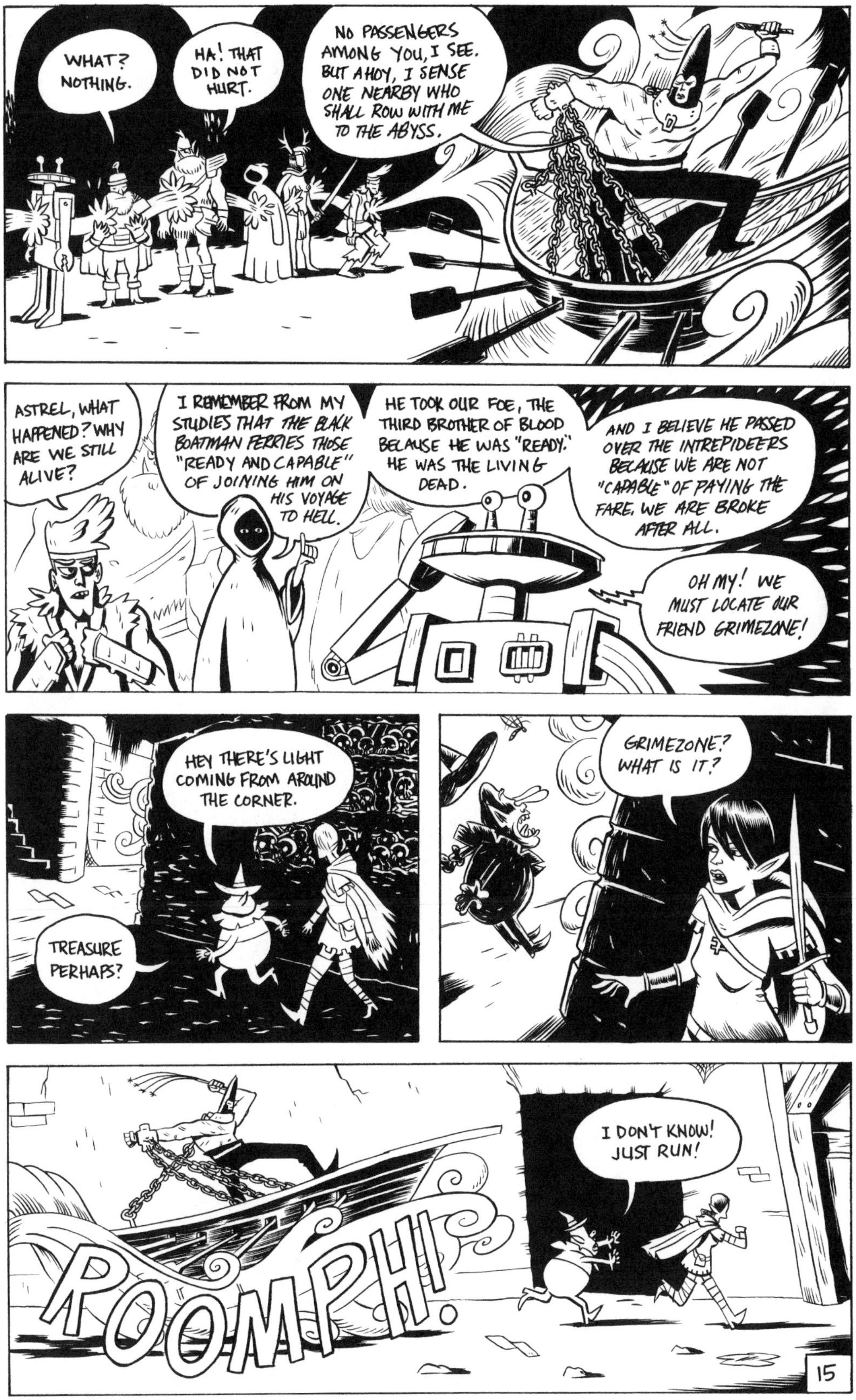
WHAT? NOTHING.
HA! THAT DID NOT HURT.
NO PASSENGERS AMONG YOU, I SEE. BUT AHOY, I SENSE ONE NEARBY WHO SHALL ROW WITH ME TO THE ABYSS.
ASTREL, WHAT HAPPENED? WHY ARE WE STILL ALIVE?
I REMEMBER FROM MY STUDIES THAT THE BLACK BOATMAN FERRIES THOSE "READY AND CAPABLE" OF JOINING HIM ON HIS VOYAGE TO HELL.
HE TOOK OUR FOE, THE THIRD BROTHER OF BLOOD BECAUSE HE WAS "READY." HE WAS THE LIVING DEAD.
AND I BELIEVE HE PASSED OVER THE INTREPIDEERS BECAUSE WE ARE NOT "CAPABLE" OF PAYING THE FARE. WE ARE BROKE AFTER ALL.
OH MY! WE MUST LOCATE OUR FRIEND GRIMEZONE!
HEY THERE'S LIGHT COMING FROM AROUND THE CORNER.
TREASURE PERHAPS?
GRIMEZONE? WHAT IS IT?
I DON'T KNOW! JUST RUN!
ROOMPH!
15

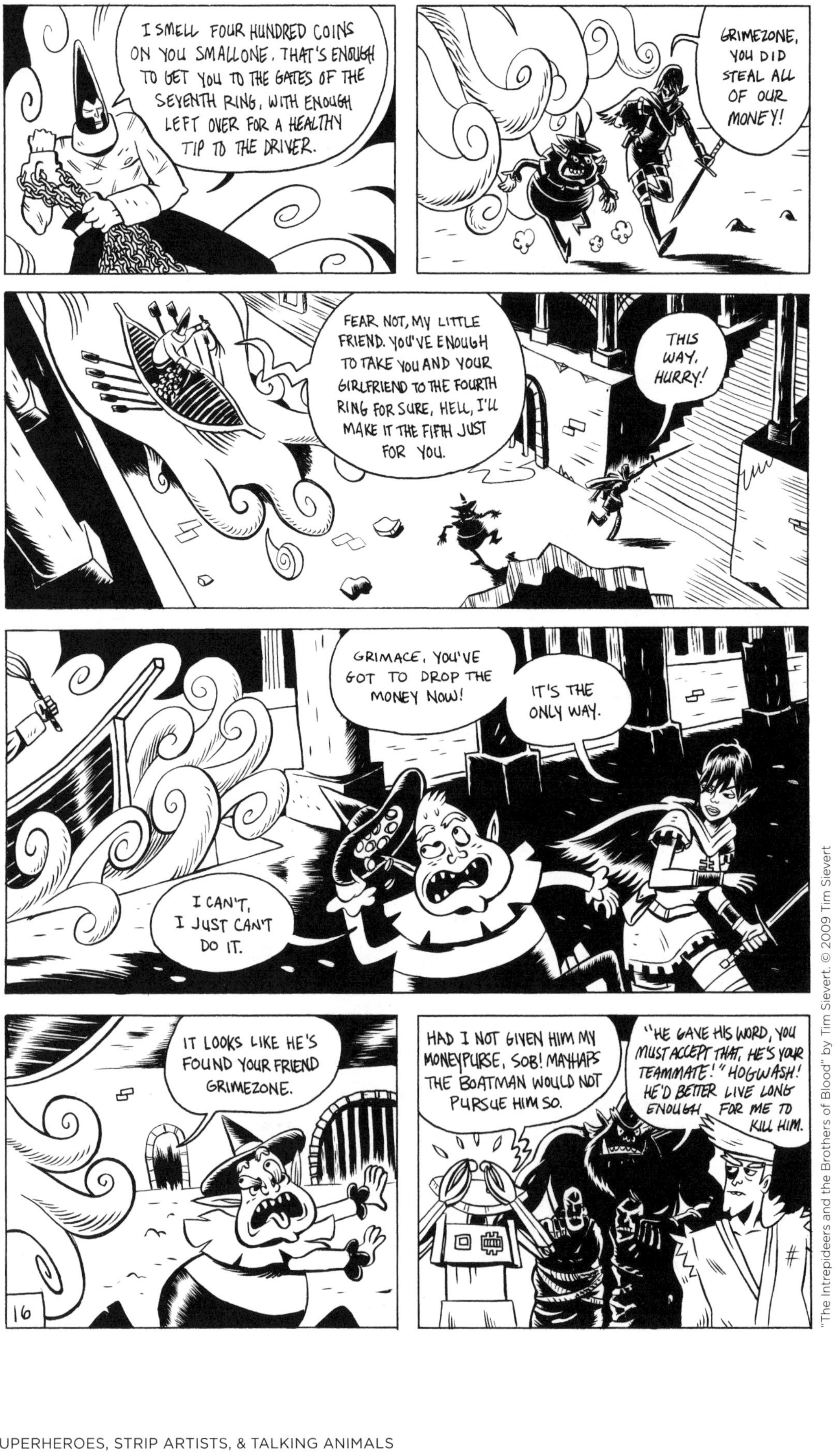
I SMELL FOUR HUNDRED COINS ON YOU SMALLONE. THAT'S ENOUGH TO GET YOU TO THE GATES OF THE SEVENTH RING, WITH ENOUGH LEFT OVER FOR A HEALTHY TIP TO THE DRIVER.
GRIMEZONE, YOU DID STEAL ALL OF OUR MONEY!
FEAR NOT, MY LITTLE FRIEND. YOU'VE ENOUGH TO TAKE YOU AND YOUR GIRLFRIEND TO THE FOURTH RING FOR SURE, HELL, I'LL MAKE IT THE FIFTH JUST FOR YOU.
THIS WAY. HURRY!
GRIMACE, YOU'VE GOT TO DROP THE MONEY NOW!
IT'S THE ONLY WAY.
I CAN'T, I JUST CAN'T DO IT.
IT LOOKS LIKE HE'S FOUND YOUR FRIEND GRIMEZONE.
16
HAD I NOT GIVEN HIM MY MONEYPURSE, SOB! MAYHAPS THE BOATMAN WOULD NOT PURSUE HIM SO.
"HE GAVE HIS WORD, YOU MUST ACCEPT THAT, HE'S YOUR TEAMMATE!" HOGWASH! HE'D BETTER LIVE LONG ENOUGH FOR ME TO KILL HIM.

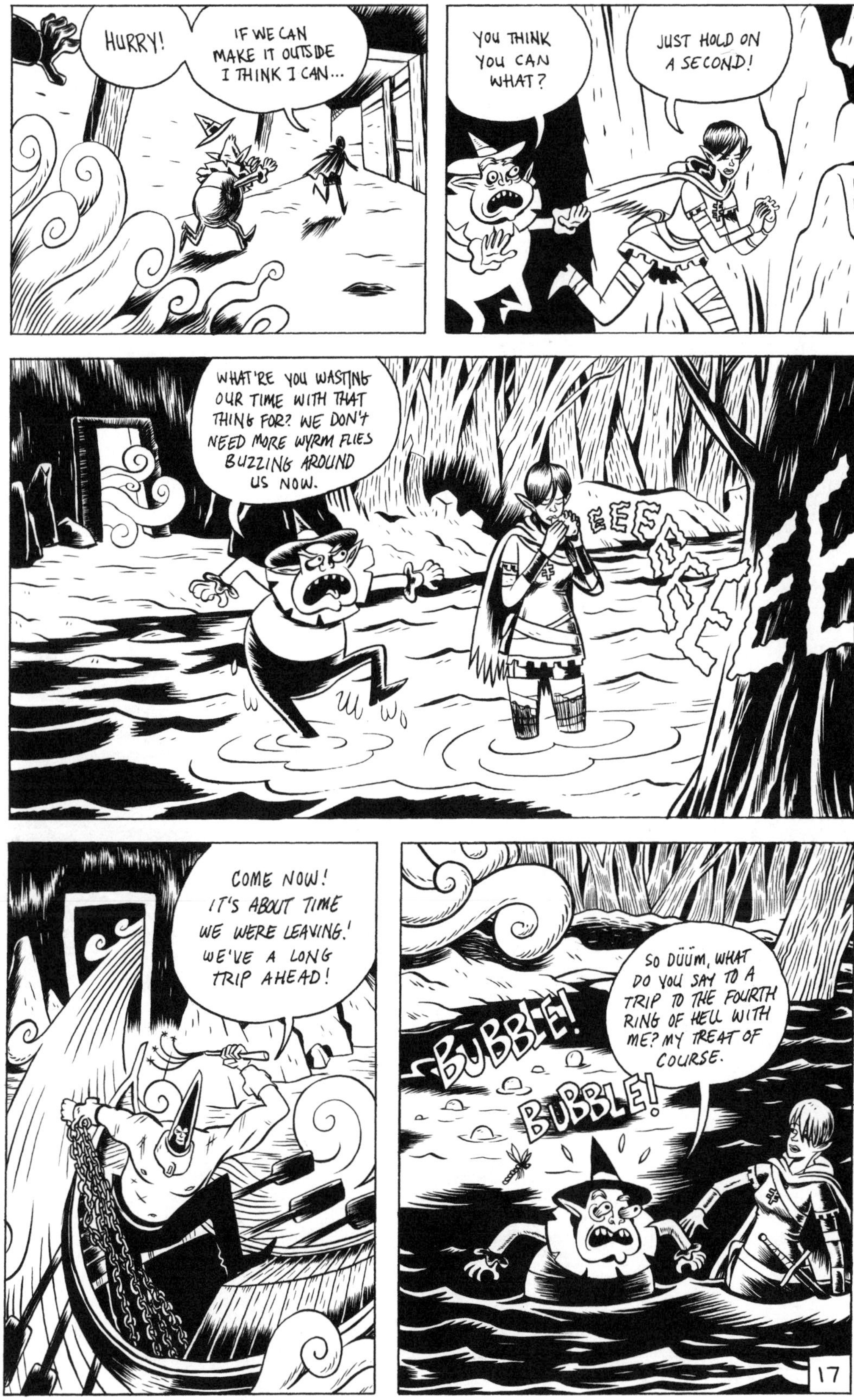
HURRY!
IF WE CAN MAKE IT OUTSIDE I THINK I CAN...
YOU THINK YOU CAN WHAT?
JUST HOLD ON A SECOND!
WHAT'RE YOU WASTING OUR TIME WITH THAT THING FOR? WE DON'T NEED MORE WYRM FLIES BUZZING AROUND US NOW.
COME NOW! IT'S ABOUT TIME WE WERE LEAVING! WE'VE A LONG TRIP AHEAD!
BUBBLE!
BUBBLE!
SO DÜÜM, WHAT DO YOU SAY TO A TRIP TO THE FOURTH RING OF HELL WITH ME? MY TREAT OF COURSE.
17

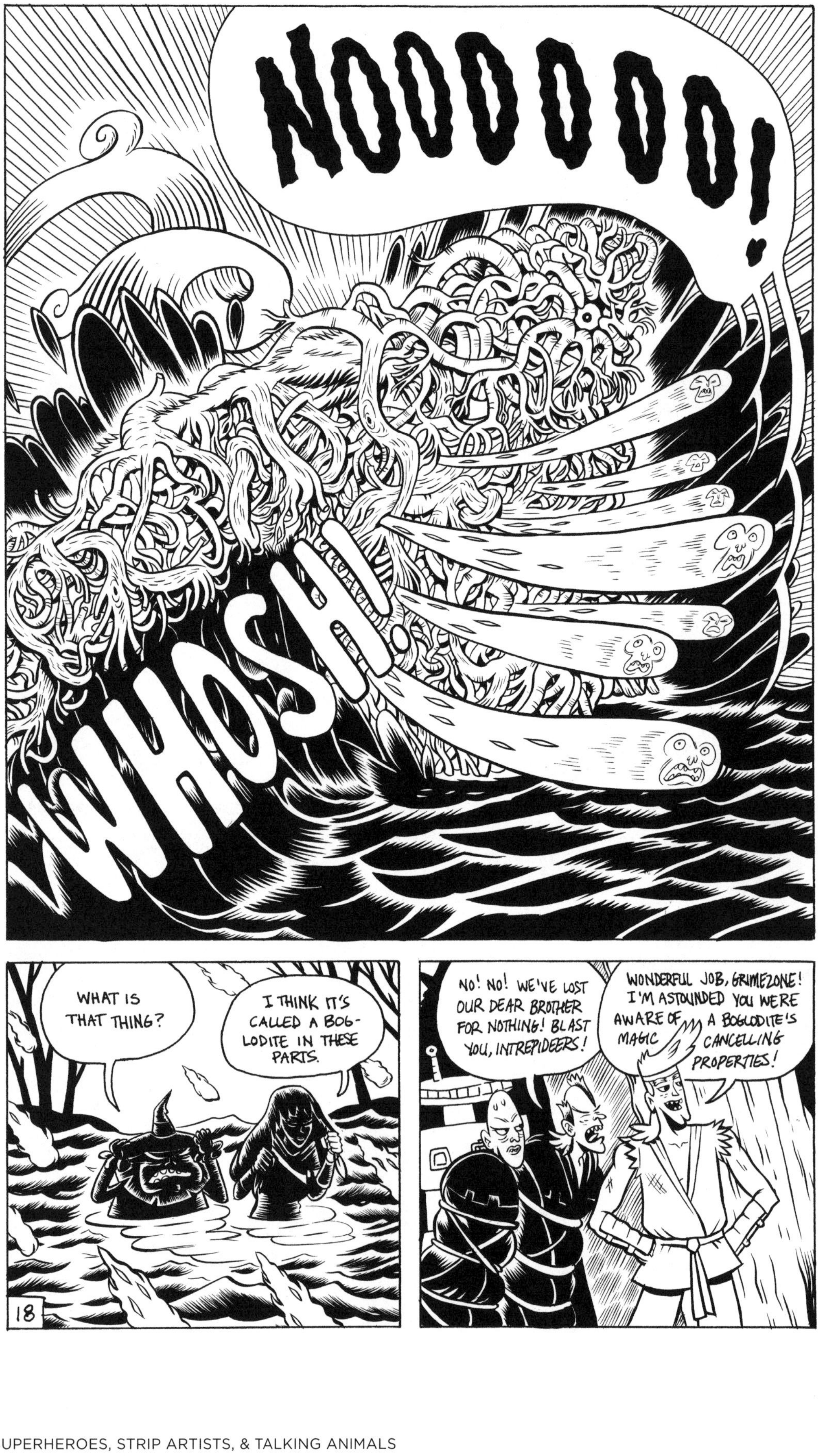
NOOOOOO!
WHOSH!
WHAT IS THAT THING?
I THINK IT'S CALLED A BOG-LODITE IN THESE PARTS.
18
NO! NO! WE'VE LOST OUR DEAR BROTHER FOR NOTHING! BLAST YOU, INTREPIDEERS!
WONDERFUL JOB, GRIMEZONE! I'M ASTOUNDED YOU WERE AWARE OF A BOGLODITE'S MAGIC CANCELLING PROPERTIES!

"The Intrepideers and the Brothers of Blood" by Tim Sievert. © 2009 Tim Sievert

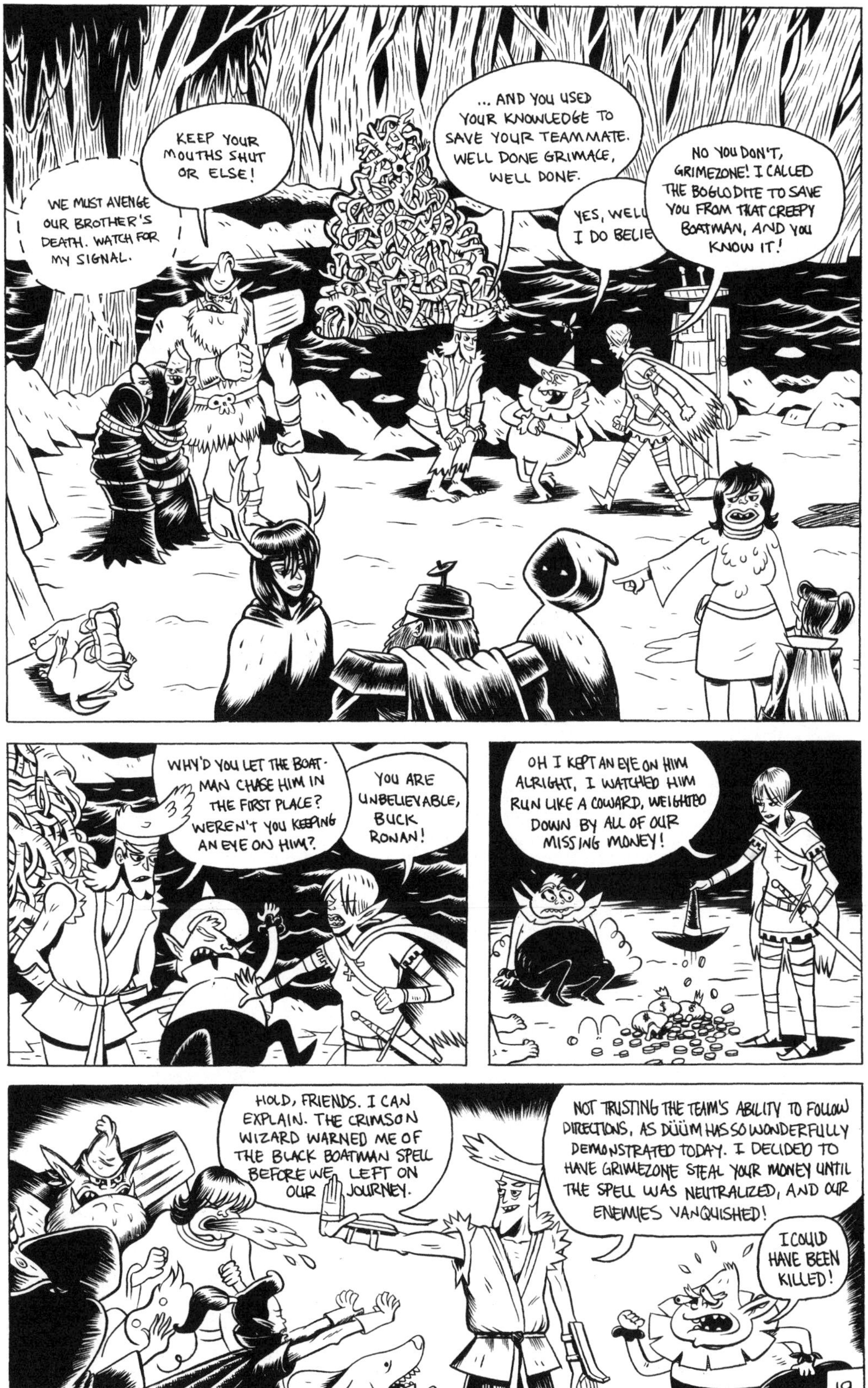
WE MUST AVENGE OUR BROTHER'S DEATH. WATCH FOR MY SIGNAL.
KEEP YOUR MOUTHS SHUT OR ELSE!
... AND YOU USED YOUR KNOWLEDGE TO SAVE YOUR TEAMMATE. WELL DONE GRIMACE, WELL DONE.
YES, WELL I DO BELIE
NO YOU DON'T, GRIMEZONE! I CALLED THE BOGLODITE TO SAVE YOU FROM THAT CREEPY BOATMAN, AND YOU KNOW IT!
WHY'D YOU LET THE BOAT-MAN CHASE HIM IN THE FIRST PLACE? WEREN'T YOU KEEPING AN EYE ON HIM?
YOU ARE UNBELIEVABLE, BUCK RONAN!
OH I KEPT AN EYE ON HIM ALRIGHT, I WATCHED HIM RUN LIKE A COWARD, WEIGHTED DOWN BY ALL OF OUR MISSING MONEY!
HOLD, FRIENDS. I CAN EXPLAIN. THE CRIMSON WIZARD WARNED ME OF THE BLACK BOATMAN SPELL BEFORE WE LEFT ON OUR JOURNEY.
NOT TRUSTING THE TEAM'S ABILITY TO FOLLOW DIRECTIONS, AS DÜÜM HAS SO WONDERFULLY DEMONSTRATED TODAY. I DECIDED TO HAVE GRIMEZONE STEAL YOUR MONEY UNTIL THE SPELL WAS NEUTRALIZED, AND OUR ENEMIES VANQUISHED!
I COULD HAVE BEEN KILLED!
19

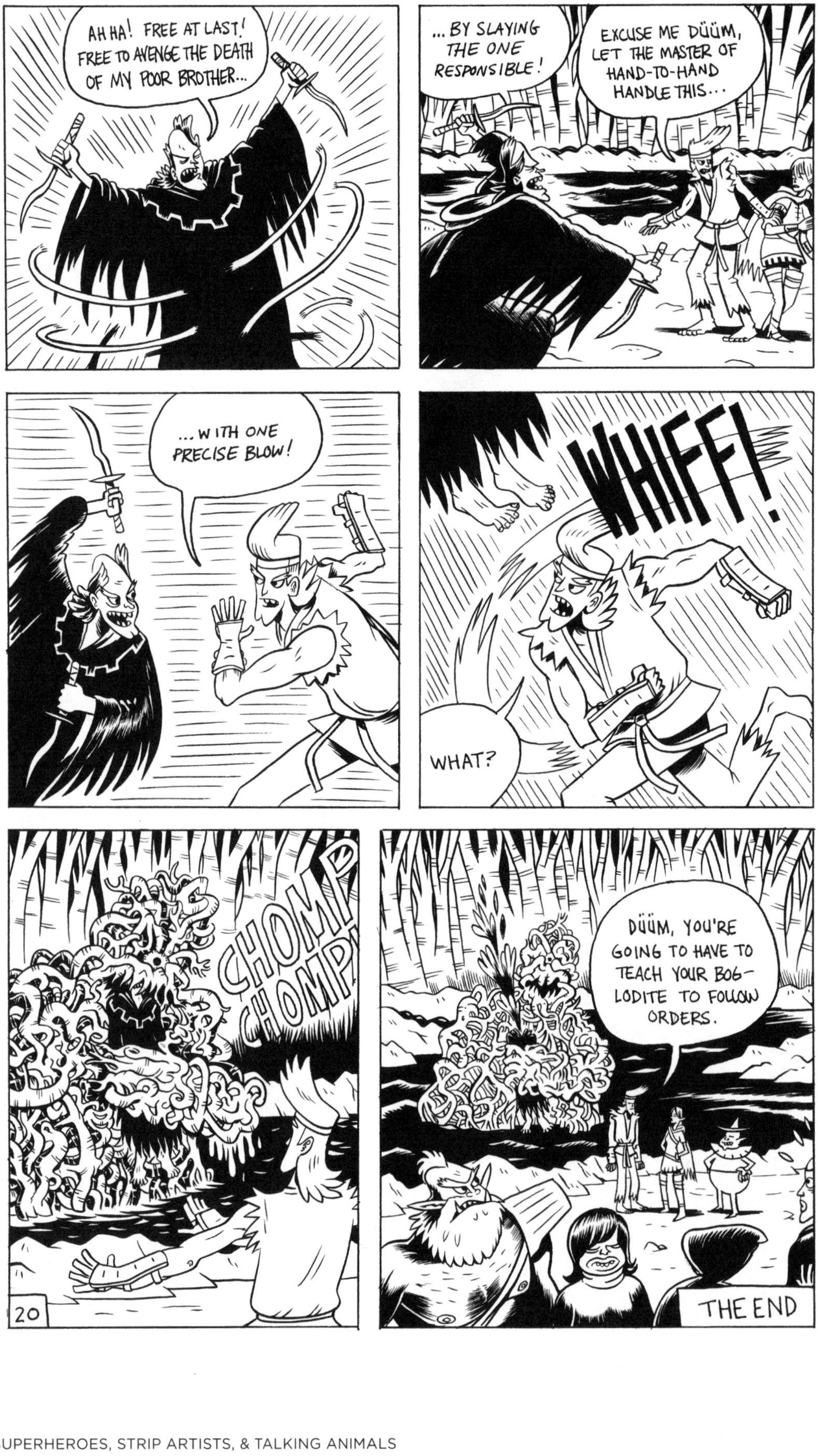
AH HA! FREE AT LAST! FREE TO AVENGE THE DEATH OF MY POOR BROTHER...
...BY SLAYING THE ONE RESPONSIBLE!
EXCUSE ME DÜÜM, LET THE MASTER OF HAND-TO-HAND HANDLE THIS...
...WITH ONE PRECISE BLOW!
WHIFF!
WHAT?
CHOMP
CHOMP
20
DÜÜM, YOU'RE GOING TO HAVE TO TEACH YOUR BOG-LODITE TO FOLLOW ORDERS.
THE END

KING MINI / VINCENT STALL

"Everyone needs a dead end box," Vincent Stall, a.k.a. King Mini, claims. He drags a box from a corner of his Minneapolis studio and throws open the lid. He details the contents. "There's a sketchbook of green-bar paper filled with page layout, page layout, page layout. There are starts of stories. There's a whole box of me trying to figure out what I'm doing artistically."

Not too long ago, Stall was a visiting artist lecturer at the Minneapolis College of Art and Design. He brought his box to class. "I told the students, 'Some of you might not need this box of dead ends. But I needed it.'"

For Stall, born and raised in 1960s Florida, the box represents history—four years of college in Florida, a long creative period in Iowa City, and the studio years at the Handicraft Guild building in Minneapolis. It also represents the early King Mini minicomics printed at Kinko's and the later minicomics printed in small press editions, as well as marriage, parenthood, and the day Stall's father died.

"My process goes back to my art school training," says Stall about his continual need to reinvent his artistic style. "It's about stepping back from your art and looking at what you're doing. If you're not satisfied, you have to retrain yourself." He has encountered creative roadblocks—dead ends—at intervals during his cartooning career. That's when he hits the books. "I set up assignments for myself. I look at other artists—Gary Panter, José Muñoz—and break down the parts. 'Okay, now I see how he's connecting the blacks. Now I understand how he's moving from panel to panel.'"

Muñoz and Carlos Sampayo's short stories of New York, *Joe's Bar,* is one of the illustrated books Stall takes down off the same bookshelf he looted as an MCAD instructor. "I wanted to expose my students to stuff they weren't seeing. At this point in my life, I have books on my shelf that have been out of print for decades. I don't know they're out of print, though, because they're on my shelf and I don't have to look for them."

Stall began collecting comics when he was six and had the mumps. The doctor didn't want him to move from the sofa, so Stall's mom bought her son a stack of comics to while away the hours. Collecting became an obsession. He even knew when the delivery van hit his comic book stores, and he'd be there waiting.

"Those days, I'd leave school with my bike and a backpack and race to catch up with the delivery man," recalls the artist. In the 1970s, before the rise of specialty comic book stores, kids like Stall had to visit a number of drugstores and retailers to find the issues they'd checked off on their monthly pull list. "Ultimately, I'd catch up with the driver and ask, 'Can I

> "IT'S ABOUT STEPPING BACK FROM YOUR ART AND LOOKING AT WHAT YOU'RE DOING. IF YOU'RE NOT SATISFIED, YOU HAVE TO RETRAIN YOURSELF."

look through your truck? Can I look through that box?' The driver was probably thinking, *There's that rabid kid who wants comics.* I was respectful enough to wait for him to at least get in the store first."

Stall's parents were practical people. They supported their son's interest in art but also encouraged him to find a career that would provide him with a 401K and health insurance. When it came time for college, "My mom was like, 'Respiratory therapy. You'll always have a job if you go into respiratory therapy,'" Stall remembers. "At the same time, my father had me take all the graphic design classes I could, so I'd have something to fall back on."

Stall took his father's advice and then some, adding more art classes. "When I graduated, I was completely directionless," he admits. But that lack of direction freed him to leave his home state for Iowa City, where his girlfriend Kathleen (now his wife) was attending the University of Iowa. This

> **STALL'S PARENTS WERE PRACTICAL PEOPLE. THEY SUPPORTED THEIR SON'S INTEREST IN ART BUT ALSO ENCOURAGED HIM TO FIND A CAREER THAT WOULD PROVIDE HIM WITH A 401K AND HEALTH INSURANCE.**

was in the early 1990s, right at the end of the black-and-white boom. Resident cartoonist Paul Tobin asked Stall to contribute backup stories to his series with Phil Hester, *Attitude Lad*.

Stall and his wife moved to Minneapolis a few years later. The move inaugurated the artist's transition to the minicomic form and introduced him to Michael Drivas, an employee at Dream-Haven Books, a Minneapolis speculative fiction and comic book store. In the mid-nineties, Drivas left DreamHaven and opened Big Brain Comics on Tenth Street in downtown Minneapolis. Stall became a Big Brain habitué.

"I remember saying something to Mike off-the-cuff like, 'I need someplace else to work on my art,'" says Stall. His drawing table was jammed against a door in the apartment. "Mike's really big into hooking people up. He knew Zander Cannon was working on *The Replacement God* [Cannon's graphic novel] underneath his bed. Zander had a bunked bed. So Mike said, 'I know this other cartoonist who's looking for space too.'"

Stall and Cannon co-leased a studio in the Handicraft Guild building on Tenth Street. The building was a mecca for Minnesota cartoonists. Kevin Cannon served his internship under Zander there. Shad Petosky, who would eventually form the illustration studio Big Time Attic with the Cannons, rented space, as did Gene Ha, a DC Comics artist now living in Chicago. Graphic novelist Sam Hiti drew *Tiempos Finales* there.

With the aid of a single-color copier at Kinko's, Stall began to produce self-published minicomics under the pen name King Mini. He crafted a story from Melville's *Moby Dick*. He generated minis with the titles *Fodder, Nonsense,* and *Gristle,* and sold them at Big Brain and DreamHaven.

Robot Investigator appeared in 2001. In the story, a robot lands on an alien world to investigate and photograph the native inhabitants. But the robot's inquiries go awry when he interferes with the ragged post-industrial society.

Everybody Takes a Turn reflects another phase in Stall's career, a phase born out of loss and an artistic hiatus that extended over three years. His daughter was born prematurely, and shortly thereafter his father fell ill and died.

The death sent Stall into a creative freeze. "I must've had the kind of nervous breakdown where you just go about your daily life and do what you have to do, but that's about all you can do." Meanwhile, he continued to fill sketchbooks and deposit material in the dead end box.

Eventually, the block passed, and Stall felt the stirrings of inspiration. He picked up the beginnings of a graphic novel, *Brass Tacks,* about a moving company that specializes in removing its customers' mental baggage. And he exteriorized the tumult of the previous few years in *Everybody Takes a Turn.* The wordless panels track through drifting clouds, silent figures, and a close-up of wood grain. A man wanders a forest of stumps. He arrives in a thicket of dream trees, dead trees with bottles tied to the limbs, and builds a cottage.

Stall printed the book on blotter paper because of the paper's impermanence; the books will eventually fall apart, like the cottage. The cartoonist wanted his mini to tell a specific kind of story, "one you could go to and find meaning in when you needed it. Maybe you haven't had the experience yet," says the artist, not giving away what that experience is. Death? Grief? Letting go? "But when you have the experience, I want this story to be there." ■

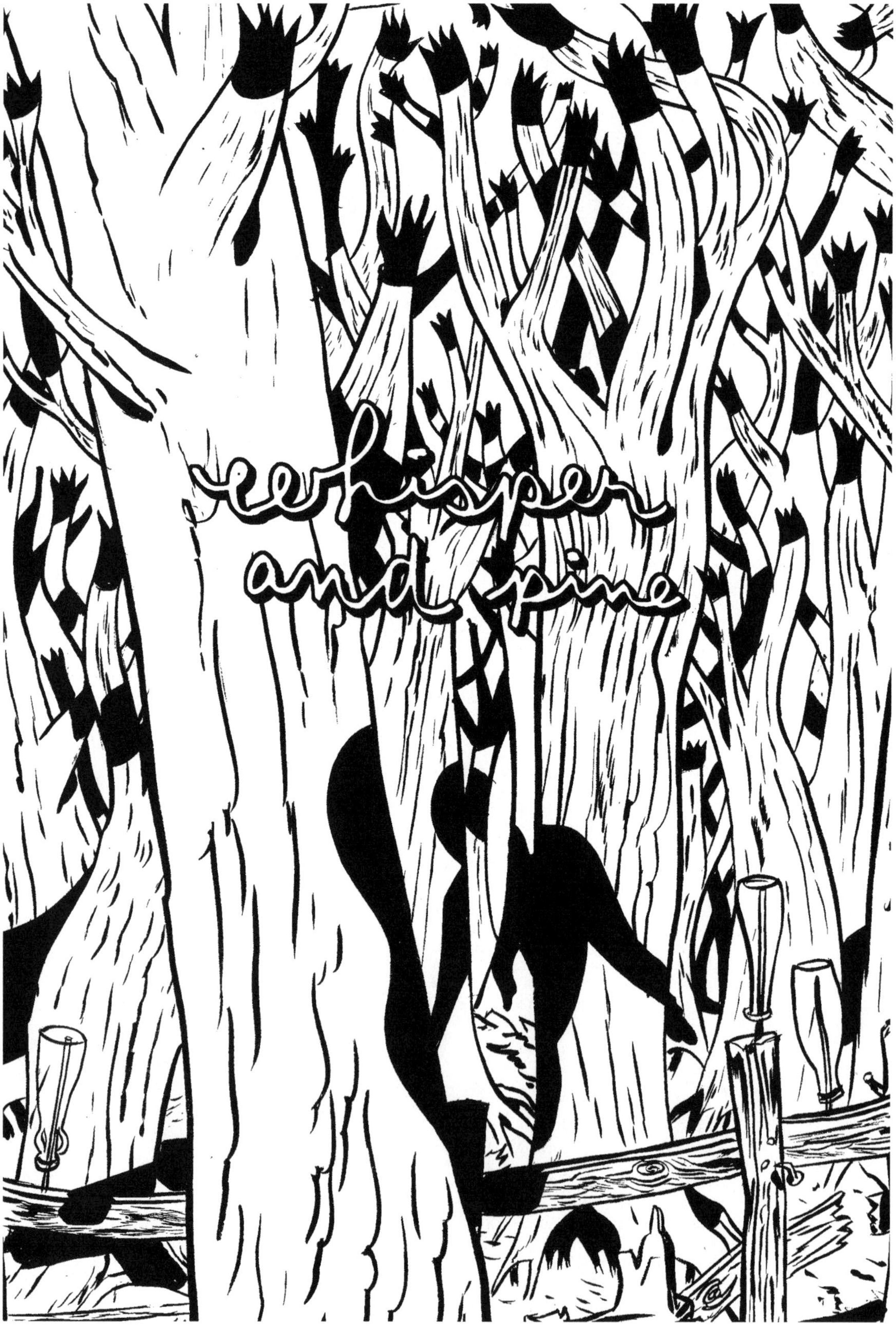
whisper
and pine

"Whisper and Pine" by King Mini. © 2005 King Mini

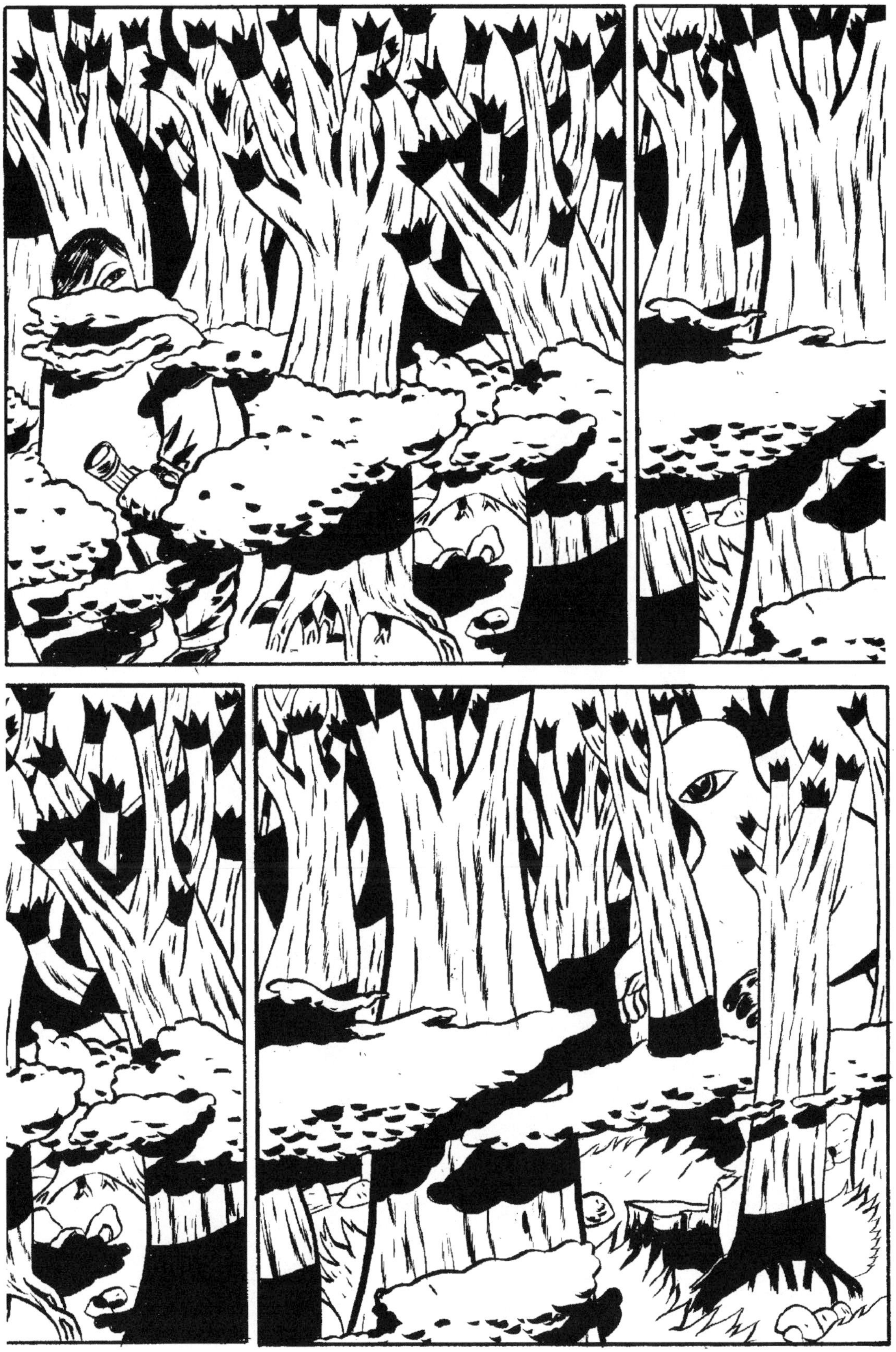

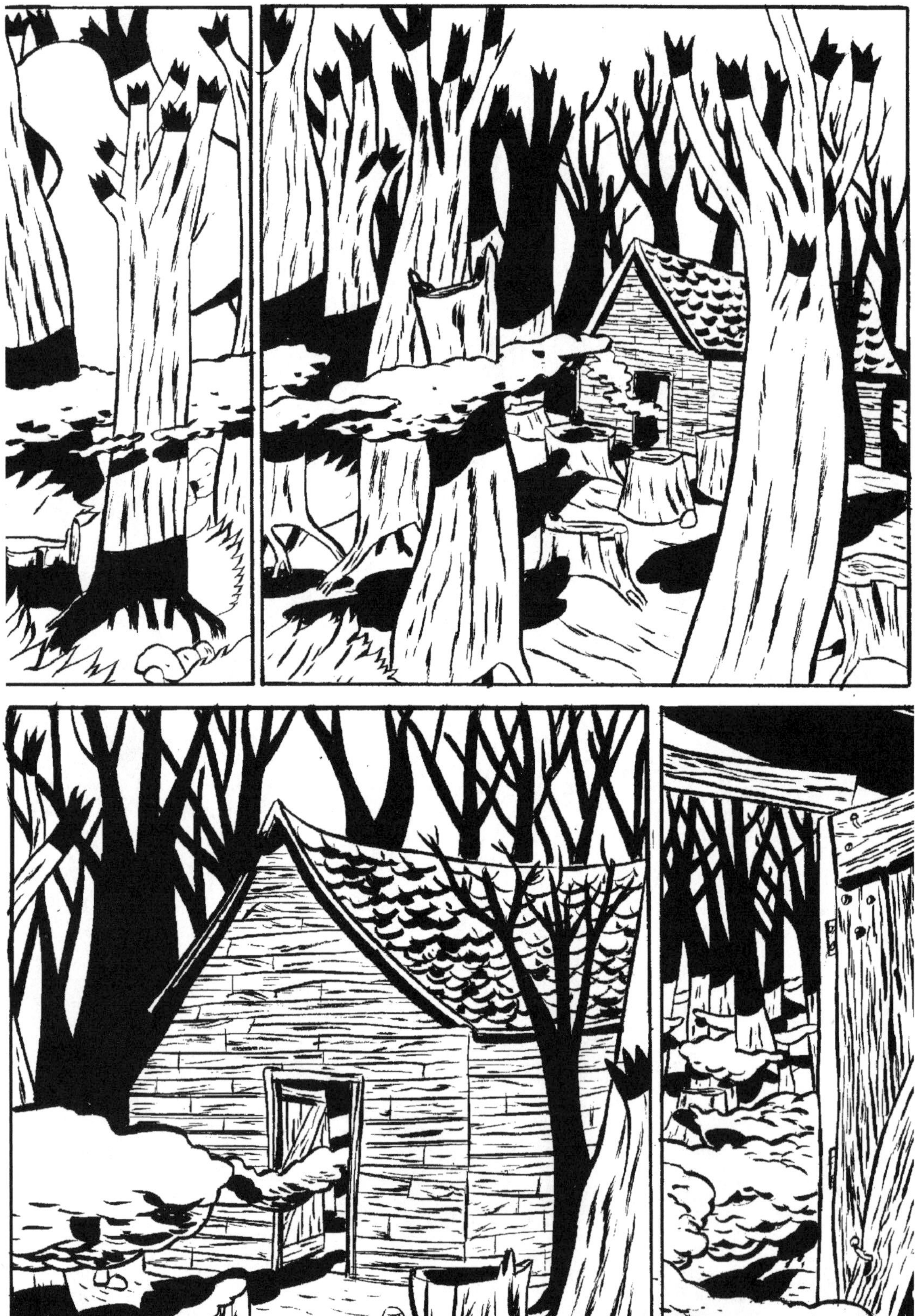

"Whisper and Pine" by King Mini: © 2005 King Mini

"Whisper and Pine" by King Mini. © 2005 King Mini

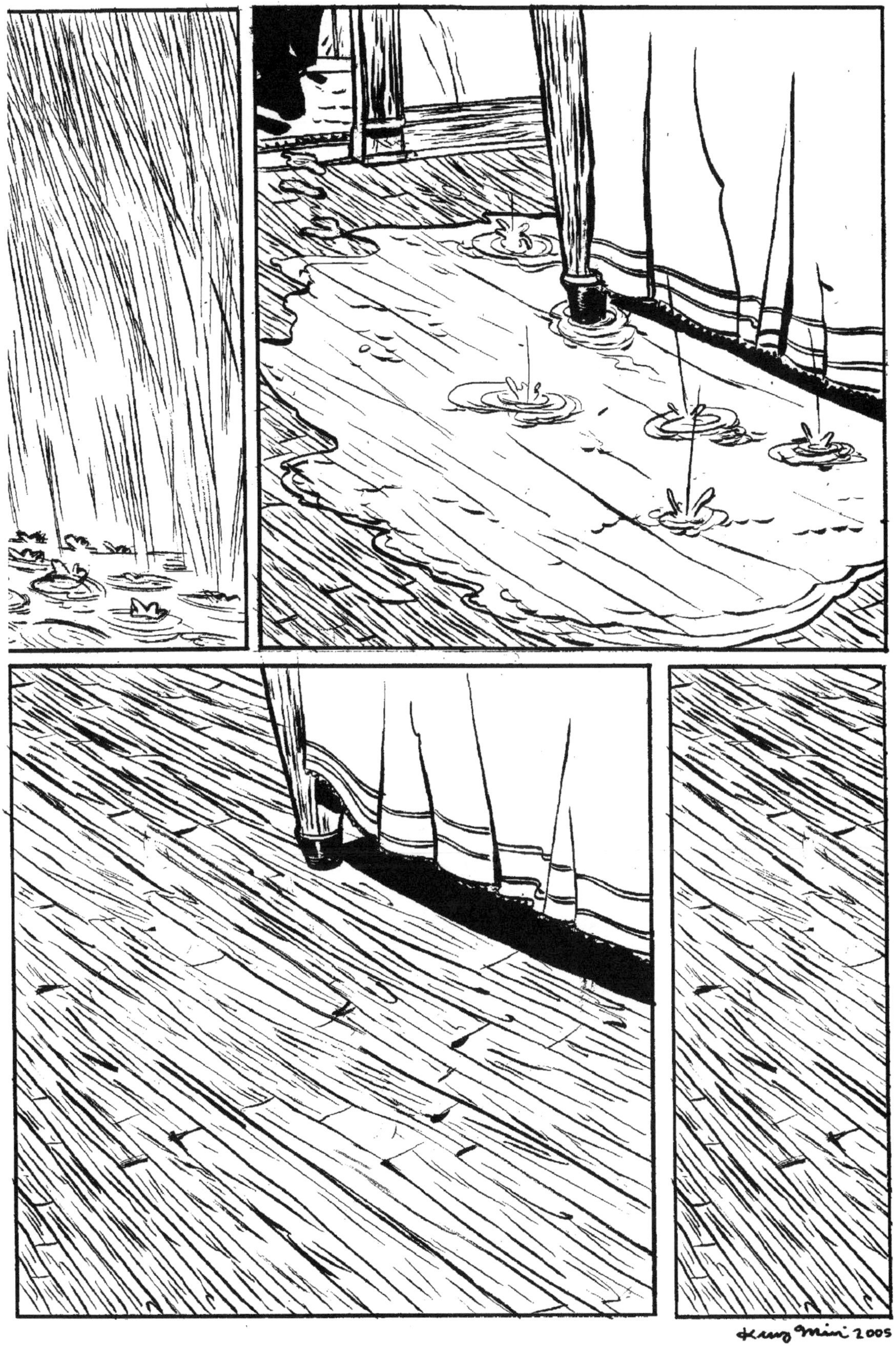

Reynold Kissling has the distinction of sharing geography with two American presidents. Born in 1986 in Midland, Texas, where George W. Bush sowed his wild oats, Kissling later spent four years in Jakarta, which also provided an address to the young Barack Obama.

The relationship to American presidents is circumstantial but significant in that, even at a tender age, Kissling sampled different worlds. He tasted the dust swept up from a lonely West Texas highway and felt the heat of an Indonesian sun. Quite the education for a future politician or a man destined to invent worlds in art.

One of those strong Texas winds blew a college fair to Houston, where Kissling was finishing his high school education. Kris Musto, a rep for the Minneapolis College of Art and Design, talked a good game with her potentials. Other reps handed out brochures, but Musto painted a picture. Kissling felt compelled to check out her school. He and his mother made an investigatory trip north. Then he and his father made another trip. No one ever said the Kisslings weren't thorough. In 2004, the high school grad began his studies at MCAD.

Kissling has a hard time talking about his comics career because it has only begun. But that's in relation to comparative veterans of the art. In terms of a beginning, Kissling sees his career springing from a near worship of Bill Watterson.

"'Calvin and Hobbes' is one of the best comic strips out there," says Kissling. "The writing is impeccable. You have a blend of intelligent, witty, and complex dialogue with humorous back and forth between the characters." No surprise, Kissling took a cue from Watterson and made a stab at his own strip, *Mad Max,* in high school.

The idea of becoming a strip artist went by the wayside at MCAD. "Syndicates run the comic strip business," he explains. "They own your strips outright, so you have no control over merchandizing; and if you quit the strip, the syndicates can bring in someone else to draw your strip."

So it was so long, stripville, and hello, minicomics and novel-length books. By the time Kissling graduated from MCAD, cartoonist Marjane Satrapi had proved the marketability of the novel form with her graphic memoir *Persepolis.* Harvey Pekar, a writer who has collaborated with a number of artists, had done something similar much earlier with *American Splendor.* Both had seen not only relatively good sales but film adaptations of their properties. And, more importantly, they retained copyright on their work.

Kissling has been working up to the graphic novel, first focusing on panels, then on the agreement of panels, then working shorter stories into longer ones. Art school pushed him through his paces.

"At MCAD, I was always at the drawing table," he says. "With the comic art classes you sometimes had to produce eight-page comics every week, on top of everything else you were doing. Comics take time because you have to be good at everything: graphic design, draftsmanship, landscape, portraiture, storytelling."

He produced a number of minis, which he now hosts on his website. In *White Noise,* he put himself in the mindset of a World War II fighter pilot. After his plane is shot down, the pilot wanders aimlessly through a dry landscape, which could be 1940s North Africa or present-day West Texas. The pilot loses touch with reality as his life ebbs. His vision flips—through the lens of Kissling's art—between a hospital bed and an atomic blast.

The mini *Kingwood Himself* was the artist's attempt "to write something happy. I noticed I was writing a lot of depressing stories, and I'm not that kind of person," says Kissling. Kingwood also happens to be the name of the Houston subdivision where Kissling spent his teen years.

"I always thought Kingwood was an ominous name for a subdivision," he says. "Some friends and I came up with this character Kingwood Himself, a giant monster who would roam around enforcing all the housing codes, eating teenagers, and controlling the roving bands of deer that were always around."

Kissling's early mythmaking enters into the comic, which begins as a girl discovers a cluster of houses hidden in a forest. The fantastical neighborhood lays claim to a population of monsters—Jambe the kid monster, Eleman the philosopher-monster, and Kingwood Himself the tree creature. The title character engages his neighborhood in a campaign to save the forest from a developer's tree-cutting crew.

"EVEN IF I GET A GRAPHIC NOVEL PUBLISHED, THAT'S STILL NO GUARANTEE I'LL BE SUCCESSFUL OR EVEN REMEMBERED. BUT I WANT TO START OUT WITH THE HIGHEST AMBITIONS POSSIBLE."

Kissling has two graphic novels in the works: a space-themed novel, *Pale Blue Dot,* and *Nils,* a coming-of-age story drawn in collaboration with writer and MCAD alum Ed Choy Moorman. *The Good Minnesotan* #4 (2D Cloud Press) anthologized portions of *Pale Blue Dot* in 2010. He has published recent short work in the comics anthology *HIVE* #5 (Grimalkin Press).

Kissling is taking a level-headed approach to his career. "Even if I get a graphic novel published, that's still no guarantee I'll be successful or even remembered. But I want to start out with the highest ambitions possible," he says. "I want to say that I'll change comics forever, because even if I strive for that goal and I don't reach it, I'll still be making some pretty good art." ∎

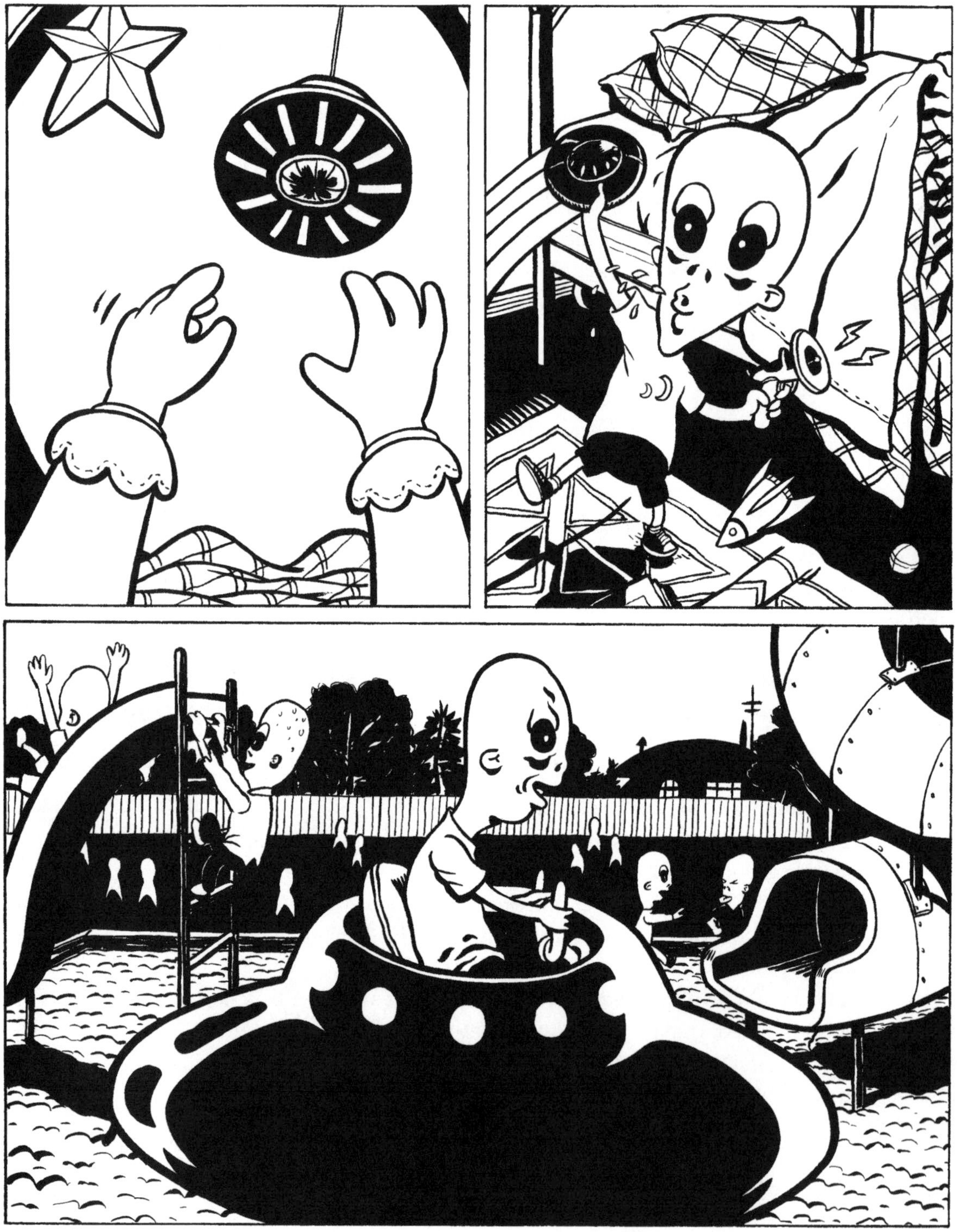

"Pale Blue Dot" by Reynold Kissling. © 2009 Reynold Kissling

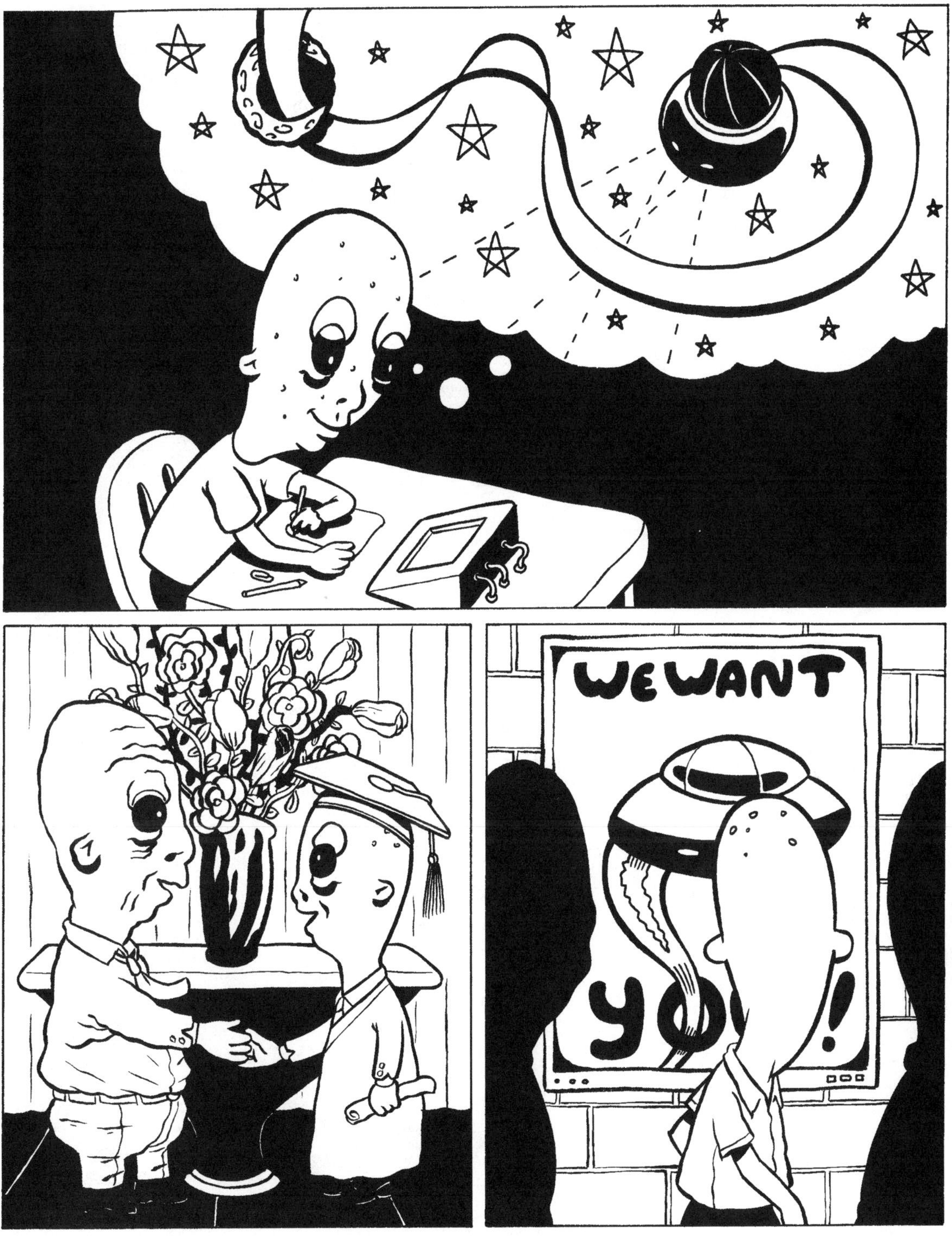
WE WANT
YO !

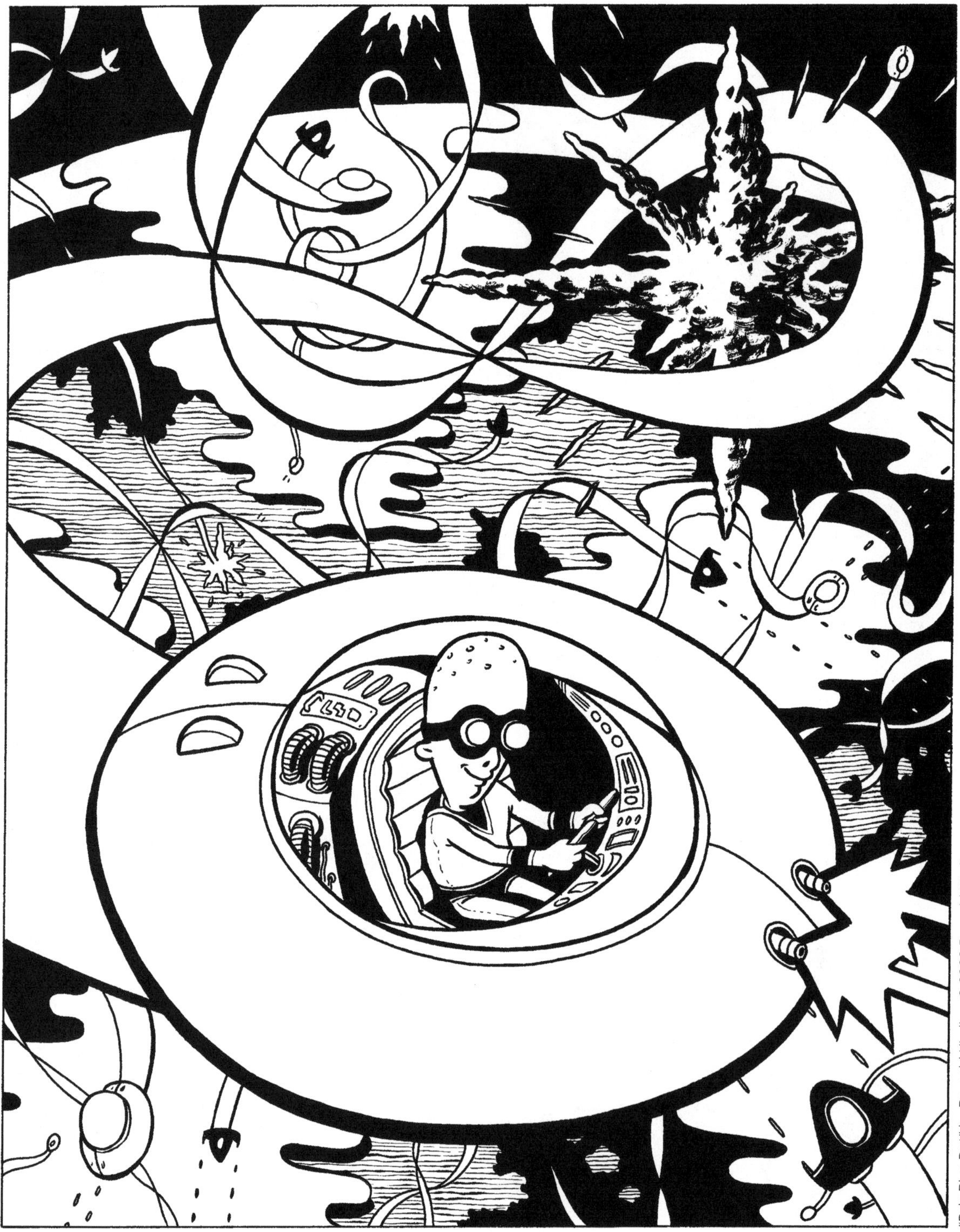

“Pale Blue Dot” by Reynold Kissling © 2009 Reynold Kissling

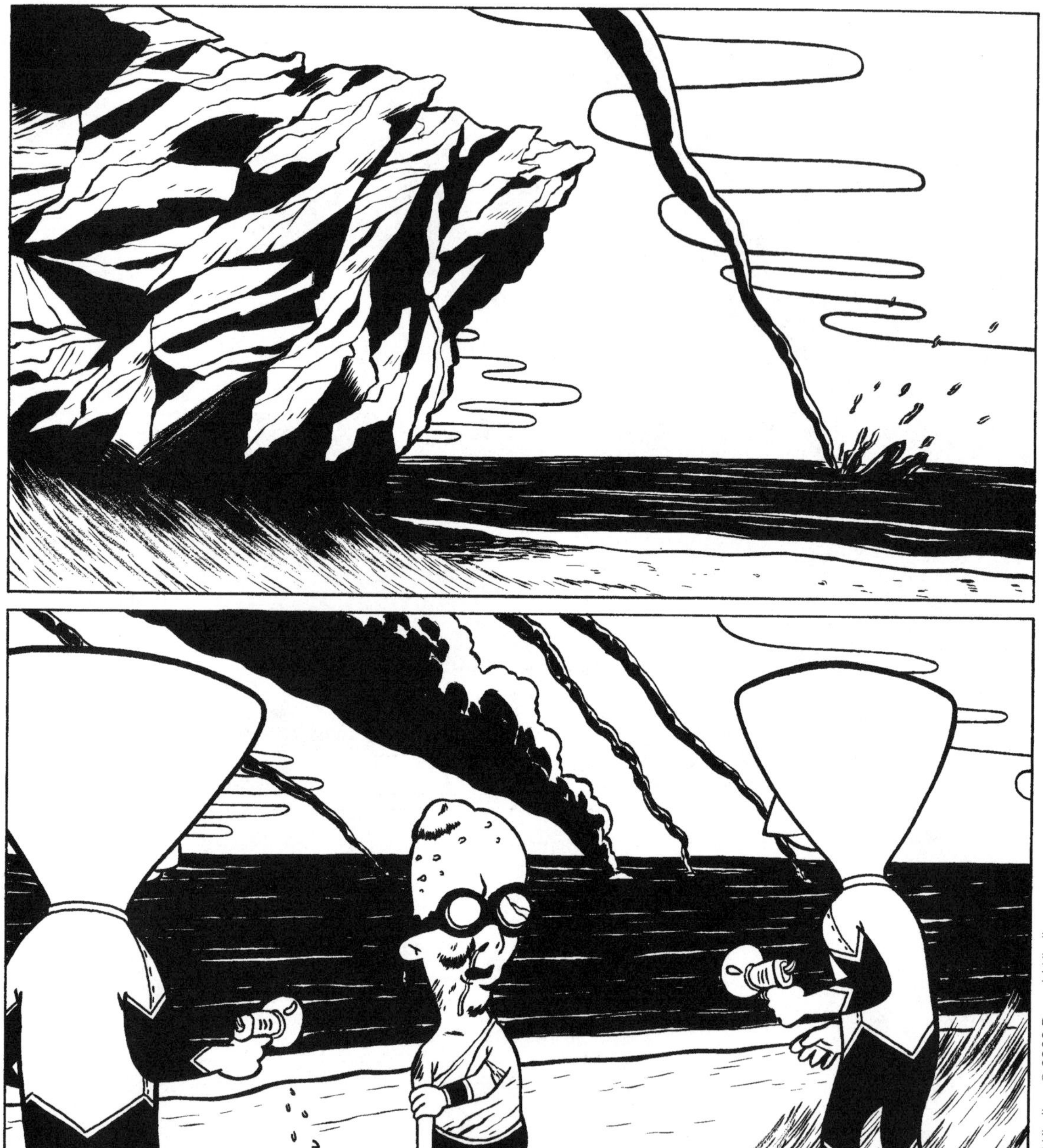

"Pale Blue Dot" by Reynold Kissling. © 2009 Reynold Kissling

DANNO KLONOWSKI / DANK!

In 1993, American cartoonist Scott McCloud published *Understanding Comics*. The graphic book has since passed through several reprints, but its impact remains undiminished. McCloud, in an economic 215 pages, explains the importance of an art that has occasionally felt the neglect of critical regard and had to defend itself against congressional committees, parent groups, and stereotypes. Comics fans and artists snapped up the book.

"My friend loaned me his *Understanding Comics,* which, when it came out, was this really important book about comics and still is," says Danno Klonowski, who goes by Danno or Dank! when penning his minicomics. "Anyway, I accidentally dropped his book in a toilet and flushed."

This put him in a bind. Because that very same friend was dropping by—in minutes—and Danno had promised to return the book. A very soggy book now.

"I was in such a panic. I tried to dry it with a hairdryer in like the two minutes I had before he picked me up," says Danno.

The friend arrived. Everything was real chummy. A little of, "Hey, how's it going?" from Danno, and "Not bad. What's going on with you?" from his friend. What's going on? Oh, nothing. Nothing at all. *What was he going to do?* Think. Think. Think. Aha! If this were a minicomic, Danno would have a light bulb over his head. He had an idea. When the friend's back was turned, Danno chucked the wet book into the back of the car. Their friendship was salvaged, for now at least.

Ideas for minicomics can come from anywhere. It helps if you're one of those people to whom things happen. Danno draws inspiration from popular culture, current events, the Minnesota cartooning multiverse, and bad luck with toilets.

Danno grew up in Coon Rapids, Minnesota, and attended college down the road at St. Cloud State University, where he drew a comic strip for the student paper. The inspiration to develop his comics work into full-fledged minicomics arose from an introduction to the work of John Porcellino and Zak Sally.

"They were the first big wave of minicomics makers," says Danno. Porcellino, Sally, and others like them had taken the initiative to self-publish their work. They read each other's minicomics, borrowed each other's characters and plotlines. In essence, they created a multiverse—separate minicomic story worlds that occasionally overlapped—as well as a loose community of cartoonists.

Danno liked the idea of community. The idea of gathering like-minded individuals together to share technique, story concepts, gallery space—that worked for him. But where was he going to find a community like that in Minnesota? In 2002, another cartoonist, Steve Stwalley, posted flyers for the first meeting of the Cartoonist Conspiracy in Minneapolis. Danno attended with eight or ten others. Then word began to spread.

"As a cartoonist, you're alone in a room all the time," says Danno. "But with the Conspiracy, you feel like you're collaborating on something together."

Literally, it turns out. Like Porcellino and Sally, Danno and his fellow conspirators adopted each other's minicomics titles. They borrowed characters.

"I was standing at the register at DreamHaven Books and my friend said, 'Hey, Dan, what's Lederhosen Punk doing on the cover of someone else's comic?'" Danno remembers. Lederhosen Punk was a character in Danno's *Staple Genius* minicomic. "I looked over, and there's this minicomic called *Uptown Girl.* One of my characters was on the cover."

The creator of *Uptown Girl,* Bob Lipski, worked at DreamHaven and just happened to be standing at the checkout. "Bob said, 'That's not your character. That's *my* character,'" says Danno. As it turned out, they were both right, and both wrong. They had ripped off the same character from Frank Miller's *The Dark Knight Returns.*

The two cartoonists decided to work together. Danno wrote and drew short pieces for Lipski's *Uptown Girl* and then became principal artist on *Tommy Chicago,* a minicomic co-created by Lipski and Brian Bastian.

Danno first conceived the idea for his minicomic series *Manly Tales of Cowardice* in 2006. "I was reading a blog by a guy who reviews old comics. He was reviewing man comics and man adventure comics. I thought, *There's no way you could write a story like that today, not with* man *in the title, not without it being shelved in the adult section,*" he says. The temptation was too great. He had to write his own manly tale.

Fleming Hazmat, the hero of *Manly Tales of Cowardice,* is a gentleman adventurer. An Indiana Jones possessed of abundant vision and zero courage. Bolstering him through his bouts of timidity are sidekicks Atlantis Lad and Betsy Rossbot.

Danno, Bastian, and Lipski later combined their multiple comic universes in a sixty-page mini, in which Fleming Hazmat, Uptown Girl, and Tommy Chicago travel through a rip in space-time. And what is the point of their noble quest? To locate the ingredients for stew.

Members of the Cartoonist Conspiracy have also joined forces on a Sunday funnies–style publication, *The Big Funny,* and gallery shows. It was a gallery show at Altered Esthetics in Northeast Minneapolis that resurrected Danno's long-ago toilet incident. The conspirators needed work to hang in the gallery's bathroom, so Danno wracked his brain for a suitable bathroom-worthy comic. Nothing came. And then it surfaced. An image of a sodden *Understanding Comics* floated to mind. *Understanding Toilets* debuted at the 2008 Lutefisk Sushi Bathroom Show.

And what about the damaged book chucked in the back of his friend's car? "Months later, my friend found the book," says Danno. "He assumed the water damage had been caused by rain getting in his car." ∎

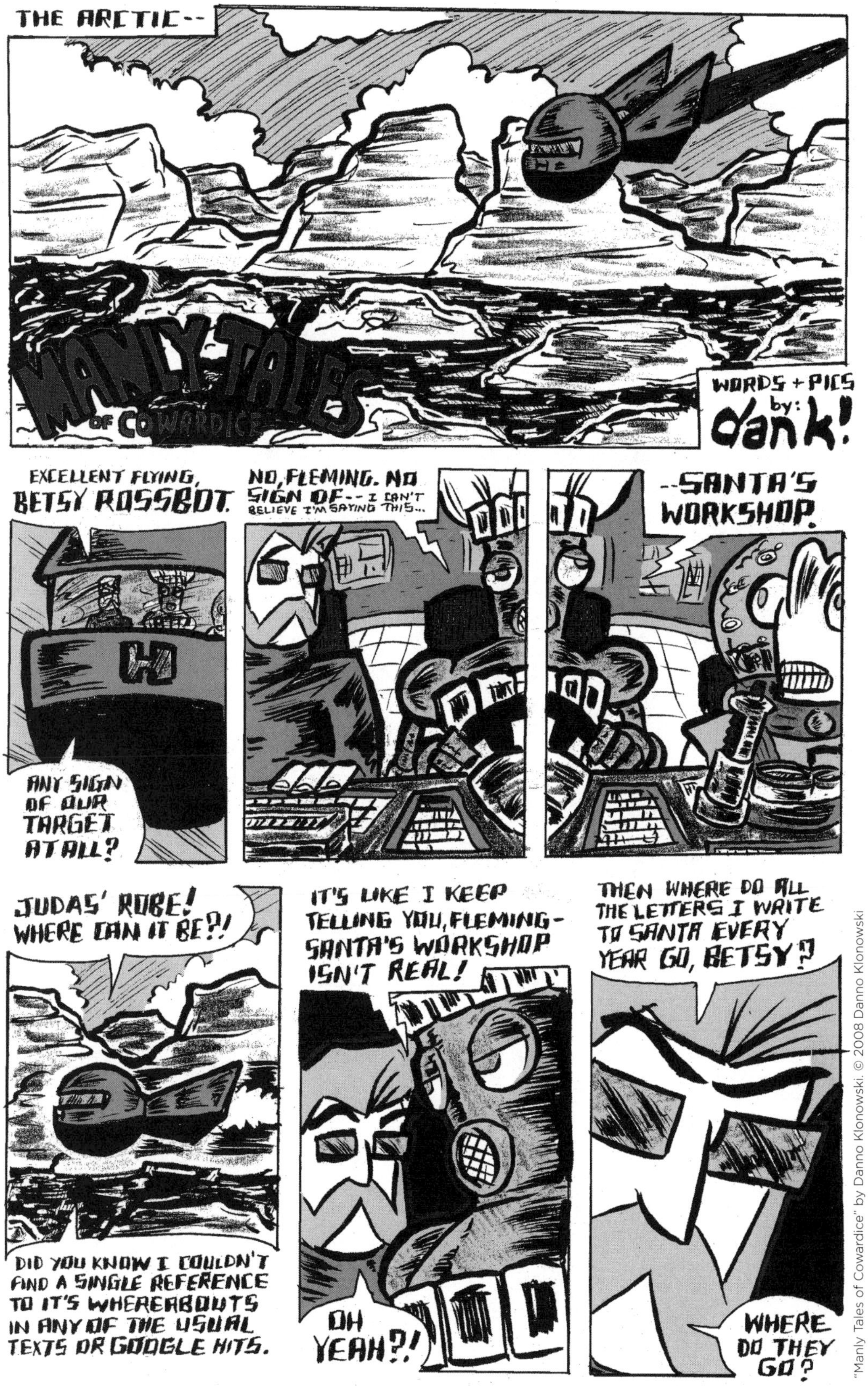
THE ARCTIC--
MANLY TALES OF COWARDICE
WORDS + PICS by: dank!
EXCELLENT FLYING, BETSY ROSSBOT.
ANY SIGN OF OUR TARGET AT ALL?
NO, FLEMING. NO SIGN OF-- I CAN'T BELIEVE I'M SAYING THIS...
--SANTA'S WORKSHOP.
JUDAS' ROBE! WHERE CAN IT BE?!
DID YOU KNOW I COULDN'T FIND A SINGLE REFERENCE TO IT'S WHEREABOUTS IN ANY OF THE USUAL TEXTS OR GOOGLE HITS.
IT'S LIKE I KEEP TELLING YOU, FLEMING- SANTA'S WORKSHOP ISN'T REAL!
OH YEAH?!
THEN WHERE DO ALL THE LETTERS I WRITE TO SANTA EVERY YEAR GO, BETSY?
WHERE DO THEY GO?

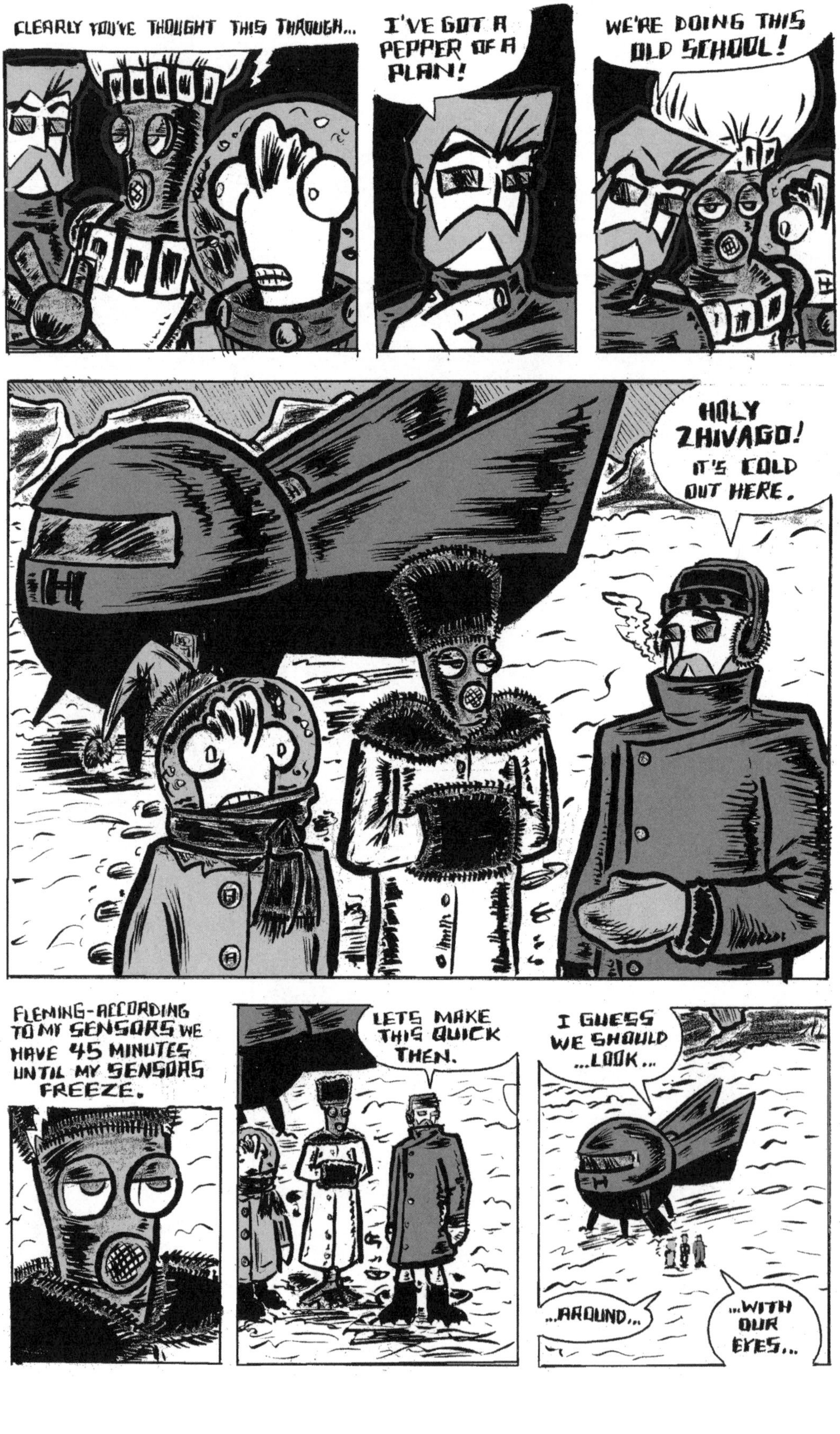
CLEARLY YOU'VE THOUGHT THIS THROUGH...
I'VE GOT A PEPPER OF A PLAN!
WE'RE DOING THIS OLD SCHOOL!
HOLY ZHIVAGO! IT'S COLD OUT HERE.
FLEMING-ACCORDING TO MY SENSORS WE HAVE 45 MINUTES UNTIL MY SENSORS FREEZE.
LETS MAKE THIS QUICK THEN.
I GUESS WE SHOULD ...LOOK...
...AROUND...
...WITH OUR EYES...

"Manly Tales of Cowardice" by Danno Klonowski. © 2008 Danno Klonowski

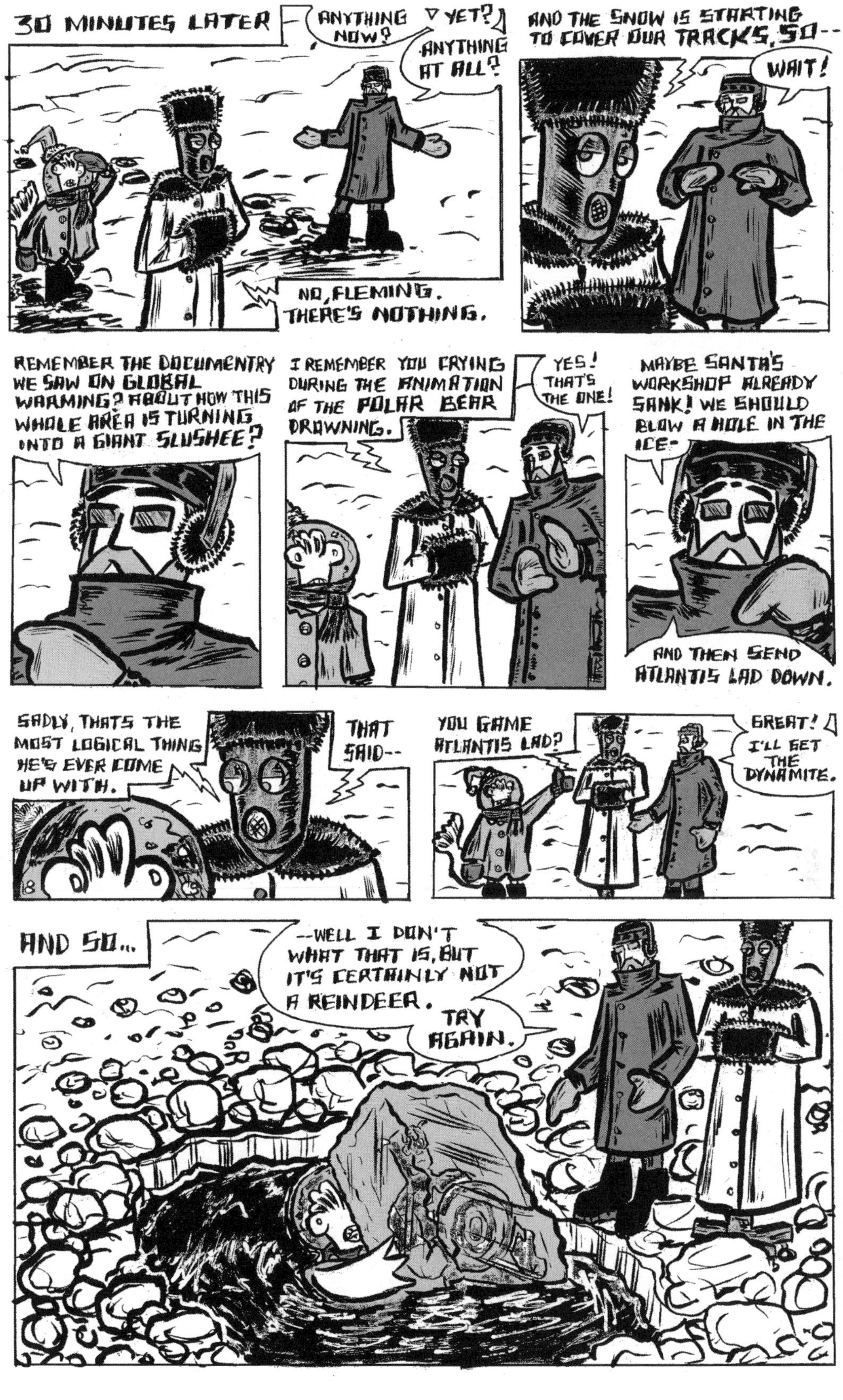
30 MINUTES LATER
ANYTHING NOW?
YET?
ANYTHING AT ALL?
NO, FLEMING. THERE'S NOTHING.
AND THE SNOW IS STARTING TO COVER OUR TRACKS, SO--
WAIT!
REMEMBER THE DOCUMENTRY WE SAW ON GLOBAL WARMING? ABOUT HOW THIS WHOLE AREA IS TURNING INTO A GIANT SLUSHEE?
I REMEMBER YOU CRYING DURING THE ANIMATION OF THE POLAR BEAR DROWNING.
YES! THAT'S THE ONE!
MAYBE SANTA'S WORKSHOP ALREADY SANK! WE SHOULD BLOW A HOLE IN THE ICE-
AND THEN SEND ATLANTIS LAD DOWN.
SADLY, THATS THE MOST LOGICAL THING HE'S EVER COME UP WITH.
THAT SAID--
YOU GAME ATLANTIS LAD?
GREAT! I'LL GET THE DYNAMITE.
AND SO...
--WELL I DON'T WHAT THAT IS, BUT IT'S CERTAINLY NOT A REINDEER.
TRY AGAIN.

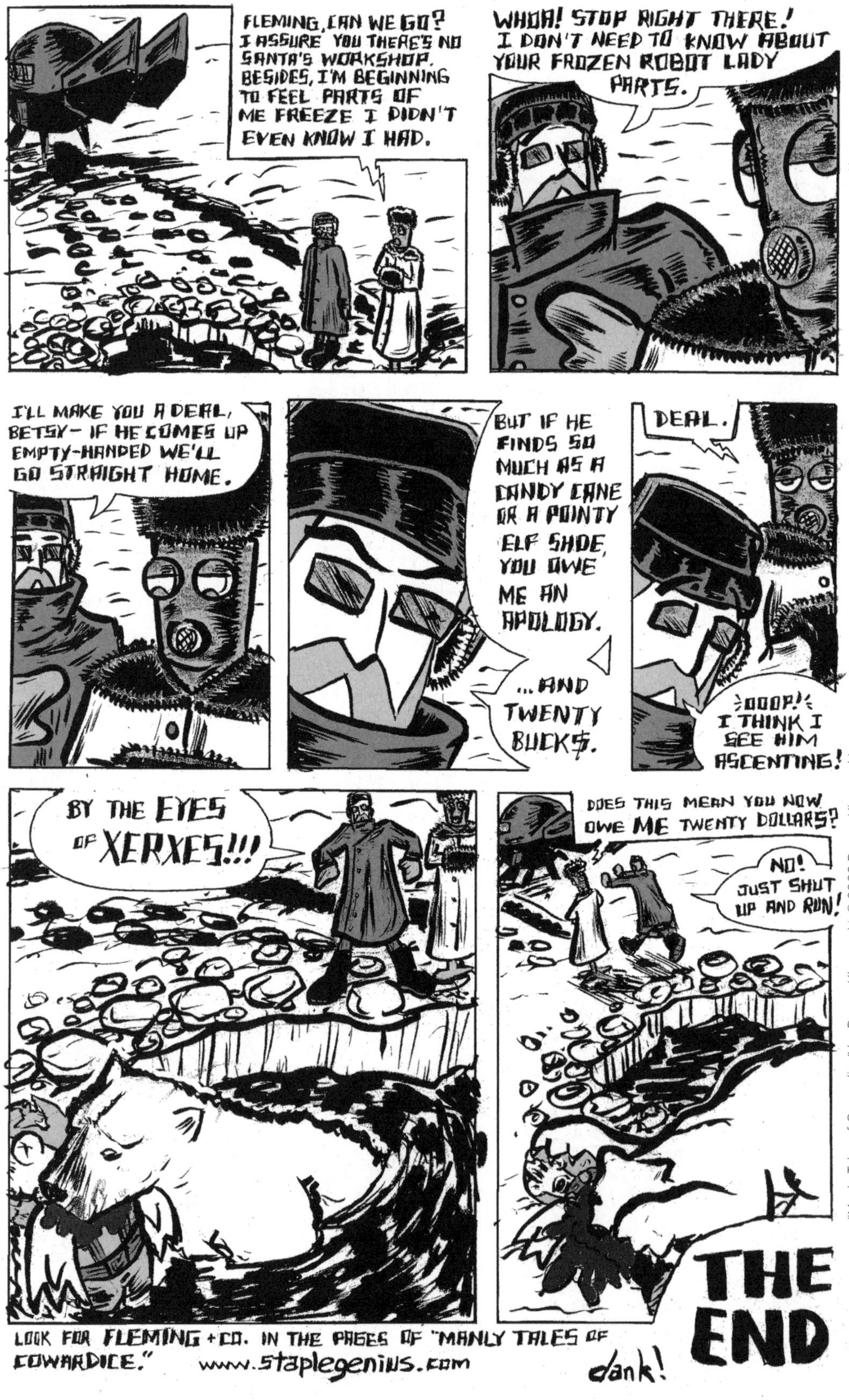
FLEMING, CAN WE GO? I ASSURE YOU THERE'S NO SANTA'S WORKSHOP. BESIDES, I'M BEGINNING TO FEEL PARTS OF ME FREEZE I DIDN'T EVEN KNOW I HAD.
WHOA! STOP RIGHT THERE! I DON'T NEED TO KNOW ABOUT YOUR FROZEN ROBOT LADY PARTS.
I'LL MAKE YOU A DEAL, BETSY– IF HE COMES UP EMPTY-HANDED WE'LL GO STRAIGHT HOME.
BUT IF HE FINDS SO MUCH AS A CANDY CANE OR A POINTY ELF SHOE, YOU OWE ME AN APOLOGY.
...AND TWENTY BUCK$.
DEAL.
OOOP! I THINK I SEE HIM ASCENTING!
BY THE EYES OF XERXES!!!
DOES THIS MEAN YOU NOW OWE ME TWENTY DOLLARS?
NO! JUST SHUT UP AND RUN!
THE END
LOOK FOR FLEMING + CO. IN THE PAGES OF "MANLY TALES OF COWARDICE." www.staplegenius.com
dank!

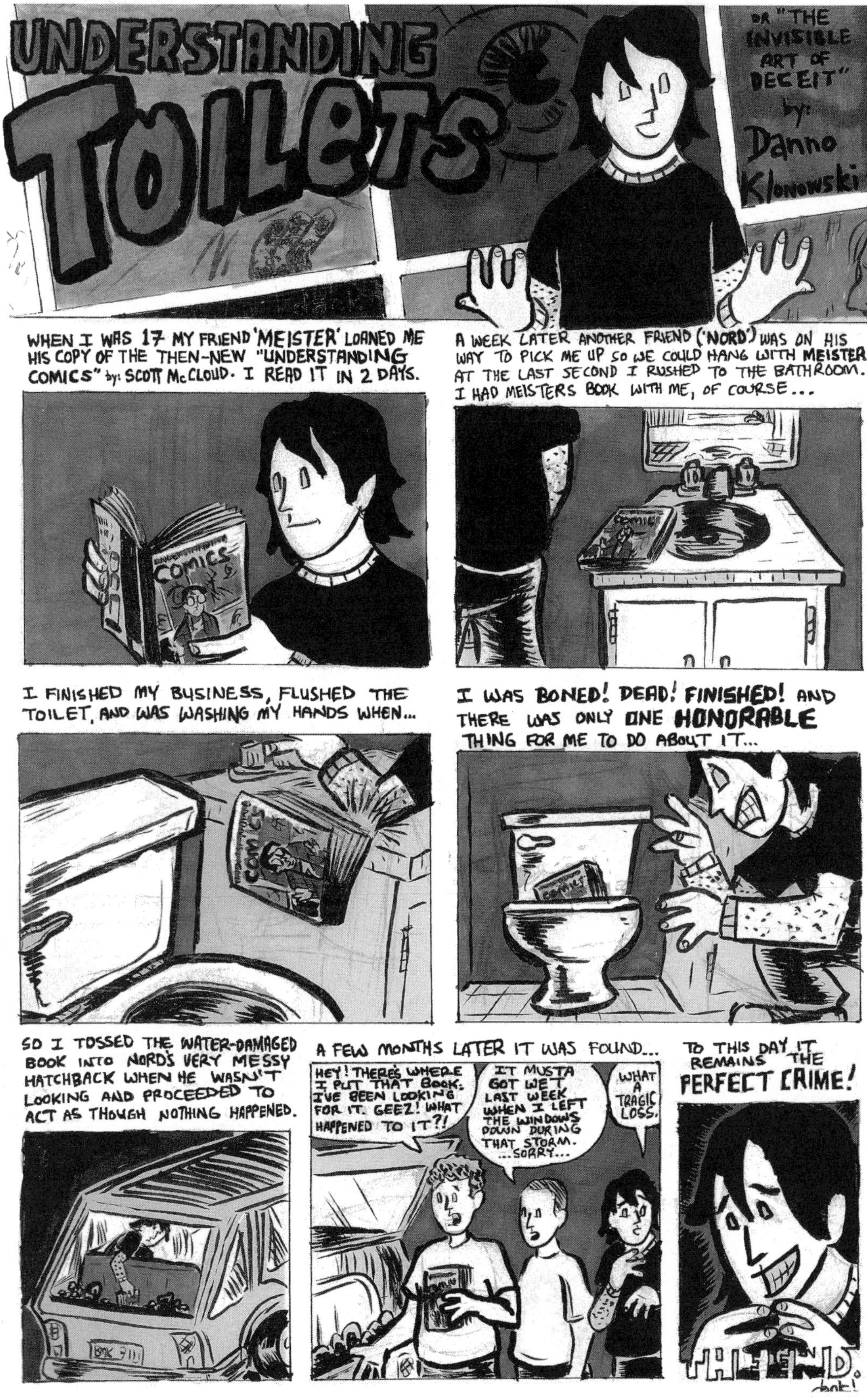
UNDERSTANDING TOILETS
OR "THE INVISIBLE ART OF DECEIT" by: Danno Klonowski!
WHEN I WAS 17 MY FRIEND 'MEISTER' LOANED ME HIS COPY OF THE THEN-NEW "UNDERSTANDING COMICS" by: SCOTT McCLOUD. I READ IT IN 2 DAYS.
COMICS
A WEEK LATER ANOTHER FRIEND ('NORD') WAS ON HIS WAY TO PICK ME UP SO WE COULD HANG WITH MEISTER. AT THE LAST SECOND I RUSHED TO THE BATHROOM. I HAD MEISTERS BOOK WITH ME, OF COURSE...
COMICS
I FINISHED MY BUSINESS, FLUSHED THE TOILET, AND WAS WASHING MY HANDS WHEN...
COMICS
I WAS BONED! DEAD! FINISHED! AND THERE WAS ONLY ONE HONORABLE THING FOR ME TO DO ABOUT IT...
COMICS
SO I TOSSED THE WATER-DAMAGED BOOK INTO NORD'S VERY MESSY HATCHBACK WHEN HE WASN'T LOOKING AND PROCEEDED TO ACT AS THOUGH NOTHING HAPPENED.
A FEW MONTHS LATER IT WAS FOUND...
HEY! THERE'S WHERE I PUT THAT BOOK. I'VE BEEN LOOKING FOR IT. GEEZ! WHAT HAPPENED TO IT?!
IT MUSTA GOT WET LAST WEEK WHEN I LEFT THE WINDOWS DOWN DURING THAT STORM. ...SORRY...
WHAT A TRAGIC LOSS.
TO THIS DAY IT REMAINS THE PERFECT CRIME!
THE END.
dank!

BOB LIPSKI & BRIAN BASTIAN

Brian Bastian and Bob Lipski grew up on opposite sides of the Mississippi River, Bastian in St. Paul and Lipski in Minneapolis. Bastian sealed his relationship with comics early. He followed Batman and Spidey in the monthly serials and donned superhero-themed Underoos at bedtime.

In elementary school, Bastian crafted detective stories starring his dog and won family drawing contests "because I was the oldest of three brothers and my youngest brother, whose job it was to pick the winner, always picked me," says Bastian. "I had almost no artistic skill."

Bob Lipski's grandmother was a teacher who would set her students a year-end assignment to be completed in spiral notebooks. Once she was finished grading, she ripped out the used pages and laid the notebooks on her grandson, knowing of his doodle habit.

Lipski doodled in the back of classrooms, in front of the TV, and during breaks at work. In high school, he clerked at Toys "R" Us. That's where he met Bastian over a job application.

Bastian was the job applicant and Lipski the clerk slipping him the application, no doubt with a heartfelt, "Good luck." A memorable moment, according to Bastian.

"Brian says I'm the one who gave him the job application," Lipski says. "I don't remember that at all."

The two ended up clerking together and over time discovered a compatibility of interests. They both wanted to create comic books, and, fittingly, one could write and one could draw. Sort of. They were still learning.

"We weren't really drawing comic books back then," says Bastian. "They were more one-page comics. But I was interested in writing longer scripts. So Bob and I started talking about making an indie comic book. We had a couple starts and stops, but then Bob created *Uptown Girl*." And once the ball got rolling, they were ready to run. That was 2002.

Uptown Girl is the story of a twenty-something reporter, Uptown Girl, and her friends Rocketman and Ruby Tuesday. The friends fall into misadventures and spend most of the twenty-four-page scripts trying to claw their way out. The events take place in Minneapolis—a Minneapolis that teeters on the border of fact and fiction. The friends bop from outings at the Walker Art Center to sword-and-sorcery exploits at the Cursed Castle, all within a ten-minute drive of their favorite hangout, Tom's Diner.

If Lipski were forced to give an elevator speech, he would pitch *Uptown Girl* as "*Seinfeld* meets *Archie Comics*. Because nothing really goes on. The characters go about their day. They have experiences, but in the end everything returns to normal."

Bastian's great contribution to *Uptown Girl* is Sulky Girl, a recurring character who absolutely refuses to see the positive side of life. Sulky Girl debuted in issue nine, the first Bastian wrote for Lipski. Sulky Girl also made a film appearance in Minnesota filmmaker Ben Mudek's 2005 adaptation, *The Uptown Girl Movie*.

Bastian and Lipski have collaborated on a second minicomic series, *Tommy Chicago*. Like the stories Bastian wrote about the family dog in elementary school, he cast his new protagonist, Tommy Chicago, as a detective—the most abysmally flawed detective ever to match wits with the criminal mind in Chilitown, USA. Bastian originally envisioned an animal-friendly, vegetarian gumshoe. But Tommy asserted himself, and Bastian gave in to his creation, scripting a rude, self-absorbed, and in truth more interesting detective, who has a habit of turning up at Free Comic Book Day events.

IF LIPSKI WERE FORCED TO GIVE AN ELEVATOR SPEECH, HE WOULD PITCH UPTOWN GIRL AS SEINFELD MEETS ARCHIE COMICS.

Every year, comic book stores observe Free Comic Book Day. Stores sponsor events and give out free comic books. Bastian has appeared at a number of these events, handing out copies of his rude gumshoe comic.

The great thing about fictional characters is they don't have to grow up if the creator doesn't want them to. Uptown Girl is as cheerfully wrinkle-free today as she was in 2002 when Lipski conceived her. But after twelve issues of *Tommy Chicago* and seventy-five of *Uptown Girl,* Lipski was starting to feel the toll. He geared back on his schedule, changing *Uptown Girl* from a monthly comic to a yearly graphic novel and turning over his drawing work on *Tommy Chicago* to Danno Klonowski.

"When I started, I was single and living alone. I could work on a comic for ten hours straight," says Lipski. "I'm married now, and I have kids. A lot of cartoonists want to work faster. But I'm at a point where I want to slow down and concentrate on my art. I'll still pour my heart into it but take it slower." ∎

UPTOWN ★ GIRL in "The Itsy Bitsy Teeney Weeney Yellow Polka Dot Bikini"

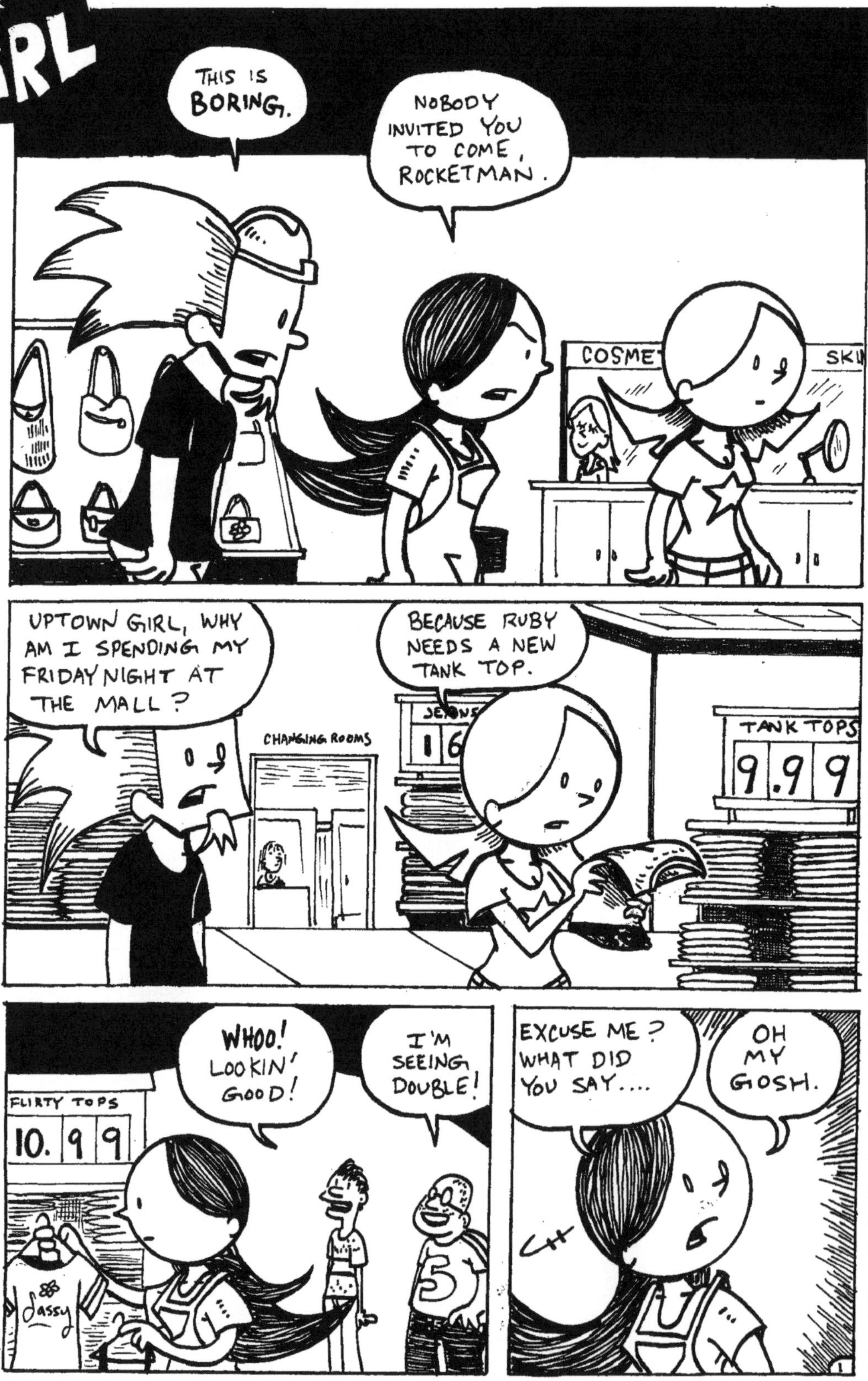
THIS IS BORING.
NOBODY INVITED YOU TO COME, ROCKETMAN.
COSMET
SKI
UPTOWN GIRL, WHY AM I SPENDING MY FRIDAY NIGHT AT THE MALL?
BECAUSE RUBY NEEDS A NEW TANK TOP.
CHANGING ROOMS
TANK TOPS
9.99
FLIRTY TOPS
10.99
WHOO! LOOKIN' GOOD!
I'M SEEING DOUBLE!
Sassy
5
EXCUSE ME? WHAT DID YOU SAY....
OH MY GOSH.
1

STORY + ART BY Bob Lipski

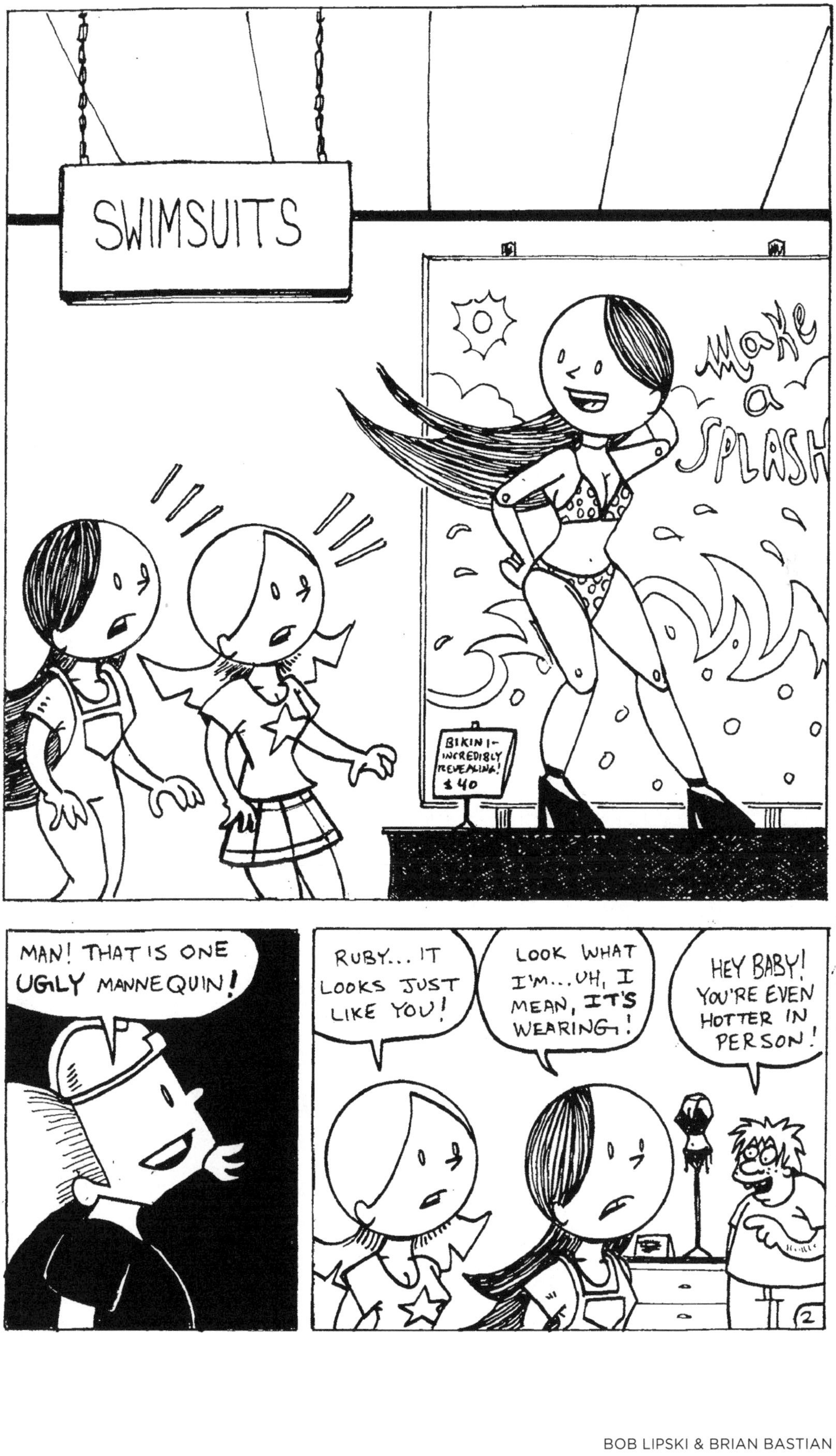
SWIMSUITS
Make a SPLASH
BIKINI - INCREDIBLY REVEALING! $40
MAN! THAT IS ONE UGLY MANNEQUIN!
RUBY... IT LOOKS JUST LIKE YOU!
LOOK WHAT I'M... UH, I MEAN, IT'S WEARING!
HEY BABY! YOU'RE EVEN HOTTER IN PERSON!
2

Uptown Girl issue "The Itsy Bitsy Teeny Weeny Yellow Polka-Dot Bikini" by Bob Lipski. © 2009 Bob Lipski

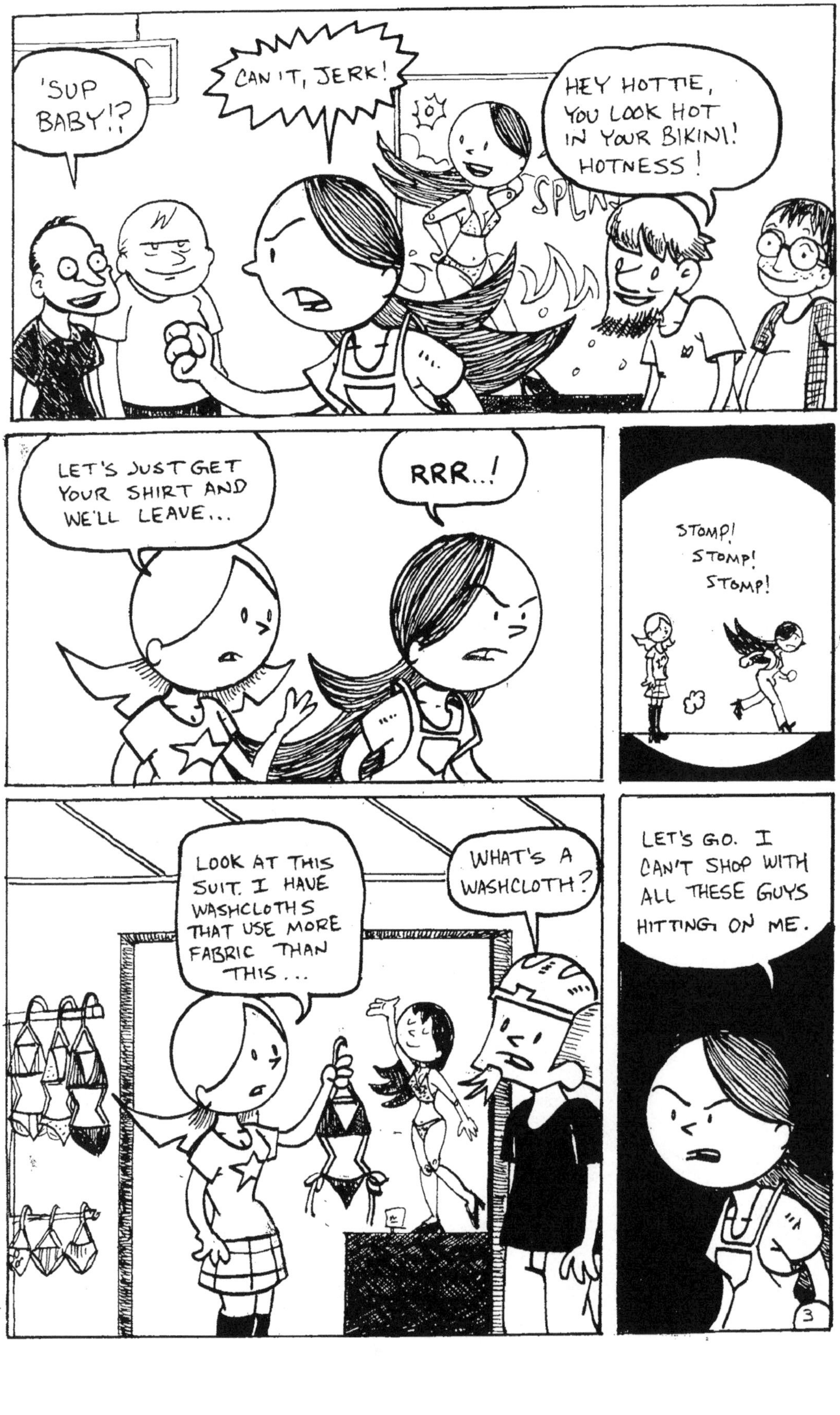
'SUP BABY!?
CAN IT, JERK!
HEY HOTTIE, YOU LOOK HOT IN YOUR BIKINI! HOTNESS!
LET'S JUST GET YOUR SHIRT AND WE'LL LEAVE...
RRR..!
STOMP! STOMP! STOMP!
LOOK AT THIS SUIT. I HAVE WASHCLOTHS THAT USE MORE FABRIC THAN THIS...
WHAT'S A WASHCLOTH?
LET'S GO. I CAN'T SHOP WITH ALL THESE GUYS HITTING ON ME.
3

Uptown Girl issue "The Itsy Bitsy Teeny Weeny Yellow Polka-Dot Bikini" by Bob Lipski. © 2009 Bob Lipski

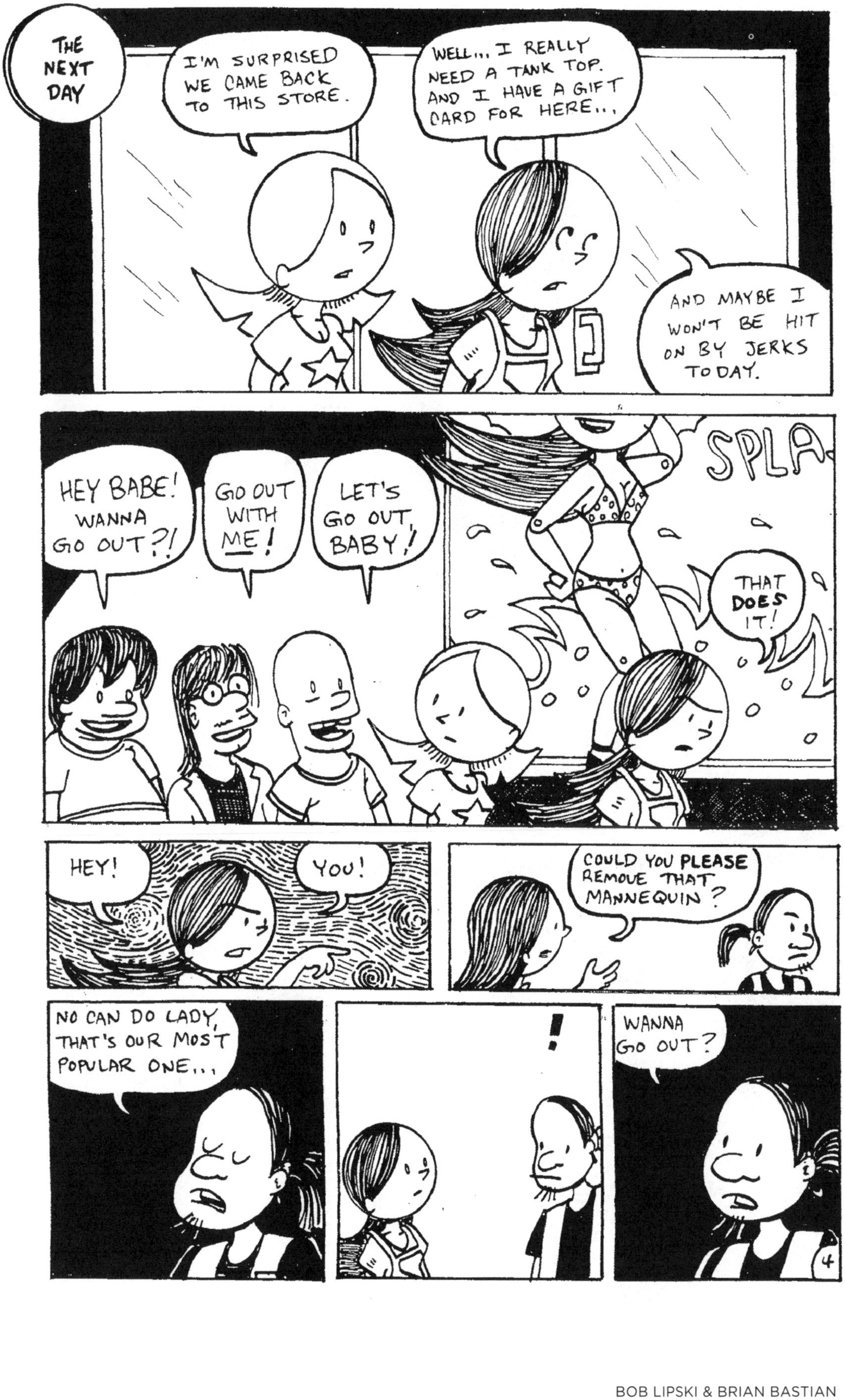
THE NEXT DAY
I'M SURPRISED WE CAME BACK TO THIS STORE.
WELL... I REALLY NEED A TANK TOP. AND I HAVE A GIFT CARD FOR HERE...
AND MAYBE I WON'T BE HIT ON BY JERKS TODAY.
HEY BABE! WANNA GO OUT?!
GO OUT WITH ME!
LET'S GO OUT, BABY!
SPLA
THAT **DOES** IT!
HEY!
YOU!
COULD YOU **PLEASE** REMOVE THAT MANNEQUIN?
NO CAN DO LADY, THAT'S OUR MOST POPULAR ONE...
!
WANNA GO OUT?
4

Uptown Girl issue "The Itsy Bitsy Teeny Weeny Yellow Polka-Dot Bikini" by Bob Lipski. © 2009 Bob Lipski

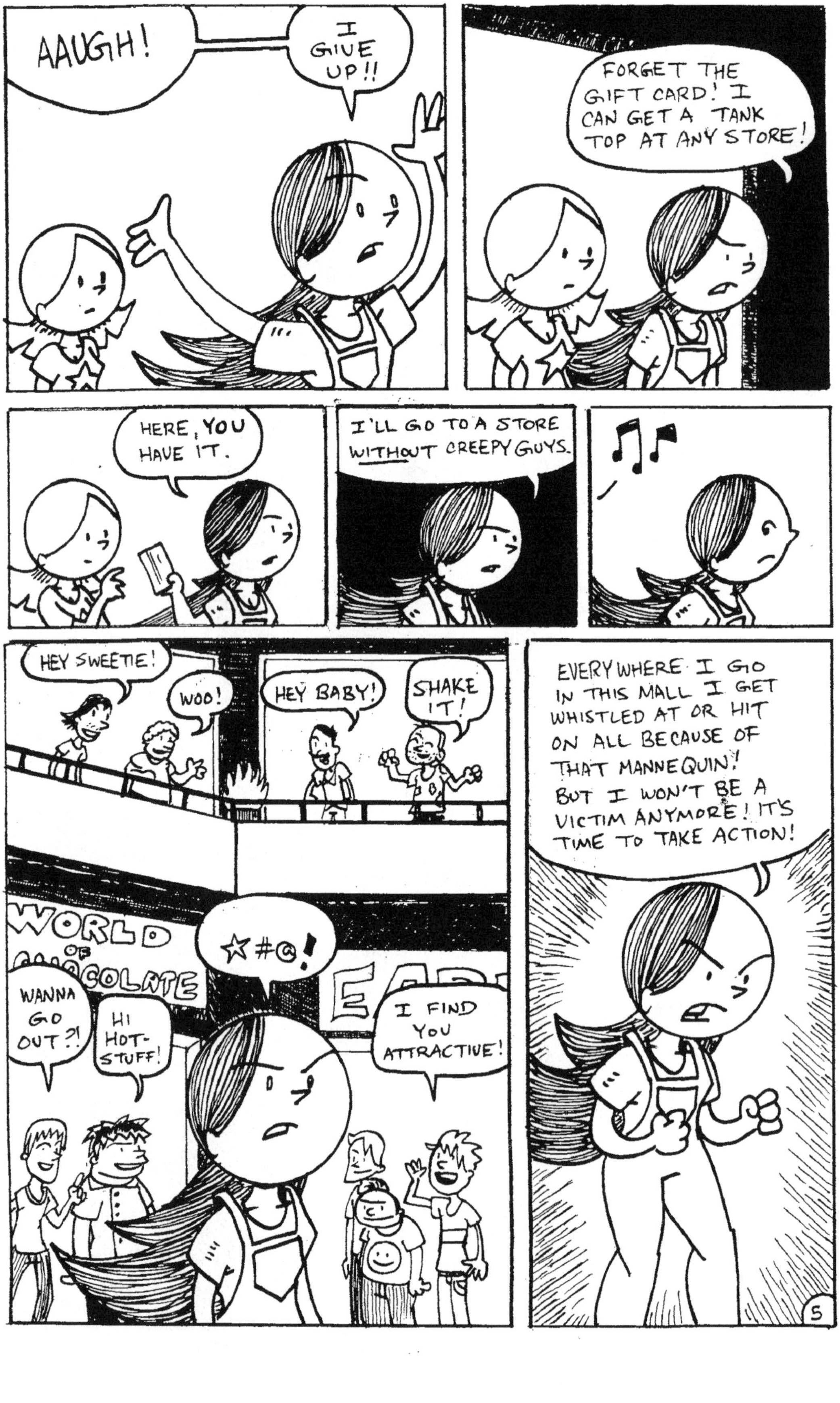
AAUGH!
I GIVE UP!!
FORGET THE GIFT CARD! I CAN GET A TANK TOP AT ANY STORE!
HERE, YOU HAVE IT.
I'LL GO TO A STORE WITHOUT CREEPY GUYS.
HEY SWEETIE!
WOO!
HEY BABY!
SHAKE IT!
WORLD OF
☆#@!
WANNA GO OUT?!
HI HOT-STUFF!
I FIND YOU ATTRACTIVE!
EVERYWHERE I GO IN THIS MALL I GET WHISTLED AT OR HIT ON ALL BECAUSE OF THAT MANNEQUIN! BUT I WON'T BE A VICTIM ANYMORE! IT'S TIME TO TAKE ACTION!
5

Uptown Girl issue "The Itsy Bitsy Teeny Weeny Yellow Polka-Dot Bikini" by Bob Lipski. © 2009 Bob Lipski

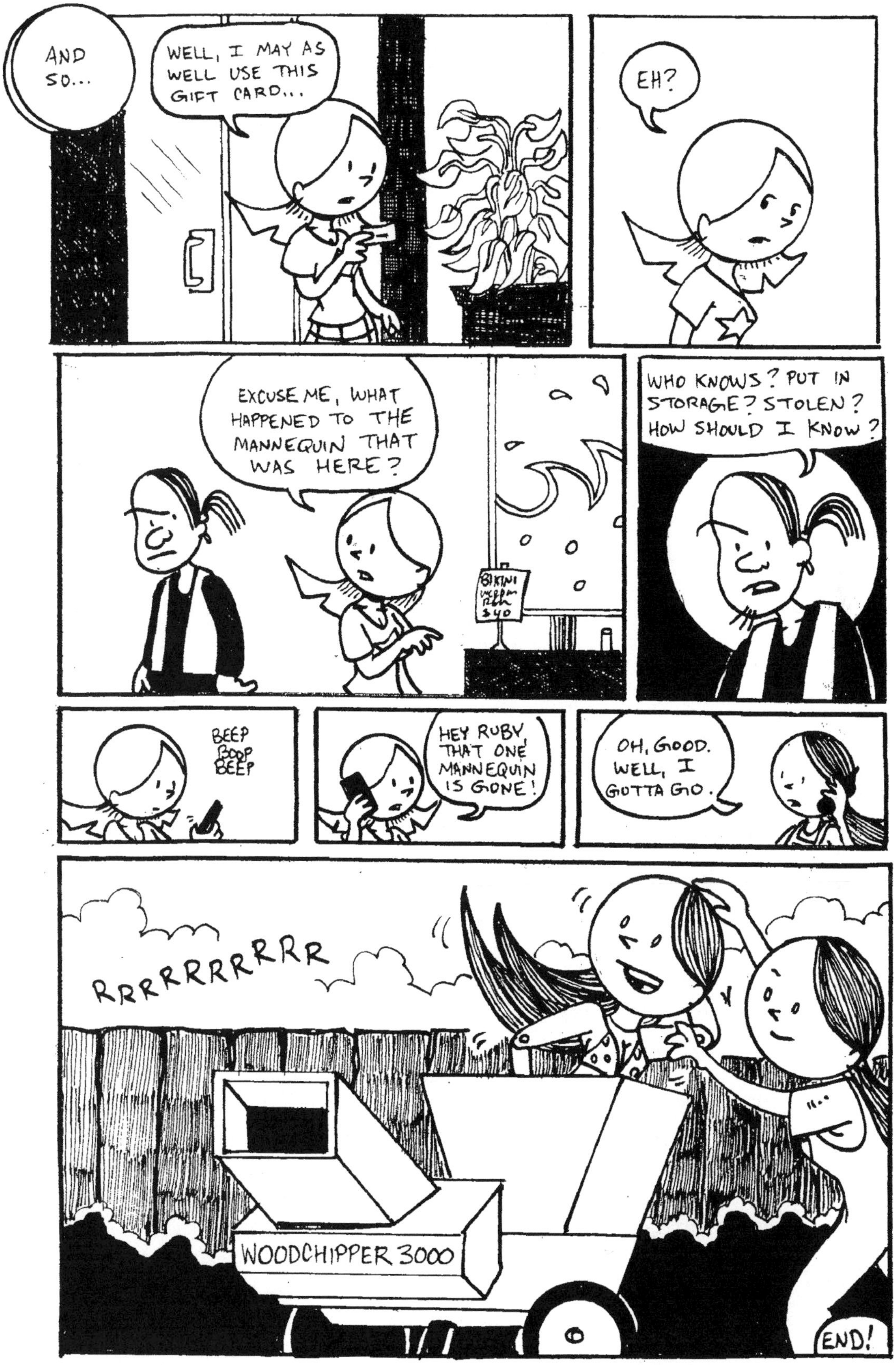
AND SO...
WELL, I MAY AS WELL USE THIS GIFT CARD...
EH?
EXCUSE ME, WHAT HAPPENED TO THE MANNEQUIN THAT WAS HERE?
BIKINI
$40
WHO KNOWS? PUT IN STORAGE? STOLEN? HOW SHOULD I KNOW?
BEEP BOOP BEEP
HEY RUBY, THAT ONE MANNEQUIN IS GONE!
OH, GOOD. WELL, I GOTTA GO.
RRRRRRRRRR
WOODCHIPPER 3000
END!

Uptown Girl issue "The Itsy Bitsy Teeny Weeny Yellow Polka-Dot Bikini" by Bob Lipski. © 2009 Bob Lipski

Brittney Sabo grew up in the computer age. In 1984, a year before her birth, the first Apple Macintosh went on sale. By the mid-nineties, e-mail had become a primary mode of communication and, for Sabo at least, the Internet had become a "portal to the world." Cartoonist and illustrator, Sabo has matured in a world of iPods, Smart Phones, hybrid cars, and webcomics (or webcomix); but her art, nearly always, takes a cue from the past. She freights her drawings with good, old-fashioned history and a splash of the supernatural.

Sabo was raised in Winona, a Minnesota river town, but attended an arts magnet high school in Durham, North Carolina. The advantage of growing up in a digital world was that even as a high school student, Sabo was able to network with artists far outside the Durham city limits. She hooked into her virtual arts community through the art-posting site deviantART and blogging platform LiveJournal. Her community provided feedback and kept her art moving forward.

In 2003, Sabo enrolled at the Minneapolis College of Art and Design as an illustration student. She was back in Minnesota—with a truckload of homework, deadlines, portfolio due dates, rushed meals, and class critiques. Art school was one part fun, four parts all-nighters.

Back in the Middle Ages and Renaissance, a student who wanted to learn painting apprenticed under a master. The great Italian fresco artist Giotto studied under Cimabue, da Vinci under Verrocchio. Even today, students learn best in the company of practicing artists. For Sabo, an influential teacher-artist was Vincent Stall, an instructor in the comic art program during her time at MCAD.

What made him good was not his depth of knowledge, his talent, or his contagious passion for artistic creation, which he had in spades. Nope. It was his scrappiness. Put this dude in the ring at a student art critique, and he'd take off the gloves.

"Kids need to hear things about their work they don't want to hear," says Sabo. Stall had no problem with that. "He'd say things like, 'What is this? This is ridiculous. It doesn't make any sense.' Some students interpreted that as, 'Oh, he doesn't like superheroes.' But that wasn't it. Vince would tell you why your art didn't work and then he'd try to get you to go to the next level."

Sabo was an illustration student. But the comic art instructor gave her advice she still carries with her. One piece was that she didn't have to create a masterpiece straight out of school. A no-brainer, right? But art students endure art history lessons too, and inevitably compare themselves to the great artists, who by some accounts conquered the art world while still in diapers. It's hard to measure up to that. Another nugget of Stall wisdom was to focus on story. He told Sabo that a cartoonist or illustrator can get away with being a mediocre artist but not a mediocre storyteller.

Initially, Sabo undertook her minicomic *Badlands* for ACT-I-VATE, an online webcomix collective based out of New York. Nikki Cook, an MCAD grad, had done work for the site and asked Sabo to submit a piece. "I started *Badlands* the first semester of my senior year, and I was like, *I'll have plenty of time to draw a page a week*," she says. But her sunny optimism fled under the pressures of art school. Too much work, too little time for anything but work.

However, the story attached itself to her and resurfaced in 2008 when Sabo needed a piece for a comic art show in St. Paul. *Badlands* opens in Depression-era South Dakota. A young farm couple scrabbles to eke out a living as the Dust Bowl sweeps over the horizon, depositing misery in heaps in every corner of the house.

Sabo's close-ups of the farm couple capture their sense of hopelessness, the way Dorothea Lange's photographs of the Great Depression captured the despair of migrant workers. But apart from the documented history of the period, Sabo provides an out for her fictional characters. She sends a touring circus into the dust storm and a circus showman who promises freedom from financial ruin, if the farm couple will only do him one teensy favor.

Badlands finds Sabo in prime storytelling mode, digging into the past and overlaying her narrative with a thin gauze of the weird and magical. Another mini posted on her website, *Shortcut,* plays out a boy's fears as he wanders down a lonely forest path. Nearby, two figures argue in a cemetery. *That's God and the Devil,* the boy thinks, hearing the men dole out the souls of the dead. "You take this one, and I'll take this one," they say. As the boy scampers off, Sabo zooms in for the reveal. God and the Devil are nothing more than old duffers tossing apples in burlap sacks.

With her graphic novel *Francis Sharp,* Sabo returns to Depression-era America and farm country. "It's allowing me to combine everything I love about storytelling into one story," she says of the project developed with writer Anna Bratton. "The idea came when I was joking with friends. I needed a story, and I said, 'What kind of stories do I always tell? Well, I tell stories about a kid lost in the woods.' But then I thought about that. I'd never actually explored *why* the kid is lost in the woods. So, in *Francis Sharp,* I'm taking that theme and turning it into a longer story."

Now employed as an assistant to Vertigo cartoonist Peter Gross, Sabo remains in touch with the Minnesota cartooning community. She provided a strip, *The Teenage Ghost Hunting Society,* for a Cartoonist Conspiracy publication, *The Big Funny.* And she continues to mull over some good advice she got not so long ago.

"I'm not into creating Spider-Man fan art or telling a story about a guy who walks up stairs for twelve pages," she says. "I want to learn how to tell a cohesive story that appeals to people. You need a sophisticated voice to tell some kinds of stories. But before that, you need to figure out how to tell a straightforward one." ■

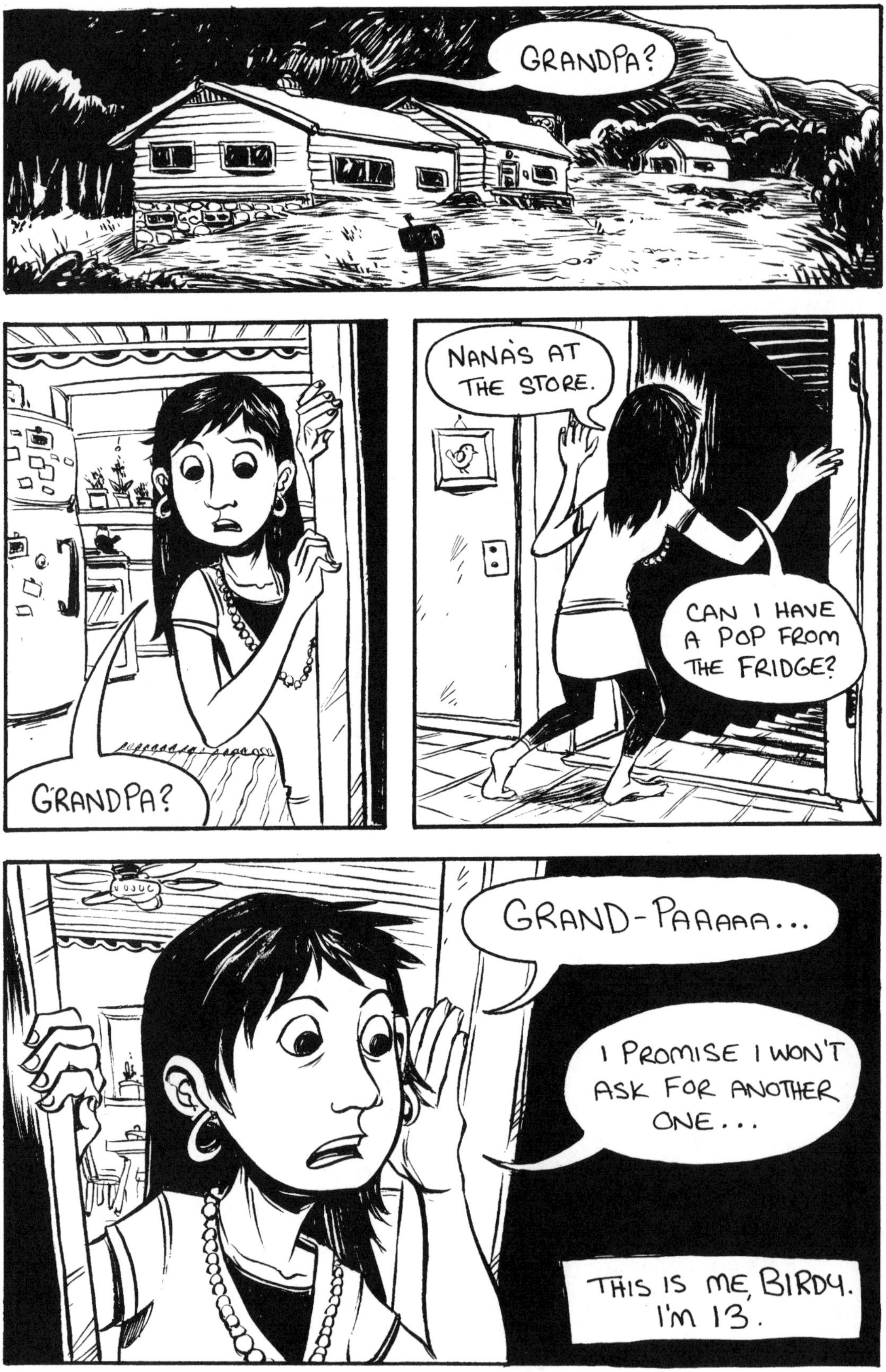
GRANDPA?
GRANDPA?
NANA'S AT THE STORE.
CAN I HAVE A POP FROM THE FRIDGE?
GRAND-PAAAAA...
I PROMISE I WON'T ASK FOR ANOTHER ONE...
THIS IS ME, BIRDY. I'M 13.

"Ghost Jars" No. 1 by Brittney Sabo. © 2009 Brittney Sabo

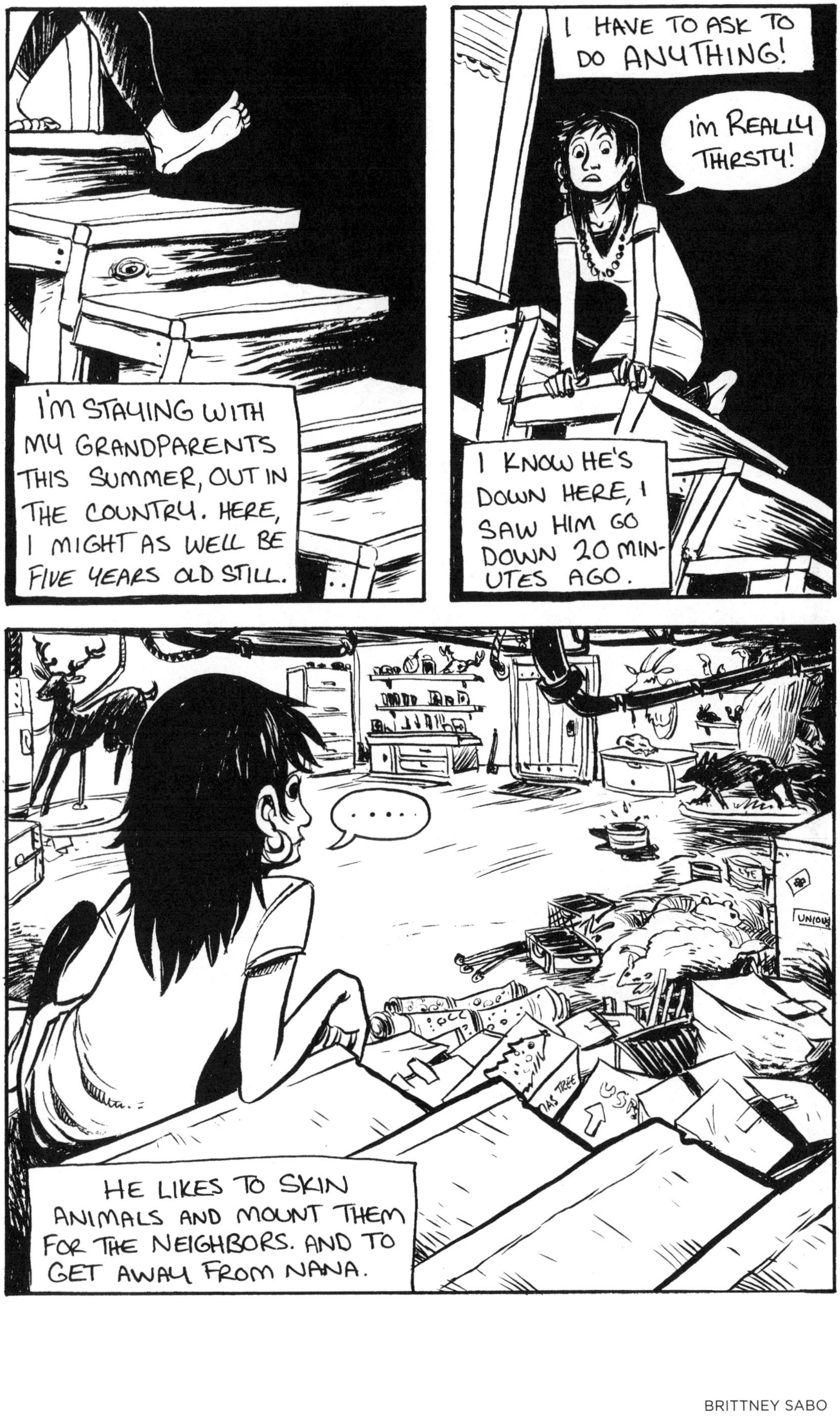
I'M STAYING WITH MY GRANDPARENTS THIS SUMMER, OUT IN THE COUNTRY. HERE, I MIGHT AS WELL BE FIVE YEARS OLD STILL.
I HAVE TO ASK TO DO ANYTHING!
I'M REALLY THIRSTY!
I KNOW HE'S DOWN HERE, I SAW HIM GO DOWN 20 MINUTES AGO.
....
HE LIKES TO SKIN ANIMALS AND MOUNT THEM FOR THE NEIGHBORS. AND TO GET AWAY FROM NANA.

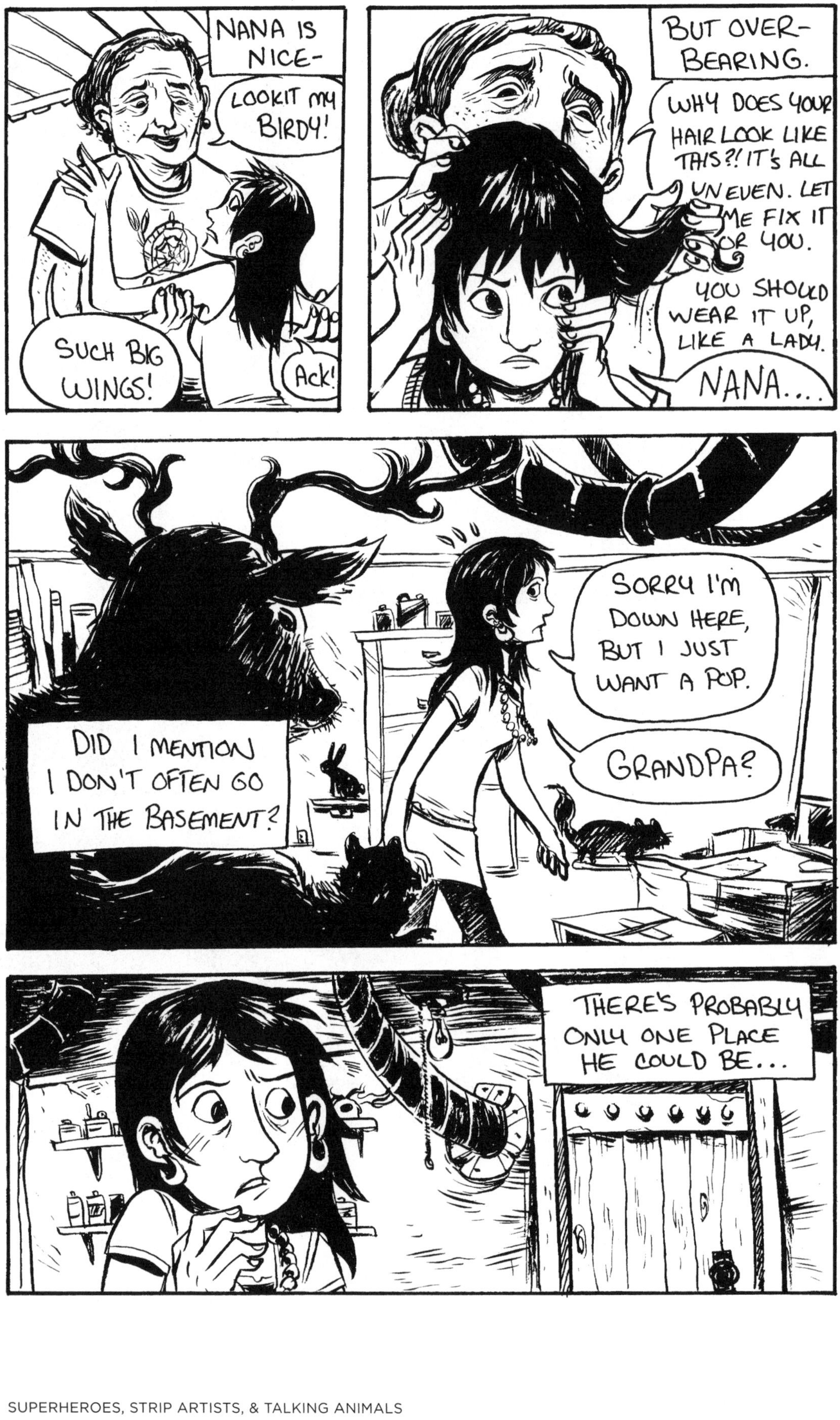
NANA IS NICE-
LOOKIT MY BIRDY!
SUCH BIG WINGS!
Ack!
BUT OVER-BEARING.
WHY DOES YOUR HAIR LOOK LIKE THIS?! IT'S ALL UNEVEN. LET ME FIX IT OR YOU.
YOU SHOULD WEAR IT UP, LIKE A LADY.
NANA...
DID I MENTION I DON'T OFTEN GO IN THE BASEMENT?
SORRY I'M DOWN HERE, BUT I JUST WANT A POP.
GRANDPA?
THERE'S PROBABLY ONLY ONE PLACE HE COULD BE...

"Ghost Jars" No. 1 by Brittney Sabo. © 2009 Brittney Sabo

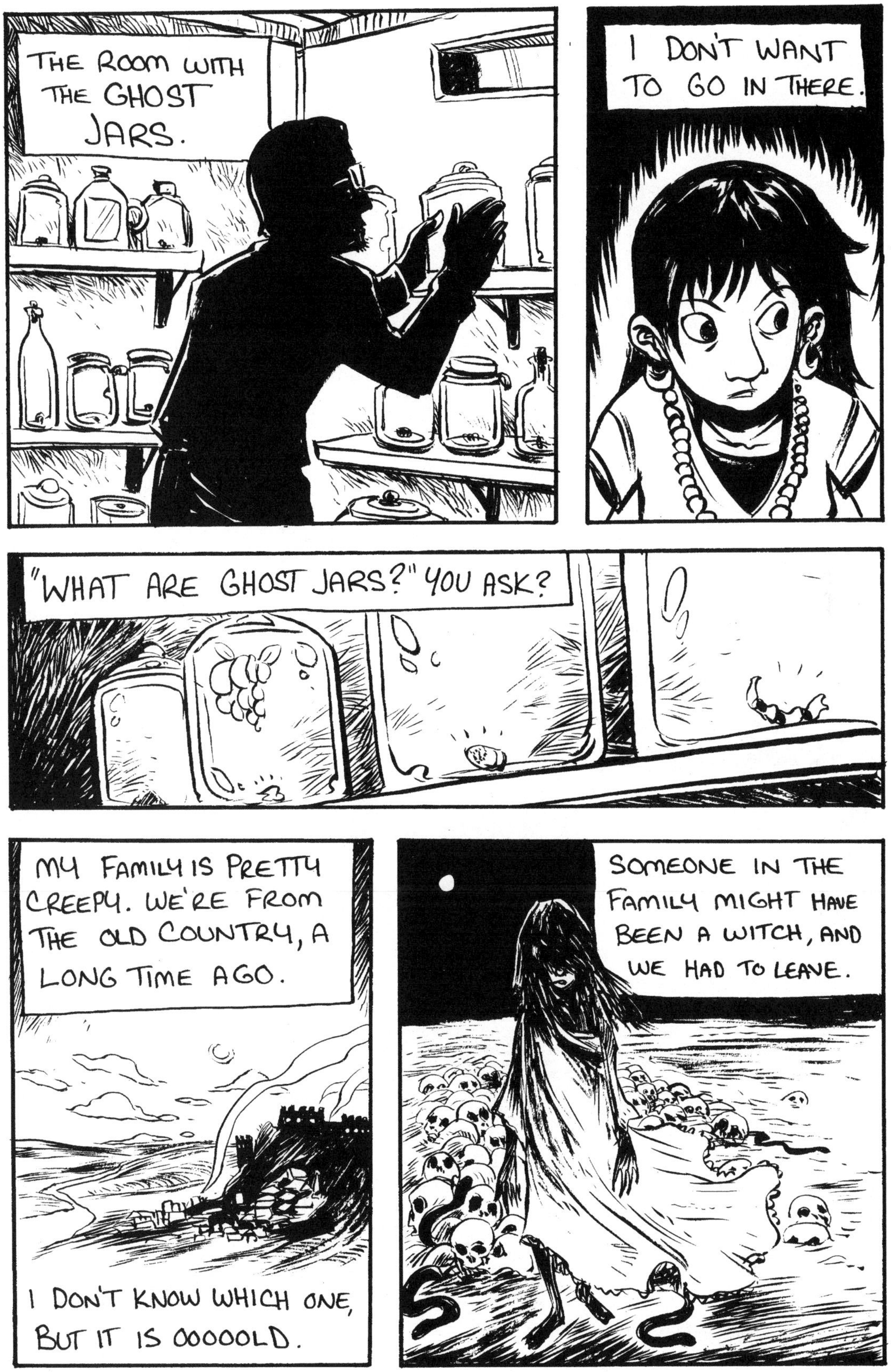
THE ROOM WITH THE GHOST JARS.
I DON'T WANT TO GO IN THERE.
"WHAT ARE GHOST JARS?" YOU ASK?
MY FAMILY IS PRETTY CREEPY. WE'RE FROM THE OLD COUNTRY, A LONG TIME AGO.
I DON'T KNOW WHICH ONE, BUT IT IS OOOOOLD.
SOMEONE IN THE FAMILY MIGHT HAVE BEEN A WITCH, AND WE HAD TO LEAVE.

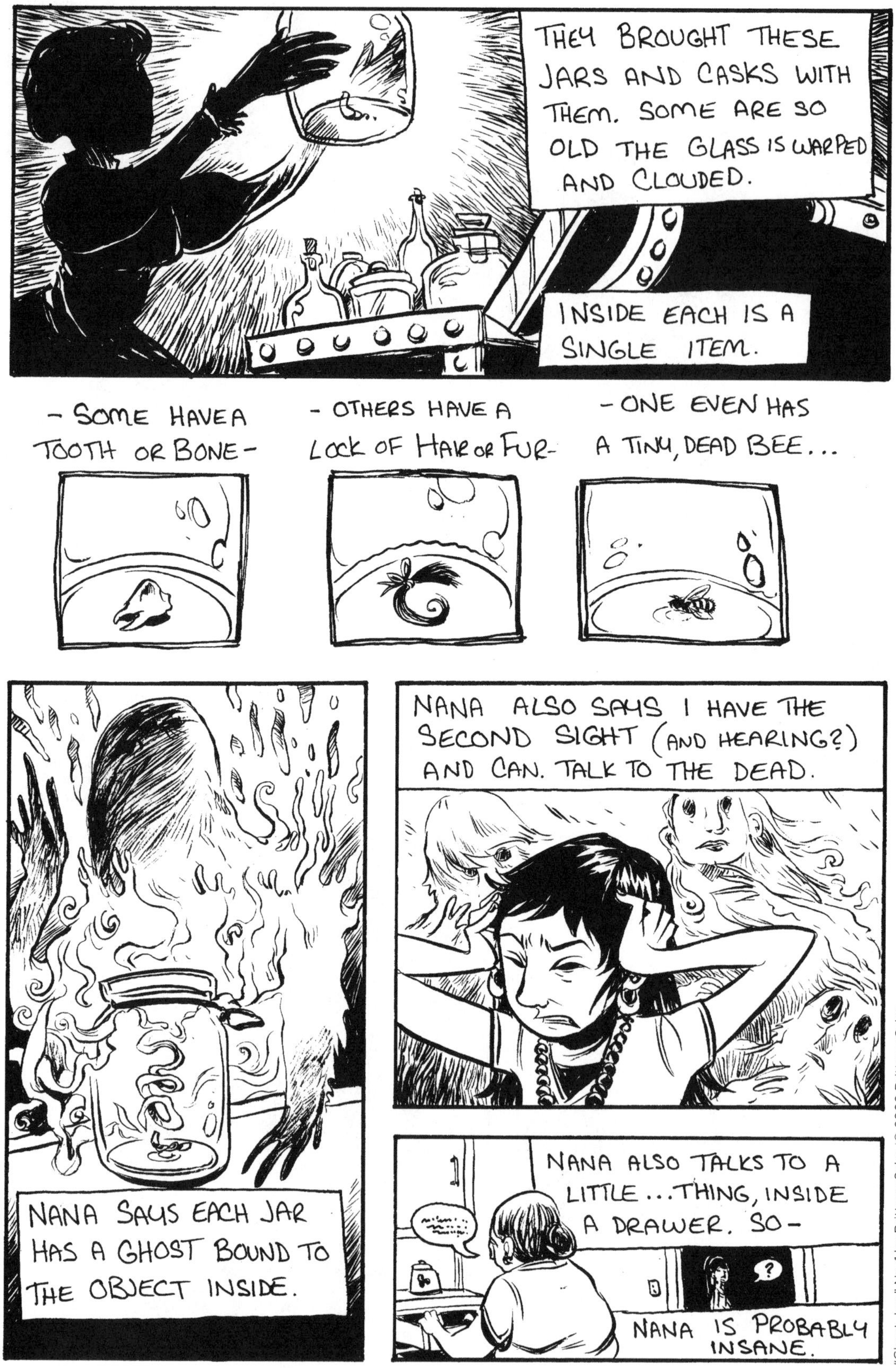
THEY BROUGHT THESE JARS AND CASKS WITH THEM. SOME ARE SO OLD THE GLASS IS WARPED AND CLOUDED.
INSIDE EACH IS A SINGLE ITEM.
- SOME HAVE A TOOTH OR BONE -
- OTHERS HAVE A LOCK OF HAIR OR FUR -
- ONE EVEN HAS A TINY, DEAD BEE...
NANA SAYS EACH JAR HAS A GHOST BOUND TO THE OBJECT INSIDE.
NANA ALSO SAYS I HAVE THE SECOND SIGHT (AND HEARING?) AND CAN. TALK TO THE DEAD.
NANA ALSO TALKS TO A LITTLE...THING, INSIDE A DRAWER. SO-
?
NANA IS PROBABLY INSANE.

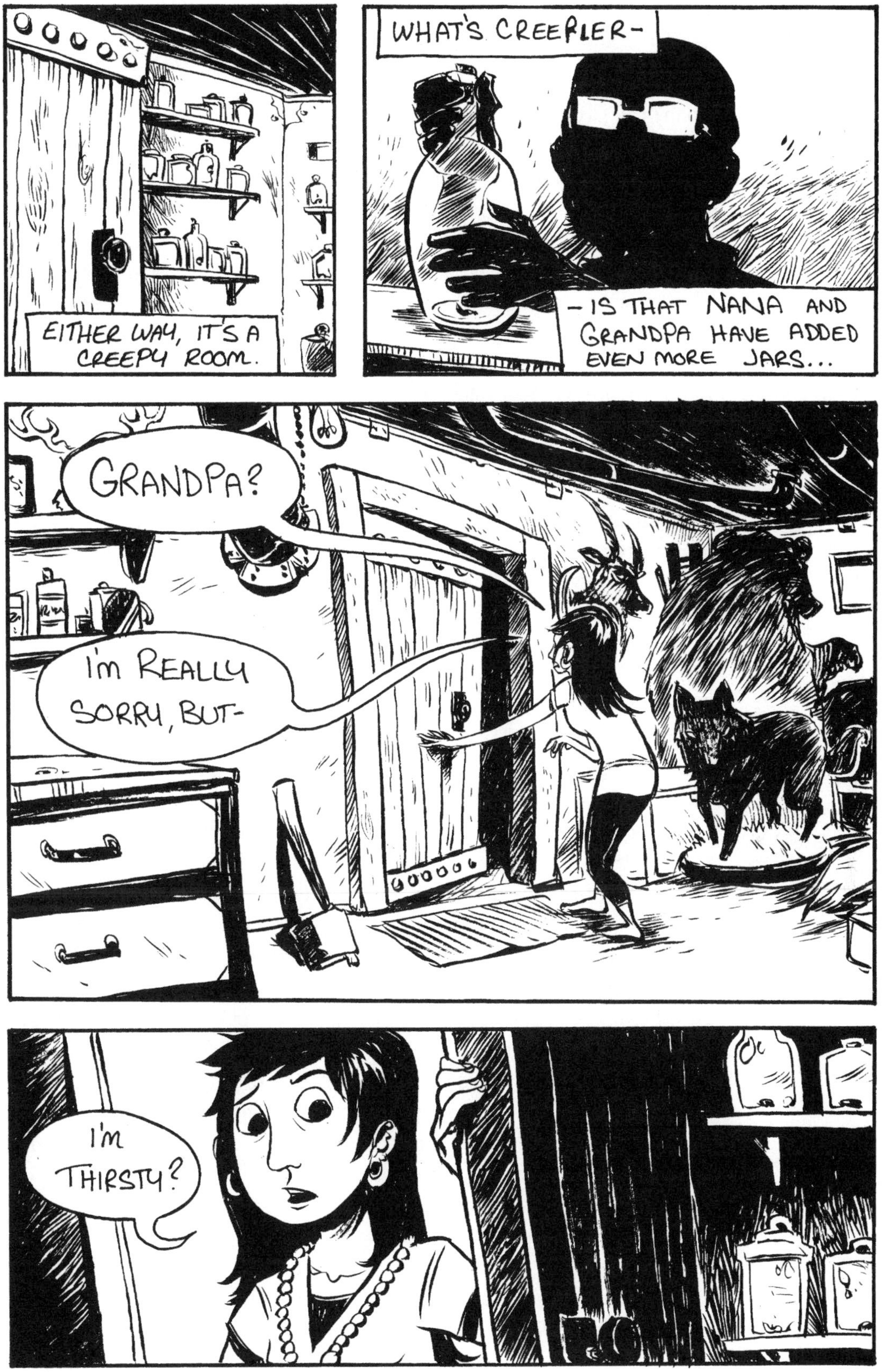
EITHER WAY, IT'S A CREEPY ROOM.
WHAT'S CREEPIER-
-IS THAT NANA AND GRANDPA HAVE ADDED EVEN MORE JARS...
GRANDPA?
I'M REALLY SORRY, BUT-
I'M THIRSTY?

STEVEN STWALLEY

Soapy the Chicken has a problem. She's dead, kicked off her comic strip like an old can of beans; and now the ducks, Quackers and Waddles, are holding elections to become the featured character in the "Soapy the Chicken" strip. Where is Bubonic the Rat when Soapy needs him? Or Frog the Frog? Well, thanks to Soapy's spending habits, a collections agent has collared Bubonic for outstanding debts. And Frog, last anyone heard, was tumbling down the alimentary canal of Quackers the Duck, ingested to silence his protests over the elections.

It's not easy being a cartoon strip character. Soapy could probably use a good therapist. If she's seeking the meaning of life or the timely reversal of her comic strip death, though, she needs to go straight to the top, to Steven Stwalley, the cartoonist behind the strip and the agent of Soapy's demise. But Stwalley, who by day works as an interactive developer and animator for a Minneapolis ad agency, can't be reached for comment. He's got a full plate, what with work, family, and a slew of extracurricular cartooning activities that—sorry, Soap—take precedence over the minor agonies of his comic characters. Busy. That's the life of a modern-day cartoonist. Soapy will have to lump it.

Stwalley's story begins in Iowa City, Iowa, where he was born in 1970. His father gave him a collection of Walt Disney comics he'd also read as a boy. Stwalley devoured the comics, and by and by transformed into the dyed-in-the-wool comics and animation fan who found himself at Minneapolis's Art Institute studying three-dimensional design. He liked school well enough, but he loved the school's library.

"I ended up working in the Art Institute's library while I was a student," says Stwalley. "It was a great job because the library needed to order new books" and the librarian asked the student for his input. No problemo. He knew exactly what the library needed—comics—and had plenty of suggestions. "I basically helped the library buy this incredible collection of comics."

After graduation, Stwalley went in search of other Minnesota cartoonists. He'd been drawing comics since he was a kid and felt a need to absorb the creativity of other cartooning gents and ladies. He waved a magic wand—and nothing. So, in 2002, he organized. He printed flyers, tacked them to telephone posts, and voila, the Cartoonist Conspiracy was born. The community has since become the International Cartoonist Conspiracy, with cells in cities across the United States and even a few abroad.

In Minnesota, the Conspiracy meets twice a month, once in Minneapolis and once in St. Paul. Altered Esthetics, a gallery in Northeast Minneapolis, regularly exhibits members' artwork, and every year, the Minnesota Center for Book Arts hosts the Conspiracy's 24-Hour Comics Day. The point of the 24-Hour Comics Day is for cartoonists to gather en masse and crank out a comic in twenty-four hours.

"Kevin Cannon would produce these amazing comics at 24-Hour Comics that were basically better than what some cartoonists would make in a lifetime," says Stwalley of another local cartoonist. He voiced a challenge in earshot of the other cartoonists. "Hey, Kevin, why don't you do one of these twenty-four-hour days every month for an entire year, but have each twenty-four-hour session be a chapter of a longer book?"

Cannon couldn't back down. Not in front of an audience. He smiled, nodded, escaped the session, and sweated over the project to which he'd just committed a year of his life. "After a long sixteen-hour sleep, after the fourth marathon, I woke up and my right arm was numb," says Cannon. "I was like, *Oh god, if this is how it's going to turn out I'm not going to do these marathons anymore.*" He ended up finishing the book but without the marathons. Top Shelf Productions published Cannon's effort, *Far Arden,* in 2009.

> "I NEVER SIT DOWN WITH A PLAN FOR WHAT I'M GOING TO DRAW," SAYS STWALLEY. "BUT USUALLY BY THE LAST PANEL, I'VE FIGURED [OUT] WHAT THE COMIC IS ABOUT."

Encouraged by his friend's success, Stwalley and other conspirators undertook what they labeled the 288-Hour Graphic Novel Challenge. Stwalley has yet to finish his submission, *Ezekiel Fishman Versus the Martians,* but the pages are posted online and feature a Stwalley-esque cast of characters: train-riding hoboes, cops, Martians, and, of course, zombies. He is also working on a children's book, *The Most Delicious Cookies in the World.*

"I never sit down with a plan for what I'm going to draw," says Stwalley. "But usually by the last panel, I've figured [out] what the comic is about." In 2005, those unplanned sessions gave birth to "Soapy the Chicken," Stwalley's recurring webcomic.

Poor Soapy. She never had a chance. She dies, and her body is cloned to provide meat for a fast food chain. Meanwhile, her devoted sidekick Bubonic the Rat goes missing. This leaves an opening in the strip. Management hires a temporary sidekick, Frog the Frog. He doesn't smoke, doesn't drink (much), and doesn't gamble. Instead, he spends his comic strip appearances searching for good old Soapy, who like Bubonic must have fallen in a hole somewhere.

Soapy's world is anthropomorphic, animals acting like human beings, with only a peppering of real humans to round out the cast. Stwalley prefers to illustrate animals, but he's also drawing from a long history of animal-centric comics. George Herriman popularized the animal love triangle in the early twentieth century with his comic strip "Krazy Kat." Offisa Pup loves Krazy Kat, Krazy loves Ignatz the mouse, and Ignatz throws bricks at Krazy's head.

Soapy too—when she's around—is involved in a love triangle. "Frog loves Soapy. Soapy loves a can of beans," says Stwalley, "but the can of beans doesn't reciprocate anyone's love." ∎

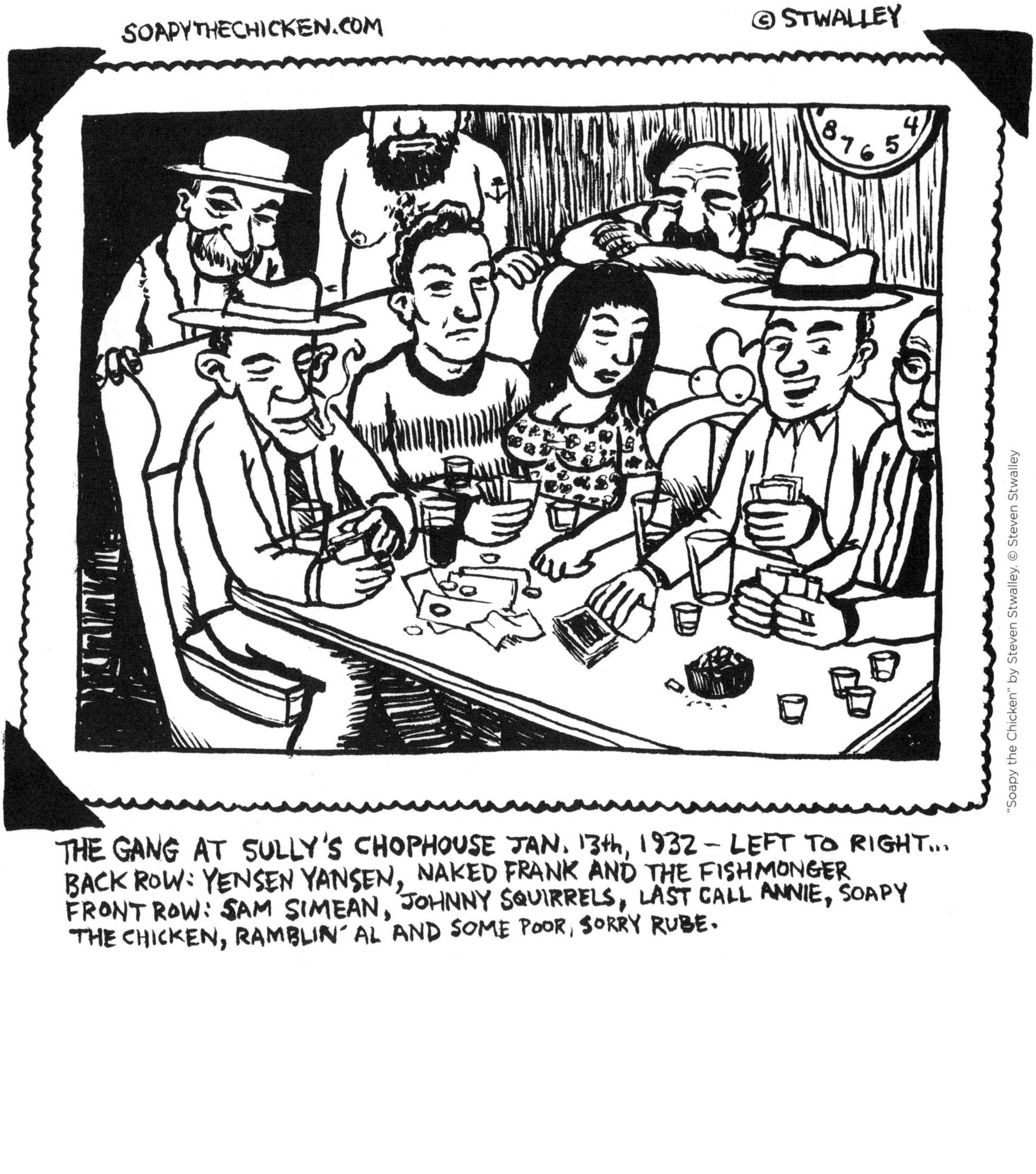
SOAPYTHECHICKEN.COM
© STWALLEY
THE GANG AT SULLY'S CHOPHOUSE JAN. 13th, 1932 – LEFT TO RIGHT...
BACK ROW: YENSEN YANSEN, NAKED FRANK AND THE FISHMONGER
FRONT ROW: SAM SIMEAN, JOHNNY SQUIRRELS, LAST CALL ANNIE, SOAPY THE CHICKEN, RAMBLIN' AL AND SOME POOR, SORRY RUBE.

SOAPY The Chicken
I CAN'T BELIEVE SOAPY IS REALLY GONE.
WITHOUT HER, MY ENTIRE LIFE SEEMS EMPTY AND MEANINGLESS.
A SIDEKICK WITHOUT A BUDDY? IT'S RIDICULOUS.
I MAY AS WELL HAVE NEVER BEEN BORN. MAY AS WELL BE DEAD.
SOB
EVEN IF I AM JUST A TEMP.
YEP. THAT'S THE ANSWER.
THERE'S JUST NO OTHER WAY.
"FOR A SIDEKICK TO RETAIN HIS HONOR WHEN HIS BUDDY HAS PASSED ON, HE MUST TAKE HIS OWN LIFE. FOR THIS IS THE WAY OF THE SIDEKICK."
PAGE 153. OF "THE ART OF SIDEKICKERY" BY GABBY HAYES.
LET'S SEE... I CAN'T AFFORD A GUN... TOO MESSY ANYHOW. I DON'T OWN A CAR SO RUNNING MYSELF OVER IS OUT. I WONDER IF YOU CAN CHOP OFF YOUR OWN HEAD WITH AN AXE?
SOAPYTHECHICKEN.COM
©STWALLEY

"Soapy the Chicken" by Steven Stwalley. © Steven Stwalley

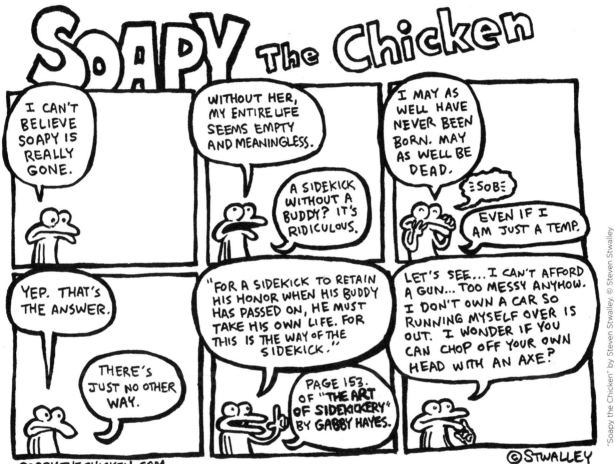

SOAPY THE CHICKEN
WELL, LOOKSH LIKE THISH ISH IT... SHOON I WILL BE DEAD.
SOAPYTHECHICKEN.COM
NO TIME TO LOOSHE I SHUPPOSH.
SHEE YA SHOON SHOAPY!
GAK!
KICK!
CLANKITY-CLANK CLANK!
WELL THAT WASH SHORT OF PAINFUL. WONDER IF I'M DEAD YET?
I'LL BE A BETTER JUDGSH WHEN I SHOBER UP...
© STWALLEY

"Soapy the Chicken" by Steven Stwalley. © Steven Stwalley

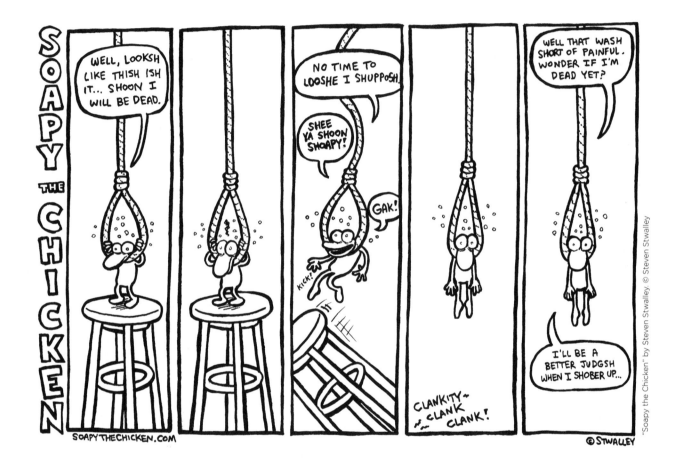

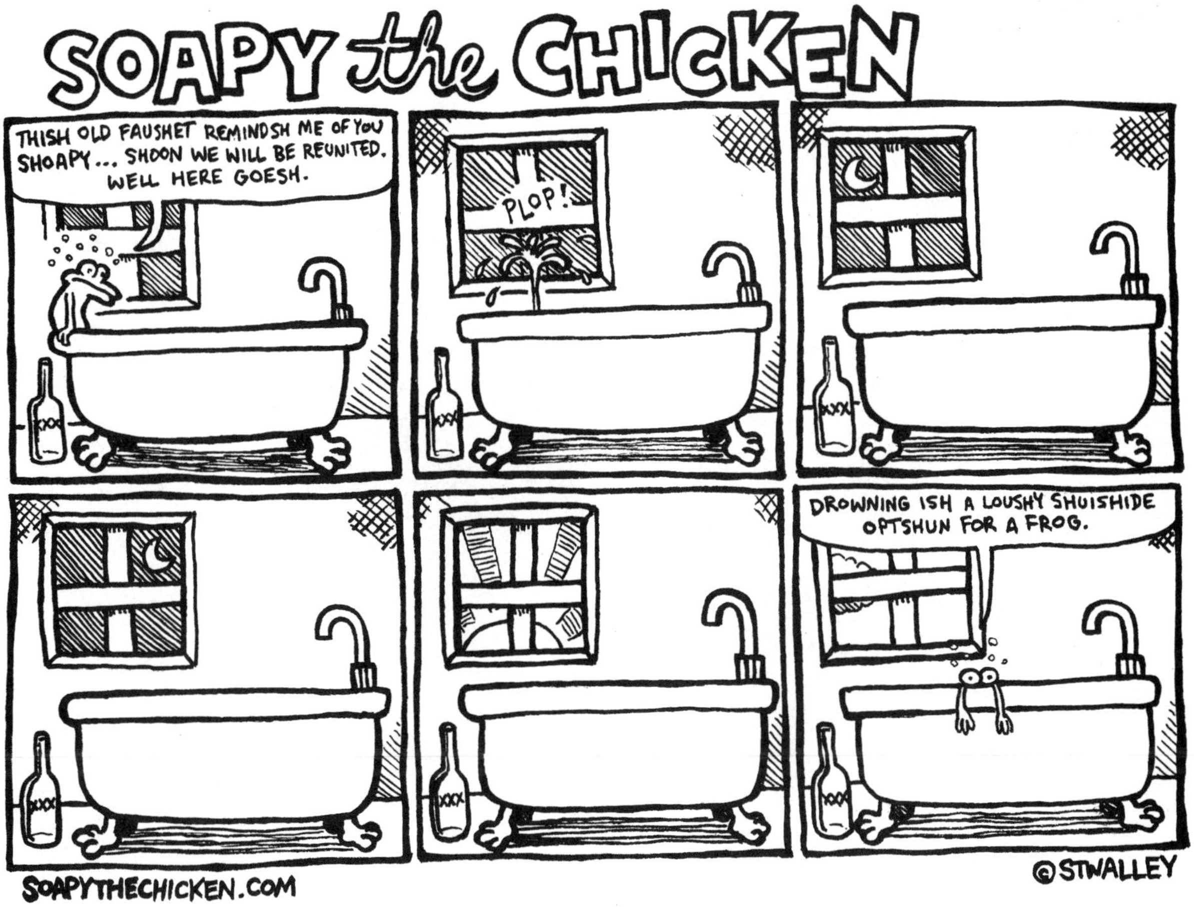
SOAPY the CHICKEN
THISH OLD FAUSHET REMINDSH ME OF YOU SHOAPY... SHOON WE WILL BE REUNITED. WELL HERE GOESH.
PLOP!
DROWNING ISH A LOUSHY SHUISHIDE OPTSHUN FOR A FROG.
SOAPYTHECHICKEN.COM
©STWALLEY

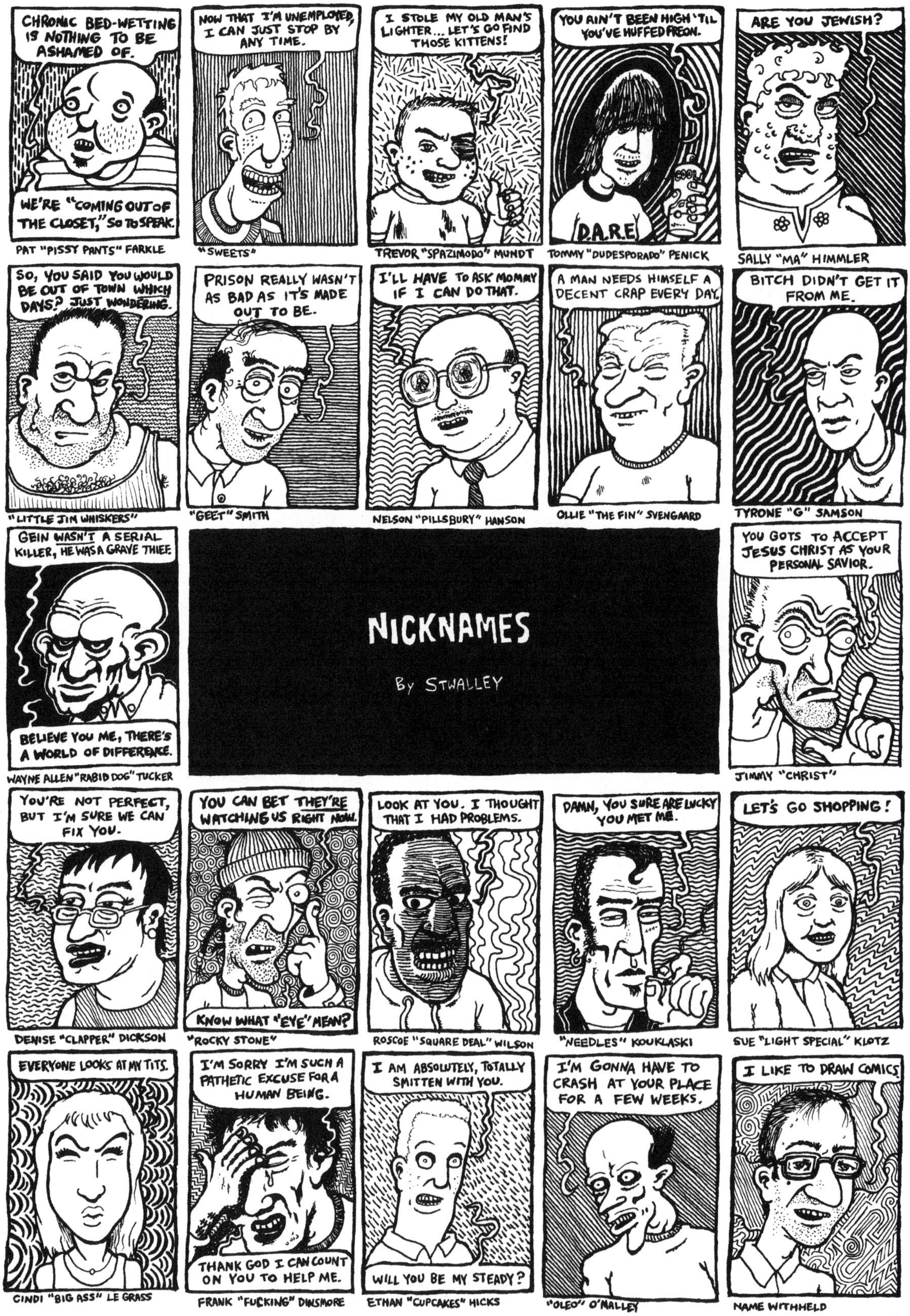
CHRONIC BED-WETTING IS NOTHING TO BE ASHAMED OF.
WE'RE "COMING OUT OF THE CLOSET," SO TO SPEAK.
PAT "PISSY PANTS" FARKLE
NOW THAT I'M UNEMPLOYED, I CAN JUST STOP BY ANY TIME.
"SWEETS"
I STOLE MY OLD MAN'S LIGHTER... LET'S GO FIND THOSE KITTENS!
TREVOR "SPAZIMODO" MUNDT
YOU AIN'T BEEN HIGH 'TIL YOU'VE HUFFED FREON.
D.A.R.E
COOL
TOMMY "DUDESPORADO" PENICK
ARE YOU JEWISH?
SALLY "MA" HIMMLER
SO, YOU SAID YOU WOULD BE OUT OF TOWN WHICH DAYS? JUST WONDERING.
"LITTLE JIM WHISKERS"
PRISON REALLY WASN'T AS BAD AS IT'S MADE OUT TO BE.
"GEET" SMITH
I'LL HAVE TO ASK MOMMY IF I CAN DO THAT.
NELSON "PILLSBURY" HANSON
A MAN NEEDS HIMSELF A DECENT CRAP EVERY DAY.
OLLIE "THE FIN" SVENGAARD
BITCH DIDN'T GET IT FROM ME.
TYRONE "G" SAMSON
GEIN WASN'T A SERIAL KILLER, HE WAS A GRAVE THIEF.
BELIEVE YOU ME, THERE'S A WORLD OF DIFFERENCE.
WAYNE ALLEN "RABID DOG" TUCKER
NICKNAMES
BY STWALLEY
YOU GOTS TO ACCEPT JESUS CHRIST AS YOUR PERSONAL SAVIOR.
JIMMY "CHRIST"
YOU'RE NOT PERFECT, BUT I'M SURE WE CAN FIX YOU.
DENISE "CLAPPER" DICKSON
YOU CAN BET THEY'RE WATCHING US RIGHT NOW.
KNOW WHAT "EYE" MEAN?
"ROCKY STONE"
LOOK AT YOU. I THOUGHT THAT I HAD PROBLEMS.
ROSCOE "SQUARE DEAL" WILSON
DAMN, YOU SURE ARE LUCKY YOU MET ME.
"NEEDLES" KOUKLASKI
LET'S GO SHOPPING!
SUE "LIGHT SPECIAL" KLOTZ
EVERYONE LOOKS AT MY TITS.
CINDI "BIG ASS" LE GRASS
I'M SORRY I'M SUCH A PATHETIC EXCUSE FOR A HUMAN BEING.
THANK GOD I CAN COUNT ON YOU TO HELP ME.
FRANK "FUCKING" DINSMORE
I AM ABSOLUTELY, TOTALLY SMITTEN WITH YOU.
WILL YOU BE MY STEADY?
ETHAN "CUPCAKES" HICKS
I'M GONNA HAVE TO CRASH AT YOUR PLACE FOR A FEW WEEKS.
"OLEO" O'MALLEY
I LIKE TO DRAW COMICS.
NAME WITHHELD

Cover for *Rogues' Gallery* No. 1 by Steven Stwalley. © 2008 Steven Stwalley

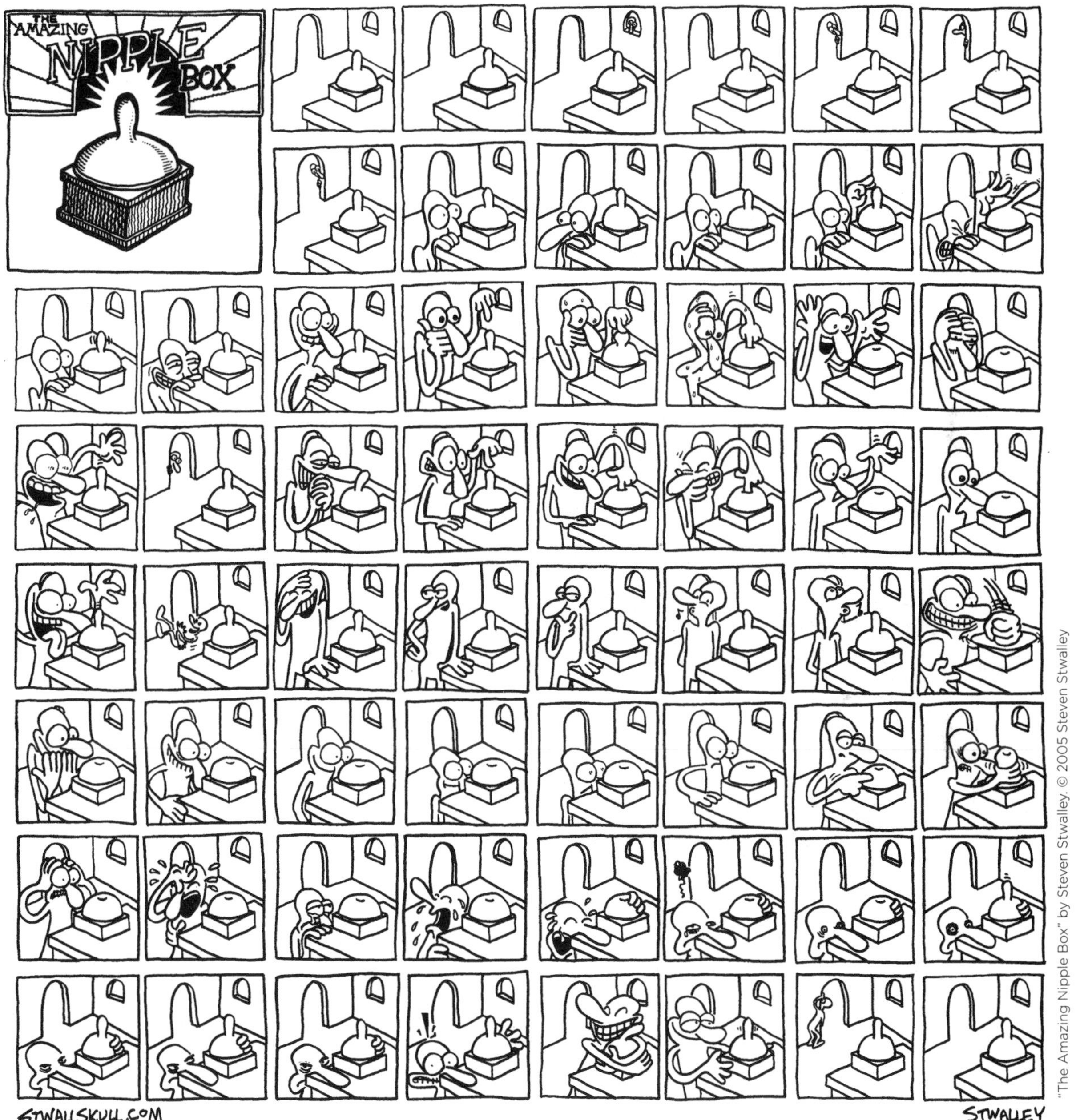
THE AMAZING NIPPLE BOX
STWALLSKULL.COM
STWALLEY

"The Amazing Nipple Box" by Steven Stwalley. © 2005 Steven Stwalley

CARTOONISTS ON THE WEB

Welcome to the end of the book. If you've made it this far, you've spent several dozen glorious pages salivating over some of the best comic art Minnesota has to offer. (Hopefully you had your hanky nearby.) But then again, some of the best Minnesota comic art never made it into the book: that would include additional art by selected artists and art by cartoonists not included in the collection. Books are notoriously selective creatures because they live in a world of page counts. Only so many cartoonists can squeeze into the pages of a book.

That's why after a barnstorm journey through the art of these contemporary Minnesota cartoonists you find yourself at a list. If you let your eyes drift to the next page you'll see a gaggle of cartoonist names alongside website addresses. That's right. Now it's your turn to take a self-directed plunge into the world of comic arts.

This particular inventory limits itself to Minnesota cartoonists and even then does not pretend to be exhaustive. New cartoonists are coming up all the time. Other cartoonists prefer to remain offline, eschewing the call to virtually archive work. Then, too, cartoonists migrate. If you read the profiles accompanying the art, you know that many so-called Minnesota cartoonists bear the imprint of other states in their biographies. And again, no list can hope to collect every living, breathing, doodle-mad cartoonist inhabiting a state that claims ten thousand lakes within its borders.

But you won't want to stop your investigations with contemporary Minnesota cartoonists. If you did, you'd miss the genius of Winsor McKay (New York) and Lyonel Feininger (Chicago), whose comic strips captivated readers in the early part of the twentieth century. And there are plenty more comic strip artists worth your hard-earned dough, but to categorize them here would entail another list and rob you of the pleasure of discovery.

Over the years, comic books have fostered an all-star roster of writers and artists who have cast and recast the superhero genre anew for their generation and expanded the medium to other genres of storytelling. The underground, alternative, and DIY movements continue to breed new revolutions that explode barriers of style, narrative content, technique, geography, and social context in the service of personal expression and art. In your quest for the cartoonists and stories that best suit your tastes, you may want to enlist comic store clerks, book store staffers, and a zealous librarian or two.

One caveat before closing. A rare few still hold that reading comics will lead, in time, to attendance at geek conventions, long bouts of anti-social behavior, and the wearing of superhero tights. The first two allegations are utterly false. The third is mostly false but can be accounted for by distracted readers, noses buried in a spellbinding comic art tale, tossing shrinkable delicates in a dryer roaring at full blast. Please read garment labels before proceeding with laundry.

Marcus Almand: www.razorkid.com
Kirk Anderson: www.kirktoons.com
Ken Avidor: www.avidorstudios.com
Tuesday Bassen: tuesdaybassen.blogspot.com
Brian Bastian: www.tommychicago.com
Terry Beatty: www.terrybeatty.blogspot.com
Hannah Blumenreich: easymetaphors.blogspot.com
Anna Bongiovanni: www.softandfleshy.blogspot.com
Curtis Square Briggs: www.comicspace.com/curtis_square
Christopher and Joseph Brudlos: www.alpha-shade.com
Bud Burgy: budburgy.wordpress.com
Kevin Cannon: www.kevincannon.org
Zander Cannon: bigtimeattic.blogspot.com
Will Dinski: www.willdinski.com
Ryan Dow: www.ryandow.com
Andrey Feldshteyn: www.cartoonblues.com
Michael Furious: uttertoadcomix.com
Neil Gaiman: www.neilgaiman.com
Patrick Gleason: www.patrickgleason.net
Peter Gross: www.petergrossart.com
Jesse Haller: jessehaller.blogspot.com
Sam Hiti: www.samhiti.com
Meghan Hogan: startledmaggie.blogspot.com
Raighne Hogan: raighne.blogspot.com
Ursula Husted: www.apocalyptictangerine.com
Michael Hutchison and Phil Meadows: www.MetroMedComic.com
Christopher Jones: www.christopherjonesart.com
Dan Jurgens: lambiek.net/artists/j/jurgens_dan.htm
Tom Kaczynski: www.uncivilizedbooks.com
Melissa Kaercher: www.tinlizardproductions.com
David Karrow: www.davidkarrow.com
Ryan Kelly: www.funrama.blogspot.com
King Mini/Vincent Stall: www.kingmini.com
Reynold Kissling: www.reynoldbot.com
Danno Klonowski/Dank!: staplegenius.wordpress.com

Maxeem Konrardy: www.maxeem.com
Matthew Kriske: matthewkriske.blogspot.com
Becky Laff: beckylaff.com
Bob Lipski: www.uptowngirlcomic.com
Vas Littlecrow: www.vaslittlecrow.com
Roger Lootine: www.residuecomics.com
Sean Lynch: tallsean.blogspot.com
Doug Mahnke: lambiek.net/artists/m/mahnke_doug.htm
Lars Martinson: www.larsmartinson.com
Ed Choy Moorman: www.edsdeadbody.com
Sarah Morean: www.smorean.com
Daniel J. Olson: www.bewilderedkid.com
Ozel: www.modurndae.com
Tyler Page: www.webcomicsnation.com/tylerpage
Evan Palmer: www.evanpalmercomics.com
David Phipps: www.phippsville.com
Gordon Purcell: home.comcast.net/~gordonpurcell
Rana Raeuchle: www.chibitoaster.com
Tom Richmond: www.tomrichmond.com
Quillan Roe: www.quillanroe.com
Brittney Sabo: www.bsabo.com
Zak Sally: www.lamano21.com
Jason Sandberg: www.jasonsandberg.com
Will Schar: 800poundcomics.blogspot.com
Barb Schulz: bschulz.blogspot.com
Mike Sgier: www.msgierillustration.com
Damian Sheridan: butcherblak.deviantart.com/gallery
Tim Sievert: www.timsievert.com
Andy Singer: www.andysinger.com
Jon Sloan: www.sa-bonjimcomic.com
David Steinlicht: www.allsmall.net
Steve Stwalley: www.stwallskull.com
Ryan Swanson: www.mnartists.org/ryan_swanson
Sean Tenhoff: www.seantenhoff.com
Mike Toft: www.cartoonistconspiracy.com/brainfood
Chaz Truog: www.chaztruog.com
Lonny Unitus: www.lonnyunitus.com
Jerry Van Amerongen: www.ballardstreet.com
Brett Von Schlosser: vonschlosser.blogspot.com
Reed Waller: www.omahathecatdancer.com/reed_waller.htm
Adam Wirtzfeld: www.wrenchintheworks.com
Kate Worley: www.kateworley.com

ACKNOWLEDGMENTS

No book is ever the creation of one mind. Thank goodness, because one mind is prone to lapse into many errors. In my case, I must begin my recitation of gratitude with an acknowledgment of the almighty force that reigns over author heaven: the editor. Ann Regan shaped my rough manuscript into a book, with the grace of one who has revised many literary flaws in the course of her professional career and lived to tell about it.

Pam McClanahan, director at the Minnesota Historical Society Press, got the ball rolling. She read an article I'd written on Minnesota cartoonists for mnartists.org and sent an e-mail saying something like, "Hey, you want to talk about a book?" I always do. Mnartists.org editor Susannah Schouweiler earns four stars for publishing the piece on cartoonists in her magazine.

Mike Hanson organized the early stages of cartoonist interviews and research. Dan Leary, lucky guy, had the questionable honor of wading through a suitcase (yes, an actual suitcase) full of comic books, graphic novels, and original art, as well as several digital files, to select the art in the book.

On the family side, Mom, Dad, and Grandma June warrant BIG thanks for supporting my desire to write, and to write for a living, during an economic recession that has placed bigger dreams than mine on the unemployment rolls. The Central Minnesota Arts Board, through funds derived from the McKnight Foundation and the Legacy Fund, has come to bat for me twice, first with an Individual Artist grant and then with a Mentorship grant. Though the grants financed other endeavors (fiction writing and screenwriting), they propped my confidence when I needed it most.

I would be utterly remiss if I didn't thank the Elk River Area Arts Alliance, the Elk River paper (the *Star News*), and its editor Jim Boyle, who provided early outlets for my writing. Then of course there are the mountain bikers and hikers at Hillside City Park and Woodland Trails Park in Elk River, who put up with my multitasking on their trails. Yes, I was the one transcribing cartoonist interviews on purple note cards as I listened to audio through earphones and rambled over the hills, head down, pen moving, trying not to knock myself out by walking into a tree. I did a couple times, but I don't think anyone saw.

Others I want to thank in no particular order: the librarians at the Elk River Library, mnlinkgateway.org, the mass communications department at St. Cloud State University, the art department at Gustavus Adolphus College, Alison Bergblom-Johnson, Jeanne McGee, Peter Gross, Kirsten and

Jon Yocum, Linda and Dave Simpkins, Linda and Jim Antil, my sis Jennifer, my brother-in-law Paul, Tom, Brianna, Nick, Tim, Nate, Elizabeth, Josh, the gang from Glenelg High School in Maryland, my air force pals, the ladies from Curves–Elk River, the YMCA for keeping me from resembling an author who sits on her duff all day, and Dunn Bros for brewing a highly addictive cold-press coffee.

Authors are told to save their highest praise for the first and last paragraphs. So this last paragraph is dedicated to David Mruz, Duane Barnhart, Sarah Morean, Greg Ketter, and the cartoonists featured in this book, all of whom rate as talented artists, generous interviewees, and fine people.

INDEX

Page numbers in *italic* refer to illustrations